CULTURAL DIVERSITY IN CHILD PROTECTION

CULTURAL DIVERSITY IN CHILD PROTECTION

CULTURAL COMPETENCE IN PRACTICE

DR. SIOBHAN E. LAIRD AND

DR. PROSPERA TEDAM

macmillan international
HIGHER EDUCATION

RED GLOBE PRESS

First published 2019 by
RED GLOBE PRESS

Red Globe Press in the UK is an imprint of Springer Nature Limited, registered in England, company number 785998, of 4 Crinan Street, London, N1 9XW.

Red Globe Press® is a registered trademark in the United States, the United Kingdom, Europe and other countries.

ISBN 978–1–352–00620–9 paperback

This book is printed on paper suitable for recycling and made from fully managed and sustained forest sources. Logging, pulping and manufacturing processes are expected to conform to the environmental regulations of the country of origin.

A catalogue record for this book is available from the British Library.

A catalog record for this book is available from the Library of Congress.

CONTENTS

LIST OF FIGURES

LIST OF TABLES

ACKNOWLEDGEMENTS

We would like to thank Peter Hooper our editor at Red Globe Press for his timely advice and guidance. Our appreciation also goes to the production team at Red Globe Press for their commitment and typesetting of this book. We are both indebted to Dorcas Boreland, Siobhan's mother, for giving so generously of her time to read through a final manuscript and for suggesting many ideas for improvement. Prospera would like to offer a special word of thanks to my husband and children for their support and understanding during the writing of this book. Also to my late father whose early encouragement has motivated me to be who I am today. Appreciation to my mother Emelia Dzang whose newly developed expertise on social media meant that she would ask for regular updates about the progress of the book. To my colleagues at Anglia Ruskin University and friends for their encouragement. Last but not least, a big thank you to Dr Siobhan Laird for her invitation to co-author this important book. Siobhan wishes especially to thank my partner Gill for her patience and nurture – my last book done.

1

An Introduction to Racial and Ethnic Diversity

Introduction and structure of the book

This book is concerned with the increasing racial and ethnic diversity evident among families involved with child protection services, due to the processes of globalisation and the movement of people across national borders escaping violence and deprivation. Based on applied research derived from an analysis of 30 Serious Case Reviews, it is designed to support social work practice with families from Black and minority ethnic backgrounds where children are considered to be at risk of significant harm. The book is aimed at social work students in the final year of their Bachelors or Masters degree programmes; newly qualified social workers during their first assessed and supported year in employment; and experienced child protection social workers who are intervening with ethnically and racially diverse families. As a study examining practice, which critically engages with theory and practice models, it will also be of interest to social work scholars and educators. While the exemplar case studies presented illustrate practice in the United Kingdom, much of the underpinning research and theory draws on an international literature. As the book addresses child protection practice with families from Black and minority ethnic backgrounds, social workers, trainers and scholars in North America, Australia and many European countries will find a great deal that is relevant to their own contexts.

This study of social work argues that culturally competent child protection assessments and interventions are integral to anti-oppressive practice with families from Black and minority ethnic backgrounds. This chapter explains diversity in the UK before elaborating concepts and theories relating to race, culture, faith and ethnic identity development. Chapter 2 focuses on Anglocentric values and the experience of belonging to the White ethnic majority in the UK. Chapter 3 by contrast is concerned with the experiences of being from a racial or ethnic minority. All three of these chapters set out reflective exercises which require readers to consider their own personal, family and community-related experiences. Chapter 4 details a number of theories and models concerned with cultural competence and concludes with a case example of applying a model to practice.

Subsequent chapters address themes arising from the analysis of Serious Case Reviews conducted in England and employ a set of exemplars to illustrate how common issues and dynamics play out between practitioners and families. Reflective exercises in these chapters concentrate on practice and are used to assist readers to broaden their knowledge base and develop their practice skills in relation to race, ethnicity and faith. Many of these reflective exercises require the reader to apply the theories or models related to cultural competence detailed in Chapter 4. Chapters 5 through to 9 each conclude with a demonstration of a worked case example incorporating cultural competence models from Chapter 4. Chapter 10, which explores risk assessment, includes an extended worked case example drawing together concepts, theories and cultural competence models from across the book.

An international perspective on child protection and diversity

The United Kingdom, United States and Australia have each witnessed an unprecedented increase in the ethnic diversity of their populations since the Second World War as people have crossed international borders to escape conflict, oppression and poverty. The creation of multi-nation free trade blocks, and regional instability in the Middle East and parts of Africa, in conjunction with the processes of globalisation, have resulted in large movements of people across national boundaries. Consequently, these post-industrialised countries have become demographically multicultural, which reflects a worldwide trend in the growth of numbers and diversity of migrants (Meissner & Vertovec, 2015). Although the UK, US and Australia have different histories, their shared experience of diversity, and the child protection challenges arising from it, offers a foundation for exploring cross-national issues and drawing on international scholarship to find solutions to protect children in ethnically varied societies.

The persistent over-representation of indigenous, Black and minority ethnic children in the child care systems of the UK, US and Australia, alongside numerous inquiries into child protection calamities, reveal shortcomings in social work theory and practice in relation to engagement with the racial, ethnic and religious diversity of families (Phillips, 2007; Chimba et al., 2012; Owen & Statham, 2009; Department for Education, 2014a; Dakil et al., 2011; Boyd, 2014; Northern Territory Government, 2007; Bilson et al., 2015; Sawrikar & Katz, 2014; Children's Bureau, 2016). Scholars in these countries have attributed this in part to a lack of expertise among practitioners when working in cross-cultural contexts (Laird, 2008; Williams & Johnson, 2010; Sawrikar & Katz, 2014; Sue et al., 2016). Some have also argued that conventional anti-oppressive and anti-discriminatory approaches, which concentrate primarily on racism, do not adequately equip practitioners to tackle the more complex issues posed by working in an ethnically diverse society (Furness, 2005; Parrott, 2009; Holloway & Moss, 2010; Laird, 2014).

Much has been written about the circumstances surrounding the murder of an eight-year-old Ivorian girl named Victoria Climbié in London in 2000 by her guardians since the public inquiry conducted by Lord Laming. The inquiry focused predominantly on organisational policies, procedures and human resources, and made multiple recommendations in relation to them (Laming, 2003). Confined to a relatively small section of the inquiry report were issues concerning race; culture; spiritual beliefs; language barriers; extended family roles; immigration status; dispersal of relatives between countries; regular movement of family members across international borders; and the racial matching of social workers to the families they work with. Yet these matters had considerable impact upon practice at the time, and as the analysis of Serious Case Reviews in this book reveals, continue to have significant ramifications for social work with families from Black and minority ethnic backgrounds.

The research method underpinning the book

In the United Kingdom, when a child who was known or suspected to have been maltreated dies or is seriously harmed, an investigation is conducted into how this occurred. It is a mandatory requirement that senior professionals unconnected to the case are appointed to objectively examine the circumstances of what happened and why, so that lessons can be learnt in order to improve policy and practice, thus reducing the risk of harm to other children in the future. Previously in England, Local Safeguarding Children Boards, composed of senior managers representing each of the agencies in an area involved in the care or protection of children, were responsible for commissioning these investigations. With the abolition of Local Safeguarding Children Boards in 2018 this process is now handled by a smaller body of local-level safeguarding partners. However, cases which raise complex issues or are likely to be of national significance are commissioned by the Child Safeguarding Practice Review Panel (HM Government, 2018).

These types of investigations were originally known as Serious Case Reviews, but from 2018 are referred to as Child Safeguarding Practice Reviews. An Overview Report is then generated, which draws out learning and makes recommendations to rectify any identified problems and prevent repetition. Similar enquiries are undertaken in the US, Canada and Australia where they are referred to as Child Death Reviews. This study draws on the Overview Reports generated by such enquiries in England, which have to date received little scrutiny regarding how race, ethnicity and faith influence child protection decision-making and practices. However, other aspects such as domestic violence, addiction, mental health and non-compliance by parents have been subject to biennial (and latterly triennial) analysis (Brandon et al., 2009, 2011; Ofsted, 2011; Sidebotham et al., 2016).

In 2013 the British Government introduced a presumption that the full Overview Reports of Serious Case Reviews conducted in England be published unless there were exceptional reasons for not doing so. Since then, these have been voluntarily placed in an online national repository administered by the National Society for the Prevention of Cruelty to Children. These reports are publicly accessible and can be downloaded from the repository located at www.nspcc.org.uk/preventing-abuse/child-protection-system/case-reviews/. In this study all the available Overview Reports concerning families from ethnic minority backgrounds available from this archive for the period 2013–2017, which are searchable using key words, were examined. Any Executive Summary Reports or heavily redacted Overview Reports which provided too little detail of decision-making or practice to provide any useable information for the purposes of this study were excluded at this point.

From the remaining 30 reports all sections or passages referring to race, ethnicity, faith, nationality, language or immigration status alongside intersecting structural factors such as poverty, gender, disability, etc., were extracted. These were converted into synopses comprising critical details linked together with relevant contexts, events and factors taken from the related Overview Report. This was a necessary first step as Serious Case Reviews are typically wide ranging in nature, covering an often disparate catalogue of issues and incidents, particularly when multiple agencies are engaged or there has been involvement by Children's Social Care Services over many years. The summaries were then thematically analysed to draw out practice-related issues which arose during intervention with the family and had contributed to inadequate child protection responses. We were primarily interested in how subjective experiences of situations and personal viewpoints affected people's responses in circumstances which raised child protection concerns. Study of the summarised Overview Reports was therefore undertaken, employing a method designed to reveal how individuals interpret the world around them including the meanings they place on objects, events and behaviour. We used Phenomenological Interpretative Analysis, an approach to qualitative data analysis of text refined by Smith et al. (2009) and Pietkiewicz & Smith (2012). This technique, which has been extensively applied to interview transcripts, works to identify themes arising from textural material. We have adapted and applied the principles of this method to the summaries of Overview Reports of Serious Case Reviews through the steps suggested by Pietkiewicz & Smith (2012) outlined below:

1. Move between emic and etic perspectives. The first anthropological term refers to the perspectives of those who are being studied, their understandings of the world and the meanings they assign to their actions and those of others in any given situation. The second term concerns the professional or scholarly perspectives of those undertaking the study. It involves the application of concepts and theories arising from different academic disciplines to understand the worldviews and behaviours of individuals, families, groups or communities. Essentially this means bringing to bear both an insider and outsider perspective on analysis of the data.

2. Close reading of the textural material a number of times. Designed to help researchers immerse themselves in the data and become highly familiar with it, this stage includes taking notes and reflecting on content, language and/or descriptions of context in the text.

3. Identify emergent themes from the data, based on movement backwards and forwards between emic and etic perspectives, while drawing on notes and reflections derived from numerous readings. A set of succinct short phrases which capture the essence of each emergent sub-theme is then developed from this process.

4. Identify connections between emergent sub-themes and form these into larger clusters of conceptual meaning under superordinate themes. This stage also involves disregarding less significant themes or outlying emergent themes.

5. Construct a narrative account derived from the content and relationships between sub-themes and superordinate themes through the application of relevant concepts and theories to deepen the data analysis in order to reveal new insights. This narrative should be supported by excerpts from the textual material to both evidence and illuminate researchers' interpretations of the data.

Overview Reports, and thus our summaries derived from them for this study, generally present multiple points of view. However, some of these viewpoints usually receive more credence and word space than others. In particular, it needs to be borne in mind that Overview Reports as essentially professional accounts of a child's death or serious injury, mean that the perspective of family members tends to be muted. Inevitably our summaries reflect this bias with much greater emphasis on professional understandings of the situation. Nevertheless, our summaries of the Overview Reports and analyses strive to retain multiple standpoints reflecting the emic perspectives of those involved in child protection cases and sometimes the Overview Report authors, while generating an etic perspective through the application of concepts and theories. The emergent and superordinate themes derived from the earlier stages of data analysis are contained in a table which can be found in Appendix 2. Concepts and theories are explained throughout the book as they become relevant and continue to be emphasised through the use of italics. This also helps to make explicit how etic perspectives are being generated through the application of various conceptual and theoretical frames.

A sub-sample of the summarised Overview Reports (listed in Appendix 1) was chosen for inclusion in this book because they provided more extensive, in-depth or explicit coverage of particular themes. These case studies drawn from the summarised Overview Reports are presented throughout the book as exemplars of common dynamics or patterns which illuminate practice. They also serve to draw together multiple sub-themes and demonstrate how these are intricately related to each other. As such, these case studies underpin the narrative account referred to by Pietkiewicz & Smith (2012) above, and assist to illuminate our findings while supporting the overall cohesion of this study and highlighting implications for practice. As all the Overview Reports had been anonymised prior to online publication, no issues of confidentiality arose. The analysis of Overview Reports took place prior to the changes introduced in 2018. Consequently references are made to Local Safeguarding Children Boards and Serious Case Reviews throughout.

Yin (1994, p. 13) promoted single-case and multi-case studies as a means of investigating situated social phenomenon in circumstances where 'the boundaries between phenomenon and context are not clearly evident'. Critical case research focuses on situations of crisis within organisations. Serious Case Review reports examine extreme circumstances and outcomes in child protection social work related to policies, processes, decision-making and practices. Arguably these are atypical instances, as critical cases by definition examine acute and often exceptional situations. Their utility lies in how these extreme instances highlight the underlying dynamics of routine child protection practice.

Thematic analysis of the Overview Reports indicates that a number of issues and tensions, which are considered in subsequent chapters, played out to a greater or lesser extent in multiple cases. Theories relating to ethnocentrism, cross-cultural interaction and cultural identity are used to explore root causes of inadequate child protection responses and learn lessons, while models of cultural competence are applied to indicate how child protection practice can be improved with families from a diversity of racial and ethnic backgrounds.

Migration and settlement in the United Kingdom

As a maritime nation the UK has historically witnessed the growth of small communities of migrants around its port cities, predominantly due to sailors, soldiers or traders settling. Over the centuries these have been augmented by those fleeing natural disaster, famine, persecution and periodic war in continental Europe, resulting in tens of thousands of Irish, German, French, Russian and Jewish migrants settling in Britain (Bloch et al., 2013, pp. 51–52). The Second World War precipitated large movements of peoples across Europe and the establishment of communities in England of Ukrainian, Russian and Polish émigrés. In the aftermath of the War devastation to infrastructure and industry alongside a labour shortage led the British government, in the 1950s, to appeal for workers from Commonwealth countries and Dependencies to come to the UK. Over 500,000 people arrived from the Caribbean, South East Asia and China (by way of Hong Kong) between 1955 and 1961, with around 75,000 arriving per year throughout the 1960s. Most settled in London, the south east, the Midlands and the manufacturing centres of northern England – places where labour was most needed (Laird, 2008).

The Treaty of Rome 1957 instituted what is now the European Union and granted free movement of goods, services, capital and people between member states. Initially this generated only limited migration from the other 15 member countries, with comparatively small numbers arriving from France, Portugal and Greece (White, 1998, p. 1729). The expansion of the European Union to encompass 10 countries of the former Eastern Bloc in the years following the fall of the Berlin wall in 1989 resulted in a significant movement of workers from these member states to the UK (Laird, 2008, pp. 138–39). The 2011 Census revealed that there were 654,000 Polish-born residents in the UK with 24% of them living in London, the largest group of migrants from a single EU country, followed by 83,000 Romanian-born residents, of whom 54% were living in London (Vargas-Silva, 2014, p. 5). While the UK's decision in 2016 to leave the EU resulted in a drop in migration from member states of the EU, many migrants from these countries continue to enjoy rights to reside and work in the UK.

The UK has, since the 1950s, hosted a small number of university students from new Commonwealth countries, some of whom decide each year to work and reside in the United Kingdom. The higher education sector has continued to attract young people from overseas to the point where during 2013–14 the UK Council for International Student Affairs (2015) reported that 125,000 EU students and 310,000 non-EU students were studying for undergraduate, postgraduate and research degrees in the UK, accounting for 18% of all students. The processes of globalisation manifested, through inexpensive instantaneous international communication, easy access to the internet's multimedia platforms for information sharing and cheap air travel, have further encouraged the movement of people across international borders. Migration to the UK has risen from around 300,000 per year during the early 1990s to an average of 550,000 per year in the period 2003–2014; of which, in 2013, approximately 42% were from other EU member states (Hawkins, 2015).

Successive conflicts around the world have displaced populations and often created oppressive regimes, generating large numbers of refugees, many of whom have sought asylum in the UK. In 1987 asylum applications stood at around 4,000 per annum, peaked at 84,000 in 2003 and dropped thereafter to under 25,000 per year due to the introduction of legislation designed to reduce the number of successful asylum applications (Blinder, 2014, p. 3). The country of origin of asylum seekers changes as war and oppression affect different populations at different times. In 1999 around 11% of asylum applications were made by Somalis, while in 2002 around 17% were made by Iraqis. More recent conflict in Syria and ongoing unrest in Eritrea, Afghanistan and Pakistan meant that these were among the top 10 countries of origin of asylum seekers in 2013 (Blinder, 2014, p. 7).

The combination of increasing numbers of asylum seekers, refugees and economic migrants from EU countries has resulted in a considerable rise in the numbers of those born overseas living in the UK, which stood at almost four million in 1993 and almost doubled to seven million in 2011 (Migration Observatory, 2012). According to the 2011 Census for England and Wales, which asked respondents to choose their ethnicity from a pre-specified list, 83% identified as White British, 6% as Asian or Asian British, 3% as Black or Black British and 1% as Chinese. These national statistics obscure the considerable regional disparity in the residence of ethnic minority communities. In Birmingham 63% of the city's population identify as White British, with 20% identifying as Asian or Asian British and 7% as Black or Black British. In London 60% of the population is White British while the remaining 40% is made up of minority ethnic communities.

The overall result of successive migrations and continuing movement back and forth across international boundaries has led to the advent of *'superdiversity'* in the UK and other advanced industrial countries such as the US and Australia. *Superdiversity* refers not just to the multiplicity of ethnicities – for example in London over 300 different languages are now spoken – but to the diversity this has engendered in relation to migration patterns and legal statuses (Cantle, 2008, p. 23; Meissner & Vertovec, 2015). Migration channels to the UK are more varied than ever before, as people arrive on work permits, through marriage, for family reunion, seeking asylum, on student visas, under the free movement rules for EU nationals, as undocumented economic migrants and as trafficked individuals. Compared to the 1960s, migrants evidence much greater variance regarding their education, training and skills. While historically migration into the UK was skewed towards young men, the ages and gender of migrants have become more diverse. The numbers of women and families relative to single young men has increased significantly and there is a wider variation in age, ranging from unaccompanied asylum seeking children and students to older people joining the families of their adult children in the UK.

Defining race

The concept of race has its origins in the period of exploration and colonisation by European nations during the eighteenth and nineteenth centuries. It was at this time that race came to be defined in terms of physical characteristics, most particularly colour. The difference in appearance between White European peoples and the indigenous peoples of the Americas, Australia and Africa were used by social scientists as a basis to attribute mental and physical failings. It is now long established that there are in fact no biological differences between people of different skin colour and, indeed, the genetic diversity between two people of the same skin colour is often greater than that between people of different ones. This means that the concept of race is a social construct and not an inherent biological variation between people. It was this social construct of race that historically vindicated and propagated assumptions that Black Africans were childlike, intemperate, lazy and less intelligent than White Europeans. These notions were widely held in the colonial era by American and European social scientists, politicians and the general public. Such negative stereotyping was used as justification for the subjugation of African peoples and their enslavement, the clearing of Native Americans from the prairies and the removal of children from Aboriginal families in Australia, which continued up until the 1970s (Smedley, 1993; Garner, 2007).

The origin of race as a concept illustrates two important points. First is that the notion of race is not actually about biological differences, but social processes, which means that differences in physical appearance lead to assumptions, usually negative, about the attributes and abilities of another person. People are thus categorised into social groups on the basis of beliefs about their common biological descent and assumed psychological, emotional and behavioural characteristics, for example that Black Africans are more impulsive and aggressive. Secondly, *racialisation* is the social process by which the economically, socially and politically dominant group (White Europeans) is able to impose its definitions on another group of people (Black Africans) in ways which maintain their economic, social and political subordination. Slavery was the most extreme manifestation of this. The division of humans into distinctive biological categories by the pseudo-science of the nineteenth and early twentieth centuries has now been discredited. But such categorisations persist among many sections of the White population in Europe, Australia and North America. For this reason race remains an important concept in understanding people's reactions, not only to those of a different skin colour, but also in relation to others of a different ethnicity, culture or religious faith from their own (Mason, 2000, p. 7; Garner, 2007).

Reflective exercise

Consider your own personal experiences.

What positive and negative stereotypes are common in society in relation to people respectively from a: Chinese, Pakistani and African Caribbean background?

Have you experienced or observed racial abuse or discrimination against anyone from a racial minority, and if so what happened?

What assumptions about people from that racial minority seemed related to the racial abuse or discrimination?

Defining culture

Culture is closely associated with the concepts of 'race' and 'ethnicity', but can be distinguished as 'the learned, shared, and transmitted knowledge of values, beliefs, and lifeways of a particular group that are generally transmitted intergenerationally and influence thinking, decisions, and actions in patterned or in certain ways' (Leininger & McFarland (2002), p. 47). A designated group is a social group that shares a common history which frames the transmission of traditions, beliefs and superordinate life goals from one generation to the next. As Matsumoto & Juang (2004, pp. 10, 12) emphasise, 'culture describes average, mainstream tendencies. It cannot describe all behaviours of all people in any culture.' Although beliefs, values and social practices are transmitted by one generation to the next, as communities encounter different conditions – perhaps caused by climate change, the introduction of new technologies or migration to another country – cultural patterns are adapted to new circumstances and therefore change over time.

Martin & Nakayama (2010, p. 87) point out that 'cultural patterns of thought and meaning influence our perceptual processes, which, in turn, influence our behaviour'. Though beliefs are strongly associated with holding a religious faith or spiritual worldview, they are not synonymous with it and people's beliefs often draw on perspectives which reflect traditions and cultural values. Lustig & Koester (2013, p. 79) suggest that 'a belief is an idea that people assume to be true about the world. Beliefs, therefore, are a set of learned interpretations that form the basis for cultural members to decide what is and what is not logical and correct.' These learned expectations are usually passed to children through social learning processes as they interact with parents, kin, teachers, people of authority and, as they grow older, their peers. *Enculturation* refers to the internalising and subjective processes of absorption, adoption and expression of aspects of transmitted culture. Some of these beliefs may be quite central to a person's self-concept while others may be more peripheral. Moreover, the beliefs a person holds which are influenced by a particular cultural heritage may change over time as they interact with people from different cultural backgrounds or due to new life experiences. Often, however, such beliefs are unconscious as they become a person's inherent way of viewing self and the world, and hence their reality.

Cultural values commonly express the ideal rather than the actual reality of people's lives, though many individuals and families may strive to live by these values. Lustig & Koester (2013, p. 81) define values as 'what a culture regards as good or bad, right or wrong, fair or unfair, just or unjust, beautiful or ugly, clean or dirty, valuable or worthless, appropriate or inappropriate, and kind or cruel'. Cross-culturally values can also differ regarding their *valence*; that is, whether something is regarded positively or negatively. Among many cultures of East Asia older people tend to be held in high esteem and respect for them is *positively valenced*. By contrast in the societies of North America and the UK it is youth which is most valued, and consequently respect towards older people is *negatively valenced*. *Intensity* refers to the importance assigned by a culture to a particular value, which can also vary cross-culturally. The *positively valenced* value of interdependence and close relationships with kin in most societies of sub-Saharan Africa has a high *intensity* because it is of considerable importance. Whereas among the ethnic majority in the UK and North America though relationships with kin are also *positively valenced*, this value generally has less *intensity* in those societies because individualism and independence are more highly prized.

Values underpin norms, which are 'socially shared expectations of appropriate behaviours' that when violated by an individual or family incur disapproval, stigma, exclusion or other forms of social sanction (Lustig & Koester, 2013, p. 81). Norms frame not only conduct but also communication. Therefore violations of social norms by cultural outsiders who are unaware of them can cause unintentional discomfort or offence. In some societies social norms require an outsider to first approach the male head of household to ask for his permission to communicate with other family members. Social practices are the combined expression of beliefs, values and norms and are manifested through the typical and therefore predictable behaviours of people from a particular cultural background, in relation to greeting, eating, sleeping, marrying, etc. (Lustig & Koester, 2013, p. 82). Individual differences mean that in fact there will be a degree of variation among people as to how they express cultural values, beliefs and norms. *Ethnocentrism* refers to the worldview that one's own culture is superior and normative, meaning that the beliefs, values and social practices of other cultures and societies should be judged against it as the standard (Neuliep, 2018). Reflexiveness is a necessary corrective to this tendency and involves recognising how one's own culture governs perceptions of what is good or bad, such as notions of appropriate parenting.

Popular understandings of culture assume that an identifiable group of people, such as those of Chinese descent living in the UK, share the same values and beliefs which are fixed over time. This common tendency to stereotype means that 'notions of cultural incompatibility' are increasingly deployed by sections of the majority White population and a number of politicians to justify exclusion of certain minority groups or restriction on their migration to countries of Europe (Mason, 2000, p. 10). Some scholars refer to this development as the 'new racism', which shifts attention from differences based on physical appearance to those of culture and religion. Other scholars argue that this allegedly new focus, which has gained ground since the 1990s, is but a cover for 'old racism' and its preoccupation with biological differences (Mason, 2000, p. 10). So, while Islamophobia centres on Muslims, the racial abuse and attacks on property and people which give expression to it, are in fact targeted at people of Pakistani, Bangladeshi and Indian backgrounds. That is to say, it is targeted on people who have brown and not white skin. Despite the many White Muslims who live in the UK, many from the former Yugoslavia, they are by and large not the immediate targets of racial abuse. Hence colour, which marks out difference in appearance, attracts assumptions about biological difference between people and continues in the twenty-first century to be a major source of racism.

Stereotyping and assumption also occur in relation to nationality, which refers to a person's country of origin or their citizenship of the country in which they currently live. 'Nationality' is frequently used interchangeably with 'culture'; for example, people commonly speak of American culture or German culture alongside notions of national character. These overlook the diversity of ethnic communities now living in North America and Europe. Therefore it is important to distinguish between 'nationality' and 'culture' as separate entities. The former refers to an essentially legal status and the latter to the expression of shared beliefs, attitudes, values and social practices. While there is often a link between a person's nationality and culture, they are not interchangeable concepts and treating them as equivalent can perpetuate a static notion of culture and hence play into stereotypes (Matsumoto & Juang, 2004).

Reflective exercise

Consider your own cultural heritage.

What are the ideals in your culture of: family organisation; rearing young children; and how adolescents should behave?

How do these ideals in your culture affect your perception of the choices and behaviours of parents, children and young people from other cultural backgrounds?

Dimensions of culture

Extensive research conducted by Hall (1989), Hofstede (2011) and Chinese Culture Connection (1987) revealed a number of *dimensions of cultural variability* described below, which comprise continuums along which different societies are positioned. These are general prevailing orientations within societies, constituting just one source of influence upon the worldviews and behaviours of individuals. Although there are dominant beliefs, values or expectations of behaviour in different societies, people inevitably vary as to the extent that they follow them. Globalisation means that families often draw on cross-national cultural influences, while acculturation experiences commonly shape how the heritage culture of people from minority ethnic backgrounds influences their lives.

Low context/High context

In *high context* cultures when individuals communicate they presume a set of shared understandings, beliefs, values and social practices and their messages may contain little information regarding these matters because it is presumed. Consequently much may be conveyed through more subtle verbal and non-verbal communication. Individuals are therefore more likely to send indirect messages in which much is implied rather than explicitly stated. *High context* cultures include those of Africa, Latin America and the Middle East.

By contrast the UK, Sweden, Germany and the US are *low context* cultures, which means that messages between senders and receivers usually contain more explicit information about beliefs, values and social practices because less is presumed. Messages therefore tend to be encoded to be explicit and direct. This happens in everyday life. For example, if people share an occupation or leisure activity such as social work or football respectively they can converse about it in a shorthand form because there is a set of common understandings. However, someone speaking to a person who does not share their occupation or leisure activity is likely to be more explicit because there is less shared context. Overall this means that reactions to messages in *low context* cultures tend to be explicit and observable while in *high context* cultures they are likely to be more reserved. In essence people in *low context* societies tend to communicate directly and those in *high context* cultures are more likely to use indirect communication.

Therefore a social worker from a *low context* culture is likely to be more direct in making enquiries and exploring matters of concern or significance with family members. If the family is from a *high context* ethnic background, the social worker can come across as rude, abrupt or even rather aggressive. The communication style of this family may appear to a social worker from a *low context* culture as evasive and they may miss the subtle conveyance of information through allusion, hint and metaphor. Conversely a social worker from a *high context* background could be more attuned to the indirect communications of these family members. But on the other hand, he or she could experience a family from a *low context* culture as forceful and insistent, when they are simply being straightforward.

Individualism/Collectivism

In countries which rank high on *individualism* such as the US, the UK and Hungary the dominant belief is that people are only expected to take care of themselves and their immediate family and individual autonomy is paramount. Consequently decisions are primarily made by the individual based on their judgement of what is good or bad for them. Conversely highly *collectivist* cultures, such as those of Pakistan, India and societies in West Africa, value loyalty to the group, which is usually kin, but can be other groupings such as work colleagues, social networks or castes. Decisions are based on what is best or good for the group as a whole, rather than what is good for a particular individual. Therefore individuals have obligations towards the group and are reliant on it for support, which includes an emphasis on belonging. This can mean that individuals are less likely to put themselves forward or articulate a point of view as humility and modesty can be valued attributions in such societies. These kinds of behaviours can be misinterpreted as reserve, shyness or indifference by individuals from cultural backgrounds which value *individualism*.

Consequently a social worker from a cultural background which prizes *individualism* is likely to expect parents, their partners and older children to take decisions largely autonomously, including making changes to reduce risk of significant harm. However, family members from *collectivist* cultures may want to consult with and be guided by others in determining what is best for the kin group as a whole. Family members may be more conformist in their outlook and both parents and children may consider that obeying adults or elders is normative. Potentially this can create misunderstandings, if social workers in such cross-cultural encounters fail to appreciate the degree to which harmony and obedience are important values in family life. This does not mean practitioners should accept cultural norms which imperil the safety of children, but it does mean ensuring that assessments accurately reflect family dynamics, motivation and inhibitors to necessary changes.

Low power distance/High power distance

This dimension refers to the approval or acceptance of inequality within a society. In *low power distance* countries such as Denmark and the UK, the dominant worldview is that power differentials are essentially unfair and should be minimised and unequal power only used when necessary, as when social work or police powers are used to prevent child maltreatment. In situations where power is exercised by people on account of their higher social status this may be greatly resented or resisted. In a *low power distance* culture the general expectation would be that older children share decision-making with parents, or at least parents are expected to justify their decisions to them, while the opinions of grandparents are likely to be of less importance. The lack of formality in such societies often indicates closeness and trust, while such behaviour might be regarded as rude or impertinent in a *high power distance* society.

Conversely in societies such as those of Saudi Arabia and the Philippines, hierarchy is more accepted and the majority of people expect authority to be exercised by those who are older, male, from a higher social class or who possess a university education. They may feel uncomfortable or confused in situations where the hierarchy is ill-defined. In these societies inequality between social groups is perceived as justified or positively valued. These differences are perceptible in family relationships. The expectation in a *high power distance* culture is that children obey their parents or parents defer to the opinions of grandparents. They are also evident in the common use of honorifics to indicate respect. In *high power distance* cultures individuals with lower social status may be reluctant to initiate conversation with, or ask a question of, someone of higher status as this might be regarded as offensive.

Parenting styles can reflect cultural influences in relation to *power distance* between older and younger people in a society. Research based on White American middle-class parents conducted by Baumrind (1971) identified three parenting styles: *authoritative* parents who set clear boundaries, are warm towards their children and encourage independence; *authoritarian* parents who value obedience and respect while discouraging independence; and *permissive* parents who set few boundaries and expect their children to self-regulate. Although further research has revealed that these parenting styles exist in other societies, there are differences in how normative they are. While in the *low power distance* society of the UK *authoritative* parenting is considered the ideal, in the *high power distance* culture of China *authoritarian* parenting is regarded as the more ideal parenting style (Chao, 1994). Parents adopting this style may perceive themselves as bringing up their children to respect their elders; be disciplined; work hard at school; and develop a sound morality reflecting that of their parents.

Since parenting styles are integral to assessment, a British social worker is likely to perceive ethnically Chinese parents following a traditional *authoritarian* parenting style as excessively strict, restrictive and insensitive, thus raising their estimation of risk to the child. But these parents may be convinced they are doing their utmost to support their child's healthy development. For them it is the relative permissiveness of British parenting which they may regard as unsupportive and failing to instil moral values. On the other hand a social worker from a cultural background where more *authoritarian* parenting styles are endorsed may fail to pick up on the warning signs of potential abuse. This may have occurred in the Victoria Climbié case when a social worker of African Caribbean heritage assumed that a young African child who was stiff and silent in the presence of her great aunt was expressing respect. In fact it was attributable to fear due to the severe abuse she was suffering at the hands of her great aunt (Laming, 2003).

Femininity/Masculinity

Gender difference is a fundamental differentiation in all societies. Along this dimension *femininity* is defined as valuing the quality of life, nurturing others, relationships and interdependence. *Masculinity* is defined as a focus on materialism, achievement, assertiveness and independence. *Femininity* in this respect is also associated with fluid gender roles and gender equality, while *masculinity* is associated with the ascription of gender-specific roles, which at its most differentiated means men financially support the family while women undertake domestic tasks. This is often associated with gender inequality, which in masculine-oriented societies is considered beneficial.

Cultures differ in the extent to which they value *masculine* and *feminine* attributes. Countries such as Italy, Japan and Mexico rank high on *masculinity* as achievement and ambition are highly prized alongside the material display of success. In such cultures men strive to be competitive, successful and visible and the expression of manliness is considered extremely important. By comparison Nordic countries such as Norway and Sweden rank high on *femininity*, as does Thailand. In these cultures service to others, actions which improve quality of life and nurturing roles for both men and women are highly valued. Men are more likely to view cooperation and solidarity with other males as more rewarding. Even in societies which score high on *masculinity* this ideal may incorporate other norms, such as the ethic of *caballerismo* in Latino cultures, which emphasises the role of men in caring for and protecting their families.

Parenting is gendered to some extent in all societies, with women expected to take on the greater proportion of childrearing and responsibility for domestic tasks. However, the majority of societies promote the involvement of both fathers and mothers in family life and bringing up children. Research suggests that social workers frequently neglect the role of fathers in assessments (Laird et al., 2017). This tendency is often compounded by professional assumptions that men from heritage backgrounds which emphasise *masculinity* play either a minimal parental role, or else one characterised by a detached *authoritarian* parental style. Much research demonstrates the extent to which fathers from many minority backgrounds value their role as fathers and are involved with their children's upbringing (Chowbey et al., 2013; Laird, 2008; Reynolds, 1997).

Low uncertainty avoidance/High uncertainty avoidance

Uncertainty avoidance is the degree to which people feel comfortable or threatened by ambiguous situations, alongside the likelihood that they will try to avoid uncertainty by creating more structure to compensate, such as more rules. The UK, along with the US, India, Jamaica and Sweden, ranks low on *uncertainty avoidance* which means most people from these countries tend to have a higher tolerance of ambiguity and are more prepared to accept dissent, institute fewer rules and take more risks compared to people from Japan, Portugal and Greece who usually prefer more rules and consensus around goals. However, increasing risk aversion and the proliferation of management performance systems in the workplace are lowering the tolerance of ambiguity in many professional contexts in the UK.

Pakistani society ranks quite high for *uncertainty avoidance* and many families from this cultural background may place importance on observing some customary forms of address and social conventions. But to a social worker from the White ethnic majority coming from a low *uncertainty avoidance* cultural background, family members exhibiting this kind of behaviour may appear inhibited and over-controlled. That perception could lead to negative professional judgements about parenting and children's behaviour, as opposed to merely recognising difference in a situation of *good enough parenting*. Ultimately these kinds of misjudgements could mislead practitioners into reckoning a higher level of risk of significant harm to a child than actually exists.

Short-term orientation/Long-term orientation

Short-term orientation is the tendency to focus on quick results and consequences occurring relatively shortly after one's actions. North American and most European societies typically have a *short-term time orientation* in contrast to those of Germany, China, Japan and Russia, which tend to be characterised by a *longer-term* perspective. Time in the UK and US is normatively highly organised with precise timescales for goal-oriented activities. *Long-term orientation* refers to a longer perspective which emphasises virtue and focuses more on conduct such as perseverance at a task, subordination to the group for the sake of a larger purpose and willingness to accept deferred gratification. Notably, in cultures which value a *long-term orientation* time is viewed more flexibly and employed more responsively to the immediate needs of a situation, such as prioritising assistance to a family friend rather than getting to an appointment on time.

Computerisation of many social work tasks, particularly assessment, care planning and care implementation combined with the introduction of management performance systems into software has accentuated for practitioners the already highly *short-term orientation* of British society. As a result, social workers tend to place considerable emphasis on time-keeping both for themselves and for families. Undoubtedly a proportion of family members and young people miss appointed meetings or are persistently late for them due to resistance. However, it is important to ponder whether for other families there may be cross-cultural differences relating to the meaning of timeliness, either in relation to attending pre-arranged meetings or in respect of care plan implementation. Without this reflexive consideration social workers may mistakenly assume that family members or young people are being resistant, when in fact they are observing a more *long-term orientation* reflecting different cultural norms.

Indulgence/Restraint

At one end of this continuum is the degree to which a society values *indulgence* in terms of deriving pleasure from living and enjoying life through such activities as eating, consuming alcohol, buying consumer goods, sexual gratification and socialising with friends. Mexico, the US and the UK tend to rank quite highly on this dimension. By contrast other cultures greatly value *restraint*, and prize self-discipline, willpower, moderation and modesty. This is more typical of countries such as Pakistan and Saudi Arabia. This can lead to conflicts when parents and children are from a heritage background which values self-control and modesty while their social worker is from a culture which values pleasure and choice. In these circumstances difference can often be interpreted by a practitioner as pathology and linked into child protection concerns. Meanwhile, family members may be highly resistant to professional insistence that children and young people be given more freedom of choice. Here there is a clash over understandings of what constitutes the 'good life' and how it should be achieved. On the other hand, a social worker from a cultural background highly influenced by *restraint* may regard a family whose outlook is shaped by *indulgence* as evidencing overly permissive or disengaged parenting, raising the estimation of risk posed to children.

Reflective exercise

Consider members of your own nuclear and extended family and their interactions with others.

Are there any commonalities or norms you notice among family members that reflect cultural influences along the dimensions identified above?

Where is your family positioned along each of these dimensions?

Has this position changed over time and does it vary, for example between different segments or generations of your family?

Cultural fluidity

More recent research indicates that as societies undergo transformation due to modernisation, technological advance, globalisation and the influence of consumerism, people in them are drawing on multiple belief and value systems to create unique cultural expressions which combine notions of, for example, *individualism* and *collectivism* or *femininity* and *masculinity* rather than regarding them as mutually exclusive opposites (Martin & Nakayama, 2010, p. 106). Regardless of cultural heritage, through the mass media and more recently the advent of the internet, almost everyone will have encountered, and may be influenced by, multiple sources of beliefs, values and practices. Many individuals pick and mix from both the culture of the ethnic majority and that of their own heritage background. They may appropriate elements of other minority cultures also living in the same country; for example, South Asian youths in Britain have appropriated African American styles of dress and Black English (Ghelani, 2001).

Cultural change also occurs where people from one country emigrate and settle in another, particularly if subsequently second- and third-generation immigrants grow up in the host country which in turn becomes their country of birth and nationality. For families which comprise parents or grandparents who grew up in or have spent most of their lives in the country of origin while the children have been born and brought up in the host country, cultural beliefs, values and social practices can be a site of conflict, negotiation, adaptation or fundamental change. Shaikh & Reading (1999) in their research describe how first- and second-generation South Asian service users often felt a pull between an emergent independent self and the more collectivist values of their family and community, with whom they also felt a strong emotional attachment and identification. The researchers documented how some family members may be endeavouring to preserve their cultural heritage through a rigorous commitment to the beliefs, values and social practices as they are observed in the family's country of origin in ways that become unsustainable in the changed environment of the host country. At the same time other members may be striving to adopt the cultural values and social practices of the ethnic majority in the host country in ways which are inapt and unrealistic. How families resolve these challenges may generate new cultural forms. Shaikh and Reading (1999, p. 53) suggest that for their South Asian service users, 'the choice is not whether to sustain traditional values or to discard these in favour of getting on in Western society but how they can effectively combine the best of both'.

Reflective exercise

Consider your recent practice with families from three different ethnic minority backgrounds.

To what extent do you recognise and explore the varied cultural and religious influences of different family members and how these affect their beliefs, values and conduct?

To what extent do you explore any tensions or conflicts arising between family members due to the different beliefs and values that they hold?

If you do not explore these matters, or only discuss them with family members at a superficial level, identify the reasons why.

Dimensions of cultural identity

Roland (1988) discovered three aspects of identity present in all cultures. These are: an *individualised identity* which concerns the sense of an independent or discrete self; a *familial identity* expressed through a sense of interdependence and connectedness to others; and a *spiritual identity* comprising both an individual's inner experience of spirituality and its outward expression through ritual, public and private observance and participation in collective acts of faith. Different cultures place different degrees of emphasis upon these aspects. In societies such as those of North America and Western Europe most attention is on the development of an independent, self-determining individualism.

By contrast in many Latin American societies much more attention is given to the development of *familial identity* and children are taught to value interdependence, reliance upon and loyalty to their family or wider social network. This means for instance that family members might play a substantial role in decisions concerning an individual's choice of marital partner, education or employment. Conversely in countries such as those of the Middle East and Africa *spiritual identity* is particularly important, as evidenced by the 97% of Afghans and 98% of Somalis who describe themselves as religious, compared to just 30% of people in the UK and 34% in Germany who do so (WIN/Gallop International, 2016).

These identities are not mutually exclusive. In many African societies both *spiritual* and *familial identities* tend to hold a higher priority than *individualised identity*. As people engage in collective acts of worship or public ritual these identities may reinforce one another. This contrasts with mainland China where culturally *familial identity* is typically emphasised, but spirituality is not (WIN/Gallop International, 2016). However, individual differences will mean that within any given society these identities may be more or less important to particular family members or may have changed in importance over time due to processes of acculturation on settling in another country (Martin & Nakayama, 2010, p. 165).

Reflective exercise

Consider your family.

Which of the above three identities tend to be more or less expressed?

Is the expression given to these three identities different between segments or generations of your family?

How are these three different identities given expression in your family?

What kinds of questions could you ask to explore these identities with family members from ethnic minority backgrounds in your practice?

Cultural identity development

Identity refers to a reflective self, comprising an individual's perception of themselves and the self-image they think they are projecting in social settings. It incorporates multiple sources of identity derived from membership of different social groups such as being female, middle class and able-bodied in addition to being Black, Christian and from an African heritage background. In all societies family and kin remain foremost in the enculturation process during which children learn and internalise the beliefs, values and customs related to their culture. Schools, peer relationships, religious institutions, the mass media and the internet are also significant sources of enculturation (Ting-Toomey, 2005). Analysing cultural identity formation, Phinney (1993) proposes a three-stage developmental model.

This commences with *unexamined cultural identity* during which cultural attributes are naturalised and taken for granted by the individual, cultural differences between self and others remain unperceived and there is little interest in exploring cultural issues or differences. This stage is particularly characteristic of childhood, but is not confined to this age group. Many adults may not move beyond this stage as they adopt an unquestioning attitude toward their own culture while employing stereotypes held by their group to understand and describe themselves. Research in the US suggests that a relatively high number of people from the ethnic majority fall into this category as a result of the power structures which privilege their cultural beliefs, values and social practices, thus making them normative, for example, through education and the mass media (Lustig & Koester, 2013).

As individuals come into contact with people from other cultural backgrounds and encounter other cultures through the mass media and internet they may embark on a process of questioning and exploration of both their own culture and that of others. This stage is referred to as the *cultural identity search* and is often accompanied by increased political and social awareness which may have an affective component (e.g. anger, confusion, hopelessness) as individuals discover the impact of culture on their lives or the effect of discrimination. This new knowledge may lead individuals to identify more or less strongly with their cultural community or may create or intensify positive or negative feelings towards other ethnic groups.

Cultural identity achievement occurs if the individual, as a result of embarking on a process of exploration, is able to resolve emergent tensions, issues and dilemmas to develop an internalised self-confident cultural identity which is associated with positive mental health. Lustig & Koester (2013, p. 133) argue that 'once formed, cultural identities provide an essential framework, organizing and interpreting our experiences of others. This is because cultural identities are central, dynamic, and multifaceted components of one's self-concept.' Since cultural identity is formed through encounters with others, potentially it can continue to develop and change over time as the individual continues to interact with people from their own and other cultures. Such encounters can reinforce or challenge stereotypes which may in turn entrench an individual in an *unexamined cultural identity*, move them into or contribute to self-exploration at the stage of *cultural identity search* or help them to reach *cultural identity achievement*.

Cultural identity development has implications for both practitioners and the families they work with. A social worker from the ethnic majority who grows up with a self-assured *unexamined cultural identity* may struggle to understand how different cultural influences govern the conduct of families from diverse backgrounds. They may constantly measure these against their own Anglocentric norms, inflating the assessment of risk for families from minority ethnic backgrounds. Conversely, social workers still in the process of a *cultural identity search* can potentially fall into the trap of *relativism*, an ideological position which regards cultural practices as equally valid. So they might be hesitant to challenge parents who refuses to permit female children to leave the home on the grounds that this exposes them to the immodest gaze of men and molestation, destroying the girls' marriage prospects, as virginity is highly prized in their culture. Alternatively, social workers may be intervening with family members who live in relatively isolated local ethnic communities, resulting in them having *unexamined cultural identities*. Awareness of this can alert practitioners to the family's potential antagonism towards people from other ethnic groups, seen as outsiders, and possibly high levels of initial reluctance to engage with services.

Bains (2001) contends that the development of a self-assured *cultural identity* can also be detrimentally affected by first-generation migrants experiencing conflict between integration of the self within the majority and minority cultures. This is particularly so if these two cultures make very diverse demands in relation to beliefs, values and social practices. Additionally, parental experiences of migration can significantly affect the development of *cultural identity* in children. Bains (2001) gives the example of first-generation migrant parents who have endured a negative acculturation experience and poorer quality of life as a consequence of their ethnicity in the UK adversely affecting their children's *cultural identity*.

Positive acculturation experiences and acceptance by the majority culture can create a less adverse environment for their children to develop a positive cultural identity. Young people's *cultural identity* can also be conflicted if they feel pressured to acculturate while at the same time retaining a *cultural identity* which reflects the beliefs, values and social practices of their family's country of origin. This can be further exacerbated if family members feel different degrees of affiliation with the country they have settled in. A confused, incoherent or conflicted *cultural identity* can also arise if a young person perceives the ethnic majority as being hostile to their minority ethnic group. An individual experiencing this may reach *cultural identity achievement* by rejecting the negative characteristics ascribed to them by those outside their ethnic minority and instead embrace the cherished attributes and practices of their family's cultural heritage. For those of mixed heritage a period engaging in *cultural identity search* may be more likely and particularly significant in reaching *cultural identity achievement*.

For adolescents particularly, cultural identity development is of considerable importance. Social workers need to be mindful of this when assessing the needs of young people from minority ethnic backgrounds. This means taking the time to explore with each child how they view their cultural identity and what the implications of this might be for their beliefs, conduct and relationships with other family members. It will also be important to be aware that for recent migrants, adult family members may also be wrestling with their own *cultural identity search* due to acculturation experiences. Putting in time to listen to how children of mixed heritage backgrounds perceive their identity will be vital to any assessment. But it also avoids the assumption that such children's identities are necessarily problematic. Their diverse cultural background may actually aid the process of *cultural identity search* and reaching *cultural identity achievement*.

Reflective exercise

Consider your own cultural identity.

What cultural identity status do you think you have and why?

Has this changed over time and if so what contributed to these changes?

How would you go about exploring the cultural identity of a young person or parent from an ethnic minority background?

Religion and spirituality

According to Mathews (2009, p. 3) all religions have a number of key characteristics, which are:

➢ A structured set of beliefs which are transmitted through teaching, rituals and holy books such as the Bible, Talmud, Qur'ān, Guru Granth Sahib or Vedas.

➢ Beliefs concerned with morality and the meaning of life.

➢ A core belief that there is a spiritual realm beyond the material world of human beings which exerts an influence upon events and individuals in that material world.

➢ A set of principal beliefs shared by a substantial number of people creating a communal aspect to religion resulting in believers coming together either in small or large numbers to worship, dance, sing, pray or spend time in individual mediation.

While organised religions may share a set of common features, there is huge variation in people's beliefs, attitudes and values even when they subscribe to the same faith. The multiplicity of denominations within Christianity, together with the various strands of belief in Hinduism and Islam, are illustrative of this. But even when family members follow the same denomination or strand of an organised religion, they may each differ considerably in their degree of spiritual devotion, commitment to observances and how faith influences their values and worldview. Merely noting that a family is Muslim, Sikh or Jewish does not actually provide information about the implications of this for wellbeing, motivation, daily routines, parent–child relationships, wider kinship dynamics or relationships between the family and local faith-based congregations or communities. It can, however, be the basis for stereotyping and a whole set of assumptions. Comprehending how people experience their faith; understanding what influence it has on their wellbeing and relationships with others; how it guides, supports and comforts; or in what ways it causes tension, can only be done if social workers explore the unique personal meaning of religion for individual family members.

While most people experience spirituality within the context of an organised religion such as Buddhism, Hinduism, Islam or Christianity, many others adhere to a more personal form of faith. This may reflect influences from the religion in which they were brought up or it may draw upon diverse religious inspirations. Increasingly people from the White majority population, and some from minority ethnic communities, derive their spiritual beliefs from a pick and mix approach to religious beliefs and secular values such as justice, equality and self-determination. Consequently, a number of individuals may have a unique set of spiritual beliefs which underpin their understanding of the world around them and guide their conduct. The growing secularisation of British society has been an acknowledged phenomenon for many decades, with steep declines in church attendance by members of the White majority community. At the same time, some people in Britain have turned to 'new age' beliefs such as those of Paganism, Scientology and Hare Krishna.

Religious belief can be an integral part of a person's cultural heritage and profoundly influence family relationships, dress, diet, behaviour, social activity and leisure. Shariah is a system of rules based on the Quran and the sayings of the Prophet Muhammad. These govern the social and economic activities of practising Muslims, although of course they may be followed to a greater or lesser extent by individual believers. Hindu beliefs can dictate the nature of social interaction between people of different castes, how food should be prepared and taboos on eating meat. On the other hand Anglican theology, with its emphasis on the individual's relationship with God and its historical view of labour as a moral activity, underpins dominant attitudes which value independence and paid work in modern-day Britain (Crompton, 2008, p. 34). Hence spiritual beliefs can sometimes be an indistinguishable part of a person's cultural heritage.

Social work as a secular profession is based on rationality and draws heavily on the social sciences, as opposed to being shaped by spirituality or morality. Therefore it has in the main ignored matters of faith (Furness & Gilligan, 2010; Holloway & Moss, 2010). This makes it quite challenging for practitioners to work with families where religion is central to many aspects of family life, including how children are brought up. The lack of consideration given to religion and spirituality in social work training can leave practitioners with an inadequate knowledge base to manage effective assessments with families for whom faith is central to their worldview, moral outlook and everyday conduct. Recognising, rather than ignoring, the importance family members place on religion in their lives and the strength of their bonds with faith communities or local congregations is a necessary first step to integrating matters of faith and spirituality into assessments.

Reflective exercise

Consider your practice with families from different faith backgrounds.

To what extent do you explore the religious beliefs and observances of different family members?

To what extent do you ask family members about the relevance or influence of their faith in different areas of everyday life?

If you spend little time discussing these matters with family members reflect on why this is so.

Why might a deeper understanding of the religious beliefs and observances of family members be important in safeguarding children?

Ethnicity and ethnic identification

Every individual is socialised during childhood into the language, faith, gender role expectations, cultural beliefs and customary observances of their parents, kin and often the immediate community in which they grow up. This process of socialisation leads individuals to identifying with others who have similar historical roots, language, religion, values and culture. At its most simple Smith (1986, p. 192) has defined an ethnic group as 'a population whose members believe that in some sense they share common descent and a common cultural heritage or tradition and who are so regarded by others'. This definition highlights several important aspects of 'ethnicity' as a concept. Firstly, it implies a common origin or history; secondly, that the members of the group hold shared cultural beliefs or observances; and thirdly, that being a member of an ethnic group is to a degree self-chosen.

Jenkins (1997, pp. 22–23) uses the notion of *group identification* to refer to a process of self-ascription by virtue of which individuals choose the ethnic group to which they belong on the basis of similarity. *Social categorisation* is defined by Jenkins (1997, pp. 22–23) as the imposition of a racial identity upon a person by a more dominant social group such as the White majority population in North American or European countries. He indicates that minority ethnic groups are created by two dynamic processes, one involving those who voluntarily associate themselves with a particular ethnic group and those from a more dominant social group who impose *social categorisation* upon them. Such *social categorisations* typically carry negative attributions, such as the caricature of established Pakistani communities in European countries as being exceptionally patriarchal and oppressive of women (Laird, 2008).

Barth (1969) argues that while the idea of a shared culture is closely associated with belonging to an ethnic group, there is no direct relationship. He contends that people associated with a particular ethnic group decide which cultural features are significant for the group and act as *markers* to distinguish them from other ethnic groups. Which cultural features become salient as *markers* of ethnicity and which are ignored depends on the interaction between different cultural groups in a society. In Northern Ireland, while English is the first language of virtually everyone, the ability to speak some Gaelic has become an important *cultural marker* among Nationalists alongside the oppositional political allegiances which also distinguish Nationalists from Unionists. Speaking Gaelic as a point of departure between Nationalists and Unionists is particularly important in a context where both social groups are White, largely of Celtic descent and share considerable similarities in their day-to-day living patterns. Conversely, since the 2001 terrorist attack on the Twin Towers in New York, young people of Pakistani heritage living in the UK have increasingly played down regional differences in cultural practices and their heritage languages while instead emphasising their common Islamic faith as a *marker* of *group identification* (Jacobson, 1997). This broader *group identification*, particularly among younger Muslims, has been driven partly by sharing the common experience of living in the UK and developing a British-Muslim identity, but also by Islamophobia. The latter is characterised by negative stereotypes of Muslims as patriarchal, fundamentalist and sympathetic to terrorism which has fuelled an upsurge of attacks on the property of Muslims and verbal abuse or assault against people of the Islamic faith (Laird, 2008, p. 5, 25).

This construction of ethnicity makes it negotiable, indicating that individuals can exert a degree of choice over their group identity. Pressures from within the group for all its members to conform to markers of ethnicity, such as a dress code, and pressures from without created by a dominant social group which assigns individuals to a racial category, regardless of actual similarities, reduce the scope for personal choice regarding ethnic identification. So, for instance, a young Pakistani man born in the UK may identify as British and have much the same lifestyle as young men from the White majority community. Yet he may still be denied British identification by a vocal and hostile section of that White majority population which perceives him to be a Pakistani immigrant subscribing to Islam, a faith regarded as hostile to their idea of the 'British way of life'. At the same time this young Pakistani man may be subject to peer pressure from some sections of the British Pakistani community to wear a prayer cap as a visible sign of his religious affiliation.

The tendency to construe culture and faith as a set of fixed values, beliefs and practices universally embraced by individuals from a particular ethnic background is true not only of people from the ethnic majority, but also of some sections of minority ethnic communities. Dominant opinion leaders from within a minority ethnic group may make demands that everyone from that heritage background adheres to a set of values and behaviours which it is claimed authentically expresses a particular culture. In circumstances where Islam as a minority religion in Britain is constantly criticised, the need to defend Muslim identity can result in the expectation of conformity and a narrowing of what it means to be Muslim, both culturally and spiritually.

Equally, many of Pakistani heritage, brought up in the Muslim faith, are comfortable with their cultural and religious identity. But they may behave differently in different social contexts. If first-generation immigrant grandparents originally migrated to Britain from a village in Punjab they may well have brought with them cultural values which stress the deference younger people should show to older people. A young man may continue to adhere to this cultural expectation and show respect to the elders of his kin group and other older people in his local Pakistani community. By contrast in college he may adopt a casual attitude in interactions with older teachers, common amongst younger people of the ethnic majority population. In other words, his ethnicity and its expression through *cultural markers* is likely to alter depending on the social context in which he is performing his identity.

Social work typically hones in on family units, and its practice is largely confined to the family home or the child's setting, such as a foster placement. But this professional norm tends to constrict social work assessments, which often make little reference to community-level interactions. Concepts of *group identification* and *cultural markers* remind social workers that their practice needs to embrace a wider set of factors and relationships. Many families from minority ethnic or faith backgrounds can be closely bound into their local communities. While avoiding stereotypical assumptions that people from minorities necessarily strongly identify or frequently interact with their local ethnic community, it is essential to explore families' relationships with wider social networks. For some family members *group identification* may be extremely important, for others less so. Some may feel pressured to conform and adopt *cultural markers* with which they disagree or which they find onerous, such as wearing a top-knot or turban in a Sikh community. Others may draw a sense of pride and positive cultural identification from their relationship with their local ethnic or faith community. Understanding these divergent feelings, attitudes and outlooks is what social work assessment is about.

Reflective exercise

Consider the local ethnic community with which you identify.

Describe the different power relationships within this local ethnic community.

How do these community-level power relationships affect you and/or members of your family?

Regardless of how an individual ethnically identifies they may be subject to erroneous assignment of their identity by others, particularly if they are a member of an ethnic or racial minority. Someone who ethnically identifies as British African Caribbean may be assumed to be a recent African migrant, an assumption based on stereotypes of Black people as immigrants rather than citizens. When people categorise others in terms of their ethnicity they rely on 'audible, visible and readable cues' which often feed into stereotypes (Hua, 2014, p. 205). Audible cues refer to how a person sounds, and can include their accent and fluency in using English. Research reveals that additional language users of English (meaning those for whom English is not their first language) are deemed less intelligent, less educated and poorer than native English language speakers. Other studies have demonstrated that people making requests in Standard English are much more likely to receive a positive response as opposed to those making the request in a vernacular such as patois or Black English. Yet being able to speak one's heritage language can be an important marker of identification with, and acceptance within, a minority community (Hua, 2014).

Visible cues concern appearance; with skin colour, facial features and hair being predominantly used by people to ascribe both race and ethnicity to others. Readable cues refer to what is written down, the most common being a person's name. If this seems to be a non-native English name the reader may assume the individual concerned is a recent migrant or 'foreigner' and in any event may mistakenly assume the person's ethnicity because they think the name looks African or Indian, etc. Similar types of ascriptions are often made when a reader peruses an email, letter, application or document from someone on the basis of how they write. Social workers are far from immune from making these same kinds of misidentifications, particularly if pushed for time. Once such a racial or cultural identification has been made, the tendency is for a set of positive or negative stereotypes associated with that identity to influence professional perceptions and practice. Assuming that a young person is Hispanic because his name sounds Spanish and so does the language he speaks may miss the fact that he is actually from Brazil and his first language is Portuguese leading to relative isolation in a context where there are far fewer Portuguese language speakers than Spanish speakers in the UK. Alternatively, assuming that a mother who communicates in halting English is a recent migrant may lead to a whole set of presumptions, when in fact she is Polish and has lived in Britain for the last 15 years. But she feels nervous during interviews with practitioners, which reduces her normally high level of English language proficiency.

Reflective exercise

Consider three family members from different racial or ethnic backgrounds that you have met or received communication from for the first time recently.

What audible, visible or readable cues did you use to identify each person's race, ethnicity, faith, first language and English language ability?

To what extent did you rely on these cues in your practice as opposed to asking direct questions of family members and getting them to tell you about these aspects of their lives?

What assumptions did you make and how did this affect your responses?

The creation of stereotypes

Stereotypes are generalisations about a group of people who may share one or more characteristic which makes them perceptible as a social group, for example, skin colour, a specific religion or the same sexuality. These generalisations may be entirely inaccurate or, even when they hold some validity, are applied indiscriminately to everyone in that social group, without attention to individual differences and the range of beliefs, values, practices and abilities that exists in any group of people, particularly if it is large. *Ethnocentrism* is one source of stereotyping, because when a person observes the behaviour of those from other cultural backgrounds, they draw on their own cultural heritage to make sense of it, interpreting the behaviour from within their own cultural frame or else censuring it, because the other person's behaviours are different from their norms. A behaviour meant to convey friendliness in one culture, such as briefly touching another person's arm, if interpreted from an ethnocentric viewpoint could be construed as over-familiarity and offensive by people from a different cultural background. Stereotypes also arise from a set of six inherent cognitive processes described by Matsumoto & Juang (2004), which help individuals to organise and make sense of the world around them. If not checked through reflectiveness, these will perpetuate perceptions of fixed and often prejudiced characterisations of people from other ethnic backgrounds. The six cognitive processes involved are outlined below.

Selective attention

Individuals must to some extent choose what to give their attention to out of all the multiple and complex stimuli and information around them. Therefore once a stereotype is created, it is easily reinforced as the individual starts to attend to the aspects of a person's conduct which appear to match the stereotype, and ignore or minimise others which conflict with it.

For example: a practitioner notices that a mother of Bangladeshi ethnic background had an arranged marriage and left school at 16, reinforcing notions of oppressive ascribed gender roles. But the practitioner does not register or explore with the mother the fact that she is the budget holder in the home and makes most of the financial related decisions, as this would disconfirm the oppressed stereotype of a South Asian woman.

Appraisal

As individuals are being bombarded with multiple stimuli, they sift through them to identify which ones have significance for them. This involves a process of evaluation. Inevitably those stimuli perceived as being of less importance will receive less attention. So the more meaningful a stimulus appears to be, the stronger the reaction it is likely to elicit.

For example: a practitioner may over-focus on the fact that a father from a Nigerian ethnic background expects his child to obey him, due to child protection concerns around disciplinarian parenting, but pay less attention to the quality of care that the child receives.

Concept formation and categorisation

In most environments people are being constantly inundated with stimuli from innumerable sources, making it impossible for the human brain to retain discrete and precise representations of each object, place, person, event and activity encountered. Instead the mind develops a set of concepts to represent classes of places, persons, events, etc.

Examples include placing people from diverse backgrounds into preconceived stereotypical categories, such as that Black young men are good at sports – a positive stereotype, or are more likely to be violent – a negative one.

Attribution

Each human being has an innate need to understand the cause of events, rationalise their own behaviour and comprehend that of other people. Attributions as to why a person is behaving as they are may coin-cide with that person's own understanding of their conduct or it may be completely mistaken.

For example, when a stereotype is in play a practitioner is more likely to make attributions based upon it, such as assuming the reason an Irish mother stays with her violent husband is because she is Catholic and thus holds religious scruples against separation or divorce. Consequently, the practitioner fails to explore with the mother other reasons why she chooses to continue living with a violent partner.

Emotion

Emotions can affect perception. If a person is feeling angry, calm or anxious when they meet someone this can affect their understanding and responses. Research indicates that people who are feeling happy during an encounter are more likely to make positive judgements about someone from a different racial background than someone who is experiencing negative emotions. Indeed, negative emotions appear to be correlated to more stereotypical perceptions of people from a different racial background (Greenberg, ct al., 1990).

For example, a practitioner who feels heightened anxiety during interactions with family members from a different racial or cultural background is more likely to engage in negative stereotyping.

Memory

What a person chooses to remember, or subconscious processes involving memory, are linked to their personal beliefs, values and expectations.

For example, a practitioner who holds the stereotype of African Caribbean families as essentially matriarchal, comprising single mothers and absent fathers, may remember when completing their case notes back in the office that the maternal grandmother shares childcare at weekends, but not that the children's father provides financial support. This is because the first piece of information affirms their racial stereotype, while the second contradicts it, resulting in a recall error and the loss of vital information.

Collectively these innate cognitive processes tend to reinforce rather than dispel stereotypes which may be positive or negative, which partly explains why they tend to endure over time and are highly resistant to change. Stereotypes, predominantly negative ones, are also perpetuated and reinforced by television, newspapers, films and the internet, particularly in relation to gender, class and race. Generally only dramatic events or significant life experiences change negative stereotypes unless individuals engage in reflection or deliberately seek out cross-cultural encounters (Matsumoto & Juang, 2004). While to some degree *ethnocentrism* and stereotyping may be inevitable given innate cognitive processes for sorting information, prejudice and discrimination are not, and can be countered by acquiring knowledge about other cultures and self-examination of one's own cultural heritage alongside an ongoing commitment to reflexive and reflective practice.

Reflective exercise

Recall a meeting with a family member from a different racial, ethnic or faith background from you.

How did you feel during the encounter?

What did you notice most about that family member? List these observations.

What assumptions did you make based on these observations?

Social work practice with racial and ethnic diversity

Race, culture, ethnicity and faith have profound implications both for social workers and families in their interactions with each other. Commonly these are perceived as fixed sets of attributes and beliefs shared by whole families, kin groups and communities. For social workers this can mean slipping into easy stereotypes regarding the motivations and intentions of parents, children and other family members in ways which curtail exploration and understanding. At the same time culture influences the worldview of those from majority ethnic backgrounds just as much as it does those from minority heritage communities. Consequently all practitioners can potentially view and assess families from the value base of their own cultural or religious affiliations. Inevitably this will distort perceptions and the accurate assessment of risk of significant harm to a child or young person.

Awareness of the close correlation between stereotypes and *racial categorisation* together with comprehending the fluid nature of *ethnic identification* can help practitioners, regardless of their own racial or ethnic background, to resist tendencies towards making assumptions, particularly in time-pressured situations. Instead they are encouraged to explore with an open mind how children, young people and family members experience their own identities. Appreciating the underlying dimensions of cultural diversity can direct social workers to ask questions about salient areas of family life in relation to child protection. Recognising that spiritual beliefs and religious observances can be an organising set of precepts in the lives of many families is an important corrective to the often inadequate attention faith receives in social work training. The concept of *group identification*, whether this concerns ethnic or faith communities, reminds practitioners that significant relationships which fundamentally shape feelings, thoughts and behaviours are not confined to the family. For many children and their parents or guardians strands of influence extend into the family from broader close-knit social networks outside of it, but in which the family is embedded.

Conclusion

The population of the UK is characterised by superdiversity in relation to race, ethnicity, faith, language and immigration status as a consequence of multiple historical and contemporary migrations alongside the variety of migration pathways from one country to another. *Racial categorisation* refers to social rather than biological processes, and involves the attribution of traits to people on the basis of their skin colour. As the White majority is the dominant social group in the UK and the US this means the ascription of negative characteristics or inferior abilities to people who have black or brown skin.

Ethnicity is commonly perceived as a set of fixed attributes shared by all people from a particular minority heritage background in relation to their culture, faith and language. However, research reveals that processes of acculturation and globalisation have resulted in hybridisation and modification of an ethnic group's values, beliefs and practices over time. Stereotypes arise from the misconception that people from the same racial or heritage background share exactly the same traits and attributes. Once formed these stereotypes are often perpetuated by innate cognitive processes which accentuate and reinforce these fixed views of people from different racial or ethnic groups. Additionally, an individual's stage of *cultural identity* development can profoundly affect how they perceive and comprehend people from other ethnic backgrounds. Those whose own *cultural identity* remains unexamined are more likely to rely on racial and cultural stereotypes in their interactions with people from different heritage backgrounds.

2

White Privilege and Anglocentric Culture

Introduction

Practitioners need to achieve a degree of detachment from their own cultural background and gain insight into the nature of their beliefs, values and traditions and how these shape their worldviews and responses to others. The UK, like other Anglocentric nations such as the US and Australia, is not a culturally neutral society. Rather the demographically large and economically powerful White middle class is disproportionately influential in determining the overarching beliefs, values and conventions in these countries (Garner, 2007). These in turn become normalised and institutionalised to the point where, for those from the White majority, the day-to-day contexts in which they work and socialise appear neutral and unremarkable. To help social workers to develop reflective and reflexive capabilities in relation to race and culture, this chapter examines Whiteness as a racial identity and explores dominant strands of British culture in order to aid those primarily from the ethnic majority, but also from ethnic minorities, to identify and explore how their cultural heritage shapes their perceptions and assumptions. The implications for social work practice are examined through three case studies drawn from Serious Case Reviews involving British White families. These specific cases are exemplars of the impact of Anglocentric values in social work practices in relation to alcoholism, adolescent autonomy and sexual exploitation. They have multiple ramifications for work with ethnic minority families across a wide spectrum of child protection issues.

White privilege

White privilege is premised on the notion that regardless of whether they consent or agree, all White people irrespective of gender, age or class are to some extent beneficiaries of being racially white. Examining the nature of *White privilege* and how all White people are advantaged by it can be a profoundly uncomfortable and disconcerting experience, particularly for individuals who are genuinely appalled by racism and whose self-concept

is constructed around a belief in fairness and equality. Therefore explor
ing *White privilege* can elicit strong defensive reactions, including denial,
anger or ridicule. Drawing on the research, Garner (2007, p. 4) contends
that 'white people frequently construct themselves as raceless individuals,
unfettered by the kinds of collective identifications that they view other
people as having'. While those from White majority populations tend to
perceive themselves as individuals, they consider people from minority
ethnic communities as having attributes and traits reflecting their collective culture. The effect of this, as Frankenburg (1993) discovered, is that
the most frequently observed approach to the subject of race adopted by
White people was the evasion of discussing race and power issues, which are
instead replaced by what she terms 'a white self, innocent of racism'. Therefore at one and the same time White people perceive difference between
themselves and those from Black and ethnic minority communities, but by
professing a colour-blind worldview deny that such differences have any
significance. Such is the depth of this conviction among White people that,
as Garner (2007, p. 4) observes, 'seeing race' is regarded as inherently racist
when articulated by White people. When articulated by a Black person, it is
often dismissed as the inability of those from racial minorities to relinquish
historical grievances and acknowledge the equality offered by democrati-
cally constituted societies.

The common expressions *'people of colour'* or *'visible minorities'*, which
refer to those of Black or Asian origins, epitomise how *'white'* is socially
constructed as neither a colour nor visible. Yet *'white'* is a noun denoting
a colour and White people, who make up the majority population in both
the UK and North America, are certainly a most visible presence. This para-
dox arises because *whiteness* is not a racialised identity, but is instead treated
as the norm from which the physical features of others diverge and against
which they are adjudged. The proliferation of research into Black and
minority ethnic groups attests to the problematising of these social groups
in ways which are not true of the White majority. Martin & Nakayama
(2010) observe that precisely because White people constitute the majority
they are oblivious to their colour and are thus unselfconscious regarding
their racial identity. The naturalising of the colour *'white'* to the extent that
it becomes socially invisible – a state of racelessness – is accompanied by the
de-culturing of the majority White population while attributing culture to
Black and Asian communities.

As a consequence social workers from White majority backgrounds may
not recognise the degree to which their own experiences differ from those of
the Black and Asian families that they work with. These practitioners can be
oblivious, not only to the pervasiveness of racial abuse in the lives of many
minority families, but unaware of how racism creates unsafe localities; limits opportunities; adversely affects self-confidence; and undermines healthy
identity development. While many White majority social workers recognise

that racism has detrimental impacts, they are often insensible to the depth and range of these impacts for families from racial minorities. For families suffering racial abuse the extent to which this may damage their relationships with people from the White majority and therefore White social workers is not always appreciated. This means that such social workers can be slow to acknowledge and reflect upon how their own positionality in relation to race affects their interaction with families from racial minorities.

The White majority in both the UK and North America is socially constructed as possessing a rational universalist set of values and beliefs coalescing around autonomy and individualism underpinned by the legislative framework of human rights. Hence marrying for love among the White majority is not merely regarded as a practice consonant with notions of self-determination, but is considered normative, meaning it is what individuals should aspire to. Conversely, arranged marriages among some sections of South Asian communities based on relationships which can bring benefits to families as a whole, are derided as a violation of autonomy. Likewise the practice of *visiting* relationships among some couples of African Caribbean heritage in which men live outside the familial home, but are long-term partners, has been construed as widespread single motherhood, with African Caribbean men characterised as irresponsible and disengaged fathers (Laird, 2008, pp. 100–101). In fact, as research conducted by Mirza (1992) and Reynolds (2001, pp. 1052–53) reveals, around 80% of women of African Caribbean heritage defined as lone mothers are reckoned to be in long-term unions, often with men who pay maintenance and take on domestic responsibilities. The fact that this family arrangement does not fit the model of co-resident heterosexual parents has led to it being denigrated relative to the normative idea of family organisation embedded in White majority culture (Laird, 2008, p. 100). What is missing from everyday social life is the notion of White ethnicity; meaning the realisation that the majority White population shares a set of influential beliefs, attitudes and traditions which in some important respects differ from those of other ethnic groups.

White supremacy is predicated on the conviction by members of the White majority that Western European norms are superior to those of Black and minority ethnic groups. So for example White British people generally adjudge personal autonomy morally superior to a worldview which positions the best interests of the group above individual freedom of choice. This inevitably leads to a whole set of other judgements, for instance that marriages based solely on attraction and love are superior to arranged marriages which involve decision-making by kin as well as the prospective couple. This means that White majority values and behaviour become the standard against which those of other racial or ethnic groups are measured and against which they may be perceived as deviant or deficient. White supremacy as a concept not only embraces the notion of *White privilege*, but also presupposes that White people have a vested interest in maintaining institutions and structures which continue to advantage them, both at a national and international level.

The universalising and normalising of key beliefs and values held by the White ethnic majority in North America and Western Europe means that social workers from this background can often be oblivious to the fact that they are from an ethnic group themselves. So over-familiar is this dominant worldview in British society that it can be difficult for social workers from the White ethnic majority to perceive themselves as holding to distinctive beliefs, values and practices. Yet in reality these are but one cultural formulation of how to organise family, rear children and live a meaningful or good life. It is for this reason that appreciating positionality in terms of ethnic identity can be more challenging for social workers from the White ethnic majority. When working with families from minority ethnic backgrounds, lack of reflexive capability can make it harder to build effective working relationships with children and family members.

Belonging to the majority White population therefore carries privileges associated with invisibility, normative lifestyles and apparent cultural neutrality. It is also the experience of not encountering difficulties predicated on race, such as employment discrimination or racial abuse. At an individual level these privileges include possessing greater cultural capital than those from ethnic minority groups. This is because it is the culture of the White majority which underpins norms widely assumed to be universally applicable, such as independence and autonomy. At a societal level these privileges include the superior political and economic power that White people wield both nationally in the UK and globally in the dissemination of normative forms of family life and childcare (Laird, 2008; Twum-Danso Imoh & Ame, 2012). According to Bourdieu & Wacquant (1998, p. 109, cited in Garner, 2007, p. 6) this kind of 'cultural imperialism rests on the power to universalize particularisms related to a specific historical tradition by making them (mis)understood as universally true'. When Western values and norms are raised to the level of universal truth, propagated historically through colonialism and currently through the global economic and political dominance of the US and the EU, then they become difficult to 'see'. Frankenburg (1993) argues that Whiteness has three dimensions, which are described below.

Normative race privilege: As the dominant social group those from the White majority accrue automatic privileges such as: being invisible and thus not attracting attention; in most settings being in the company of their own race; and one's beliefs, values and behaviours being treated as normative and therefore not being required to acculturate.

A worldview: A perception of self, others and society from the standpoint of being a member of the White majority which is often profoundly different from the perceptions of people from minority ethnic groups, for example around issues of inequality and discrimination.

A set of cultural practices: As the culture of the White majority is omnipresent and constitutes the economic, social and political fabric of society, their cultural practices are often unrecognised as distinctive cultural practices; an example is the emphasis on individualism and independence.

Reflective exercise

Consider your own experience.

In what ways is *White privilege* or supremacy evident in aspects of your social and work life?

How is *White privilege* or supremacy displayed in your neighbourhood or in relation to your community?

At a broader societal level, what aspects of *White privilege* or supremacy influence your values, beliefs or behaviours?

White diversity

The White population of the UK comprises a diversity of ethnicities, languages and faiths. While the 2011 Census revealed that 82% of the population identified as White British, out of this total 64% identified as Christian, 0.5% identified as Jewish and 0.4% as Muslim. While these percentages appear small they equate to 226,000 White Jews and 181,000 White Muslims. In the UK, out of those describing themselves as White, 55,000 identified as Gypsy, Traveller or Irish Traveller while 500,000 identified as White Irish and 2,500,000 as 'White other'. Of those identifying as 'White other' the majority were from other European countries, while a smaller number were from North America and Australia. In terms of native languages among White people, 530,000 spoke Polish, 120,000 Spanish, 91,000 Lithuanian, 84,000 Italian, 75,000 German and 66,000 Romanian (Office for National Statistics, 2011).

There has been push-back against the proposition that all White people are equally privileged. In particular those from working-class and lower middle-class backgrounds may perceive themselves as having lost out to Black and minority ethnic groups as they confront poor housing, over-stretched public services and the educational achievement of some categories of White children dropping below those of Black and Asian minorities in Britain. Often such groups argue that political concern and resources have been focused on supporting minorities rather than deprived indigenous communities (Cantle, 2008). Many British and American White people on low incomes, with poor educational qualifications and confined to low-paid casual employment would argue that for them being White is not privilege-bearing. They perceive ethnic minorities as having been the beneficiaries of racial equality and community cohesion policies. Often they blame their own predicament of unemployment and deprivation on minorities rather than on economic structural changes or the retrenchment of government welfare policies (Garner, 2007). This neglects their freedom from racial abuse in contrast to the sense of permanent vulnerability created by the visibility of having black or brown skin in a predominantly White society.

Many White minorities in the UK appear to no longer share in the same *White privilege* and may hold worldviews and engage in cultural practices which are different from those of the White majority population. Increasingly White migrants from Eastern Europe face prejudice, discrimination, exploitation, deprivation and abuse in the UK (Fox et al., 2015; The Migration Observatory, 2013, 2014). Garner (2007) argues, based on scholarship in the US, that individuals from White immigrant minorities can over time move from their *'in-between'* White and Black status to assimilation into the White majority population in ways which are not open to those with racially different features from the White majority. So while White immigrants may be initially disadvantaged, though often not to the same extent as Black and Asian minorities, they have the option of melting into the White majority in ways impossible for individuals from Black and Asian backgrounds. In terms of acculturation, people from White minorities generally have a real choice to identify with, and be accepted by, the White majority in the medium to longer term (Garner, 2007). Moreover, while White minorities from Eastern Europe may not share in the *White privilege* of White British-born majority group members, they will nevertheless enjoy those privileges in their home countries, as is evident from the high level of racial prejudice, ethnocentrism and discrimination evident in many Eastern European countries (The Conversation, 2017).

This debate does lead to the recognition that context and positionality can change the extent to which *White privilege* can be exercised and that people may be more or less advantaged by it depending on their immigrant status, gender, disability, sexuality, religion and class. Indeed, Garner (2007, p. 11) acknowledges that 'a person racialized as white can be ideologically exiled from this privilege, or may pursue values seen as antagonistic, or adhere to a minority religion, or are from a different country, for example (e.g. Travellers/Gypsies, "white trash", Jews, various migrant groups such as the Irish in Britain)'. But he proceeds to argue that an over-focus on White divisions and diversity begins to obscure the pervasive overarching dominance of *White privilege*.

Social workers from the White ethnic majority and from Black and ethnic minority backgrounds need to recognise the intersectionality of social class, poverty, ethnicity and religion with Whiteness. Plainly not all White people are able to exercise *White privilege* to the same degree and many may actually be profoundly disadvantaged. But precisely because children or family members are White, there is a danger of simply treating them all the same without exploring how Whiteness intersects with other structural aspects of their lives. A Jewish White family may be confronted by anti-semitism, while White Traveller families face considerable hostility from sections of settled communities. Similarly, many White Romanian and Polish families are subject to verbal abuse and intimidation in often predominantly White neighbourhoods. Conversely, social workers also need to bear in mind how the intersectionality of disadvantage in the lives of children and family members may also fuel their prejudicial attitudes towards people from minority backgrounds.

Notions of White supremacy influence perceptions of 'respectability'. Skeggs (1997, p. 1) suggests that the idea of respectability is 'one of the key mechanisms by which people are othered and pathologized'. This includes its deployment by people in more dominant social groups as a marker to distinguish between classes, races and ethnicities. Research reveals examples of people from a White British working-class background objecting to the behaviour of Asians on the grounds that they held strange beliefs, were noisy, had multiple relatives visiting and ate strange meat (meaning halal). This was contrasted with White working-class people who by comparison were quiet, held mainstream views and ate 'normal' meat. This notion of respectability was also deployed to differentiate between those defining themselves as decent, honest, self-sufficient, industrious working-class people in contrast with White youth sub-cultures, which were characterised as jobless, idle and delinquent. Additionally, young people's adoption of Black forms of music, dress and language were perceived by many working-class adults as deviating from respectable White norms. The comparisons that 'respectability' creates act both to laud the beliefs, values and practices of one's own racial or ethnic group or social class while essentialising and devaluing those of others (Garner, 2007, pp. 59–60).

Anglocentric values

This section presents an overview of Anglocentric values and demonstrates how deeply embedded they are in British society. Throughout they are contrasted with the varied worldviews of other cultures, many of which remain influential among the ethnic minority communities settled in the UK. How Anglocentric values affect the perspectives and practices of social workers is explored in the next section through three Serious Case Reviews. These describe the circumstances which led to the deaths or gross abuse of children and young people and reveal the extent to which Anglocentric values underpin social work decision-making and interventions in ways which can skew practice.

Like the colour white, which has become socially invisible, many belonging to the majority population in the UK think of culture as something which characterises the lives of others, but not their life. Culture is perceived to shape the lifestyles and actions of those from minority ethnic groups while *'mainstream'* society is experienced as possessing neutral or universal values and being cultureless. This is because as the dominant and most influential group in the UK (as in North America and Australia), the White majority determine the standards for appropriate behaviour by others. In doing so the culture of the White majority has thereby become normative. The Department for Education (2014b, p. 5) describes 'fundamental British values' as comprising 'democracy, the rule of law, individual liberty and mutual respect and tolerance of those with different faiths and beliefs'. British culture is often caricatured as cohering around the class system, personal reserve, popular music, the arts scene and such traditional foods as fish and chips and Yorkshire pudding. This superficial perception of British values and culture obscures pervasive and deep-rooted influences on everyday life. Laird (2008, pp. 44–45) and Lattanzi & Prunell (2006, p. 25) draw on the literature to identify a number of values and beliefs which underpin social expectations and lifestyles in the UK and US and are evident in the dominant norms of British society. These are considered each in turn and compared to those of other cultures.

Influenced by the Protestantism adopted by the state in the seventeenth century, which places the individual's relationship with God at the centre of worship and religious practice, autonomy and self-determination have become highly prized attributes among the White British majority. The significance given by Protestantism to reading the Bible also placed new emphasis on printing and communication through the written word, a mainly private activity. Consequently, great importance is assigned to a person's ability to exercise self-determined choices which meet their desired goals and achieve outcomes valued by them personally. Freedom of choice is a central tenet of their social lives, derived from the strong influences of libertarian ideology in Britain from the eighteenth century onwards. This strand of political thought gives primacy to individual autonomy unless a person's choices infringe the rights of others to make choices, violate their rights or pose a danger, in which case the state steps in to arbitrate these conflicts through the rule of law. The overarching principle of rights attaching to individuals (reflected in the integration of the Convention on the Rights of the Child into British law) grants protections to individuals, while domestic legislation underpins security of personal property and physical safety. Since everyone is equally entitled to exercise their individual rights, tolerance and restraint are considered important human qualities in social relationships and encounters. While equality has been undermined in the UK by poverty, prejudice and discrimination against many social groups, it still remains an ideal which informs legislation and expectations of conduct.

It encompasses equality between people of different genders, sexuality, race, ethnicity, age and ability.

Other societies are more collectivist in orientation and place greater emphasis on the group rather than the individual. Among many Asian cultures the wellbeing of the kin group or sometimes the local community can take precedence over individual preferences. Acting on purely individual considerations may be viewed as selfish. Therefore individual family members may be expected to subordinate their desires to the needs and aims of the household as a whole. Many decisions may be based on collective deliberations rather than only individual choice. In some societies, such as those of India and Pakistan, deference to elders, males and those in positions of authority is often more important than equality. In these contexts a lack of deference can be perceived as rude or transgressive. In Hispanic countries such as Spain (which has similar equality legislation to the United Kingdom) the cultural constructs of *caballerismo* (referring to male dignity and nurturing family) alongside *machismo* (concerning self-reliance and masculine superiority), still shape gender relations and undermine equality.

The attention given to the individual within the dominant culture means that the development of personal identity and respect for individuality are highly valued among the majority community in British society. The corollary of such emphasis on the individual is the expectation that people will be independent, largely self-sufficient and manage their problems primarily through self-help. The entitlement to personal privacy which follows from the attention given to the individual in British society, while increasingly challenged by social media, particularly among younger people, nevertheless remains an important influence in people's interaction with one another and the state. There is a presumption that an individual's thoughts and feelings are private matters, which they may decide to disclose to a few chosen family members, friends or work colleagues. This makes the maintenance of confidentiality an important aspect of interactions both between individuals and between the state and its citizens.

This emphasis on the individual contrasts with the influential cultural values of numerous other societies. In China complex social and economic support networks known as *guanxi* are fostered over time and relied upon during periods of difficulty or for favours. Among many African peoples and those of African origin, emphasis is laid on mutual assistance and reciprocity. There is a presumption that individuals within the kin group, and often the community, will help each other out rather than everyone having to rely essentially on themselves. There is an expectation that difficulties will be discussed and managed at the level of the family or wider kin. In this setting privacy and confidentiality may be considered less important, while the sharing of experiences, concerns and personal details is both anticipated and encouraged. Adopting reserve can seem secretive or mistrustful and be isolating.

Self-expression, assertiveness and direct communication are the behavioural corollaries of the cultural emphasis on individuality. Since the mid-twentieth century deference between people of different statuses such as older and younger, employer and employee and middle class and working class has given way to greater value being placed on informality in social interactions. However, in many other societies individuality is de-emphasised relative to preserving harmony between people. In Filipino culture maintaining smooth relationships, referred to as *pakisisama*, is highly valued as opposed to self-assertion. Respect for and deference to authority figures remains influential, while formality, especially between people of different statuses, is an observed norm. Moreover, like North American and Australian societies, the dominant culture in the UK is *low context*, meaning that individuals tend to be relatively explicit in conveying meanings in their communications. By contrast, French, Spanish and Greek societies are higher context than that of Britain and consequently more interpersonal communication may be implicit, with shared understandings assumed rather than expressed. Chinese, African and Indian societies tend to be higher context than European ones, resulting in even more communication reliant on a common worldview and multiple meanings implied rather than spoken.

The Age of Enlightenment of the eighteenth century was an intellectual movement in Europe which set rationality over religious faith; displaced belief with empiricism; and promoted deductive reasoning to extrapolate theories about the observable world. From these origins, secularism and positivist science not only underpin technological advances alongside control over the environment, but in the UK also influence the wider culture. British society is task-oriented and prizes practicality, efficiency, prompt action and keeping to time. It is also achievement-oriented, with individuals earning respect for demonstrating competence and obtaining results. While controversy surrounds poor social mobility in the UK, it nevertheless remains a country which conceives of itself as a meritocracy, encouraging competition between individuals and rewarding those who achieve, with promotion, higher earnings, greater social status or acclamation. The combination of individualism and positivist science means that in relation to outcomes, British society tends to assign credit and culpability to individuals rather than other factors. This is evident in the tendency to blame individual social workers, police officers or doctors for the deaths of children known to these services rather than inadequate systems within or between agencies or broader structural factors such as poverty or discrimination.

By contrast, in numerous societies religion remains extremely influential in most people's lives. In Pakistan, Islam embodies a set of rules which shape legislation and determine proper conduct in both economic matters and social life, including family relationships. Among some sections of the population in Nigeria evangelical Christianity makes their faith a vital source of guidance and church congregations close-knit communities. In many societies religious belief is blended with scientific and technological advances rather than being eclipsed by them. While British culture focuses on individual achievement and reward, other societies place more importance on spirituality, social relationships and the environment. Many ethnic Chinese who practise Buddhism or Taoism deem harmony within the family and with their physical environment vital considerations when making decisions. For a number of first nation peoples such as native Americans and Australian aborigines the relationship between communities and their natural environment is viewed as a reciprocal one. In many African and Chinese societies, fulfilling obligations to family members, or those owed a favour, may take precedence over other considerations, resulting in a relative or friend being given employment who is not as competent as others. Among cultures which place more emphasis on *'being'* rather than *'doing'* and on maintaining relationships rather than individuality, time may be of less importance. Consequently, keeping to time may be sacrificed to meeting social obligations; for instance a mother staying longer on a visit to a family member, rather than leaving in time to attend a health appointment with her child.

The scientific underpinning of the economy has created a high technological dependency in the UK, as is true of other post-industrial societies. Additionally, the combination of capitalism (itself an expression of individualism, freedom of choice, competitiveness and personal gain) and the position of the UK as one of the foremost economies, has resulted in hyper-consumerism, predicated on materialism and status based on ownership and patterns of consumption. As a culture greatly influenced by empiricism and scientific thinking, dominant strands in British society tend to be future-oriented, open to change and adaptable, placing less emphasis on the past and tradition. Cultural tropes in other societies such as Ghana and Pakistan are more concerned with tradition and continuity than is the case in the UK. In countries such as Spain and Greece, although individualism and consumerism still shape social relationships, the extended and nuclear family remain more central to social life than is so for the majority of White British people.

Reflective exercise

Consider your own ethnic background.

How much influence do Anglocentric norms have on your values, attitudes and behaviour?

What other cultural or spiritual influences are there in your life?

How do you synthesise these different sources of influence and/or manage any conflicts they create?

Anglocentric values and beliefs therefore revolve around scientific positivism, secularism, individualism, independence, self-reliance and freedom of choice. As foundational tenets these encourage self-expression, directness and informality and support notions of personal space and privacy, while fostering competitiveness and achievement. They are values which underpin a capitalist market system where consumer choice is paramount and material possessions are articulations of success and social status. Technological advances combined with self-expression through patterns of consumption have driven hyper-consumerism in the UK as in other Anglocentric countries. The market system and individual responsibility also mean that societal norms place a premium on the efficient use of time and task-oriented occupations. Equal rights and equality of opportunity, alongside merit-based advancement, all guaranteed by the rule of law, remain ideals strongly embedded in British society.

However, Anglocentric values, beliefs and practices have long escaped scrutiny in child protection social work. The notion of culture as imbuing the perspectives and habits of ethnic minorities, but not those of the ethnic majority whose beliefs and behaviours are obscured by assumptions of normativity, can blindside practitioners. The Serious Case Reviews discussed in the second half of this chapter are concerned with three examples of ethnic majority culture related to parental alcohol consumption, decision-making by teenagers and adolescent sexuality. These have been chosen to demonstrate how dominant British values and norms modify professional perceptions and frame social work intervention with families. Not only do they illuminate interactions with families from the ethnic majority, but indicate how by shaping social workers' practices they can also influence engagement with families from ethnic minorities.

Alcohol in ethnic majority British culture

British attitudes towards, and patterns of, alcohol consumption have ramifications for child protection. In the UK as a whole it is estimated that 2.6 million children live with a parent whose alcohol consumption puts them at risk of neglect (Manning et al., 2009). An audit of Child Protection Registers in London found that 75% of parents whose children were on the Register, and therefore had a Child Protection Plan in place, misused alcohol (Hayden, 2004). In their analysis of 174 Serious Case Reviews for the period 2011–14 Sidebotham et al. (2016, pp. 69, 85) found that parental alcohol misuse was a factor in 37% of cases, while among abused or neglected 11–15 year olds 18% misused alcohol, rising to 50% for children over 16 years of age.

The prevalence of high alcohol consumption in modern-day Britain has historical roots. By the late sixteenth century technological advances in fermentation and the expansion of alehouses meant that stronger affordable beer became available on a much larger scale than before. Drunkenness started to emerge as an acknowledged social problem, with commentators of the era observing that drinking to excess had become embedded in English everyday culture. The Anglican Church and later many evangelical protestant denominations viewed drinking as sinful, occasioning immoral behaviour (James, 2009). By the late nineteenth century the medical profession was becoming increasingly influential, resulting in the rise of the 'disease' model of excessive alcohol consumption, which defined it as a form of physiological and psychological dysfunction to be treated in hospital or the asylum. The increasing dominance of psychiatry in the twentieth century, paralleled by the decline of religious faith, replaced moral culpability for drinking with helpless addiction.

This tension continued until the 1960s, when the counterculture of that era focused on individualism and pleasure-seeking, with government emphasising freedom of choice rather than political action to curb intoxication. The strong association of alcohol with sporting fixtures, particularly football, has increased its widespread acceptability and expectations of social drinking in both the UK and US (Gilchrist et al., 2014, p. 11; Alcohol Concern, 2014, p. 3). Further technological advances and deregulation of the retail drinks industry during the 1990s and 2000s has made alcohol cheaper and accessible 24/7. The cultural preoccupation with individual freedom in an era of hyper-capitalism witnessed a shift of emphasis to economic rights and lifestyle choice, prioritising the entitlement of consumers to choose what products they wish to buy and consume. While *'binge drinking'* remains an acknowledged social problem, closely linked to violence and domestic abuse, successive governments have treated it as essentially a public health issue, exhorting people to drink responsibly (Institute of Alcohol Studies, 2013).

Research indicates that 29% of men and 15% of women *'binge drink'*, defined as a man drinking above eight units and a woman above six units of alcohol in any one day (Royal Geographic Society, 2010, p. 3). Approximately 33% of men and 24% of women are classified as hazardous drinkers in England, while British drinking culture is evident across social classes with 38% of professionals and 29% of manual workers exceeding the daily recommended amount (Alcohol Concern, 2014, p. 1; Royal Geographic Society, 2010, pp. 5, 19). In their survey of the population in England NHS (2017) asked respondents whether they drank in excess of 8/6 units (depending on gender) on their heaviest drinking day of the week and found that around 18% of those in each of the age groups 16–24, 25–44 and 45–64 reported imbibing levels of alcohol consistent with binge drinking.

This overview of the literature reveals how alcohol consumption has become a pervasive aspect of social and leisure activity in the United Kingdom. It evidences the interaction of capitalism, technology, individualism, autonomy, consumer choice and secularism (neutralising notions of immorality) in creating a high incidence, high consumption drinking culture. This is despite the long known detrimental health consequences of heavy drinking, such as memory loss, poor concentration, depression and liver disease alongside a raft of anti-social and risky behaviours including aggression, impaired judgement and loss of sexual inhibition. The widespread acceptance of high levels of alcohol consumption among those from the ethnic majority inevitably influences the attitudes and actions of practitioners interacting with parents where children may be at risk of significant harm. This is illustrated in NSPCC (2016) *Serious Case Review No. 2016-C5807 Children U, B and V*, which concerned the neglect of two children fathered by Mr R and the death of a six-week-old baby in November 2014 fathered by Mr W.

NSPCC (2016) *Serious Case Review No. 2016-C5807 Children U, B and V*

Two fathers, Mr R and Mr W, and the mother, all White British, resided in separate properties. But there were frequent visits and overnight stays between them, their relationship being characterised by alcohol misuse. In 2011 the mother reported heavy drinking related to insomnia to her GP. In early 2014 Mr W was admitted to hospital on several occasions suffering from suicidal ideation and was known to consume excessive alcohol. Although he was encouraged by the hospital and his GP to engage with services to address his alcohol misuse, he refused assistance. At around the same time Mr R was repeatedly admitted to hospital due to health conditions associated with heavy drinking, including severe depression. During a prenatal appointment in April 2014 the mother disclosed high levels of alcohol consumption and feelings of depression to the midwife. The nursing practitioner made a referral to Child Protection Services, but it was rejected as of insufficient gravity to merit assessment. When invited to engage in an assessment for their alcohol misuse both mother and father denied they had drink-related problems and refused additional support services. In September 2014 Child Protection Social Services received an anonymous call, and in early November contact from the police, regarding the mother's excessive drinking while in charge of her children then aged 13 and 15 years. Amid increasing concerns from various agencies an initial Child Protection Conference was held on 17 November and Child Protection Plans put in place for all the children. The baby died a week later before these could be fully implemented. The cause of death could not be ascertained and both parents pleaded guilty to child neglect and received short custodial sentences.

During 2014 Mr R, Mr. W and the mother between them had 70 separate contacts with agencies, predominantly in relation to their chronic alcoholism. This compares to the older children only being seen several times by professionals (excepting for teachers at school) over the same period. Explaining to the Serious Case Review why they did not intervene earlier with the family, Child Protection Services attributed this to 'the fact that alcohol is a socially acceptable drug and argue[d] that this may have been a factor in the failure to explore the issues further' (NSPCC, 2014, para.6.1.14). The Serious Case Review Panel accepted this reason, albeit that they concluded poor multi-agency information sharing contributed to this.

In relation to the lack of uptake of addiction support services by the parents the Overview Report suggested that professionals should have made more effort to engage the parents in support services for their addiction. In this instance all the parents had health treatment due to the detrimental effects of alcohol misuse, particularly in relation to severe depression. They were offered addiction services, which each parent refused and was not com-pelled to accept, reflecting notions of autonomy and the paramountcy of freedom of choice. Indeed, alcohol is widely described by drinkers in positive terms as a leisure activity, improving sociability and relieving stress (Gilchrist et al., 2014). The widespread social acceptance of alcohol con-sumption and the normalising of 'binge drinking' may explain the finding of Sidebotham et al. (2016, p. 80) which noted a sometimes sluggish social work response to the co-occurrence of domestic violence and alcohol abuse, which also seems to have occurred in NSPCC (2016). It is as if the high prevalence of excessive alcohol consumption across social classes, ages and genders together with its widespread social acceptance among the ethnic majority has made it invisible. In child protection social work this seems to translate into very high thresholds for intervention in families where alco-hol consumption is affecting the standard of childcare.

NSPCC (2016, para.5.1.3) *Serious Case Review No. 2016-C5807 Children U, B and V* noted that the agencies involved with the White British family had provided minimal information regarding their socio-economic background, beliefs or cultural identity. Yet in the UK there is ethnic variation, with those from Irish and Scottish backgrounds evidencing a higher level of alcohol consumption than those from English ones (Royal Geographic Society, 2010, pp. 5–7; Hurcombe et al., 2010). However, compared to all non-White minority ethnic communities, White British people abstain less and drink more. Just 4% of people from Pakistani backgrounds and 5% from Bang-ladeshi backgrounds living in the UK consume alcohol, compared to 68% of White British people (Hurcombe et al., 2010; Royal Geographic Society, 2010, p. 6). In other words there is a cultural influence at work among the White ethnic majority population, making high alcohol consumption and the adverse behaviours that flow from it highly acceptable – an attitude not shared by other ethnic groups.

This exploration of the centrality of alcohol – an addictive, but legal and socially accepted drug in the daily life of most people from the eth-nic majority – articulates cultural values and beliefs regarding freedom of choice, informality, consumerism and the de-stigmatisation of alcohol con-sumption through the adoption of secularism. Cultural perspectives affect not only the outlook and actions of parents who reframe their alcoholism as 'social drinking', but also of the professionals who interact with them and are so accustomed to high levels of alcohol consumption that this is per-ceived as a lifestyle choice and so normalised that only in the most extreme circumstances is it assessed by practitioners as putting children at risk of significant harm. But alcohol is not the only aspect of British cultural life which has adverse ramifications for the safety of children and the responses of professionals endeavouring to safeguard them.

Reflective exercise

Consider the circumstances in NSPCC (2016).

What are your own attitudes and behaviours relating to the consumption of alcohol?

How might these attitudes and behaviours influence your perceptions and practice responses to a family in similar circumstances to those in NSPCC (2016)?

The social construction of teenagers in White British culture

In all societies the onset of puberty in girls and boys is accompanied by a process of psychosocial development as physiological changes signal the process of sexual maturation. In Anglocentric societies the normative expectation is that it is a period of 'storm and stress'; a concept first discussed by Hall (1904), an American psychologist, in his seminal work during which adolescents commonly experience emotional volatility, engage in risky behaviour, and are frequently in conflict with parental figures. Later developmental theory elaborated by Freud (1969), an Austrian neurologist, further emphasised the role of sexual impulses in the acting out of strong instinctual forces. Blos (1962), an American psychoanalyst, conceptualised adolescence as a second individuation process as the older child now needed to weaken ties with the family in order to develop affective bonds and explore sexuality with others. Erikson (1963, 1968), a German-born American psychoanalyst, and Marcia (1966), a Canadian psychologist, theorised that the primary developmental goal of adolescence was the forging of a coherent self and elaboration of personal identity. In order to achieve this, parents needed to provide adolescents with greater freedom while they became less tightly bonded to family and more interested in interacting with their peers. Taken altogether, these highly influential theories of adolescence, which conceptualise it as a period of turmoil, individuation, identity development and reliance on peers rather than family, have been universally applied to young people. However, much research now demonstrates that they refer to culture-bound behaviours particular to Western societies and most particularly children of the White ethnic majority (Robinson, 2007; Twum-Danso & Ame, 2012).

In many African societies children often move from childhood into the workforce or take on adult domestic tasks without experiencing a period of adolescence, if this is rightly understood as a social transition and not merely a biological process. Among many families in Asian and African societies where *high power distance* between older and younger people remains influential, young people may be much more likely to respect the authority of their parents or elders rather than rebel against it. Racial and ethnic identity development is missing from the work of these North American and European theorists, who were all from the White majority. Yet for those from racial and ethnic minorities, racialisation constitutes a formative experience (Robinson, 2007; Twum-Danso & Ame, 2012). Consequently the underpinning child development theories used by social workers to inform their observations of family life, assessments of need and care plans are based on a particular, though dominant, worldview. Nevertheless, social work draws extensively on social science theories in relation to child development, family dynamics and inter-generational relationships, creating paradigms which both guide and skew practitioners' interpretation of what they see (Daniel et al., 2010; Sudbery, 2009). In Anglocentric societies, teenagers as a social group fall awkwardly between childhood and adulthood in ways which often lead to confusion over their status. This is evident in Gloucestershire Safeguarding Children Board (2016) *Serious Case Review Lucy*, which investigated the circumstances surrounding the murder of 16-year-old Lucy by her 18-year-old male partner, who was subsequently sentenced to life imprisonment.

Gloucestershire Safeguarding Children Board (2016) *Serious Case Review Lucy*

For much of her life Lucy had lived between her White British mother, father and maternal grandparents. By the age of 14 years due to her challenging behaviour, including self-harm, going missing from home, school truancy, alcohol misuse and aggressive outbursts, her relationships with family members faltered to the extent that they became unwilling to accommodate her and by the age of 15 she was effectively homeless. At this point Children's Social Care became involved. Notably this agency had received earlier referrals regarding Lucy's misuse of alcohol which, despite the well-established strong correlation between self-harm, depression and aggression with heavy drinking, did not meet the threshold to initiate a *child in need* or *child protection* assessment. Nor, apparently, was Lucy referred to an addiction service; instead she was later referred for counselling. This agency's response reflects prevailing British cultural attitudes towards alcohol consumption, even by those under the legal drinking age, as notions of freedom of choice predominate in conjunction with expectations of risky behaviour and conflict with authority figures among adolescents.

▶

◀

Social workers did attempt to negotiate accommodation for Lucy on a one-to-one basis with individual family members, but they did not call a family group conference. This is a forum which brings together involved family members to deliberate on concerns regarding a child's health, development or safety in order to find a solution facilitated by professional support. Social workers attributed this decision to Gloucestershire's Family Group Conference Policy which at that time stated 'the young person has to be in agreement for the conference to take place, if they are considered to have the maturity to make the decision for themselves, independent of those with *parental responsibility*'. The perception of some practitioners was that Lucy was resistant to the prospect of such a conference and in accordance with her wishes none was called.

Lucy moved to live with her male partner against the advice of the student social worker allocated to her, by which time it was known that this male partner was controlling Lucy's communications by smashing her phone, ensuring she had little money, engaging in coercive behaviour and continuing to assault her. There was no discussion with Lucy as to how she might safely separate from her violent partner and the policy framework that was in place was for adult victims of domestic abuse, which required them to voluntarily engage with the process. Thereafter the focus of Children's Social Care was on the safety of Lucy's unborn child rather than Lucy, who was herself a vulnerable child requiring protection from a violent coercive partner. A subsequent Child Protection Conference held to address the safety of the unborn child made it subject to a Child Protection Plan on the grounds of risk of emotional and physical abuse. Lucy's parents were not invited to this conference, although her partner was, and indeed he was praised by professionals at the conference for attending. In retrospect it is likely that he attended in order to control Lucy's participation. Subsequently Lucy moved back to live with her mother, but was shortly afterwards killed by her male partner who was found guilty of murder and received a life sentence.

The professional decision not to call a family group conference, and the agency policy which supported it, illustrates how Anglocentric culture relegates kinship and bonds of interdependence relative to individualism and freedom of choice. In accordance with notions of individuation, separation and selfhood premised on the developmental theories of Erikson (1963, 1968) and Marcia (1966), Lucy is treated here as a standalone individual who not only makes decisions for herself independently from her family, but can prevent even parents and grandparents from intervening in her life by refusing consent for them to be involved. This is a power professionals bestowed upon her based upon cultural precepts. This is at odds with the cultural values and beliefs dominant in many other societies, which emphasise the interdependence of family members and the rights of parents, guardians or other authority figures (embedded in social mores and sometimes in legislation) to guide and direct children during their teenage years and often into early adulthood.

Dominant constructions of the British family as essentially nuclear in form appear to have influenced who social workers invited to a pivotal

Child Protection Conference. The parents (grandparents to the unborn child) are not invited to participate in the decision-making process relating to their teenaged child's safety, but the violent father is. This atomised version of the family unit as discrete from wider kin relationships is at variance with influential mores around family organisation in other societies and often replicated by minority communities in the UK (Laird, 2008). The fairly light guidance provided to Lucy by a student social worker also illustrates how teenagers, who are legally children in the UK until the age of 18 years, are nevertheless treated as if they were adults. This follows from developmental theories of adolescence as a period that requires teenagers to be given more responsibility and freedom in order to achieve a healthy autonomous identity status.

Gloucestershire Safeguarding Children Board (2016, para.3.2.1) noted that 'Lucy exposed herself to a greater level of risk when she moved to live with [her partner] and professionals considered she had the autonomy to take this step despite the increased risk to herself and [the unborn child]'. The Serious Case Review argued that social workers did not adequately take into account the degree to which being in an intimate abusive and controlling relationship impaired Lucy's ability to exercise self-determination. By letting Lucy be the decision-maker social workers assumed she knew how to keep herself safe. As Gloucestershire Safeguarding Children Board (2016, para.2.2.2) acknowledges, 'there is a balance to strike when practitioners work with teenagers, between respecting and supporting their autonomy and their need to be protected as children'. Gloucestershire Safeguarding Children Board (2016, para.3.6–3.6.3) concludes that:

> The challenge for professionals is how to safeguard a teenager who is making choices that put themselves at risk. There must be a point in safeguarding systems when the child's vulnerability outweighs their ascertainable wishes...If professionals lose sight that a teenager is a child, with all the inherent vulnerabilities that being a child brings, they fall out of being afforded adequate protection, as younger children are, because they are seen as ultimately autonomous.

However, this balance is exceptionally difficult to achieve in a society where values and beliefs, alongside culturally driven developmental theory embedded in social work training, prize separation from parents, the development of autonomy and exercising freedom of choice. These are perceived to be integral to the 'good life' in the UK and therefore the desired end state of adolescent maturation. It is unsurprising, therefore, that professionals will seek to support these developmental processes through permitting teenagers to make choices in much the same way as adults; and then to become confused regarding intervention when young people make highly risky decisions. Dominant notions of normative family relationships and child development undoubtedly influenced the perceptions of social workers and the actions they took in relation to Lucy. Some of these elements are also evident in the next case study, concerning professional decision-making in relation to teenage sexuality.

Reflective exercise

Consider the circumstances in Gloucestershire Safeguarding Children Board (2016).

What are your own beliefs and views about how adolescents should be parented?

What are your own beliefs and views about how much choice teenagers should be given and over which aspects of their lives?

To what extent are your beliefs and views influenced by Anglocentric norms?

How might any Anglocentric norms you adhere to influence your perceptions of and practice responses to a family in similar circumstances to those described in Gloucestershire Safeguarding Children Board (2016)?

Adolescent sexuality in White British culture

The decline of Christianity in the UK and with it prohibitions on premarital sex, alongside the advent of contraception and emphasis on individual choice, has resulted in a tendency towards serial monogamy in what are often short-lived sexual relationships between young people (Moore & Rosenthal, 1993, p. 98). The decoupling of sex from reproduction, permitting the postponement of parenthood, has also meant that first sexual activity occurs at a younger age than was true of previous generations. Research indicates that in Western countries the average age of first intercourse has dropped from 18 years to 16 years over the last few decades (Moore & Rosenthal, 1993, p. 7; Powell, 2010, pp. 14–15). Consequently in Anglocentric societies there are presumptions that teenagers will distance themselves from parental figures, spend more time with friends, have casual sexual experiences and exercise much greater autonomy compared with childhood. For girls their psycho-sexual–social development anticipated during adolescence is further complicated by gender expectations and consumerism.

The mass media and advertising visually present to girls and young women that their bodies are and ought to be sexually desirable objects. Moreover, they convey messages relating to expectations of heterosexual desire and activity (Frost, 2001; Griffin, 2004; Papadopoulos, 2010). Advertising has used sexualised images of women to sell products since 1900. However the spending power of teenagers and the pester power of tweenies (8–14 year olds), alongside the multiplication and diversification of digitalised media in an era of hyper-consumerism, has culminated in the earlier sexualisation of children (Griffin, 2004; Papadopoulos, 2010). Sexualised and gender-stereotyped childrenswear for girls regularly appears as scaled-down versions of clothes imbued with adult sexuality (Entwistle, 2000). This in turn influences girls' understanding about what they should wear and the male attention they should seek to elicit, even when their intention is not to initiate sexual activity. Gleeson & Frith (2004), in their exploration of 12–16-year-old girls' choice of clothes, found that they chose garments with very low necklines, extremely short hemlines and/or revealing slits to convey adultness and solicit attention, predominantly from boys. The girls concerned were ambivalent and circumspect in acknowledging this as their intent. As Papadopoulos (2010, p. 5) concludes in her review of the research, girls from the ethnic majority feel under increasing pressure to adopt attire and mannerisms which make them appear sexually available. Papadopoulos (2010, p. 6) summarises this phenomenon as follows:

> While sexualised images have featured in advertising and communications since mass media first emerged, what we are seeing now is an unprecedented rise in both the volume and the extent to which these images are impinging on every-day life. Increasingly, too, children are being portrayed in 'adultified' ways while adult women are 'infantilised'. This leads to a blurring of the lines between sexual maturity and immaturity and, effectively, legitimises the notion that children can be related to as sexual objects.

Against this cultural backdrop of hyper-sexualisation, girls' sexual behaviour remains much more closely policed than that of their male peers. While post-feminist discourse around *'girl power'* promotes the right of females to please themselves in their choice of clothing and sexual interactions with males, casual sex among girls continues to be censured and often regarded as indecent, in contrast to the approval commonly given to male youths. Despite much greater sexual permissiveness in British society since the 1950s, this double standard continues to shape gendered attitudes towards adolescent sexuality among both teenagers themselves and adults (Moore & Rosenthal, 1993). Girls who have a number of short-term partners or engage in brief sexual encounters are characterised as promiscuous and sluttish, and from a child protection perspective often perceived as beyond parental control (Frost, 2001, p. 197). Moreover as Moore & Rosenthal (1993, p. 69) observe, the prolongation of the transition between childhood and adulthood in conjunction with the differentiation of adolescents into a separate social space has produced a youth culture, which influences teenagers' behaviours and choices particularly around fashion, music, leisure activity and sexual mores. Frost (2001, p. 86) alludes to this as the myth of the teenager as 'style-conscious, street-sussed, confident, socially bonded with other like-minded teenagers, oppositional to adult "authority" in minor or major ways, with clearly demarcated tastes and interests'. These influential elements of culture among the White ethnic majority are evident in social work responses to the sexual exploitation of girls in a northern English town.

Rochdale Borough Safeguarding Children Board (2013) *Serious Case Review in Respect of Young People 1,2,3,4,5 & 6* investigated the child sexual exploitation of six young people known to Children's Social Care, health services and the police, from three different families over a six-year period by a group of eight men, of whom seven were British Pakistani. At the time of the court case in 2012, which resulted in custodial sentences for all the men involved, the media focused exclusively on the ethnicity of the perpetrators. This analysis of the related Serious Case Review examines the cultural background of the six White British girls who were sexually and physically abused by the men. It considers how their culture, and that of the White majority society in which they grew up, influenced both their own actions and the generally ineffectual response of professionals responsible for protecting them from significant harm.

Rochdale Borough Safeguarding Children Board (2013) *Serious Case Review in Respect of Young People 1,2,3,4,5 & 6*

All of six young people who were sexually exploited grew up in economically disadvantaged families living in one of the most deprived districts in England. There was a history of child neglect, domestic violence and substance misuse in most of the families. All the young people had considerable involvement with Children's Social Care, health services and the police over many years. From early teenage years they presented to health services with a variety of sexually related issues, including sexually transmitted infections, pregnancy and requests for emergency contraception or terminations. There were also repeated admissions to Accident and Emergency departments of hospitals due to injuries or overdoses and presentation to mental health services for self-harm and depression. However, this did not elicit concerted coordinated intervention by police, health and Children's Social Care.

According to Rochdale Borough Safeguarding Children Board (2013) the lack of intervention from public agencies was influenced by the perception of the girls as ambiguous towards the men who were exploiting them, for example returning to them even after being brought back to their families by police, and making and then withdrawing allegations of sexual abuse. They were also plied with drugs and alcohol by the perpetrators and were often intoxicated or under the influence of drugs. Many of the girls appeared reluctant to engage with the police or social workers, and even when they did, for example in cooperating with an earlier police investigation, they were dismissed as unreliable witnesses or perceived as *'rebellious'*. Multiple references were also made in agency documentation to the young people *'engaging in risky behaviour'*, suggesting that they were choosing to put themselves in hazardous and harmful situations while ignoring social work advice (Rochdale Borough Safeguarding Children Board, 2013, para.4.4.53, 4.4.59). Practitioners tended to focus on the problematic behaviours of these teenaged

▶

◄

girls rather than their vulnerability and need for protection from sexually abusive adult males. After a subsequent police investigation it was found that six girls had been sexually exploited by eight men over a period of six years. The perpetrators were found guilty of sexual assault and received custodial sentences.

The dominant *'storm and stress'* model of adolescence portrays older children as transitioning to adulthood through breaking away from parents and other authority figures in an endeavour to achieve separation and mould their own self-identity. Teenagers are expected to experiment with new life experiences including engaging in risky behaviour around alcohol and sex alongside other forms of self-expression such as choice of clothing and leisure activities. In this case, the cultural expectation of conflict with authority figures as these girls began to exercise their freedom of choice, in conjunction with norms supporting experimentation in developing a unique self-identity, contributed to practitioners not perceiving the girls' behaviours as exceptional. Even when the girls engaged in activities which put them at risk of significant harm, professionals viewed these as occurring along a continuum of behaviours to be anticipated from teenagers. As such they failed to elicit sufficient alarm among social workers to initiate child protection procedures. But this widely recognised period of rebellion against authority figures so embedded in Western concepts of child development does not necessarily happen in other societies where reciprocity in family relationships is normative and interpersonal harmony highly valued (Arnett, 1999).

The Serious Case Review concluded that even though social workers and their managers knew that sexual abuse was occurring, they believed that the young people were making a *'lifestyle choice'* and therefore choosing to engage in sexual activity with the men. As the Serious Case Review observes, this label was often used judgementally and as shorthand to cover a collection of behaviours encompassing early sexual activity, alcohol and drug misuse, teenage pregnancy and insalubrious friendships. As such, the label reflected wider pejorative societal attitudes towards girls engaging in these activities, as opposed to eliciting professional responses aimed at understanding these behaviours. Rochdale Borough Safeguarding Children Board, 2013, para.4.7.15 noted that practitioners, 'by summarising them as "lifestyle" with its implications of free choice and the potential for moral judgement, ... betrayed and reinforced the concept that the young people had the freedom to make meaningful choices about the way they could live their lives. Given their economic, social and family backgrounds and the corrosive effect on the self of sexual exploitation this was fundamentally misconceived.'

Despite the decline of Christianity among the ethnic majority, females who have short-term or multiple sexual relationships are adjudged promiscuous and stigmatised. This viewpoint, combined with notions of adolescent individuation, separation from parents and the high value placed upon exercising free will in British society, led to the girls being perceived by professionals as choosing risky sexual encounters and to misuse alcohol, while deciding to ignore the advice of authority figures. The girls themselves were resistant to cooperating with social workers because often they did not perceive themselves as being at risk. In part this was because adolescents among the ethnic majority are encouraged to exhibit independence and self-reliance. To admit being at risk of significant harm is to undermine the societal expectation of teenagers as increasingly capable decision-makers who can exert control over their lives. This, however, omits the impact of hyper-consumerism and early sexualisation in British society, which is increasingly amplified through social media. These place considerable pressures on girls to appear sexually attractive to men and ultimately to engage in often premature sexual activity. Both teenagers and professionals alike seem confused by the sexually active adolescent who is a child and yet construed as somehow an adult in Anglocentric societies. These cultural patterns can obscure the nature of sexual exploitation, making it difficult for professionals to differentiate between consensual sex and sexual abuse. Conversely, in other societies children remain bound into their families and parental authority while sexual activity is confined to marriage. Among many cultures the virginity of girls and young women is highly regarded and may be monitored and protected by kin or other authority figures (Laird, 2008).

Reflective exercise

Consider the circumstances in Rochdale Borough Safeguarding Children Board (2013).

What are your own beliefs and views about the sexuality of teenaged girls?

To what extent are these beliefs and views influenced by Anglocentric norms?

To what extent might the responses of social workers in Rochdale Borough Safeguarding Children Board (2013) have been influenced by notions of 'respectability' in British society?

How might stereotypes of White working-class culture have intersected with attitudes towards female teenage sexuality in the perspectives and responses of professionals in this case?

Social work practice and Anglocentric values

Secularism, the nucleation of the family, individualism and freedom of choice as demonstrated in the Serious Case Reviews discussed in this chapter profoundly affect how social workers intervene with the family. Many of the norms which underpinned intervention, or indeed sometimes the lack of it, are demonstrably particular to the ethnic majority and are not necessarily shared by other cultures. While Anglocentric norms are often perceived as either neutral or normative, in these instances it can be seen how, like social norms in other societies, they can sometimes impair more objective assessments about the best course of action to protect a child or young person.

The utilisation of positivist conceptions of child development and their universalisation through global structures of power, undergirded by *White privilege* and supremacy, perpetuates fixed notions of children. The social construction of adolescence as a period of *storm and stress* characterised by experimentation as teenagers develop their independence and individualism is a very particular conception of those aged 10–19 years. It is not a social phenomenon necessarily observed in other societies. But the cultural expectation that teenagers will engage in risky behaviour and rebel against authority figures can obscure from practitioners the real distress and danger some young people face.

Materialism, consumerism and the early sexualisation of girls also means that social workers may not be sufficiently sensitive to early signs of sexual exploitation or sexual abuse by a family member. While alcoholism may be a coping mechanism for parents and young people in abusive or deprived circumstances, the widespread social acceptance of high levels of alcohol consumption alongside freedom of choice means that often it is not picked up as an indicator of distress. These problems are not particular to social work with White British families. This cultural backdrop will equally exert influence over practice with families from racial and ethnic minorities.

Reflective exercise

Consider your own personal experiences.

Identify how dominant Anglocentric norms and values influence your interactions with members of your own family, friends and strangers.

How do dominant Anglocentric norms and values frame your interactions at work with parents, parental partners, guardians and children?

How are your relationships with colleagues and managers at work influenced by dominant Anglocentric norms and values?

Conclusion

White privilege means that people from the White majority tend to experience their values, beliefs and behaviours as natural and normative. Therefore White people commonly lack insight into the extent to which their worldview is influenced by particular cultural values and perspectives, which differ in important ways from those of other societies or ethnic minority communities in the UK. White supremacy refers to the dominance of Anglocentric values and perspectives which are often disseminated and reinforced through the greater economic, social and political power wielded by White people. This includes the power to determine racial categories and create normative expectations of appearance or behaviour.

Anglocentric values have become naturalised within British society and are therefore often perceived as part of a neutral underpinning of social life, as opposed to the cultural frame in which it takes place. Historical examination of key influences in British society demonstrates the degree to which many taken-for-granted values, beliefs and behaviours are in fact particular to the White majority population and are articulations of aspects of their culture. Social workers from both majority and minority backgrounds are influenced by Anglocentric norms, which shape their perceptions of families, understandings of social dynamics and interventions with parents, their partners, children and young people. These norms, and the assumptions or expectations they engender, often unconsciously underpin work with White British families and those from minority ethnic communities.

3

Race, Ethnicity and Anti-Oppressive Practice

Introduction

There is much research evidence from the US, UK and Australia to demonstrate that discriminatory decision-making in the child protection system is resulting in a disproportionate number of families from Black and minority ethnic communities being subject to investigation and intervention (Tibury & Thoburn, 2009). Explaining this, Birchall & Hallett (1995) found that in the UK social workers assigned higher levels of risk of child abuse to African Caribbean families than White families in similar circumstances. Conversely, positive stereotypes of capable African Caribbean matriarchs resulted in misguided assumptions about strengths and consequently less intervention (Munro, 2008). In the US racism and discrimination alongside higher rates of poverty and residence in disadvantaged neighbourhoods among Black families have been identified as causal factors in the disproportionate numbers of Black and ethnic minority children in the American child protection system (Fluke et al., 2011). In Australia the disproportionate numbers of indigenous children and those from racial and ethnic minority backgrounds in the child protection system was linked to the colonial legacy; poverty; lower educational levels; social marginalisation; and racism (Tibury, 2008; Tibury & Thoburn, 2009).

Stereotypes based on race, ethnicity or socio-economic status have also been found to influence social work assessments of risk to children and young people (Miller et al., 2012; Morton et al., 2011). A number of studies have found, after controlling for poverty, that risks of child maltreatment among minority ethnic families are no greater than those of the ethnic majority (Children's Bureau, 2016a). However, in the UK Owen & Statham (2009) documented the under-representation of children from Asian backgrounds and over-representation of those from African heritage backgrounds and mixed race children – indicating a racial or ethnic element in interactions between child protection services and families from different minority communities. Patel & Strachan (1997) found that the availability of media stereotypes of people from South Asian backgrounds affected causal attributions made by practitioners concerning their problems and behaviours. The demonstrable tendency of all humans to rely on intuitive rather than analytical reasoning in situations of high uncertainty also means that where evidence is equivocal or incomplete the perspectives of practitioners are susceptible to personal bias predicated on cultural differences. Findings from Enosh & Bayer-Topilsky (2015) suggest that in situations of ambiguity child protection social workers are likely to estimate higher risk for families of African or Asian ethnicity or those from low-income groups than for White families and those on higher incomes.

This chapter analyses the ways in which race and racism manifest in child protection practice. The aim is to introduce anti-racist theory and practice and examine their application to social work with children and families from Black and minority ethnic groups. A particular focus is placed on the Critical Race Theory and the ways in which social work practitioners might draw upon this framework to not only make sense of the experiences of Black minority ethnic families, but also ensure that families from these backgrounds are not discriminated against during the course of their work. The second part of this chapter examines the experiences and roles of social work educators, social work students and qualified practitioners in driving forward anti-racist practice as good social work practice.

Anti-racist and anti-discriminatory practice

Anti racist paradigms for social work education and practice are important for a number of reasons. Singh (2013) has suggested that anti-racist practice can raise awareness of differential treatment and racial inequalities, and identify the complex dynamics of everyday personal, institutional and structural racism while challenging the values, attitudes and behaviours of practitioners which are racist. This paradigm focuses on the power structures of *White privilege* and how they disempower and discriminate against people from Black minority backgrounds, as opposed to focusing on Black minority families and communities. Dominelli (1997, p. 3), as a committed advocate of anti-racist practice, observes that 'racial inequality has not disappeared because White people understand better the customs, traditions and religious activities of ethnic minority groups'. Therefore any work with family members in relation to issues of ethnic identification, cultural beliefs and matters of faith must integrate an anti-racist perspective, which recognises structural inequality evident in education, employment, housing, income, access to amenities and conditions in the neighbourhood.

The operation of racism at different levels can be understood through Thompson's (2016) Personal, Cultural and Social (PCS) model, which links personal experiences and beliefs to specific social and cultural groups in the context of the wider society and community. The personal or psychological analysis of oppression and discrimination operates on an individual level where feelings, actions, thoughts and attitudes are of a discriminatory or oppressive nature. The *'C'* or *cultural level* of oppression and discrimination functions on a shared consensus about what is 'normal', desirable or acceptable. This also reflects the influence of culture on people's assumptions and the ways they think and perceive events. The *structural or 'S' level* refers to the social divisions within a society, which create power relationships between different social groups, advantaging some and disadvantaging others. An ethos of intolerance spurred by discriminatory attitudes and behaviours may permit racism to fester unchallenged.

At the *personal level* it is important that that the role of language is considered when discussing race and ethnicity within the context of child protection work. Language forms can be discriminatory and so it is incumbent on social workers to use language which is acceptable and not derogatory towards families from racial and ethnic minorities. Overtly derogatory terms such as 'Paki' are rarely heard in social care settings. However, more insidious forms of discriminatory language may be used, such as referring to a British African Caribbean child as 'quite intelligent' when the qualifier 'quite' would not be used for a White British child in the same context (Robinson, 2007, p. 132). Conversely, family members should maintain respectful and non-discriminatory language when talking to social workers and could be challenged for using language which might offend, exclude or disrespect others.

At the *structural level* social workers need to pay close attention to the socio-economic circumstances of children and families. Many of the Serious Case Reviews involving families from racial or ethnic minorities reveal that practitioners often record little information about their economic or social circumstances, as exemplified in Kingston Local Safeguarding Children Board (2013) *The Serious Case Review Relating to Tom and Vic* examined later in this chapter. Even when this kind of information was more detailed, typically links were not made between race and ethnicity on the one hand and aspects of disadvantage on the other. Generally, Serious Case Reviews indicate that families' experiences of racism or sectarianism are rarely explored, yet as Brighton and Hove Local Safeguarding Children Board (2017) *Serious Case Review: Siblings W and X* (discussed later in this chapter) reveals, racial abuse can have profound impacts on children. Without fully exploring the *structural level* of family life, assessments of need will be based on incomplete information and consequently care plans will fail to sufficiently address the circumstances contributing to the risk of significant harm to a child.

At the *cultural level* social workers need to develop a critical approach to the positivist scientific theories underpinning their work with parents and children. As Chapter 2 has already demonstrated, the dominant culture of Western post-industrial societies places considerable authority and confidence in positivist science, which is applied not only to the natural sciences, but also to aspects of social life. To take a primary example in relation to child protection social work, attachment theory was developed by John Bowlby (1951, 1953) a White British psychologist and psychoanalyst. He based his research on experiments with birds and mammals alongside observations of human infants. Bowlby asserted that a continuous dependable maternal relationship with the child was essential for normal development. This comprised four developmental phases: pre-attachment (0–3 months) – the infant does not distinguish the primary caregiver from others; attachment-in-the-making (3–6 months) – the infant forges a bond with the primary caregiver; attachment (6–12 months) – the infant has sufficient motor skills to physically seek out and move towards the primary caregiver; and the goal-corrected partnership (12–24 months) involving the negotiation of the toddler's need for autonomy with the primary caregiver's need to protect the child by setting limits. Based on his research Bowlby asserted that *stranger anxiety*, meaning the infant's wariness of strangers, peaked at 8–10 months while *separation anxiety*, meaning distress caused by the absence of the primary caregiver, was most intense at around 12 months. These were regarded as psychologically healthy reactions during these stages of development. Where the development of the maternal bond was interrupted, according to Bowlby disruptive and anti-social behaviour would ensue in adolescence and then in adulthood increase the likelihood of criminal activity. While Bowlby's original theory focused on the maternal bond, subsequent elaborations of his theory have emphasised bonding with a primary caregiver, who could be the father.

Bowlby's colleague Mary Ainsworth (1978), a White Canadian psychologist, who later pursued her career in the United Kingdom, expanded on Bowlby's work through empirical research. She focused on observations of infants aged 12–18 months by introducing 'the strange situation', which examined the reactions of children to separations and reunions with their mothers. This social psychology experiment involved a mother and child in a room which a stranger then entered and began a conversation with the mother. The mother then left and the stranger attempted to engage the child, after which the mother re-entered the room to reunite with her child. Dependent on their responses to these interactions children were categorised into *anxious/avoidant*, who are those apparently indifferent to whether the primary caretaker is present or not and may seek comfort from the stranger; *anxious/resistant* children who stay close to their primary caregiver, exhibit high anxiety when she leaves the room and take a long time to calm down even when comforted by their mother on reunion; *securely attached* children who remained settled with the stranger while their mother was also present, became distressed when she left the room, were not comforted by the stranger, but were quickly calmed by their mother on reunion. *Securely attached* children are regarded as the ideal and as exhibiting a healthy maternal bond. Ainsworth (1978), like Bowlby (1951, 1953), argues that these early responses to the presence or absence of the primary caregiver have profound implications for child development. Subsequent research, while confirming the findings of Ainsworth, has like her original experiments been conducted predominantly with middle-class Euro-American parents (Robinson, 2007). However, cross-cultural research relating to the 'strange situation' challenges a number of precepts embedded in the work of Bowlby and Ainsworth.

Drawing together studies conducted in countries outside North America and Europe Robinson (2007) shows how culture influences the expectations of children, parenting strategies and the goals of different childrearing practices. In Western European countries relatively more children were categorised as *anxious/avoidant* compared to Japan, where they were more likely to be *anxious/resistant*. As Le Vine & Miller (1990) argue, the experimental basis of the 'strange situation' assumes that it is culture-neutral, whereas international variations suggest that in fact the meaning of the 'strange situation' for the child, and consequently their responses to it, is different in different cultural contexts. Among the ethnic majority in Western European and North American countries independence from a young age is encouraged, including infants being weaned relatively early and typically sleeping separately from their parents. This can mean that they are less likely to miss a parent in the 'strange situation'. Conversely, in other cultures such as those of Japan the continued physical closeness of mother and infant is considered extremely important and consequently in the 'strange situation' a child will suffer correspondingly more distress because the absence of the mother is atypical.

Research in China has produced similar results to that conducted in Western Europe in terms of a high representation of children in the *anxious/avoidant* category. However, Chinese scholars argue for a different interpretation of what this means. In China it is common and culturally sanctioned for children to be reared to become relatively independent from an early age, but also to be looked after for extended periods by other family members, typically grandparents. In the 'strange situation' children used to receiving care from individuals other than a primary caregiver, and therefore more used to care by others, are more likely to engage with a stranger and less likely to be distressed by parental absence. So the observation of *anxious/avoidant* behaviour in this cultural context does not suggest that the child is insecurely attached to his or her parent. In China it is actually the *anxious/avoidant* category which is indicative of healthy child development and not the *securely attached* category normative in Western Europe and North America. Similarly in the societies of sub-Saharan Africa and India multiple family caregivers are often involved in bringing up young children, and there may be much less emphasis on parents as primary caregivers (Robinson, 2007). Families with origins in Japan, China, India or sub-Saharan Africa settled in the UK may continue to be influenced by these cultural norms. Correspondingly, the behaviour of children around their parents may reflect these patterns of socialisation. Parent–child interactions can therefore be misconstrued in the absence of a reflexive approach to the application of attachment theory to work with families from minority ethnic backgrounds.

More broadly, social workers need to appreciate that much of the research into child and adolescent development is predicated on an essentially ethnocentric developmental model originating in North America and Europe, against which modes of childcare common in other cultures are adjudicated. As a result, normative conceptions of childhood and how children should be properly treated become the standard against which other understandings of childhood or approaches to the upbringing of children are appraised. This in turn creates a deficit model in relation to parenting by those from other cultural backgrounds, whereby deviation from the norms of an Euro-American conception of childhood development and approaches to childrearing is devalued, dismissed or deemed harmful (Monaghan, 2012; Robinson, 2007, pp. 8–9). It is therefore incumbent upon practitioners to critically examine theory in terms of its cross-cultural applicability and to consider how discrimination at the *cultural level* may be skewing their assessments of risk.

Critical Race Theory

Critical Race Theory (CRT) adopts the view that colour-blind approaches are inherently racist and discriminatory. It was originally developed in the US as a progressive approach to the slow pace with which racial discrimination and inequality was being addressed. According to Taylor (1998, p. 122) 'It challenges the experiences of whites as a normative standard and grounds its conceptual framework in the distinctive experiences of people of colour'. It attempts to place the 'Black' voice and experience at the centre and to challenge discrimination, racism and oppression, and is underpinned by social justice and fairness. Critical Race Theory espouses a number of principles, five of which appear to be particularly suited for working with Black and Asian minority children and families and are outlined below.

1. Critical Race Theory sees racism as endemic – a daily occurrence for Black and minority ethnic groups and therefore not an abnormal experience. Proponents argue that if racism is seen as being produced and reproduced in systems, organisations and processes it often goes unnoticed by people who are racially privileged. Understanding this principle will perhaps guide social workers to understand why some well-meaning child safeguarding processes are viewed with hostility and apprehension by Black families. Indeed it is important that social workers request information from Black families about how the fear of racism or indeed the experiences of racism impact on their daily lived experiences and family functioning. In a number of cases discussed in this book where minority ethnic families were experiencing racism (Birmingham Safeguarding Children Board, 2010; Bradford Safeguarding Children Board, 2013; Brighton and Hove Local Safeguarding Children Board, 2017) what ought

to have taken place was a dedicated period of rapport building with family members by professionals and some acknowledgement of their experiences of racism. This may have influenced the way in which social workers approached these families and may also have shed some light on the actual reasons for the non-engagement of family members.

2. Another tenet of Critical Race Theory is that it promotes and advances the voices of the otherwise voiceless and marginalised. This view further argues that marginalised people are better placed to *'tell their story'* than dominant groups who have the tendency to re-tell the stories using a *'White'* lens. Feeling able to tell one's story very much relies on a strong and professional relationship between service users and social workers. This principle should encourage social workers to develop positive relationships with the families they work with. There is synergy between this tenet and the previous one in that this enables Black service users to talk about their experiences, using language and expressions which they are familiar with, and to people they feel safe to speak to. It may be the case that if Victoria Climbié was given the opportunity to speak in private to the social workers who were working with her family, she may have been able to express her experiences in French through an interpreter.

3. A third dimension of Critical Race Theory is that of *differential racialisation* in which dominant groups possess the power to decide which groups are deserving and undeserving, the *'in'* group who benefit from resources, opportunities for success and other privileges while the *'out'* group lack access to similar opportunities for success and associated privileges. In using this element of the theory, social workers must reconsider the factors that influence their biases and decision-making. Self-reflection about issues such as which families meet eligibility criteria is important, alongside social workers being accountable for their decisions and their actions. It has been widely established that social workers are more likely to adopt punitive approaches when working with Black children and their families than with those from the ethnic majority. Consequently their numbers in the child protection process are often disproportionately higher than those from the ethnic majority, who appear more often to be offered family support and non-statutory intervention.

4. Another principle of Critical Race Theory relates to what has been called the *intersectionality of identities*. While race is the main concern of Critical Race Theory, it recognises the importance of social class, religion, sexuality, gender, disability and the implications for outcomes for Black families. Referring to Kyhra Ishaq, for example, who is discussed in more detail in Chapter 5 (Birmingham Safeguarding Children Board, 2010), it would not be sufficient to view the family simply as a Black family. Their faith (Islam), their social class and other areas of their diversity would have to be considered. *Intersectional analysis* of ethnicity examines the

way in which dimensions of difference are constructed through social interactions. It is also true to say that social workers must give careful consideration to these factors when they are working with children and families from Black and minority ethnic backgrounds.

5. *Interest convergence*, another principle of Critical Race Theory, proposes that in order for the interest of Black communities and groups to be considered important, these interests must align with a clear gain and benefit for the racial majority. Leigh (2003, p. 277) explained that when the interests of Black people are in opposition to or at 'odds with those in power' it becomes increasingly difficult to expose racism and to pursue racial equality. One could argue therefore that the increasingly concerning reports about the growing numbers of Black children who are looked after and the disproportionate numbers of Black families going through child protection processes has led to the need for a closer interrogation of how this has been left to continue. Embedding Critical Race Theory in family assessments and child protection procedures is therefore vital and would require social workers to:

> Understand previous statutory and other involvement with a family.

> Understand their experiences of racism and discrimination.

> Recognise the uniqueness of each family in terms of their structure and functioning.

> Understand and respect the impact of the family's culture and traditional beliefs.

Reflective exercise

Consider your recent social work practice with families from minority ethnic backgrounds.

How might you use elements of Critical Race Theory to inform your work with Black children and families?

Identify ways in which your practice might change through the application of Critical Race Theory.

African-centred approaches

When Black people are exposed to significant adversity, resilience becomes necessary to enable them to navigate the available resources and opportunities. In order to achieve this, one's family and wider community become important in securing the resources and maintaining health, wellbeing and safety (Ungar, 2008, p. 225). There are cultural variations in how people do this; however, for Black people of African heritage, it is argued that extended family networks serve as *social capital* while linguistic and cultural capital are harnessed through the feeling of belonging, identity and acceptance. Mosley-Howard & Burgan Evans (2000) used systems and African-centric theories as the framework for their research and wanted to move from a deficit model of understanding African American families to one based on the strengths of the family from a cultural and indigenous perspective. African-centric approaches value the integration of cultural practices and ways of thinking in everyday family life. They recognise governance systems and the respect accorded to elders and community leaders.

This approach values the interconnectedness between people and the idea that people are spiritual and connected to each other through a belief in a supreme being. This idea authenticates the rationale for the involvement of community leaders and family elders and relations. African-centric approaches argue that using ethnocentric concepts when working with people of African origin may not yield positive outcomes, particularly when there is little attempt by social workers to understand the cultural heritage of families they work with (Graham, 1999). The notion of step-siblings and half-siblings is largely non-existent in many African families and consequently Graham (1999) has argued that the use of ecomaps does not capture the reality of some Black and ethnic minority families. Instead she insists on a strengths-based social work orientation that recognises, supports and develops the strengths of families of African heritage, which Graham (2002, pp. 107–9) describes and is reproduced in an abridged form below.

Survival of Black families: Historically, black families have survived the distinctive forces such as enslavement and colonialization that have sought to destroy Black family life. The continued presence of Black families is testament to their enduring strengths and a cause for celebration.

Strong religious and spiritual orientation: Spirituality is a common cultural value framing the worldviews of black peoples throughout the world. There is an acceptance of a non-material higher force present in all life's affairs. Expression of spirituality has often taken place in religious organisations and the social practices have been identified as key factors in sustaining families, promoting resilience, and nurturing spiritual values.

Strong achievement orientation: Black families have traditionally placed great value on education and knowledge. Black parents have rejected the limitations placed upon their children by educational systems. The importance of education in black communities has been explained as a way of counteracting the effects of oppression and discrimination.

Strong kinship bonds: In traditional societies, all family members were involved in the parenting process. The community shared responsibility for all children;

children belonged to the community. Older siblings and significant others are an integral part of the parenting process…Concepts of family include members who are not biologically related, including an extensive network of cousins.

A tradition of communal self-help: Has featured as an integral part of African cultural value systems. Self-help is built upon notions of exchange and reciprocity which are active social patterns found in black communities.

The adaptability of family roles to new social structures and environments: Was another key factor in survival. This approach to family functioning includes the sharing of responsibility and decision-making to meet the needs of the family. This orientation towards flexibility in performance of family roles may involve for example older siblings caring for younger siblings.

Reflective exercise

Consider your practice with families who have African roots.

To what extent do you explore and identify the strengths of families of African and African Caribbean heritage?

List the strengths you typically identify during your assessments and compare them to the ones outlined above. What gaps are there in your own practice?

To what extent do you design interventions which help support and build on these strengths?

How might you change your practice to work more effectively with the strengths of these families?

Islamophobia and ethnic minorities

Anti-racist practice, Critical Race Theory and African-centred strengths-based approaches, if integrated into social work approaches to Black families, could improve practice. However religious intolerance, albeit often linked to race, is also important to consider as a distinctive form of prejudice and discrimination. Attacks on Muslims have been found to have increased in the UK and many other European countries (Bayrakli & Hafez, 2016; Tell MAMA, 2017). The growing concern about the 'war on terror' and its associated policies implemented in a number of countries, including the UK, has resulted in the 'othering' of people of Muslim faith. It has also been noted that anti-Muslim sentiment has resulted in attacks on Muslim places of worship, and females wearing the scarf (*hijab*) and the veil (*niqab*) have been targeted. The UK media has also been blamed for fuelling the increase in Islamophobic attacks by its sensationalist and stereotypical reporting (Lambert & Githens-Meizer, 2010). Islamophobia is based upon an unfounded hostility towards Islam and the people who practise this religion. Anti-Muslim oppression, discrimination and prejudice is based upon views that Islam is inferior, different and at odds with the dominant normative values of Western societies. This has been exacerbated by the introduction of government policies in the wake of the 9/11 terrorist attacks in New York which have securitised issues of community integration for Muslim faith minorities living in the US, the UK and elsewhere in Europe.

The 'Prevent' programme was first introduced in the UK in 2003. It is part of a wider counter-terrorism strategy funded by government and designed to assist early identification of individuals at risk of becoming radicalised. This can manifest in extreme views opposing democracy, individual freedom and tolerance towards other social groups and/or advocating violence. Prevent includes anti-radicalisation programmes, and thwarting children and young people from leaving the UK to join jihadi militias in the Middle East. This approach relies on information being forthcoming from members of Muslim faith communities. Teachers, doctors and social workers are under a statutory duty (popularly known as the Prevent duty) to report to the local Prevent body any suspicion that a child or young person is at risk of joining an extremist organisation or engaging in terrorist activity.

Individuals deemed at risk of being drawn into terrorism or joining jihadists abroad are referred on to 'Channel', a multi-agency process of assessment and support. Home Office (2017) figures show that in the period April 2015 to March 2016 approximately 2,100 children under the age of 15 years and 2,200 between the ages of 15 and 20 years were referred to the Prevent programme, mainly because of fears regarding Islamic extremism. Of these referrals over one third were received from schools and colleges, while another third came from the police. There have also been instances of children being removed from their families by children's social care due to their radicalisation and preparation to join Islamic jihadists (Stevenson, 2015). These are actions taken by public authorities in an attempt to protect society, but they are also likely to discourage members of those minority communities affected to come forward to disclose their concerns regarding child maltreatment, or to engage with social workers, teachers and police officers. Stanley et al. (2017) contend that it is important for social workers to move beyond the debate of whether or not this duty is 'right' or 'wrong' but rather to focus on how the profession might seek to work ethically within it. Brighton and Hove Local Safeguarding Children Board (2017) *Serious Case Review: Siblings W and X* provides insight into the inter-relationships between radicalisation, racism and Islamophobia.

Brighton and Hove Local Safeguarding Children Board (2017)
Serious Case Review: Siblings W and X

Muslim Libyan parents left Libya for political reasons and moved to the UK where they had a family of five children who were all British nationals. The father was frequently abroad and the mother felt isolated and rarely left the home. The children were brought up Muslim, spoke both English and Arabic and spent considerable periods of time back in Libya where part of their extended family remained. Some of the older children also had friends in that country. Four of the siblings were known to Education, Police, Youth Offending and Children's Social Care due to their poor school attendance, substance misuse, anti-social behaviour and criminal activities. The eldest sibling went to fight in Syria where he was later joined by two of his brothers and a friend. Both the brothers were killed in Syria, one of them aged 17 years and the other 18. Prior to the discovery that three of the brothers had left the UK to fight in Syria no professionals had assessed them as at risk of radicalisation.

In Libya the parents had belonged to that country's elite and enjoyed a high standard of living. On moving to the UK they experienced a dramatic reduction in this and later experienced racism, Islamophobia and hostility from the predominantly White British local community. Some of this appeared connected to the fact that an uncle had been detained by authorities in the US on suspicion of terrorism, which was publicised by the media. Incidents were often on a daily basis and included: racial abuse; racist graffiti; verbal abuse on social media; threats to kill; physical assaults; and stone throwing at the family home. Much of this was targeted at the children. The family moved on a number of occasions to try and avoid these attacks. The police became involved but were unable to press charges against suspects for lack of evidence. This led to an increasingly poor relationship between the police and the family. It appears that around this time the siblings began retaliating against people in the local community. They became involved in drug dealing, unprovoked assaults on others, burglary and other forms of anti-social and criminal behaviour.

The siblings spoke to a youth worker and disclosed physical abuse perpetrated by their father due to their lack of observance as Muslims. Child Protection Plans were put in place for all the siblings and the mother was supported to leave her husband with her children. These allegations were later retracted and the Child Protection Plans became Child in Need Plans. It was thought that as the father was often abroad he had little contact with the family and was no longer a direct risk. According to the Review there was little understanding among professionals as to the place of religion in the lives of the children. When two of his sons later left the UK, the father tracked them down to Turkey and travelled there to try and persuade them not to continue on to Syria, but did not disclose any of this information to the authorities. Children's Social Care, although aware of the two children's absence from the home, were given to understand that they were in the family's country of origin. Media reports of the death of one of the three brothers in Syria eventually alerted professionals to their whereabouts.

There are no direct cause and effect relationships in this case. As Brighton and Hove Local Safeguarding Children Board (2017) concludes, the domestic violence in combination with persistent racial abuse and faith-based attacks on the children made them vulnerable to radicalisation. Four of the siblings were involved in risky activities, were disaffected and had suffered years of physical and verbal abuse from members of the local community. The police were at best perceived by the family as ineffectual and at worst of having sympathies with the perpetrators. The traumatic impact of these daily incidents made the children vulnerable to risky behaviour which, together with radicalisation, culminated in their decision to join jihadist fighters in Syria. The father's decision not to inform the police of his two sons' presence in Turkey, where they might still have been apprehended and returned home, may have been attributable to his family's adverse experience of the police and/or those of other Muslim community members in his neighbourhood. In contrast to the father's non-disclosure to the police, the mother of the friend who accompanied the brothers to Syria informed the police when she suspected the destination of her absent son. This demonstrates that despite community-level suspicion of the police, issues of divided loyalties and worry about adverse reaction from the local ethnic community, family members make individual decisions which reflect a constellation of influences. What emerges from this case study is the importance of exploring and understanding the impact of structural factors such as racism and Islamophobia on families and how this affects their experience of living in a community or for children their experiences of using public transport, attending school or simply walking down their own street.

Identity markers such as accent, birthplace, nationality, heritage and so on can disadvantage groups of people. In addition to what seems to be differential treatment of Muslim males, it would appear that Muslim women experience Islamophobia in a variety of ways. Allen (2015, p. 289) has suggested that 'visual identifiers' have resulted in Muslim females being more susceptible to attack. These identifiers are described largely as *hijab* and dress such as the *abaya*. (Among men identifiers may be having a beard or wearing a prayer cap.) Very little appears to be known about the exact numbers of Muslim women who have been racially targeted, because such incidents are under-reported. However, it is known that of the 233 reported anti-Muslim attacks occuring in public spaces during the first six months of 2018, 58% of the victims were female (Faith Matters, 2018). Islamophobia is therefore a real and present threat to all Muslims, and Muslim women in particular – with further assumptions about them being oppressed, disenfranchised and accepting of domestic abuse. Social workers must ensure that they understand the lived experiences of family members linked to faith generally and Islam particularly. Culturally competent practice would mean that social workers fully understand the female Muslim experience and must attempt to provide a service which is empowering and supportive and does not undermine their beliefs and their faith. This relates to the importance of intersectionality in exploring and understanding the experiences and motivations of family members taking into consideration aspects of race, religion, gender and geographical location in terms of environment.

Reflective exercise

Consider your practice with children and their families who identify as Muslim.

To what extent do you explore the meaning of religion in their lives?

To what extent do you ask about and explore any experiences of racism or Islamophobia?

If you often do not ask about, or fully explore, aspects of religion and discrimination, reflect on why not.

Minority identity development

As demonstrated in Brighton and Hove Local Safeguarding Children Board (2017), discussed above, prejudice and discrimination can have powerful effects on children and young people. Racialisation and racism, together with ethnic or faith minority status, can affect individuals' understanding and conception of themselves. It is the view of Fook (2012) that identity formation is in a process of constant change and that often our descriptions of ourselves are very much reliant on how we view ourselves or how we would like others to view us. Martin & Nakayama (2010) propose that that there are four stages through which people from ethnic minority backgrounds develop their identities.

Stage 1: *Unexamined Identity*. During this period there is little exploration of racial or ethnic identity and often there is a lack of interest in considering this aspect of the self-concept. At this stage people from minority racial and ethnic backgrounds typically accept the beliefs, values and social practices of the White ethnic majority. This may include internalising positive attitudes towards the majority and negative ones towards their own minority group. For children and young people at this stage their racial or ethnic identity can appear unproblematic to them. A child of a family accepted as refugees from Syria might identify closely with pupils from the White majority school they attend and want to speak English all the time as opposed to communicating in Arabic or Kurdish. They may also express this identity status by seeking to spend time exclusively with White British youths.

Stage 2: *Conformity*. This involves internalisation by those from Black and minority ethnic groups of the core beliefs, values and norms held by the White ethnic majority, resulting in efforts to assimilate into the dominant group. Often this is expressed through negative attitudes and perceptions of self and one's own minority racial or ethnic group. Alternatively, attempts may be made to obscure or hide aspects of one's background which suggest deviation from the White majority culture, such as having been born in another country, or rejecting aspects of minority culture or religion; for example a Sikh boy refusing to have long hair and wear a topknot. At the same time generally positive views are held towards the White ethnic majority; that White people are fair-minded or that competition is good. Sometimes this can attract contempt and derision from members of their own minority group, typified in such derogatory expressions as 'acting white' or being a 'coconut' (i.e. black on the outside and white on the inside).

Stage 3: *Resistance and Separation.* Often this stage is triggered by adverse experiences, such as being criticised by members of one's own racial or ethnic group for admiring or assimilating into the majority White culture, or through experiences of prejudice and discrimination perpetrated by people from the White majority. Alternatively this stage can be initiated when an individual with a weaker minority racial or ethnic identity encounters someone who has a much more robust sense of their identity in this respect. It may be due to witnessing events through the media or internet taking place nationally or internationally. The individual may experience a period of confusion as they begin to question their own perception of the dominant culture's beliefs, values and social practices as necessarily positive. A person at this point becomes more preoccupied by issues of racial and ethnic identity as they start to discern between beliefs, values and practices and to decide which may be detrimental to their minority group. This can lead to a period of separation from the majority group and seeking out of places to encounter other minority members. It can also result in individuals viewing their minority group as holding superior beliefs, values and social practices to that of the White majority culture, followed by rejection of most dominant group norms. This can be a positive process, as when children or young people from a family of Black African heritage come to appreciate the support of strong kinship bonds and the racial affirmation from their local predominantly Black African ethnic community, together with the mutual assistance and shared spirituality offered by belonging to a Black-led church. *Resistance and separation* can also be expressed through extreme and dogmatic identities, as in Brighton and Hove Local Safeguarding Children Board (2017) *Serious Case Review: Siblings W and X* discussed above regarding the decision of three teenaged brothers to join jihadists to fight in Syria

Stage 4: *Integration.* This is regarded as the ideal outcome in relation to minority racial and ethnic identity development. Those achieving this identity status have a strong positive identification with their own minority group. Rather than choosing isolation from the majority group they engage with members of this group and may draw on some of their beliefs, values and social practices, integrating these with aspects of their own racial and ethnic background. Integration includes recognition of the legitimacy of the beliefs, values and social practice of other minority racial and ethnic groups alongside those of the majority. Individuals who achieve this identity status may also seek to reduce prejudice and discrimination towards their minority group by engaging in activism as opposed to only feeling great anger or resentment towards members of the White ethnic majority. This identity can be expressed through a confident self-assertiveness around issues of race and ethnicity, and family members may rightly challenge the assumptions, prejudices or racism of social workers. Such families or individuals draw on multiple heritages to enrich and inform their beliefs, values and practices.

Reflective exercise

Consider the stages of minority identity development described above.

If you are from a minority racial or ethnic background, think about to what extent these stages reflect your own experience of identity development; what stage do you think are you at?

If you are from the White ethnic majority, to what extent do you consider these stages of minority identity development in your work with children and families?

How might consideration of minority identity development and its exploration with children and significant family members improve your practice?

Families of mixed heritage

Issues of racism and discrimination can also emerge when families are of mixed heritage, which can affect the lives of parents, partners, children and wider family as illustrated in Bradford Safeguarding Children Board (2013) *A Serious Case Review: Hamzah Khan*. This involved the death of a four-year-old child through neglect and starvation. His body was not discovered until two years after his death, in the family home. His siblings were gradually withdrawn from contact with universal services and also suffered severe neglect. The Serious Case Review report has been widely cited to explain the difficulties which can arise as a result of disregarding racial, cultural and religious issues or nuances which form part of the experience of racial and ethnic minority families and their communities.

Bradford Safeguarding Children Board (2013) *A Serious Case Review: Hamzah Khan*

Hamzah's mother, Amanda Hutton, is described as White British and his father as Asian British and Muslim. They met in the 1980s when they were both 16 years old and had

▶

◀

eight children together. Domestic abuse characterised their relationship until the father was excluded from the family home under a non-molestation order in 2008. Both parents were noted to be resistant to engaging with services. Hamzah Khan lived in Bradford, which has been described as one of the poorest and most deprived districts in England. He was never enrolled into Early Years Provision and his mother had made up a number of stories to explain this, including the fact that the children were living with relatives outside Bradford. As Amanda Hutton's dependence on alcohol increased, exacerbated by isolation caused by the death of her own mother and separation from the father, her *parental capacity* deteriorated. She was unable to provide safe care for Hamzah and his siblings, who did not have access to education and were not registered with a GP. Their home environment was characterised by neglect, poor hygiene and alcohol dependency and Amanda experienced periods of depression. Hamzah died in December 2009 but his body was not discovered until almost two years later.

Little detail was ever recorded by agencies regarding the parents' backgrounds or wider families, nor was there information on their religious affiliation. Bradford Safeguarding Children Board (2013, pp. 9, 52) considered that the mother's social isolation was also associated with 'the reaction from some people in the community to a relationship that involved partners from different cultures and religions'. According to the Serious Case Review this meant that Amanda was isolated from both White and Asian communities and 'the victim of racial or cultural inspired violence'. Bradford Safeguarding Children Board (2013, p. 52) concluded that 'The cultural and religious complexity of the family was not enquired into'.

The reference to Amanda Hutton being isolated from both White and Asian communities is one that requires further analysis and discussion. It has been found that the educational development of children is enhanced by strong *social capital* and other resources which are often embedded in their communities and within their families. It is also well documented that isolation and exclusion can have detrimental effects on people. Mixed heritage families may face more challenges around acceptance by their wider families and the local ethnic communities they identify with and/or live in. Consequently they can be more vulnerable to isolation and possess little *social capital*. Recognising this can be an important starting point for social work intervention. As always, this is not to assert that families of mixed heritage are inherently problematic. Rather it is to alert social workers to the possibility that where partners are from different racial or ethnic groups, they may experience racism or sectarianism in ways which have a negative impact on wider social networks and family dynamics, and may affect individual family members differently. Indeed, Harman (2010) noted the tendency of social workers to focus on the problems of identity among mixed heritage children in families rather than giving consideration to the isolation of parents as a result of relationships which cross racial and ethnic divides, which can result in even White parents experiencing racism via association with a Black partner.

Children of mixed heritage

There is a duty on individual social workers to ensure that they embed anti-discriminatory and anti-oppressive principles into their work with children and their families. Yet according to Owusu-Bempah (1994, p. 133) many social workers 'accept the view that Black children would rather be White as self-evident. This seems to be particularly the case when so called mixed-race children are involved…This often leads otherwise well-intentioned social workers to pathologise even those children with well-balanced personality.' Research indicates that such children are as likely to identify as mixed race as Black and that many develop positive biracial identities (Robinson, 2007). However, if young people of White and Black parentage, initially identifying as of mixed race or mixed heritage, are exposed to racism, this tends to result in *social categorisation* and the *racialisation* of their identity (see Chapter 1) resulting in young people's self-identification as Black (Tizard & Phoenix, 2003). The acknowledgement, therefore, that dual heritage or mixed race children are and should be a distinct group in relation to assessment and intervention is a useful reminder and social workers should be encouraged to move away from stereotyping. Along similar lines, Goldstein (2002) recognises that in families where there are Black children with a White parent, any social work intervention must incorporate the reality of the world of that child, which will invariably include their parents from Black and White racial backgrounds. In addition to race, their gender, disability, sexuality and culture will have to be considered. Kingston Local Safeguarding Children Board (2013) *The Serious Case Review Relating to Tom and Vic* examines intersectional issues around dual heritage, identity and racism which concerned two young people who sustained life-threatening injuries.

Kingston Local Safeguarding Children Board (2013) The Serious Case Review Relating to Tom and Vic

Tom, a teenager of dual heritage born in Britain, whose first language was English, lived with his parents. He experienced problems at school, was excluded on many occasions and was involved in a number of fights. He also engaged in challenging behaviour at home and frequently went missing. His parents agreed that he be placed in foster care, from which he repeatedly absconded often being returned by the police; sometimes after committing further offences while absent, including carrying an offensive weapon. Periodic school exclusions continued due to his ongoing challenging behaviour in class. While initially there was frequent contact between Tom and his parents this tailed off. By this time he appeared to be using drugs and was often in the company of Vic, another teenager, also of dual heritage, for whom English was an additional language. Vic, who lived with his mother, also had a history of anti-social behaviour, school exclusions and

▶

◄

going missing. He started to live with another family when his mother felt unable to cope with him. Like Tom, he was charged with a succession of offences, including drug dealing. Tom and Vic had begun to commit offending behaviour together, including carrying offensive weapons, and appeared to be on the periphery of gang-related activity.

Both young people were stopped and searched by the police on repeated occasions, sometimes several times in the same day. According to the Serious Case Review this appeared related to the fact that they were both Black young males. Kingston Local Safeguarding Children Board (2013, p. 26) observed that

The effectiveness of this intervention to prevent these young men from committing crimes is questionable and it is unclear what positive outcomes it achieved. It probably contributed to these young men having little confidence in the criminal justice system as a positive process that could protect them as well as controlling their actions; as witnessed by Vic's unwillingness to co-operate when a victim [of violent crime].

Tom and Vic subsequently sustained life-threatening injuries in an incident involving another young person.

Conceivably, these two young people had entered the minority identity stage of *resistance and separation*, resulting in their very close bond with one another and rejection of people from other backgrounds. It is possible that this could have been triggered by some or all of the following: confusion about their identities as a consequence of their dual heritage backgrounds; prejudice from other pupils; numerous exclusions from school; and repeated 'stop and search' encounters with police. Children and young people of dual heritage may face additional challenges in terms of being accepted by the local communities in which they live, or may be in families unsupported by disapproving relatives. As discussed in Chapter 6, which focuses on communities, many neighbourhoods are multiracial and multi-ethnic, as a result of which children of dual heritage are unremarkable and accepted. In this case it is clear that racial and ethnic identity was an important aspect both of the bond between the two young people and also in relation to their experience of criminal justice and education. Kingston Local Safeguarding Children Board (2013, p. 33) concluded:

It is clear that for the young people their ethnic identity and life experience … was a key factor in their relationship with each other and this was acknowledged by the [Youth Offending Team] and [Multisystem Therapy Team] workers. There is little evidence however of this being taken into account in their work with the young men and little consideration of how a better understanding of the young men's feelings about their ethnic and cultural identity might assist in working with them and influencing their behaviour.

Emerging from this Serious Case Review are multiple intersectional issues relating to economic disadvantage, education, ethnic identity, the criminal justice system and racism. Poverty – which disproportionately affects families from racial and ethnic minorities – places additional stresses on all families and may make it difficult for children and young people to access educational support and leisure activities, leaving them bored and frustrated. Consequently they are more at risk of being drawn into anti-social behaviour. Yet the Serious Case Review found that little was actually recorded by practitioners about the socio-economic background of these young people's families. It seems that routinely working with predominantly disadvantaged families can blind social workers to the importance of this aspect of family life and how it intersects with other structural inequalities.

As the Serious Case Review report recognised, the use of 'stop and search' by police tends to disproportionately funnel Black young men into the criminal justice system. This was the predominant approach used, as opposed to a multi-agency preventative strategy involving coordinated interventions with the families around educational experiences, challenging behaviour and offending. Consequently it was the police who had most contact with both adolescents as opposed to direct social work contact with Vic and Tom to explore and address problematic behaviours. Racial profiling by the police through the repeated use of 'stop and search' reflected the disproportionate use of this in relation to Black and South Asian male youths, accompanied by a greater likelihood of arrest and more severe sentences than for White youths (Sveinsson, 2012).

Unsurprisingly research indicates that young people from Black and South Asian backgrounds are less likely to trust the police than other young people. This was demonstrated in Vic's unwillingness to cooperate with the authorities even when he was the victim of violent crime (Sveinsson, 2010, 2012). School exclusions also combined to create space and time for these two young people to engage in anti-social activities and associate with other out-of-school youths, possibly in organised gangs. As many gangs can involve ethnic or racial affiliation this may have raised further issues of identity and belonging for Tom and Vic. To be effective, multi-agency work with these young people and their families would need to have taken into account the intersectional nature of their experiences and circumstances.

Reflective exercise

Consider your practice with families and children of mixed race or dual heritage backgrounds.

How much information do you gather about this aspect and how much attention do you give it in assessment, analysis and care planning?

▶

◀

How might you gather more detailed information, improve your depth of understanding and be better at drawing out the implications for children and young people when their families are of mixed race or dual heritage?

How might you improve intersectional aspects of your assessments and analyses in relation to racial and ethnic identity?

Social work training

This discussion would not be complete without giving consideration to social work education itself. In terms of pre-qualifying training Singh (2013) raised concerns about social work education, including a Eurocentric bias; structures of racism; and discrimination and the dilution of anti-racism in generic approaches. He notes the reluctance of educators to fully integrate teaching about race and ethnicity into the curriculum for fear of their over-emphasis and generating stereotypes. This has also resulted in the lack of a substantive Black perspective in social work education. As Williams & Johnson (2010, p.163) argue, this lack of sufficient attention to race and culture in social work training is evident in the shortcomings of professional practice witnessed in a series of Serious Case Reviews concerning the deaths of Black children.

Edmonds-Cady & Wingfield (2017), writing about the ways in which they enable learning about race and ethnicity on their social work programme in the US, draw upon various media reports into the disproportionately high number of deaths of unarmed African American people following what has been described as police brutality. They introduce Critical Race Theory, Critical Feminist Theory and Critical Disability Theories as part of an introductory module on the social work programme, arguing that this early introduction enables student social workers to better understand other social justice concepts linked to intersectionality, race, ethnicity and other forms of diversity. Edmonds-Cady & Wingfield (2017) make an interesting observation that as Black female academics, their presence in the classroom challenges White students' stereotypes of Black people. Despite being faced with what they describe as *'resistance'*, the use of intersectional approaches enables students to analyse categories of oppression and examine the ways in which they impact on their own lives. This strategy also enables the interrogation of concepts such as unearned *White privilege*, beginning with an understanding of political and historical factors which have shaped community relations in the US. Students are subsequently required to identify an *'indigenous expert'* from a minority community and attempt to understand the difficulties they may be experiencing. Students must then attempt to unpick the problem or concern and explore possible approaches to the intervention. This strategy prioritised a bottom-up approach which meant that students would reach solutions offered by the bearers of a particular experience. This would stand them in good stead in future professional practice.

In another example, Nixon & McDermott (2010) examine their experiences of teaching race and ethnicity in England. Both social work academics from outside England, they demonstrate ways in which race and ethnicity are central to their experiences and identities. This, they argue, enables race to become visible and to inform future discussions. They do not expect their Black and ethnic minority students to share their experiences for the ethnic majority to learn from. Instead Nixon & McDermott (2010, p. 7) make it clear to students that 'Whiteness is not a lack of race' – which they suggest has the benefit of 'decentring Whiteness' – and examining unearned *White privilege*. Issues related to race are identified and continued in other modules across the whole programme and not located in a single module. The benefits of this approach for social work students are that their learning is not compartmentalised and is applicable across a range of learning. In practice, this learning is transferred into the understanding of processes which create discriminatory attitudes, and lead to social exclusion and isolation for many minority service users. This project also found that Black students sometimes struggled to articulate their experiences of racism and discrimination while White students had a tendency not to see race as problematic, which could then be used to seek out safe positions.

The role of social work educators in extending and enhancing the knowledge base of their students has been described as crucial to producing social workers who are non-oppressive, inclusive and non-discriminatory. That said, conclusions reached by Black and ethnic minority social work educators indicate that they have been made to feel like bodies out of place in higher education institutions. Edmonds-Cady & Wingfield (2017) concluded that race does matter when it comes to interactions between students and educators. Social work educators should also be added to the list of professionals who need to reflect upon and reconsider the language they use because, in preparing students to work in a multicultural society, teaching about race, ethnicity, whiteness and oppression must itself model the type of practice being promoted. Singh (2013, p. 37) argues that social work educators need to be committed to ensuring that practitioners reflect upon and challenge themselves to:

➢ Identify and name racism

➢ Challenge representations of Black people as 'dangerous', 'violent' and 'less intelligent'

➢ Raise awareness of racial and other inequalities

➢ Address and transform unequal social relations.

Understanding the experiences of discrimination among students and practitioners is equally vital, as is exploring their contribution to culturally competent practice. There is a plethora of research about the experiences of Black and ethnic minority students of social work and the ways in which they progress through their training to become qualified social workers. Students from ethnic minority backgrounds report less satisfaction about their social work training than those from the ethnic majority. They also experience discrimination, oppression and racism which often results in delayed progression, failure or underachievement (Bernard et al., 2013; Tedam, 2014, 2015). Students of Black African heritage have been identified as being on the receiving end of disparaging and negative perceptions linked to accents. 'Non-standard' accents have been viewed by the ethnic majority as different and undesirable. In a situation examined by Tedam (2015) a social work practice educator is alleged to have put the telephone down on a Black African student, stating that her accent was difficult to understand. Similar results have been found in Australia, while in the US the more disadvantaged backgrounds of many minority students presented additional challenges to study and academic success during their training (Gair et al., 2014; Yok-Fong, 2015). The relevance of this for the profession of social work is that insufficient attention may have been paid to the problem of undervaluing the contributions of Black and minority ethnic students to the future workforce, particularly in a context of *superdiversity*.

Black and minority ethnic social workers

It would appear that the difficulties faced by Black and ethnic minority students continue well into practice once they have qualified. Black and ethnic minority social workers are known to have experienced varying levels and forms of discrimination and racism in the course of their pre-qualifying studies and in their work as qualified practitioners. These experiences have impacted negatively on these social workers' confidence and self-esteem, culminating in feelings of inferiority and powerlessness (Goldstein, 2002; Mbarushima & Robbins, 2015). In more recent years the UK has seen an increase in the numbers of Black and minority ethnic social workers, largely because of a recruitment drive in Commonwealth countries such as Zimbabwe, Ghana, India, Pakistan, New Zealand, Australia and Canada (Hussein et al., 2011). These overseas recruits were found to require additional support and learning, which was not always available. Revans (2003) concluded that there was often a lack of commitment and will on the part of employers to ensure that social workers who trained abroad possessed the required skills and expertise to work within specific areas of specialism in the UK.

There is sufficient evidence to suggest that fear of victimisation often results in social workers not making formal statements or complaints in relation to experiences of discrimination and racism. Maiter (2009) considers that it is often assumed that the worker is *'culture free'*. This thinking is problematic, as social workers' understanding of families' circumstances is shaped by social workers' own culture. Writing about work in the social care sector more broadly, Hussein and Manthorpe (2014) have found that British Black and minority ethnic staff sometimes experienced racism and discrimination not only from colleagues and managers but also from service users. In terms of employment Hussein and Manthorpe (2014) found that Black and minority ethnic workers were more likely to be recruited through employment agencies than White British workers. While on its own this may not be taken to be significant, there is some evidence to suggest that in employment agencies opportunities for promotion and acceleration were often curtailed (Hussein et al., 2011).

It may be easy to think that Black and minority ethnic social workers may be better able to work with Black and minority ethnic children and families in the area of child protection. Such reasoning can be dangerous, and requires thorough consideration for managers and supervisors who find themselves aligned to this way of thinking. Ahmed (2012, p. 5) suggested that, 'becoming the race person means you are the one who is turned to when race turns up. The very fact of your existence can allow others not to turn up.' There have been concerns that many Black and minority ethnic social workers in teams and organisations have been referred to as experts or have been called upon to work specifically with Black and minority ethnic service users and families. While there may be some merit in asking Black and minority ethnic colleagues for support in specific areas of practice and cultural knowledge, it must be reiterated that this sort of *'ethnic matching'* does not always yield desirable outcomes for families. Indeed, such a situation could be construed as discriminatory and a very clear rationale would have to be provided if a pattern develops within an organisation. The findings of a public inquiry which followed the death of an African child in the UK well illustrate this problem.

In February 2000, an eight-year-old West African girl known as Victoria lost her life in London following a period of sustained abuse, torture and neglect meted out by those who were meant to protect her. She sustained 128 injuries to her body and her temperature was said to be so low that it could not be recorded on the standard thermometer. What followed was a long and thorough public inquiry into Victoria's death culminating in the Laming Report (2003). Overall, the inquiry found that: poor communication between professionals; lack of training and competence on the part of social workers; staff vacancies and shortage; inadequate management and supervision all contributed to the outcome for Victoria. Crucially, Laming (2003, para. 16.1) concluded that:

> Victoria was a Black child who was murdered by her two Black carers. Many of the professionals with whom she came into contact during her life in this country were also Black. Therefore, it is tempting to conclude that racism can have had no

part to play in her case. But such a conclusion fails to recognise that racism finds expression in many ways other than in the direct application of prejudice.

Many have expressed disappointment that Black practitioners could have failed to protect a Black child to this extent, while others have come to the realisation that racial matching of practitioners to services users does not always produce effective, safe and positive outcomes. Laming (2003, para.16.7) also noted that 'Fear of being accused of racism can stop people acting when otherwise they would. Fear of being thought unsympathetic to someone of the same race can change responses.' This suggests that effective anti-racist practice has to build upon, but extend beyond, the paradigm of White on Black discrimination, which remains at the core of structural accounts of racism. Laming (2003) suggests that being from a racial or ethnic minority does not immunise practitioners from making assumptions based on cultural stereotypes.

The allocated social worker of Black African Caribbean heritage for Victoria, who was of Black African heritage, noticed that Victoria was quiet in the presence of adults. In fact at the time Victoria would have been petrified of her great aunt (and primary caregiver), who was physically abusing her. The social worker assumed that Victoria's behaviour was 'because respect and obedience are very important features of the Afro-Caribbean family script' (Laming, 2003, para.6.300). Victoria's parents, who remained in West Africa, later explained that there was no expectation that she should stand to attention or behave in a formal manner towards adults (Laming, 2003, para.16.4). Tackling the issue of child discipline in African families Nzira's (2011, pp. 98–100) research describes its roots in notions of obedience to elders, but illustrates cultural adaptation in the wake of migration and settlement in the UK leading to a multiplicity of childrearing practices. Lewis (2000, p. 129) attacks the '*Black staff model*' (which possibly influenced the allocation of practitioner in Victoria's case) as predicated on essentialised notions about culture, describing how

> Black staff were thought to ensure equality of service provision, free from racist and cultural misunderstandings, because they would be like, indeed replicate, their clients regardless of divisions of class, gender, age, locality or indeed even the professional/client relation. No learning process would be required because in the social worker/client encounter like will meet like.

At the same time practitioners from the White ethnic majority, often apprehensive about working with families from Black and minority ethnic backgrounds, tend to over-rely on their Black colleagues and may dodge opportunities to work cross-culturally (Goldstein, 2002, pp. 771–2; O'Neale, 2000, p. 3). These professional behaviours, even if subconscious or unintentional, can be collusive in perpetuating racially based case allocations within organisations. Shared experiences of racism between Black social workers and families from racial and ethnic minorities alone are not sufficient to secure anti-oppressive and culturally appropriate assessment or care planning, as findings from Laming (2003) illustrate. In an era of superdiversity the multiplicity of backgrounds from which social workers and those they seek to safeguard are now drawn, requires that all practitioners reflect upon their own racial and ethnic backgrounds. Only then are they likely to be able to identify the assumptions emanating from their backgrounds concerning the values, beliefs and behaviours of families from different backgrounds to themselves. Models of cultural competence, which are explored in the next chapter, are therefore vital to supporting the anti-oppressive practice of social workers regardless of their racial or ethnic backgrounds.

Reflective exercise

Consider experiences in your own social work agency.

To what extent does racial and ethnic matching of social workers and families take place in your agency?

If this does take place in your agency, what effects does it have on White British and minority ethnic social workers in relation to their practice and relationships as colleagues?

What effect does this type of matching have on you personally and on your practice, and if this is adverse how might you go about changing this situation?

Conclusion

Social workers will need to engage in critical reflection which, according to Mlcek (2014, p. 1992), promotes consciousness through thinking and working towards 'valuing, identifying, acknowledging, recognising and respecting' lived experiences of family members linked to colonialism, migration and settlement. This then promotes a kind of *'racial awakening'* (Sue & Sue, 2008) which should impact on students in very personal and profound ways. Critical Race Theory is a relevant explanatory framework which can help social workers to understand the perspective from which Black and minority ethnic children and their families experience and cope with the dailyness of racism and discrimination. It can aid practitioners to explore with Black and minority ethnic children and families their strengths and the range of coping strategies they employ to navigate and negotiate oppression. To actively challenge and resist the effects of racism, Islamophobia and structural inequality, social workers can champion engagement from statutory and government agencies with Black and minority ethnic communities to ensure fairer and more sustained strategies to cope, empower and enhance their own wellbeing.

4

Concepts and Models of Cultural Competence

Cultural competence

This chapter brings together a number of cultural competence models which can be used in social work, right through from initial meetings, to assessments and reviews and through ongoing intervention with children and families. It is acknowledged that social care and health professions are particularly well placed to draw upon tools which enhance their work with people from a range of diverse backgrounds. Cultural competence is said to affect the cognitive, emotional, behavioural and environmental dimensions of a person. 'It is a complex know-act because it involves knowledge, skills, and know-how that, when combined properly, lead to a culturally safe, congruent, and effective action' (Blanchet-Garneau & Pepin, 2014, p. 12). Reflective exercises in this chapter are focused on guiding practitioners to develop cultural awareness in relation to themselves and the organisations which employ them. A worked case example at the end of this chapter and each subsequent chapter will illustrate how different models of cultural competence can be used to improve practice with families from racial and ethnic minorities.

It is argued by Papadopoulos (2006) and Sue et al. (2016) that cultural competence is achieved when a practitioner is able to integrate awareness, skills and knowledge alongside a developmental perspective. Cultural competence is therefore an ongoing process of learning and improvement in cross-cultural abilities and not an endpoint that is achieved because a practitioner has worked extensively with some minority ethnic groups. Cultural competence does not involve the deployment of specific information about each ethnic group, which necessarily makes presumptions about other people's lives. Rather it is founded on a comprehensive understanding of the broad nature of potential differences between people of diverse ethnicities. It is these which are explored in subsequent chapters and integrated into a cross-cultural approach to assessment and care planning in child protection work. The following international models and frameworks are introduced in this chapter and their application to practice is demonstrated throughout the rest of this book.

- ➤ Cultural Safety (New Zealand and Australia)

- ➤ Cultural Competence Attainment Model (USA)

- ➤ Majority identity development (USA)

- ➤ A Process Model of Cultural Competence (USA)

- ➤ Organisational Cultural Competence (USA)

- ➤ Culturagram (USA)

- ➤ Cultural Web (UK)

- ➤ Social GGRRAAACCEEESSS (UK)

- ➤ Papadopoulos, Tilki and Taylor model (UK)

- ➤ Standards for Cultural Competence (USA)

Dimensions of cultural competence

Sue et al. (2016), in their Multidimensional Model of Cultural Competence as applied to social work practice in the US, contend that the foci of cultural competence must exist on four different levels if service delivery is to be culturally appropriate. These are the individual, professional, organisational and societal levels. Sue et al. (2016) identify the obstacles to cultural competence which can manifest at each of these different levels, and these are outlined in the text box below. Chapter 2 addressed the societal level by exploring Anglocentric norms and how they are manifested in aspects of social work decision-making and practice in child protection. This chapter considers the individual, professional and organisational levels of cultural competence.

The Foci of Cultural Competence

Individual level – concerned with the practitioner's level of cultural awareness, knowledge and skills and the degree to which their prejudices, misunderstandings and stereotypical assumptions can result in discrimination.

Professional level – encompasses Anglocentric codes of ethics and standards of practice, alongside the integration of culture-bound theories drawn from the social sciences which inform understandings of human development, motivation and behaviour.

Organisational level – social work agencies and those they cooperate with, such as mental health services, the police and education providers, may have in place mono-cultural structures, policies and procedures which reflect Anglocentric norms. These can lack sensitivity to the culture or religious beliefs and practices of those from minority ethnic groups.

▶

◄

Societal level – an Anglocentric worldview can become invisible at this level because it is so naturalised and paradigmatic, determining how current events are perceived and history is interpreted. This degree of ethnocentric mono-culturalism channels how people comprehend themselves and their society. Ultimately it constitutes the power to define reality.

Cultural competence attainment model (CCAM)

The first focus proposed by Sue et al. (2016) is the *individual level* and requires practitioners to examine their own attitudes regarding diversity and equality. The Cultural Competence Attainment Model (CCAM) of cultural competence proposed by McPhatter (1997) refers to a grounded knowledge base alongside cumulative and affective skills which were deemed necessary if the over-representation of ethnic and linguistic minorities in child welfare investigations in the US was to be successfully addressed. The CCAM presupposes that in order to achieve competence, a developmental approach must be adopted as practitioners cannot simply attain competence without engaging in a process of raised awareness and accumulating new knowledge. Consequently, the components of the model include *enlightened consciousness; grounded knowledge base* and *cumulative skill proficiency*. None of these three dimensions is standalone and each must be considered to be 'mutually influencing the whole' (McPhatter, 1997, p. 262).

Enlightened consciousness, the first domain, requires social workers to re-orientate their worldviews in order to accept others on the basis of fairness, equality and a sense of shared humanity. This transformational process can be unnerving as social workers challenge their own feelings and beliefs of superiority by virtue of ascribed positive attributes and/or privilege. Once this consciousness has been achieved, social workers should begin to experience affective changes and should be able to embrace genuine acceptance and respect for diversity.

Grounded knowledge base is the second domain, which involves social workers critically questioning the knowledge on which their education and training has been based. It is widely acknowledged that social work training in the UK privileges a Eurocentric worldview to the detriment of worldviews and knowledge about ethnic and other minorities. In order to be able to work cross-culturally, McPhatter (1997) suggests that childcare social workers should develop in-depth understanding about social problems impacting on specific minority groups, and also the source of these problems, in order to better target the intervention. In addition, social workers are required to develop their understanding of the communities and neighbourhoods in which minority groups reside, alongside being aware of the community resources available to signpost and recommend for intervention. The impact of discrimination, oppression, classism and sexism is also an area where social workers need to become attuned in order to better understand their service users from a range of backgrounds. Knowledge of customs, history, preferred language, religious preferences and traditions is also important for social workers seeking to develop cultural competence.

Importantly, social workers should be familiar with ethnic minority service users' experiences of statutory intervention and must consider this when they are working with them in a variety of circumstances. This is because many service users from a minority background have experienced degradation, humiliation and discrimination from state and public services and consequently could perceive any future involvement as likely to reinforce and repeat oppression and discrimination. Social workers must understand therefore that in order to work effectively with minority service users, they must be empathic and use the utmost sensitivity. Overall a grounded approach is required.

Cumulative skill proficiency, the third and final domain, is achieved through engaging with people from different cultural contexts regularly. It relies on social workers not expecting all their service users to understand and speak the dominant language expertly, and ensuring that professional jargon is eliminated from their interactions with minority service users. Culturally competent practice requires effective cross-cultural communication skills in relation to building rapport, assessment, care planning and care plan implementation.

Majority identity development

Achieving *enlightened consciousness,* the first domain of the Cultural Competence Attainment Model, can only occur through a process of self-examination, but this can be particularly challenging for someone from a White majority ethnic background. The reasons for this relate to being a member of the dominant culture, which naturalises one's own worldview and makes it appear neutral or unremarkable (see detailed discussion in Chapter 2). Identity development differs in important respects between people who are from a dominant social group compared to those who are from a minority one. This applies particularly to racial and ethnic groups, but also other social divisions such as religion, sexuality and disability. Commonly, individuals belonging to the dominant social group tend not to think about their identity because is it so familiar, routinised and normative within society. By contrast (as discussed in Chapter 3) those from a minority group tend to become aware of their difference from the majority early on in life, often through witnessing or experiencing negative stereotyping, prejudice and discrimination towards their social group. Therefore examining their identity usually occurs at a younger age than is true for people from a majority group. Based on extensive research Helms (1990) developed a widely accepted model of White racial identity, detailed below, which describes majority identity development. People do not necessarily move through all the stages outlined and a high proportion of people become arrested at one stage or another. These can therefore be considered both as stages in terms of a developmental process, but also as a set of identity statuses which may characterise a person's identity over a prolonged period or throughout their lifetime.

1. *Contact status*: At this point members of the White majority are oblivious to racism and discrimination, believing that everyone has an equal chance in relation to, for example, education, employment and public life. They tend to have little interaction with people from minority racial or ethnic backgrounds. While the significance of race and ethnicity in relation to equality is minimised, such individuals hold stereotypical (predominantly negative) views of people from minority communities. They are generally convinced that their unexamined White majority cultural beliefs, values and social practices are superior to those of minority groups. Often this is articulated through a form of psychological compartmentalisation, with the White majority group member simultaneously deeming race and ethnicity unimportant, while being uncritical of their own cultural heritage.

2. *Disintegration status*: The individual from the White majority starts to recognise that there is unequal treatment of people from minority racial or ethnic groups. This can create internal conflict as the individual both acknowledges the wrongness of discrimination, but at the same time for instance objects to their child having a friend from a racial or ethnic minority. As these dilemmas proliferate and intensify, the individual can be conflicted between loyalty to, and identification with, their majority group on the one hand and on the other articulating support, expressing positive attitudes towards, and spending time with, people from minority groups. Some individuals may endeavour to resolve this by avoiding contact with people from minority groups, seeking affirmation from majority group members which buttresses a belief that they are not responsible for racism or avoiding discussion of subject matter concerned with race and ethnicity.

3. *Reintegration status*: Where individuals choose to retreat from contact with people from minority backgrounds and rely on affirmation from majority group members, they are likely to develop this White identity status. It is articulated through a worldview of White superiority and minority racial or ethnic group inferiority. Typically it manifests as

an idealisation of White culture and can be expressed through White nationalism alongside racist attitudes and intolerance towards minority groups. Inequalities are either denied or blamed on the attitudes, values and behaviours of people from minority groups.

4. *Pseudo-independence status*: This phase tends to be initiated by some personal experience or encounters with people from minority groups which pushes the individual into re-evaluating their White supremacist worldview. Individuals holding this status become aware of the unfair treatment of other racial and ethnic groups and experience discomfort as a White person associated with a group that holds racist or Anglocentric views. This commonly leads the individual to become concerned about the plight of people from minority communities subject to racism and discrimination. Often their endeavour to interact with and understand the experiences of people from minorities is hampered by a White majority frame of reference in relation to people from minority racial or ethnic groups. This means that they continue to be evaluated from an essentially dominant group normative perspective. Therefore understandings of minority experiences in relation to discrimination tend to remain at the level of intellectual recognition.

5. *Immersion/emersion status*: Where the tentative moves towards understanding the experiences of minority groups are supported this can lead to a deeper self-exploration of what it means to have a racial identity as a White person. This involves a questioning of how one is advantaged by and takes advantage of *White privilege* in everyday life. An individual reaching this identity status is willing to confront and explore some of their own racial and ethnocentric biases. They move from trying to change others from minority backgrounds to trying to change themselves. In doing so, they move from a purely intellectual appreciation of racism and discrimination to a much deeper empathetic understanding. This may be accompanied by feelings of guilt and shame. However, it is only at this point that an individual has the potential to develop a non-racist White identity.

6. *Autonomy status*: Achievement of this status occurs through increasing self-awareness of having a White majority racial and ethnic identity. This is reached by acknowledging how one's acquiescence or participation in structures within society can perpetuate racism or dominant group ethnocentrism. It also involves relinquishing acute feelings of guilt or shame; a reduction in defensiveness; and embracing active ways of reducing inequalities. Individuals who achieve this status are knowledgeable about minority issues and experiences while being comfortable with racial and ethnic diversity. They also actively seek out inter-racial and inter-cultural encounters.

Reflective exercise

If you are from the White ethnic majority, consider your own identity development.

What identity status best describes you at present?

Why do you think you have this identity status?

How does this identity status influence your perceptions of and relationships with people from your own racial or ethnic group and those from other racial or ethnic groups?

How might this identity status affect your professional practice with families from Black and ethnic minority backgrounds?

Developing cultural self-awareness

At the *individual level* social workers also need to examine how their own cultural inheritance affects their worldview. The inculcation of values, beliefs and practices which coalesce around secularism, science, capitalism and individualism in the experiences and perceptions of people from the White majority population obscures the degree to which culture influences are at work in dominant norms of British life. As a consequence of dominant Anglocentric values and practices being incorporated into daily experiences, recognition of the cultural constructs embedded in one's own worldview is hampered. This is a difficulty not only for those belonging to the White majority, but also for many from minority ethnic backgrounds who have integrated these dominant cultural elements into their lives and outlook. Moreover, the incorporation of Anglocentric precepts into theory, and the inculcation of those theories through professional training, hampers the ability of practitioners from both the White majority and minority ethnic communities to comprehend the culture-bound norms which these articulate.

Cultivating self-awareness in relation to one's own heritage is therefore essential as a first step in developing the ability to practise effectively in cross-cultural contexts. Culture is often hidden in the everyday, the routine and the over-familiar and makes cultural self-awareness an effortful enterprise which requires guided reflection to uncover often unconsciously held assumptions. It is a necessary process for all practitioners, but is perhaps more challenging for those from the White majority who are often accustomed to thinking of British society as underpinned by essentially neutral values which revolve around tolerance of multiple ethnic groups. Cultural awareness needs to be understood as one component in a multi-faceted model of competent practice with families from diverse ethnic backgrounds.

Campinha-Bacote's (2002) transcultural nursing model, known by the acronym ASKED, embeds cultural awareness within a set of related capabilities and is adapted for child protection social work in the box below.

A Process Model of Cultural Competence (ASKED)

Cultural awareness – involves recognising how our values and beliefs shape our interpretation of the observed and experienced, including our perceptions of people from a different cultural background. It also requires a meticulous self-examination of the practitioner's own cultural heritage and professional ethos alongside their own biases, prejudices, and assumptions about people from minority ethnic communities.

Cultural skill – is the ability to collect, comprehend and accurately analyse cultural information regarding beliefs, values and practices relevant to a family's needs and problems as part of the assessment and care planning process. It includes understanding how this ability is affected by personal or agency factors or the characteristics of the family or local community.

Cultural knowledge – comprises searching for and acquiring detailed information about other cultures and ethnic groups while avoiding stereotyping. Broadly it includes accumulating knowledge about settlement patterns, family structure, childcare, inter-generational and gender relations, faith and important traditions.

Cultural encounter – means going beyond mere interaction with families from culturally diverse backgrounds. It requires meaningful cross-cultural engagement which modifies the practitioner's existing beliefs and perceptions regarding a particular ethnic group. Genuine encounter should challenge and dispel stereotypes.

Cultural desire – this concerns the practitioner's motivation to *want* to, rather than *have* to, engage in the above four processes. It comprises an authentic willingness to accept differences, recognise similarities, and learn from family members by treating them as cultural informants.

Campinha-Bacote's (2002) ASKED model above incorporates the three key elements of *cultural awareness, cultural skills* and *cultural knowledge,* which are potentially enhanced through each cultural encounter with families from ethnic backgrounds which vary from that of the practitioner. Reflection during cultural encounters modifies and deepens the practitioner's own understanding of people from different ethnic backgrounds. This can only happen if there is *cultural desire,* meaning a genuine willingness on the part of the social worker to engage in all four of these processes.

Achieving cultural self-awareness is immensely challenging because it is inherently problematical to reflect upon one's own beliefs, values and practices when these are experienced as the *'normal'* way of thinking or doing things, most particularly if your heritage is that of the dominant social group in society. Such dominance naturalises one's own cultural heritage and acts as an obstacle to achieving objective distance. Cultural influences are embedded in family relationships, lifestyle choices, beliefs and aspirations and commonly change over time. To make these discernible and develop their own cultural self-awareness practitioners need to ask themselves the following kinds of questions reproduced from Laird (2008, pp. 156–57) in the text box below.

Reflective exercise

Social Organisation

- How is my family organised?
- What are the important relationships in my family?
- What are the expectations of different family members?
- Who makes what kind of decisions in my family?
- What is considered proper or improper behaviour?
- Who is expected to take on caring responsibilities?
- What sort of relationship does my family have with other people in the neighbourhood?

Values and Beliefs

- What are important values in my life?
- What are important aspirations for members of my family?
- Do I have spiritual beliefs and if so what are they?
- How do my spiritual beliefs influence other aspects of my life?
- What are the common health beliefs among members of my family and how do these influence my behaviour?

Lifestyle

- What sort of foods or beverages do I consume and why do I make these choices?
- What sort of clothes do I choose to wear and why?
- What choices do I make in relation to social and leisure activities and why?

Coping Mechanisms

- What coping strategies do I typically adopt and where did I learn these?
- What social networks do I call upon for assistance?

▶

◀

Change over Time

- In what ways is the current social organisation of my family similar to or different from that of previous generations, and what is the explanation for this?

- In what ways are my values and beliefs different from or similar to those of my parents, grandparents or great grandparents and what are the reasons for this?

- In what ways is my lifestyle different or similar to those of previous generations of my family and what is the explanation for this?

Knowledge for cultural competence

Attaining insight into one's own cultural heritage and how it shapes social relations, aspirations, morality and lifestyle of itself is an insufficient basis for developing *cultural awareness*, which additionally involves identifying one's own assumptions and prejudices regarding people from other ethnic backgrounds. Indeed, greater comprehension of one's own heritage and values can merely reinforce chauvinism regarding those of others. At the *individual level* of cultural competence it is also necessary for practitioners to consider what knowledge they have of other minority ethnic groups and to examine whether this is shaped by prejudice, assumptions and stereotypes rather than a real-world engagement and comprehension of the diversity between and within minority ethnic groups. Wilson (1982), addressing social workers in particular, identified a number of broad *cultural knowledge* areas which practitioners need to be conversant with in order to deliver culturally competent interventions with families from a diversity of heritage backgrounds. These categories are cross-cutting and relevant regardless of which ethnic group or groups a family belongs to. These broad areas of *cultural knowledge* are:

➤ Cultural influences

➤ Impact of class and ethnicity on beliefs, values and behaviour

➤ Help-seeking behaviours

➤ Communication styles

➤ Impact of social services on ethnic minorities

➤ Resources including formal and informal support systems and services that can be utilised for people from minority ethnic backgrounds

➤ Ways in which professionals values may conflict with or accommodate the needs of people from minority ethnic backgrounds.

➤ Power relationships in communities, institutions and/or agencies which impact on people from minority ethnic backgrounds.

Cultural safety

Cultural knowledge needs to infuse social work practice in ways which help to affirm the ethnic identity of parents, their partners, family members and children, rather than de-valuing or criticising it. *Cultural safety* is a concept originally developed by Maori nurses and refers to being able to protect the beliefs, practices and values of different cultures. Williams (1997, p. 2) suggests that it has come to be defined as 'an environment, which is safe for people; where there is no assault, challenge or denial of their identity, of who they are and what, they need. It is about shared respect, shared meaning, shared knowledge and experience, of learning together with dignity, and truly listening.' According to Duffy (2001), it involves understanding, supporting and respecting the cultural rights of people from diverse backgrounds. Used largely in the context of nursing, we argue that its applicability to social work holds value for the professionals involved and for families they work with. This is because the aim of being culturally safe has the benefit of reducing stigma and marginalisation, as well as responding to the impact of colonisation (Johnstone & Kanitsaki, 2007). Ramsden (2002) has outlined the stages involved in developing cultural safety.

Cultural Security

Cultural Safety (applied)

Cultural Sensitivity (legitimising the difference and care planning)

Cultural Awareness (identifying the difference)

Working from the bottom upwards, social workers are advised to begin with being culturally aware when working with their service users. That means to recognise and respect diversity such that blanket approaches are not used. The next step in the process is that of cultural sensitivity. Being culturally sensitive involves social workers understanding the 'self', recognising that differences between them and their service users are not perceived from a deficit perspective and do not cloud the nature and scope of their intervention in terms of offering quality of services. It includes giving consideration to social workers' own positionality and how this might affect *cultural encounters*. The more understood families from racial and ethnic minorities feel, the more likely they are to trust and to discuss significant matters. *Cultural safety* is achieved when social workers practise safely. It extends beyond cultural awareness and sensitivity and requires social workers to actively ensure dignity, respectfulness, autonomy and the human rights of family members. It is important that social workers recognise the social inequalities within which people live and operate. A lack of recognition of difference can reinforce oppressive practice and could result in culturally unsafe social work practice. Culturally safe social work practice puts the child and family at the heart of all interventions and ensures, for example, that interpreters are accessed to secure improved communication with people for whom English is an additional language. This means that lack of resources and scarcity of funds cannot be used to deny users of a service such means as interpreting, since this could likely result in unsafe practice. Coffin (2007) has argued that there is a fourth level – cultural security. However this is much more difficult to achieve because it proposes that social workers actively ensure that no harm is caused to service users as a result of culturally inappropriate or discriminatory practices.

Consider your practice with three families each from a different racial, ethnic or faith background.

How might your own positionality in relation to race, ethnicity and religion have facilitated or inhibited *cultural encounter* with each of these families?

What kinds of things might family members find more difficult to disclose or discuss with a social worker from a different racial, ethnic or faith background to them and why?

To what extent do you seek out new *cultural encounters* in your personal and professional life and what strategies could you use to increase these to demonstrate cultural desire?

Professional culture and norms

Knowledge of underpinning beliefs, practices and norms which may influence a family from a minority ethnic background and the interplay of this with other structural factors is crucial, but not sufficient of itself, for cultural competent work. Social workers also need to take account of their own professional culture and how this facilitates or inhibits effective inter-cultural communication and practice. Sue et al. (2016) refer to this as the *professional level* in relation to cultural competence. The attainment of formal professional recognition for an occupation demands that it is a bounded activity, by virtue of entailing a range of distinctive complex tasks requiring an extensive knowledge base and specialist skills to perform. The acquisition of such knowledge and skills necessitates a period of extended training, which involves the study of a systematic body of knowledge and standardised ways of carrying out tasks. Normally this precludes untrained people from acting as recognised professionals, as is the case regarding doctors, police officers, school teachers and social workers. Professional training is also a normalising process which exposes trainees to a set of values, beliefs and norms which support established structures, paradigms and methods of service delivery. Many of these, such as individualism are articulated in BASW (2014, pp. 8–9) *The Code of Ethics for Social Work*; for example, 'respecting the right to self-determination' and 'treating each person as a whole', albeit that 'recognising diversity' is also included. These create a social work professional culture which articulates many tenets of an Anglocentric worldview as evident in the predominant characteristics of social work encounters with family members, summarised by Laird (2008, p. 45) and reproduced in the text box below.

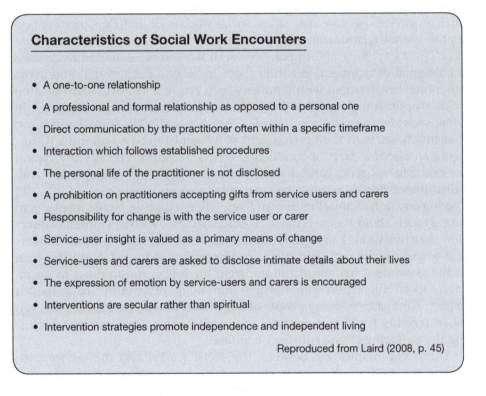

Characteristics of Social Work Encounters

- A one-to-one relationship

- A professional and formal relationship as opposed to a personal one

- Direct communication by the practitioner often within a specific timeframe

- Interaction which follows established procedures

- The personal life of the practitioner is not disclosed

- A prohibition on practitioners accepting gifts from service users and carers

- Responsibility for change is with the service user or carer

- Service-user insight is valued as a primary means of change

- Service-users and carers are asked to disclose intimate details about their lives

- The expression of emotion by service-users and carers is encouraged

- Interventions are secular rather than spiritual

- Intervention strategies promote independence and independent living

Reproduced from Laird (2008, p. 45)

These modes of interaction are not neutral, but are culture-bound and may create confusion, discomfort or conflict with people from minority ethnic backgrounds. The emphasis on a one-to-one relationship which often results in social workers asking to interview and often assess family members individually rather than in a group, runs counter to the traditions of collectivist cultures which privilege the interests of the group over those of individuals. Collective cultures put more emphasis on group goals and joint decision-making, often setting the needs of the group as a whole over those of particular individuals within it. Members of an extended family of Indian heritage may share material and monetary resources across households and expect everyone to contribute to this, rather than family members using funds for their own personal ends. Likewise, arrangements in relation to childcare may be decided by the wider family rather than simply be a matter for the parent. Therefore the tendency of casework to individu-alise family members and largely ignore wider kin in the conduct of child protection work can create unrecognised tensions from the outset, because the notion of developing one-to-one relationships with different family members presupposes the primacy of the individual over group-related considerations.

While building rapport, conveying empathy and demonstrating accept-ance of service users are core skills, social work is nevertheless premised on a professional relationship as opposed to a personal one with family mem-bers. During training and in practice social workers are exhorted to develop professional detachment, enabling them to be non-judgemental and avoid emotional involvement with families which can result in over-identification or over-optimism alongside other forms of dangerous practice. However, in some societies, personal relationships commonly straddle formal and infor-mal situations, with the development of a friendship based on mutual trust being an essential facet of conducting official business. This is fairly typical for example in Greek, Turkish and Filipino cultures. The reserved and stand-offish impression which can be created by a social worker primed to avoid sharing any details about their own lives, while requiring family members to reveal much about theirs, is likely to exacerbate this kind of cultural disjunc-tion. Relatively short procedural timescales, time pressures on practitioners due to large workloads, and the early imposition of formal processes, such as the assessment framework, all undercut the longer run-in times to mean-ingful social interaction which people from many other ethnic backgrounds expect. For instance, many people of Nigerian ethnicity anticipate that even when meeting for formal purposes, time will be spent greeting and discuss-ing the wellbeing of one another's families.

Direct communication between the social worker and the service user, parent or child is also assumed, meaning intermediaries are not used. In many societies there can be expectations that people from outside the kin group communicate through family elders or the male head to con-verse with women or children, as is the case among some families of Paki-stani heritage. In others, such as Filipino culture, third parties might be expected to seek introduction to the family via someone who is already known to them. Similarly, there may be cultural norms around negotiation with more powerful figures in families, such as a mother-in-law in some multi-generational households of South Asian heritage, or a father from an Azerbaijani background, in order to obtain permission to speak with other family members.

While the emphasis on individuality and personal identity among peo-ple of White British ethnicity encourages self-reflection and the expression of emotion, in other cultures concern for harmonious social relationships and the wellbeing of others may take precedence. For some people from a

Filipino or Chinese ethnic background saying 'no' to something can be difficult for fear of causing disharmony. So the tendency is for some people from such backgrounds to explicitly agree even when they actually disagree or are unsure, in the interests of avoiding confrontation. This is because the importance placed on conflict avoidance commonly varies between cultures and is often related to a longer-term view of relationships as built upon reciprocity.

The long history of the written language in the United Kingdom, combined with the emphasis on individualism and the rule of law, means that printed material is often the medium of communication or of formalising verbal deliberations. In numerous societies face-to-face communication is much more central to working relationships and regarded as the principal means of discussing and agreeing matters. Many African societies have a long oral tradition and bestow considerable importance on verbal exchanges as opposed to written communication. In other places where less value is given to reading and writing, as in some rural areas of India and Bangladesh, people may rely on verbal communication and be non-literate in their own language. For such societies, face-to-face communication is vital in the development of trust, as opposed to the influential Anglocentric norm of giving greater credence to what is written down such as contracts or minutes of meetings.

The prohibition on practitioners accepting gifts from service users and family members might be problematic when working with people from those cultural backgrounds where gift giving is a valued aspect of building interpersonal relationships. In the UK and the US gift-giving in formal situations, such as those of commerce or employment, is perceived as a form of corruption. However, among many ethnic Chinese giving a small gift denotes thanks for a favour or can be bestowed in expectation of receiving assistance in the future. Refusing such a gift or failing to reciprocate at some point can be regarded as rude and undermining of friendship. While gift-giving among the White majority is largely restricted to family members and generally then only on significant occasions such as Christmas and birthdays, in other societies gift-giving can be much more widespread.

The principles underpinning social work assessment and intervention are also predicated on Anglocentric norms. In the first instance they are secular in orientation, not spiritual. This can create some disjunction for practitioners when working with families for whom religion frames not only their spiritual life, but also aspects of their social relationships, their understanding of problems and the strategies they use to manage difficulties. In many families of Pakistani or Nigerian Hausa descent, Islam is not confined to a matter of faith. Sharia, a system of rules based on the Quran and the deeds and saying of the Prophet Muhammad, regulates social, political and economic activity. Consequently, relationships between male and female, and older and younger family members, alongside what is considered acceptable or objectionable behaviour, may be governed by an appeal to religious tenets.

For the majority of Anglicans in England faith is pursued separately from day-to-day life, but for many Christians in other societies, and indeed those practising other faiths, religion is an integral aspect of how they view the world, comprehend events and seek comfort or assistance. An international survey found that out of 65 countries the UK ranked 60th, one of the least religious with just 30% of respondents describing themselves as religious, compared to 94% in Thailand, 93% in Bangladesh, 86% in Poland and 71% in Greece (WIN/Gallup International Survey, 2015). In the UK itself Christianity is practised in many different ways. Some ethnically White British evangelical Christians might regard the illness of a child as God's will and therefore prioritise prayer over action in bringing about improvement to their health. In this instance faith is central for the family, but tangential to professional practice.

Intervention in child protection revolves around persuading parents and carers to change their attitudes and behaviour towards children. Social work places the responsibility on specific family members to make stipulated changes, since it is predominantly individuals who are assigned blame and credit in Anglocentric countries. In a number of other cultures, culpability and therefore the target of change may be attributed to other sources. In more collectivist cultures such as those of India and Pakistan, the harmful or reprehensible behaviour of one family member may be attributed to the family as a whole. The expectation may be that the family makes changes, rather than particular individuals. Moreover, social work intervention seeks to promote independence and places considerable emphasis on personal growth and actualisation. This runs counter to overarching objectives in numerous other cultures, which seek relational interdependence, and advance consideration for the needs and goals of the family as a whole over those of individual members. Many collectivist societies, such as those of Vietnam and the Philippines, are influenced by these social expectations.

It is not only people from minority ethnic communities who may experience social work norms and modes of intervention as disjunctive, but also members of the White majority community. The organising principle in British society of individuality and the overarching value attached to individual self-expression and autonomy alongside the right to privacy run directly counter to social work intervention in families which violates these norms. Child protection interventions by their very nature involve interference in the private sphere, demand disclosure of personal information and typically require parents and carers to follow regimes of change stipulated in formal child in need and Child Protection Plans. Culture clashes therefore can occur not only between social workers and those from minority ethnic communities, but also between practitioners and those belonging to the White majority population. Nevertheless, work with families from a minority ethnic group can sometimes add a further layer of complexity and additional considerations in relation to communication, assessment, care planning and its implementation.

Reflective exercise

Consider your own professional experience.

What culture clashes have you observed between families and social work practices?

How did these culture clashes affect your relationships with different family members?

Organisational cultural competence

Even if practitioners address the *individual level* and *professional level* regarding cultural competence, they will still be greatly impaired in their work if they are employed by a mono-cultural organisation. At the *organisational level* agencies also have to become responsive to the needs of an ethnically diverse clientele of children, parents, partners, kin and community members. In the US research has been undertaken to establish how to evaluate the degree of cultural competence at an *organisation level*. According to the Health Resources and Services Administration (2007), part of the US Department of Health and Human Services, the cultural competence of organisations needs to be assessed across four elements of their operation as follows:

Capacity and Structure – includes appropriate staffing, facilities, equipment, funding, information systems, administration and organisational architecture.

Process – concerns the cultural competence of the organisation's activities in terms of its policies, procedures, practices and methods of intervention.

Impact and Outcome – relates to the degree to which cultural competence contributes to a successful outcome regarding the provision of care, the service users' responses to that care and the outcome of the care.

Organisational Viewpoint – comprises the values, principles, attitudes and perspectives of an organisation which are espoused and enacted in relation to cultural competence.

Adapting measures suggested by the Health Resources and Services Administration (2007), the reflective exercise in the text box below asks practitioners to answer a series of questions relating to their own employing agency to gauge how culturally competent it is. These questions are divided across the four elements.

Reflective exercise

Capacity and Structure

Do priorities for funding include language and translation services?

How often are language and translation services available at the first point of contact?

How effective is your agency at disseminating information to ethnic minority communities?

How adequate are structures to guide practitioners faced with ethical dilemmas created by a family's cultural or religious beliefs and practices?

What resources are available to assist family members from minority ethnic groups to access culturally competent providers?

What capacity does your agency have to conduct a self-assessment of its cultural competence?

Process

What proportion of staff are bilingual or multilingual?

What proportion of staff are from minority ethnic backgrounds?

How easily available are interpreters and translators?

How frequently do service users receive information in their primary language?

Does your agency offer training in cross-cultural social work practice?

How often are culturally defined needs addressed in care plans?

What proportion of care plans incorporate minority ethnic community resources

Impact and Outcome

How satisfied are service users from minority ethnic backgrounds with the cultural sensitivity of the service they receive?

To what extent does the service address culturally specific arrangements and activities?

How over-represented or under-represented are different minority ethnic groups in the service provision of your agency?

Organisational Viewpoint

Does your agency's mission statement reflect a commitment to deliver culturally and linguistically competent services?

To what extent does information about services designed for service users reflect different languages, literacy levels and modes of communication?

To what extent does your agency promote and support attitudes, knowledge, behaviour and skills consistent with effective work in an ethnically diverse environment?

To what degree does your agency demonstrate attitudes consistent with respect for the settlement, migration, colonisation and acculturation experiences of service users?

Culturagram and Cultural Web

Even if good progress is made at the *individual, professional* and *organisational levels* towards cultural competence, practitioners will still need tools to assist them in realising culturally competent forms of assessment, care planning and care plan implementation. Congress (1994) proposed the Culturagram as an effective tool for assessing families, taking into consideration their unique sociocultural locations. This was further adapted for social work by Parker & Bradley (2007, pp. 51–57) who suggest the 10 areas outlined below to enable a social worker to understand the different aspects of culture in relation to a specific family. The Culturagram provides a unique opportunity for social workers to initiate discussions adapted to a particular family and which could better inform their assessments and interventions. In addition, the tool supports practice which is tailored to the needs of individual families and minimises the risk of generalisations and stereotyping.

➤ Reasons for immigration

➤ Length of time in the community

➤ Legal or undocumented status

➤ Age at time of immigration

➤ Language spoken at home and in the community

➤ Contact with cultural institutions

➤ Health beliefs

➤ Holidays and special events

➤ Impact of crisis events

➤ Values about family, education and work

Tedam (2013) developed the Cultural Web, arguing that the web of relationships within families mean that social workers must understand the intricate and complex nature of individual family members and their cultures. It draws out the need for social workers to explore the often ignored unique elements of families. This will go some way in minimising the risks posed to vulnerable children by ignoring or misunderstanding the relevant issues in relation to a child or family's situation. The Cultural Web has the added benefit of being relevant to contemporary English social work practice in that it effectively connects the elements of the web to relevant domains of the professional capabilities framework (PCF), which underpins social work training and professional development. The Cultural Web, by suggesting additional areas of enquiry and consideration, can therefore support

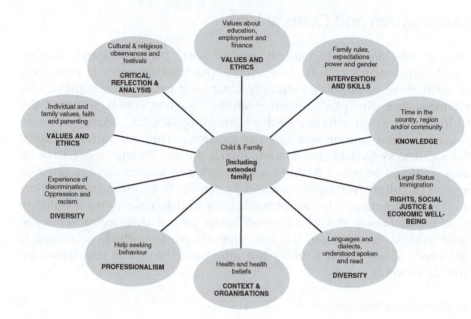

Figure 4.1 The Cultural Web

Tedam (2013, p. 55)

practitioners to exercise the totality of their professional values, knowledge and skills in working with families from ethnic minority backgrounds (Figure 4.1).

Social GGRRAAACCEEESSS

The *societal level* of cultural competence is addressed in Chapter 2 through a consideration of how expectations of children, parents, partners and family members are significantly influenced by an Anglo-centric worldview. This level also requires knowledge of how structural factors impact on individuals and families. GGRRAAACCEEESSS is an acronym that stands for Gender, Geography, Race, Religion, Age, Abilities, Appearance, Culture, Class, Ethnicity, Education, Employment, Sexuality, Sexual Orientation and Spirituality. It is a conceptual frame developed by Burnham (2012) and has been popularised in family therapy and social work as a framework for reflection in supervisory contexts. By simultaneously highlighting all facets of social differences in this comprehensive way, practitioners can be asked to explore in supervision which aspects of a family stand out the most or which are least understood. Such questions can be important starting points for effective reflexivity. This approach, Burnham (2012) suggests, can help to make visible what is invisible and help the practitioner to voice what has been unvoiced in terms of their experiences with different families. A practitioner may not have noticed a visual clue or recognise why a particular stereotype has been activated until they are guided through the social GGRRAAACCEEESSS Framework. It can be employed to explore the significance of different identities for both family members and social workers. Consequently the framework can uncover experiences of both disadvantage (e.g. due to being working class or a migrant) and advantage (e.g. due to being male or from the ethnic majority).

This is a tool for both exploring reactions to family members and also highlighting why family members might have responded to the practitioner as they did. It helps practitioners to understand how they bring to bear perceptions of visibility and invisibility due to family members belonging to similar or dissimilar social groups to themselves. Consistently using this framework to guide reflexive deliberation can, over time, increase the perceptual capacity of workers (Burnham, 2012). The social GGRRAAACCEEESSS framework can also be used by practitioners in their work with families to make the invisible, visible and the unvoiced, voiced by asking questions about race, culture and spirituality alongside ones about class, gender and sexual orientation to develop an understanding about the inter-sectoral nature of the lived experiences of different family members. We argue here that this Framework through its inter-sectoral focus will very much inform work with families in a manner that is culturally sensitive, respectful and non-oppressive.

Since its inception, the concept has grown to encompass a wider range of differences. Social workers should by the end of their training be able to work effectively with people from a range of backgrounds and life experiences. In terms of its relevance to cultural competence, this concept can develop social workers' skills in working cross-culturally and its use is both a process and experience. Understanding service users in these contexts is important because it enables social workers to assess and analyse: the power dynamics; areas of privilege; and areas of disadvantage that the various components of the model prove for them. In minimising this feeling of *'otherness'*, the model assists social workers to explore culture, diversity and difference in ways that are structured, meaningful and relevant in enhancing culturally competent practice and which take account of the intersectional nature of people's lives as a result of belonging to multiple social statuses.

Reflective exercise

Consider your recent practice with one family from a racial or ethnic minority.

Apply the social GGRRAAACCEEESSS framework to each family member and identify intersecting aspects of their lives.

▶

◄

In what ways do these intersecting aspects advantage or disadvantage different family members?

How does the application of this framework help you to understand family dynamics or the impact of structural factors in family life?

Cultural competence

A model designed by Papadopoulos (2006) and her colleagues furthers international developments in nursing in relation to culturally appropriate health care and incorporates dimensions of *cultural awareness* and *cultural knowledge* and into a wider framework. The Papadopoulos, Tilki and Taylor (PTT) model for developing *cultural competence* has four components which build on each other. Although designed primarily for health care professionals, its core components are clearly transferable to social work. *Cultural awareness* is the starting point for any professional seeking to work effectively with people from Black and minority ethnic backgrounds. *Cultural knowledge* follows from this as a practitioner able to reflect on their own cultural heritage and ethnocentrism is much better positioned to engage with the cultural heritage of others. *Cultural sensitivity* concerns the relational aspect of practice based on knowledge and awareness and reflected in effective communication and the ability to negotiate difference with people from diverse ethnic backgrounds. If awareness, knowledge and sensitivity are brought together *cultural competence* is then expressed through appropriate skills of assessment, intervention and care planning. These should explore, acknowledge and integrate significant aspects of culture, faith and ethnic identity. Maintaining *cultural competence* requires commitment to continuous reflexiveness and an ongoing effort to expand capacity in each of the four components. *Cultural competence* is therefore not a finally achieved endpoint.

The British Association of Social Workers (BASW) does not have a code of conduct related specifically to *cultural competence*; however, a number of other professional social work organisations do, including those of US and Australia. The National Association of Social Workers (NASW), which is the American professional body, in their standards for cultural competence pull together the multiple strands of good practice in this area. NASW (2015, pp. 4–5) sets out 10 cultural competencies which are reproduced below. Taken altogether these encompass what is meant by *cultural competence* in social work policy and practice and give expression to this at the individual, professional, organisational and societal levels (Sue et al., 2016).

Standard 1 Ethics and Values: Social workers shall function in accordance with the values, ethics, and standards of the NASW (2015) Code of Ethics. Cultural competence requires self-awareness, cultural humility, and the commitment to understanding and embracing culture as central to effective practice.

Standard 2 Self-Awareness: Social workers shall demonstrate an appreciation of their own cultural identities and those of others. Social workers must also be aware of their own privilege and power and must acknowledge the impact of this privilege and power in their work with and on behalf of clients. Social workers will also demonstrate cultural humility and sensitivity to the dynamics of power and privilege in all areas of social work.

Standard 3 Cross-Cultural Knowledge: Social workers shall possess and continue to develop specialized knowledge and understanding that is inclusive of, but not limited to, the history, traditions, values, family systems, and artistic expressions such as race and ethnicity; immigration and refugee status; tribal groups; religion and spirituality; sexual orientation; gender identity or expression; social class; and mental or physical abilities of various cultural groups.

Standard 4 Cross-Cultural Skills: Social workers will use a broad range of skills (micro, mezzo, and macro) and techniques that demonstrate an understanding of and respect for the importance of culture in practice, policy, and research.

Standard 5 Service Delivery: Social workers shall be knowledgeable about and skillful in the use of services, resources, and institutions and be available to serve multicultural communities. They shall be able to make culturally appropriate referrals within both formal and informal networks and shall be cognizant of, and work to address, service gaps affecting specific cultural groups.

Standard 6 Empowerment and Advocacy: Social workers shall be aware of the impact of social systems, policies, practices, and programs on multicultural client populations, advocating for, with, and on behalf of multicultural clients and client populations whenever appropriate. Social workers should also participate in the development and implementation of policies and practices that empower and advocate for marginalized and oppressed populations.

Standard 7 Diverse Workforce: Social workers shall support and advocate for recruitment, admissions and hiring, and retention efforts in social work programs and organizations to ensure diversity within the profession.

Standard 8 Professional Education: Social workers shall advocate for, develop, and participate in professional education and training programs that advance cultural competence within the profession. Social workers should embrace cultural competence as a focus of lifelong learning.

Standard 9 Language and Communication: Social workers shall provide and advocate for effective communication with clients of all cultural groups, including people of limited English proficiency or low literacy skills, people who are blind or have low vision, people who are deaf or hard of hearing, and people with disabilities.

Standard 10 Leadership to Advance Cultural Competence: Social workers shall be change agents who demonstrate the leadership skills to work effectively with multi-cultural groups in agencies, organizational settings, and communities. Social workers should also demonstrate responsibility for advancing cultural competence within and beyond their organizations, helping to challenge structural and institutional oppression and build and sustain diverse and inclusive institutions and communities

This chapter, together with the examination of Anglocentric values and beliefs alongside structural inequalities in earlier chapters, has provided an overview of the different foci of cultural competence in relation to the *individual, professional, organisational* and *societal levels*. Table 4.1 summarises this exploration and categorises the concepts and models discussed according to which level of competence they address. The case study for practitioners which concludes this chapter illustrates how one of these models can be applied to assist assessment at the *professional level*.

Table 4.1   Cultural Competence Models and Frameworks

Foci of cultural competence	Related concepts and models	Dimensions of model
Individual	Cultural Safety (interpersonal)	Cultural awareness
		Cultural sensitivity
		Cultural safety
		Cultural security
	Cultural Competence Attainment Model (CCAM) (interpersonal)	Enlightened consciousness
		Grounded knowledge
		Cumulative skill proficiency
	Process Model of Cultural Competence (ASKED) (interpersonal)	Awareness
		Skill
		Knowledge
		Encounter
		Desire
	Papadopoulos, Tilki and Taylor (PTT) Model (interpersonal)	Cultural awareness
		Cultural knowledge
		Cultural sensitivity
		Cultural competence
	Majority Identity Development (intra-personal)	Contact status
		Disintegration status
		Reintegration status
		Pseudo-independence status
		Immersion/emersion status
		Autonomy status

Professional	Anglocentric Social Work	Anglocentric embedded values
		Anglocentric practices
	Culture Bound Theory	Anglocentric child development theory, concepts of family organisation and family dynamics
	Cultural Web	Values on work, education etc
		Family rules and expectations
		Time in country
		Legal status
		Language
		Health and health beliefs
		Help seeking behaviour
		Experiences of discrimination
		Individual and family values Cultural and religious observance
	Standards for Cultural Competence	Ethics and values
		Self-awareness
		Cross-cultural knowledge
		Cross-cultural skills
		Service delivery
		Empowerment and advocacy
		Diverse workforce
		Professional education
		Language and communication
		Leadership to advance cultural competence
Organisational	Dept. of Health USA – Organisational Competence	Capability and structure
		Process
		Impact and outcome
		Organisational viewpoint
Societal	Ethnocentrism	Hegemonic Anglocentric values, beliefs and social practices
	Dimensions of Whiteness	Normative race privilege
		Worldview
		Set of cultural practices
	Social GGRRAAACCEEESSS	Gender, Geography, Race, Religion, Age, Abilities, Appearance, Culture, Class, Ethnicity, Education, Employment, Sexuality, Sexual Orientation and Spirituality

Case study for practitioners

Abdullah is a 27-year-old man who has become the guardian of his 14-year-old half-sister following the recent death of their father. Abdullah's mother passed away many years ago. Abdullah is originally from Somalia, and his half-sister Miriam is dual heritage Somali and White British. Miriam's mother, Shazia, is terminally ill and unable to care for Miriam, who is beginning to display risky behaviours and has been seen in the company of older men in their local town. School has reported that Miriam's grades are slipping and that she no longer wishes to play sport for the school. Shazia is worried about whether Abdullah will be able to meet Miriam's needs, especially as he works full time as well as volunteering at the local mosque. Shazia considers whether Miriam will be better off with her aunt Grace, who also has a daughter around Miriam's age. When Shazia informs Abdullah about the proposal, she is told that Islamophobia is rife in the area where Grace lives and that Miriam will be unhappy there as she wears the hijab. Miriam informs the school about her mother's plans for her to live with her aunt Grace for a period of time. A teacher telephones Children's Social Care to advise them of this.

Social workers who will be working with Miriam and her family can use the *culturagram* described earlier in this chapter to make some sense of, and assess, her situation. This process will involve discussions about the family's reasons for migrating to the UK, length of time in the community and their legal status in relation to immigration. Languages spoken at home will be examined as well as health-related and cultural beliefs. The family's views about education, work and career will be explored, as will the impact of crises and other significant events.

Abdullah's concerns about the neighbourhood where Grace lives will have to be sensitively explored, as well as his own role in the local community mosque and how that might provide additional support for Miriam and Shazia, particularly as research suggests that within Muslim communities there is an emphasis on caring, cooperation, interconnectedness and social support (Graham et al., 2009). In all of this, Miriam's welfare is of paramount importance and her wishes and feelings remain central to any proposed interventions.

The culturagram is a tool and therefore a means to an end rather than an end in itself. Social workers are encouraged to be creative in its use and not approach it from an inflexible position. The family's narrative will be co-constructed by its members and the social worker, whose main aim is to understand how to safeguard Miriam in particular whilst respecting the uniqueness of her family circumstance, their loss of a father and husband and the ill health currently experienced by her mother.

Conclusion

Models of cultural competence have been designed in the US, Australia and the UK to support practitioners in developing cultural awareness and capabilities in work with families from minority ethnic backgrounds. Using reflective exercises to develop self-awareness in relation to one's own cultural heritage is an essential component of all models of cultural competence. This is crucial as social work is predicated on Anglocentric norms, which can create culture clashes with families during practice. It is important to recognise the values and beliefs which underpin practice and how these may impinge on building relationships with families. Social work agencies or partner organisations can be mono-cultural in their systems, services and worldview. This can create challenges for practitioners even when their interactions with families are culturally sensitive. These situations may require workers to explore how policies, procedures or services can be modified to reflect greater cultural sensitivity. The *Cultural Web* is a tool which can assist practitioners to develop an overview of a family's situation and dynamics. These integrate aspects of culture, faith, language and immigration status into an understanding of wider socioeconomic circumstances which affect family members. But it is essential to recognise that regardless of what models or tools are used, cultural competence is a learning process and method of working, not an endpoint to be achieved.

5

Family Organisation and Childrearing

Introduction

Families are central institutions in society often providing care; inclusion; support; and cooperation with, and to, each other. Through socialisation and nurturing, children learn to recognise families as central to their growth, development and wellbeing. In this chapter a thorough examination of the concept of the family is undertaken alongside a more general discussion about different family forms across ethnic groups. The implications of patriarchy and gender roles on family functioning are explored alongside an overview of various inter-generational obligations and responsibilities. The strengths of different family arrangements is examined, together with forms of abuse linked to culture or faith. A worked case study at the end of the chapter applies culturally sensitive approaches underpinned by anti-oppressive practice principles.

The diversity of family form

It has been suggested that there is no easy way to define a family, because families are complex, dynamic entities and are also culturally mediated. The term 'family' holds varying degrees of significance for different people and so it is important that a fixed and inflexible definition of a family is avoided. According to Murray & Barnes (2010, p. 533), 'the family as a specific blend of social relations has been constructed and re-constructed in many forms throughout history...The myriad conceptualisations of family reflect socio-cultural, economic, political, temporal and spatial contexts. Family can be kin and non-kin, and is often about care and trust in the context of enduring relationships.' An important suggestion in this perspective relates to the use of the term 'social relations', which encompasses interactions between people who are not related by blood. The idea that these social relations are constructed and re-constructed infers the lack of stability in social relations as its members move in and out of their relationships, thereby altering its purpose, structure and composition. Families are continually affected by social, economic, political and cultural changes (Murray & Barnes, 2010, p. 533). Therefore it is important that individuals within a family are given the opportunity to self-define rather than impose any specific definition on a family.

It is crucial that there is a clear understanding of who has responsibility for the child. The context of *parental responsibility* is one that has developed and changed over time in the UK context. The *Children Act 1989* introduced the concept in a bid to recognise and acknowledge a responsible adult who would maintain the care and decision-making for a child. Section 3 defined this as 'all the rights, duties, powers, responsibilities and authority which by law a parent of a child has in relation to the child and his property'. It made the parent(s) responsible for ensuring for example that a child attended school. *Parental responsibility* is not gender specific, although it has been noted by UK organisations such as Fathers for Justice and Families Need Fathers that it appeared to be favourably biased towards mothers and not fathers. This was perceived to be because mothers regardless of marital status automatically have *parental responsibility* and only fathers who were married to the mother of the child when the child was born could have *parental responsibility*. Unmarried fathers could acquire *parental responsibility* by either jointly registering the child's birth with the mother or by registering the birth of a child including the father's name and details and through several other legal processes. Social workers' views of families will have implications for their interventions.

Everyone is born into a family of one form or another. However, whether or not individuals perceive themselves as belonging to a family is open to debate. Many people who have been alienated and isolated from their families find themselves on their own and often homeless as adolescents. Smith (1998) found that females and Black young people were more at risk of youth homelessness than males and those from the White majority. These youths were more likely to sleep in the homes of friends and extended family. More recently, Watts et al. (2015) found that young people from minority ethnic backgrounds were more likely to become homeless than young people from the ethnic majority. Discussion of homelessness makes it necessary to distinguish between a family and a household.

The UK's Office of National Statistics (2017, p. 2) defines a family as 'a married, civil partnered or cohabiting couple with or without children, or a lone parent, with at least one child, who live at the same address. Children may be dependent or non-dependent'. Dependent children are considered those under 16 years of age or under 18 years if still in full-time education. The Office of National Statistics (2017, p. 2) defines a household as 'one person living alone, or a group of people (not necessarily related) living at the same address who share cooking facilities and share a living room, sitting room or dining area. A household can consist of a single family, more than one family, or no families in the case of a group of unrelated people.'

This differentiation is useful for social workers who should be making a clear distinction in their assessments and interventions with children and families. There are variations in the household structures between and among cultures and not only in terms of nuclear and extended family forms.

The fragmentation and reconstitution of families is increasing, most particularly among the ethnic majority as greater numbers of birth parents separate; live apart; have a series of other partners, who may or may not adopt a parental role towards existing children, and may have children themselves with the original parent. When several generations of parents have split up and had second families or more, the generational structure of families becomes exceptionally complex. For established ethnic minority communities in the UK, and recent migrants, close family may be spread across several different countries. These families can also be extremely fluid with multiple people moving in and out of the family system in the UK who can create benefits and/or dis-benefits for children. So practitioners must take account of extended families and understand how these affect children's welfare and day-to-day experiences.

While family form among the ethnic majority predominantly revolves around the nuclear family, among many ethnic minority communities family forms are more varied. In India, Pakistan and Bangladesh the ideal household is termed a *ghar*. This is a joint family unit comprising three or more generations residing together; pooling their resources; sharing a single budget; and holding property in common, while accepting the authority of the eldest male member. Such a household is formed when married sons follow custom and continue to live in their parents' home. On the death of their father, married and unmarried brothers continue residing together in the joint household (Warrier, 1994, p. 201). Notably, this family arrangement is an ideal and is often neither feasible nor desirable for family members. The basis for it is the norm of *virilocal* and *patrilocal* residence, meaning that women on marriage move to live with or near their husbands' families. In the UK the constraints on house size and the expense of purchasing property, together with acculturation experiences and the separation of kin through migration, means that such family structures are less common. Nevertheless they may still exert some influence: for instance when the families of brothers live in the same locality and pool their finances while their households remain fluid with children and other relatives moving between them; or when extended family members frequently come together to cook, eat or socialise at the one house (Laird, 2008).

In the Caribbean a variety of family forms exist. These include *friending* or *visiting* relationships in which men, although they do not live with their female partners or children, are frequent visitors and many value their roles as fathers, provide material support and some share domestic tasks. Alongside these arrangements nuclear and extended family living is common, as is the formalisation of unions (Brown et al., 1997, p. 93; Miller, 1994, pp. 193–40; Wyss, 2001, p. 406). Families of African Caribbean heritage in the UK actually draw upon a range of family forms. Contradicting *matrifocal* preconceptions of the archetypal African Caribbean family, there are in fact fairly equal numbers of male- and female-headed households among the African Caribbean community (Peach, 1998, p. 1677). Significantly, almost 80% of women of African Caribbean heritage in the UK defined as lone mothers are reckoned to be in long-term unions, often with men who pay maintenance and contribute to domestic responsibilities (Mirza, 1992; Reynolds, 2001, pp. 1052–53). At the same time for families of African Caribbean and Black African descent lateral kinship relationships can be significant, meaning that children may enjoy close relationships with aunts and uncles to a much greater extent than is the norm among the ethnic majority (Phoenix & Husain, 2007).

These examples of family form illustrate a number of points. Firstly, stereotypes of South Asian families as multi-generational or African Caribbean households as composed of single mothers can mislead social workers. Conversely, so can Anglocentric norms which assume that families are essentially nuclear and consist of co-resident parents, thus minimising the importance of wider kin or parents or partners who do not reside in the household or where households are fluid with family members moving in and out of them. Laird et al. (2017), Strug & Wilmore-Schaeffer (2003) and Lonne et al. (2012) note the tendency of child protection social workers respectively in the UK, US and Australia to neglect wider family systems. The conflation of family with the household exacerbates this tendency. It is crucial that social workers start from a position of complete open mindedness on the nature of each family and explore this extensively with different family members.

Inter-generational families

Inter-generational families involve people from different generations who are closely affiliated for a variety of reasons. A great-grandparent, a grandparent, a parent and a child would constitute four generations and in some cultures this is highly valued and celebrated. Understanding the value of family members across generations is as important as acknowledging the help and support they offer to children. It has been argued by Nzira (2011) that grandparents play a significant role in many families of African origin in the UK, a view corroborated more recently by Tedam & Adjoa (2017), who view grandparents as often being in the position to offer their children financial and/or emotional support to enable them to raise their children effectively. Grandparents are seen to play a mediation role between their children and grandchildren and this element of their role is highly regarded, encouraged and largely welcome. This is also sometimes expected of older people, regardless of blood ties to the family. Having said that, it is also important to consider situations in which grandparents can be ineffective and may in some ways collude with the abuse and maltreatment of children in a family. Tedam & Adjoa (2017) argued that grandparents have significant power within a family, so much so that their advice and views are highly respected. This has the tendency to create a powerful hierarchy within a family where the views and ideas of grandparents are taken seriously. Similarly, Chowbey et al. (2013) identify the significant role of grandparents among many South Asian families right across ethnic, religious and class divisions.

Writing about Bangladeshi communities in London, Ruby (2012) suggests that the extended family network is commonly close-knit and that many families still live in three-generational families within one household or in close proximity to each other. Indeed, the majority of older people from South Asian ethnic communities reside with their extended families although such multi-generational households are becoming less common than they once were (Laird, 2008). Many other minority ethnic groups hold social norms valuing multi-generational living, which may be realised to a greater or lesser extent as affordability of larger homes; finding employment elsewhere; the curtailment of kin networks due to migration; familial conflict; or personal preferences, result in the fragmentation of extended family groups. So while extended family may be significant for parents, partners, other primary carers and children, equally they may not. It is for the social worker to discover this, not to assume it. In a child protection context, therefore, to neglect the views and contributions of grandparents or other older relatives is ill advised as this may result in the loss of vital information which could contribute to professional decision-making. While Tedam & Adjoa (2017) highlight the value attached to older members of the family. They also observe that while extended and wider family networks are important, their role in keeping children safe from harm can often be tenuous. Grandparents can be torn between allegiance to their own children on the one hand and the care of their grandchildren on the other hand.

Reflective exercise

Ikeru is an 11-year-old girl of dual heritage as her father is Nigerian and her mother is White British.

She lives with her father and stepmother (who is Nigerian) and her siblings who are six- and four-year-old girls. Ikeru has recently joined her father after falling out with her mother, who she had lived with since she was seven years old. Her paternal grandparents have recently migrated from Nigeria and live with the family. Ikeru has come to the

▶

◄

attention of her teachers because she has become withdrawn and quiet in school. When asked about her home environment, Ikeru informed her teachers that she was unhappy at home, that her grandparents had arrived from Nigeria and 'couldn't be bothered to do anything for themselves, always asking her to get this and do that'. Worryingly, Ikeru states that she has been asked to sleep in the living room and give up her room for her grandparents. When she challenged her father about this, she was told she did not have a choice and had to agree. Recently, Ikeru was forced to sit up until very late one night as relatives had come to see her grandparents. Ikeru informs the teacher that if the situation does not improve, she will run away from home.

Children's Social Care receives a referral from the school and you are asked to conduct an initial assessment.

What aspects of family organisation would it be important to explore and understand in this situation?

What information would you want to find out from different family members and how would you go about asking for this?

How would this knowledge assist you in working with this family?

Polygamous families

Polygamy refers to an arrangement where a man can legally or culturally have more than one wife. This should not be confused with the offence of bigamy in an unlawful marriage situation involving two wives in countries such as the UK where marriage is confined to having just one partner. Polygamous marriage practices vary across the globe and so caution is advised when working with families who are involved in some way with polygamy. It is practised in many Arab countries under Islam and a number of sub-Saharan African societies where customary law as well as Islam permits more than one wife.

Islamic scholars are not united in their interpretation of the laws which permit only men to have more than one spouse. The disagreement exists because of the interpretation of specific verses in the Quran which state that a man can marry up to four wives provided he treats them equally. This clause has been referred to as impossible to adhere to, thereby putting in doubt the applicability of the verse. It has also been acknowledged that migrants to the UK have lived in multiple locations and that this may create new opportunities for parallel partnering, thus contributing to the variety of polygamous possibilities. Writing from a global perspective, White (1988, p. 558) observes that polygamy 'is not a single syndrome but is produced by diverse strategies under a range of different conditions and comprises different systems of meaning and function'.

Nzira (2011) suggests that polygamy in Africa is widespread and that it appears to be less common among educated couples, particularly women.

Anecdotally, it appears to be the case that these kinds of arrangements continue to exist among some communities with one 'wife' legally recognised in the UK and the other existing without the legal backing of the British system. Such a situation gives rise to uncertain family dynamics, particularly within the context of child protection. Writing about polygamy amongst British Pakistani Muslims, Charsley & Liversage (2012) argue that UK law accepts polygamy which exists outside of its borders but, for the purposes of migration to the UK, the law will only recognise one spouse. This has meant that in the past, either families have been 'split' or that families have had to keep their polygamous relationships 'unofficial' and secret. Such situations could have negative effects on children who may be at risk of harm within the context of polygamous families which professionals and authorities are unaware of.

While monogamy is widely practised across societies, serial monogamy is the situation in which a person has multiple partners, one after the other, arising from divorce, bereavement, or a series of temporary sexual relationships. This is widely practised in the UK, US and Australia among the ethnic majority, with increasingly high numbers of cohabiting rather than married couples. Serial monogamy can lead to frequent changes in family structure as a succession of partners move in and out of families or households creating reconstituted families, which may later be dissolved. Casual sexual encounters may also result in offspring, child maintenance obligations, and complex situations regarding *parental responsibility* and parenting. The overarching influence of ethnic majority cultural norms (through processes of acculturation) means that within any ethnic group there will exist a wide variety of family structures, ranging along a continuum from customary forms to those reflecting serial monogamy and single parent households.

Transnational families

Globalisation in terms of cheap air travel, improved telecommunications and the internet, has meant it is much easier for family members in different countries to maintain contact with one another than has been previously possible. Consequently, there may be frequent visits by relatives from abroad who stay in the household for short or extended periods. Even when visits are fewer, kin living in the family's country of origin(s) may be in daily or weekly contact, playing central roles in decision-making or influencing the deliberations of family members. Many parents or guardians send remittances back to relatives still living in the country of origin, often to support other family members. Sometimes these financial obligations can have significant implications for the standard of living of the family in the UK (Laird, 2008).

While Anglocentric norms tend to focus on the nuclear family, those of other ethnic communities can give great weight to the opinions of extended family members, even if abroad, particularly if they are older, male, or hold a significant role, such as being a mother-in-law. The decisions of parents or guardians may have wider implications for relatives elsewhere in close-knit extended families. These often extensive kin networks can be a source of emotional, social and material support; but also a source of scrutiny, censure and obligation. Parents and children may be reliant on them; be alienated from them; or simply feel ambivalent towards them. This underlines the need to avoid conflating families with households, a mistake common in practice with social workers largely confining their assessment to those residing in the home of the children (Laird et al., 2017).

Kinship care

Kinship care, also known as *friends and family care*, involves family members and friends taking care of a child or children. Finch & Mason (2000, pp. 164–65) argue that kinship should not be seen as a structure or system but rather as 'constituted in relational practices'. Around the world, circumstances arise in which parents are unable to raise their children and have to place them in the care of friends and wider family members. These kinds of arrangements are known as *'kinship care'* and constitute the relational practices of children requiring parenting and adults available to provide parenting. *Kinship placements* are a viable and useful alternative to foster care provided by the State, as instead a child is assessed by social workers and matched with someone from within their wider family. In this regard, *kinship carers* have been said to have stronger emotional bonds to the children they are looking after than foster carers, although there can also be more friction in these arrangements. While there has been a growth in relation to *kinship care* in the UK, research about the experiences and outcomes for children and *kinship carers* is sparse (Nandy & Selwyn, 2013).

Kinship care can be a private arrangement within the family. If a social work assessment indicates that children are at risk from their parents or someone with *parental responsibility*, they can assess family and connected persons to become carers for the child. The exact number of children in kinship arrangements in the UK is unclear, but it is known that the vast majority of them are not classed as 'looked after' and therefore have not been formally assessed and placed in public care by social workers. This means that most children in *kinship care* are living in unregulated and informal arrangements and are disproportionately to be found in deprived families and disadvantaged neighbourhoods (Nandy & Selwyn, 2013). The lack of assessment by social workers implied by children not being categorised as 'looked after' has negative implications for financial support to *kinship carers* and contributes to the poverty experienced by these households.

Private fostering in the UK context needs to be distinguished from *kinship care* as in the former the foster carer is not a close relative (i.e. a grandparent, sibling, uncle, aunt or step-parent). Parents or those with *parental responsibility*, together with those proposing to privately foster a child, must notify the local government authority. This provides an opportunity for social workers to ensure that the proposed care arrangements are in the best interests of the child. In these circumstances *parental responsibility* remains with the parents or legal guardian and is not transferred to the private foster carer. While in the UK it is the responsibility of local government to publicise the regulations around private fostering many parents, particularly if they are recent migrants, may not be aware of them or through desperation choose to ignore the legal requirement to notify local government. City of Salford Local Safeguarding Children Board (2007) *Executive Summary Report of the Serious Case Review Panel into the Death of a Child: C Aged 17 Months* illustrates the unregulated use of private fostering arrangements and the risks they can pose to children.

City of Salford Local Safeguarding Children Board (2007)
Executive Summary Report of the Serious Case Review Panel into the Death of a Child: C Aged 17 Months

In this case a mother aged 16 years came to the UK from China on a student visa, although she did not attend the college at which she was to have studied. She gave birth to her first child aged 17 years and thereafter claimed asylum, which was refused. Her child died of hypothermia aged 17 months after his care had been compromised by being left with a succession of different carers. The Serious Case Review found there to be no materials available in the mother's language to explain regulations concerning private fostering arrangements either to her or those caring for her child. Those professionals with whom the mother came into contact also appeared poorly informed about private fostering regulations and therefore were not sufficiently curious, observant, or concerned when actually aware of the caring arrangements made for the child. Insufficient attention was paid to the mother's growing detachment from her infant son, apparent in suggestions she made to professionals of leaving her child long-term with unrelated carers or that he be adopted. The Serious Case Review noted that this 'was the child of a vulnerable young, single immigrant mother who while in the UK lacked support from her family, had been working illegally, had few friends and spoke little English' (City of Salford Local Safeguarding Children Board, 2007, p. 3). Despite the combination of risk factors inherent in this situation, it did not trigger a referral to Children's Social Care from any of the professionals who came into contact with mother and son.

Customary kinship fostering or *child-shifting* exists in a number of societies including some of those in Latin America, the Caribbean and sub-Saharan Africa. It was once widely practised in West Africa although, as Twum-Danso Imoh (2012) observes, it is now in decline. She notes that historically, childrearing was a communal responsibility and children were brought up by friends and family, primarily, she argued to 'redistribute the costs of raising children', provide companionship for adults whose children had left home or to instil specific sociocultural values in children (Twum-Danso Imoh, 2012, p. 352). Such cultural norms could in part explain the sometimes apparent ease with which some ethnic minority parents pass on caring responsibilities to members of their wider families. When these childrearing practices are customary in the country of origin or such cultural norms remain strongly influential in the UK, there can be confusion about *parental responsibility*. Among those societies in sub-Saharan Africa that engage in *customary kinship fostering*, the general assumption was that responsibility for the child's upbringing passed to the family member who was looking after them. In the UK only a legal process through the court can relieve a parent of *parental responsibility*. Divergent cultural understandings and practices concerning arrangements for substitute care can result in confusions for both practitioners and family members. It is therefore imperative that social workers explore with family members who cares for the child; what their relationship is to the child; and under what formal or informal arrangements care is being provided.

Reflective exercise

Consider the situation of the Chinese mother in City of Salford Local Safeguarding Children Board (2007)

What *cultural knowledge* would assist you to work with a family in these same circumstances?

Appling the culturagram explained in Chapter 4, list the questions you would ask such a mother to explore her circumstances.

Patriarchy

Patriarchy refers to the economic, social and political dominance of men over women, which reinforces inequality between men and women. Within the context of communities and families, *patriarchy* has been cited as a main reason for violence against, and negative treatment of, girls and women (Crittenden and Wright, 2012). According to Pease (2016, p. 49) there are six main areas where patriarchy exists, contributing to gender inequality.

These are:

1. The Household (where women's household labour is exploited by husbands and male partners);

2. Paid work (where women are excluded from high-status jobs, receive less pay and are often employed in segregated sections of the labour force);

3. The State (where there is a systematic bias in favour of men's interests);

4. Male violence (which is legitimated by the state);

5. Sexuality (where compulsory heterosexuality and sexual double standards reign)

6. Cultural institutions (which represent women in negative ways in the media, religion and education).

It is important to examine the impact of *patriarchy* on the lives of children and families, particularly within the context of child protection enquiries and processes. The most relevant area here is *patriarchy* within the household as it impacts on family dynamics and individual family members. Ahmad et al. (2004) found that the level of a man's education had direct bearing on their sexist and/or patriarchal attitudes and beliefs. In addition, the factors that existed to endorse patriarchal beliefs include levels of religiosity and cultural or neighbourhood influences. De Keseredy & Schwartz (2013, p. 54) differentiate between what they refer to as *familial patriarchy*, which refers to men's control of women in domestic settings and *social patriarchy* (involving men's domination at the societal level). While *social patriarchy* exists in all societies, *familial patriarchy* may be greater in some families than in others. There is considerable diversity within ethnic groups in this respect and social workers need to avoid making assumptions about the degree of *familial patriarchy* in any family on the basis of their ethnicity. Peach (2005) observed that many families from a South Asian background tended to follow a *'patriarchal model'* where concepts such as social control, family honour and status are crucial, and men are meant to be the main providers. Women in these communities might be more disadvantaged in access to employment or in the types of jobs they can perform, making them more dependent on family and staying at home while relying on the income of their husbands (Brah, 1993; Dale et al., 2002). There is also considerable evidence to show that at the same time in South Asian heritage communities, support for women's education, pursuing a career and participation in decision-making can be consistent with maintaining cultural values which validate different roles for men and women within the family (Laird, 2008). *Patriarchy* is influential in many families, whether from the ethnic majority or a minority community. However, even where fathers or partners, male in-laws, uncles or grandfathers appear to exercise control, it is important not to assume that they necessarily determine all kinds of family decisions.

Decision-making in families

According to Scanzoni & Polonko (1980) decision-making refers to a process through which individuals make judgements and choices that guide their futures. Family decision-making therefore implies judgements and decisions made by more than one person within a family. Understanding where children are in relation to family decision-making is an important consideration for child protection work. Clearly not all children are able to be involved in decision-making for a variety of reasons, and so it is important that social workers ascertain why this might be the case. Moreover, they need to understand how families make different kinds of decisions and who is involved in these or influences them.

Noller & Fitzpatrick (1993) propose five classes of decisions that can be made within the family: *affective; instrumental; social; technical;* and *economic. Affective decisions* refer to those areas relating to feelings and emotions such as decisions about getting married. *Instrumental decisions* are those which focus on health, shelter, food, money, etc. *Social decisions* are those linked to the values and goals of a family, for instance whether or not children should be raised in a specific religion or decisions regarding a parent remaining at home to look after the children. *Technical decisions* are smaller decisions made to achieve an overarching goal, such as when a child should stop education in order to work in the family business. *Economic decisions* mainly relate to finances and income and include decisions about when a young adult is expected to seek employment and contribute to the family's expenses. Various family members may have a greater or lesser say in these different categories of decisions. It is essential for practitioners to fully explore patterns of decision-making and avoid curtailing this through Anglocentric notions of family form or stereotypes regarding *power distance* between males and females or adults and children in the family. It is quite possible that while a grandfather or father might be dominant in the *social decision* concerning the values instilled in the children, he may defer to the mother, grandmother or other female relative making *instrumental decisions* regarding children's health. Moreover, family decision-making needs to be explored outside of the narrower Anglocentric constructions of essentially nuclear family forms. Critical decision-makers may well in fact be grandparents, aunts, uncles, cousins or in-laws.

Domestic violence

Male violence, exhibited through domestic abuse, which is the fourth area of *patriarchy* identified by Pease (2016), is also salient to social work practice. Marriage exists in all societies and is used to express affection, sexual intimacy and childrearing. Despite this, marriages and cohabitation between partners have been known to also be sites of various forms of abuse, targeted largely at women but also children and other relatives within the family. Across societies women can come under considerable social pressure from relatives or community members (if there are strong collectivist norms) to remain with violent male partners. They may also remain due to fear of losing custody of their children, poverty and homelessness (Burman et al., 2004). For women from Black and minority ethnic backgrounds who are disproportionately on low incomes, and especially if they are recent migrants dependent on the immigration status of their husbands for the *right to remain* in the UK, separating from a violent spouse may be particularly difficult. Physical assault is not the only form of domestic abuse defined by the Home Office (2018) as it encompasses,

> any incident or pattern of incidents of controlling, coercive, threatening behaviour, violence or abuse between those aged 16 or over who are, or have been, intimate partners or family members regardless of gender or sexuality. The abuse can encompass, but is not limited to: psychological; physical; sexual; financial; emotional.

This broader definition can assist practitioners to recognise domestic abuse in a wider variety of family forms. Where traditional gender roles place great emphasis on men as providers and women as homemakers (resulting in women not taking up paid employment) this can contribute to women's vulnerability to financial abuse. If collectivist norms are influential the notion of family *'honour'* and maintaining the family's status in the local ethnic community can motivate controlling behaviour towards women and children, such as when a teenaged girl of Indian Sikh background is punished for spending time with a boy outside of her kin group. As Gill (2004) has argued, *'shame'* and *'honour'* are *patriarchal concepts* which revolve around female sexual behaviour and place responsibility upon girls and women for upholding the family's standing. Often children internalise these beliefs and values at a young age and they can therefore be deeply held.

Among some ethnic groups extended family forms also mean that families may include multiple female relatives living together in the same home or between households. A family of Pakistani origin practising customary arrangements may comprise a young mother with children who moved on marriage to live with her husband's family. Not only might she be living with her in-laws, but the household could include the families of her husband's brothers. Research reveals that in such circumstances mothers-in-law or other female relatives may exploit the unpaid labour of a new wife and mother to undertake excessive domestic tasks. This may be accompanied by controlling behaviour (e.g. preventing a mother from attending English language classes) intimidation or violence. Women joining the family in the UK from a country of origin who are therefore recent migrants are more vulnerable to domestic abuse if they are dependent on their husband for the *right to remain* in the UK; do not speak English; are unfamiliar with the welfare system; and/or are largely confined to the home due to strict gender roles (Mama, 1996; Thiara & Gill, 2010). Female relatives are known to sometimes be perpetrators of, or complicit in, abusive behaviours towards women and children designed to maintain family *'honour'* (Choudry, 1996; Kim, 2002). Such controlling and abusive behaviour towards mothers by their female relatives can be exacerbated when *high power distance* norms are observed between older and younger family members. As a result, older family members can feel entitled to control younger women in the household, while young mothers correspondingly feel deference is owed to their elders.

Abuse which occurs in the domestic spheres of ethnic minority families can appear hidden to practitioners behind what has been described as a *'culture of silence'*. This *'culture of silence'* has often been attributed to ethnic minority families being unsure of the repercussions of disclosing abusive practices within their communities. While this may be the situation for a number of women, there is also evidence that many turn to wider kin and networks within their local ethnic communities for support and assistance (Danis & Bhandari, 2010). According to Pohjola (2016) in order for practitioners to be culturally sensitive there needs to be a recognition and understanding of the particular contexts of those women, and sometimes men, who are being abused. Islington Safeguarding Children Board (2012) *Services Provided to Child B and Child C January 2008 – February 2011* provides an insight into the cultural and sometimes religious pressures upon mothers which can inhibit them from seeking outside help in situations of domestic abuse.

Islington Safeguarding Children Board (2012) *Services Provided to Child B and Child C January 2008 – February 2011*

The parents, both originally from West Africa, met in the UK in 1997 and married the following year. They had two children together. The mother described her husband as generally jealous, suspicious and controlling, but it was only in 2008 that he started to become violent. After a series of physical assaults the court granted a non-molestation order against the father, but did not require him to leave the family, and the domestic violence against the mother continued. Children's Social Care became involved and supported the mother to leave the family home to live in a women's refuge where she resided with her children for 18 months. Her children attended a local church school and became integrated into the associated faith community. The mother and children were eventually rehoused, at which point the father applied for and obtained a joint Residence Order whereby the children were to live with him at weekends. No risk assessment of the father's potential violence towards the children was undertaken and the case was closed to Children's Social Care. The father started to send abusive text messages to the mother the week before killing both the children while they were staying with him during a weekend. He attributed this to receiving notice of repossession of his flat from his social landlord due to the children being in the custody of their mother, who he blamed.

The Serious Case Review acknowledged that while domestic violence occurs across all ethnic groups, the father expressed patriarchal attitudes towards women which appeared to be drawn from his cultural background. He found it difficult to accept the norms associated with *lower power*

distances between men and women and between children and parents dominant in UK society. An exploration of these by professionals might have
assisted in an accurate assessment of risk. The Serious Case Review also suggested that the mother's reactions to the domestic violence may also have
been influenced by her own upbringing in West Africa. Islington Safeguarding Children Board (2012, para.6.33) noted that

> The support of family members and the sanctions from family and community
> that could have come into play had such incidents happened in West Africa did
> not exist in the UK. The mother may have placed too much faith in the non-
> molestation order, which the father disregarded. She believed that in the cir-
> cumstances she knew best, a similar directive would have been obeyed with the
> support of the wider family and community.

It was also evident from a number of the mother's remarks to professionals that she held strong religious beliefs which could have influenced her
behaviour in relation to the domestic abuse and keeping the family together.
These were not explored by social workers in this case. Fortune et al. (2010)
acknowledge the spiritual, emotional and material resources that religious
belief and faith-based communities can offer to families in distress. But
they also demonstrate how religious texts can be misused to reinforce *high
power distance* between men and women and to justify exploitive or controlling behaviour by men. In fact, as these scholars reveal, most religious texts
promote mutually respectful interaction between marriage partners. Bent-
Goodley et al. (2010) argue that among families of African heritage faith-
based communities can be important sources of assistance, consolation and
mediation, but also sometimes a source of sexism and the maintenance of
rigid codes of conduct. Moreover, while organised religions offer meaning in
the midst of suffering, they also generally urge the faithful to seek its allevia-
tion. The expectation that women suffer in silence is therefore often a misuse
or misunderstanding of scripture (Fortune et al., 2010). Although forgiveness
for wrongdoing is a central precept in most world religions, as Fortune et al.
(2010) point out, it does not necessarily follow that it should be automatic or
immediate or offered in the absent of sincere repentance and change on the
part of the abuser. However, pressure may be exerted on women by devout
family members or clerics to simply forgive. Consequently, the spiritual
beliefs of family members alongside their relationships with local faith communities are crucial elements in assessment and safeguarding children.

Yet, as the Serious Case Review observed, 'It may have gone unnoticed
by professionals who in a predominantly secular society are less likely to
encounter service users whose religious beliefs significantly influence their
attitudes and behaviour' (Islington Safeguarding Children Board, 2012,
para.6.34). This final point returns to issues raised in Chapter 2 relating to
the secular nature of dominant norms in British society and the replication

of these norms in social work models of practice. A culturally competent approach must avoid reliance on stereotypes and instead involve an open-minded, sensitive exploration of the cultural and religious beliefs and values which matter to family members. The practice focus needs to be on under-standing how these shape family members' interpretations of, and reactions to, events in their lives concerning the welfare and safety of children. This is emphasised by Islington Safeguarding Children Board (2012, para.6.35) which insisted that 'It is impossible to know how important the influence of religious and cultural factors will be in any given case and this makes it important to explore them in detail. Cultural aspects need to be considered and discussed with women because is it a legitimate and essential compo-nent of the assessment of risk.'

Reflective exercise

Consider the circumstances described in Islington Safeguarding Children Board (2012)

How might professional culture and norms have impaired effective social work with this family?

What alternative approaches might have been more effective with this family?

Parenthood

While parenthood within Anglocentric cultures tends to revolve around mothers and fathers, in some cultures particular family members can have special roles in relation to childbirth and childrearing. In some African soci-eties, for instance, a newborn baby's maternal grandmother is expected to be the first person to bathe the baby by way of a massage, and to care for mother and baby for the first few months of the baby's life. The belief is that the maternal grandmother will extend her experience, technique and knowledge about childbirth and post-natal care to her daughter. The situ-ation is slightly different in the absence of a maternal grandmother as the maternal grandmother's sister or other female cousin will be asked to fulfil this role. Nzira (2011) found that that while the traditional African kin sys-tem is often greatly truncated among families of African heritage living in the UK, nevertheless among many, extended family members continued to perform important supplementary and substitutive parenting roles. Robin-son (2007) in her overview of the UK and US literature concluded that for many parents with family roots in sub-Saharan Africa, South Asia or Latin America (all collectivist societies) living with or near relatives carried a high positive valance. In these families grandparents and other relatives were often involved in childcare.

In many non-Western cultures, from birth, infants are regarded as belonging to their extended kin group rather than their parents, which has implications for their care and decisions about their welfare, as a number of adults may be involved in this (Nsameng, 1992). In the UK children are legally the responsibility of their parents and a court may make further rulings on this when parents separate or are in dispute. In other societies children may customarily or lawfully be the responsibility of maternal or paternal relatives. So it is important that social workers explore with family members how they understand the responsibilities of parenting and whether these are shared by other relatives. The test is *good enough parenting* and the extent to which the child's needs are being met. Practitioners need to be careful not to prescribe to families which relative should deliver this care, motivated by Anglocentric notions of parenting within nuclear family forms.

Returning to discussion in Chapter 1 regarding the dimensions of cultural variability along the continuum of *femininity–masculinity*; allocated gender roles vary across ethnic groups and between families within the same ethnic group. While *patriarchy* is influential in structuring all societies, the extent to which this shapes gender roles and in turn childrearing practices in any given family will differ. It is therefore imperative not to rely on cultural stereotypes to make assumptions about the parental roles of parents or other relatives, for instance assuming that African Caribbean families are matriarchal and fathers, particularly if non-resident, have minor roles in family life, while grandmothers provide substitute childcare. Another example might be assuming that women are oppressed in families of South Asian background and men are dominating and controlling, when in fact grandmothers, mothers and mothers-in-law may have pivotal roles in decision-making, particularly around children's upbringing (Laird, 2008).

It is also important to avoid taking public displays of traditional masculinity, such as adult male members of the family being protective and hostile, or females being diffident, as necessarily reflecting family dynamics. These public displays may or may not coincide with private realities. It is for social workers during assessment to fathom this out. But they cannot be objective and thorough in such assessments if they consciously or inadvertently rely on stereotypes. The result will be to foreclose on gathering information by drawing conclusions early on in interactions with families from minority ethnic communities.

The social work profession has been heavily criticised for its focus on the mother–child dyad and its virtual exclusion of fathers and mothers' male partners from engagement, assessment and intervention (Laird et al., 2017). The intersectionality of gender, race and ethnicity can result in even greater exclusion of men from consideration as fathers holding key parenting roles. Yet it is well established that father involvement in children's lives is associated with improved cognitive development; higher self-esteem; fewer behavioural problems; enhanced social skills; better peer relations; positive attitudes towards education; and emotional wellbeing (Halme et al., 2009, pp. 103–104). Research conducted by Salway & Chowbey (2009) suggests that fatherhood for most men of South Asian heritage whether Muslim, Hindu or Sikh is a vital aspect of their identity and that many contributed to basic childcare tasks or to childrearing activities such as reading and playing. Their research challenges stereotypical constructions of South Asian fathers as authoritarian and distant from their children. The choices that fathers make regarding their inputs into parenting may reflect priorities in relation to other responsibilities, such as employment, or may be constrained by structural factors. Poverty for instance precludes fathers from engaging in organised leisure activities with their children, such as swimming, due to the cost, although this would be normative among ethnic majority middle-class fathers (Chowbey et al., 2013). Likewise, often social workers' professional preoccupation with the absence of African Caribbean men from the family home neglects their contribution as fathers, grandfathers, uncles and brothers and also ignores the support of men involved in long-term *visiting* relationships with mothers as both partners and parents (Reynolds, 1997, p. 105; Laird, 2008). This again points up the mistake practitioners can make in conflating the household, i.e. who is present in the home, with who is actually a family member and exploring what their contribution is to parenting and the household overall.

While religion in the secular context of the UK has for most ethnic majority families largely ceased to play a role in children's upbringing, for many families among some minority communities it remains a basis of parental values; guidance on childrearing; ideas as to what constitutes a good childhood; the transmission of morals; a basis for cohesive family relationships; and a source of complementary and supplementary care. Faith schools are the most obvious expression of this inter-relationship between religion and parenting and provide not only formal education, but typically play a key role in relation to instilling moral values, guiding right conduct and ethnic identity development. For some children, whether attending faith schools or secular state schools, religious teaching may continue after school or at weekends. Families differ in their commitment to sending their children for religious instruction or at what age they involve children in religious activity, reflecting parental choice and sometimes gender expectations (Horwath et al., 2008; Petro et al., 2018).

Faith can be a source of guidance and comfort for parents, children and kin. Family members may also draw upon the support of their religious community. While research indicates that children of religiously devout parents are no more likely to be maltreated than those from secular families, it also reveals that neither does faith protect children against abuse (Furness & Gilligan, 2010). As social work methods are the product of a secular profession, spirituality and its implications for parental motivation and childrearing practices are frequently overlooked. Precisely because religion in family life is largely absent from social work training and often of minimal influence in the day-to-day lives of many social workers, it is often left unexplored (Holloway & Moss, 2010). As many Serious Case Reviews included in the study underpinning this book reveal that the religion of parents or children is often not recorded by social workers, and even when it is, rarely is this followed through in terms of assessing its implications for childrearing.

Challenges for minority families raising children

Literature regarding Black and minority ethnic families has historically focused on deviant and pathological conceptions which have been challenged by many scholars as distorted, racialised and unfair perceptions often resulting in exclusion, isolation and discrimination. A key area of importance in these families is the area of *racial socialisation,* which ethnic minority families and not the ethnic majority have to develop for themselves and their children. According to Lesane-Brown (2006, p. 402) *racial socialisation* is 'specific verbal and non-verbal (e.g. modelling of behaviour and exposure to different contexts and objects) messages transmitted to younger generations for the development of values, attitudes, behaviours and beliefs regarding the meaning and significance of race and racial stratification, intergroup and intragroup interactions, and personal and group identity.' The central theme in this definition is about coping in an oppressive and racist environment, creating an additional area of childrearing which the ethnic majority do not routinely have to consider and address. *Racial socialisation* is also instrumental in helping children to develop a positive racial identity in a predominantly White society that is often discriminatory towards them (Robinson, 2007).

In relation to Black parenting O'Reilly (2001) proposes the term *Black mothering* and argues that this differs significantly from other forms of mothering due to the emphasis of Black mothers on imposing a sense of awareness of a racially oppressive society, and how to survive physically, mentally and emotionally in an environment often hostile to the existence of Black people. While across societies childrearing is normatively the responsibility of mothers or female relatives, this concept can be extended to Black fathers involved in childrearing and indeed to parents from racial minorities living in any majority White population. Chowbey et al. (2013) in their research into the parental roles of South Asian fathers found that they were engaged in helping their children to navigate daily life in racist environments. Parents from Black and minority ethnic communities often seek to protect their children from the detrimental impacts of racial abuse while assisting them to develop coping strategies (Robinson, 2007).

For children born into ethnic minority families, both they and their parents may need to navigate dual cultures and sometimes multiple heritages. Primarily this involves negotiating between a heritage culture and faith on the one hand and the Anglocentric norms and dominant secular ideas of British society. Much research has focused on culture clashes between generations. Parents and grandparents are said to typically adhere to cultural values and religious observances of the family's country of origin, while children are conflicted between these and the attraction of Anglocentric norms and the secular values of their ethnic majority peers. More recent research casts doubt on this interpretation and reveals children and young people to be adept at moving between minority and majority cultures and often picking and mixing cultural forms (Laird, 2008).

Identifying and emphasising the strengths of minority ethnic families should be the first step towards providing an equitable, respectful and empowering service. The limited research about Black families' strengths makes this difficult for social workers and other child care practitioners. Social workers are encouraged to continually evaluate the standards by which ethnic minority families are measured and assessed. The expectation that all stimulation and play with a child must be in the form of toys is not only inaccurate but also not universal. Social workers should ask the parent to explain how they play and provide stimulation for their children within the home. The responses could be varied and may not necessarily reflect the worldview of the ethnic majority. In many families of African heritage children may be exposed to other community resources such as religious study groups, which may provide different forms of spiritual stimulation. There can also be large family get-togethers which serve to create cohesion and further stimulate children in these families. These forms of support and stimulation should not be undermined or disregarded by social workers but instead be acknowledged, respected and examined. Research by Bernard & Harris (2016) has identified a number of shortcomings in social work with Black and minority ethnic families which are outlined below.

> Black and minority ethnic families in the UK have been found to be under represented in families being offered Family Group Conferences.

> Social work assessment of Black families have been found to be less rigorous and of poor quality.

> Family support intervention is usually shorter than that offered to other families.

> Fear of Black men and racialisation often places Black fathers outside their immediate family regarding child protection related social work assessments.

Conceptions of childhood

Childhood in post-industrial societies has evolved into a distinct life stage set apart from adulthood; a state of need, vulnerability and dependency; a suspension of responsibility replaced by schooling and play; and a period requiring close guidance and supervision to ensure healthy moral, mental and physical development (Jenks,1996, p. 123; James et al., 2007, pp. 16–17; Hendrick, 1997). This construction of childhood not only defines what constitutes a good childhood, but acts as a standard against which to assess whether the care of a child by a parent or guardian is good, adequate, neglectful or abusive. This hegemonic concept of childhood claims for itself a correct understanding of the child derived from scientific studies of children from which has been distilled positivist theories regarding the developmental stages of children and their corresponding needs .This dominant Western version of childhood tends to dismiss, devalue or denigrate other perspectives on childhood and therefore other ideas as to how children should be appropriately treated.

The dominant notion of childhood in post-industrial societies construes it essentially as a state of incompetency relative to adulthood. Therefore the overarching developmental task of children is to attain the faculties of adults. These reflect Anglocentric values and comprise rationality; self-awareness; autonomy; self-sufficiency; individual identity; ability to make informed choices; and self-responsibility (Archard, 2015). These sharply differentiated constructions of adulthood and childhood are not shared by all societies. Helpfully, Archard (2015, pp. 35–38) proposes three constituents of childhood that may differ across historical periods or cultures.

The first of these is *boundaries*, which concern the chronological age when being a child is deemed to end. This boundary often marks the point at which a child assumes the roles and responsibilities of an adult in terms of productive and domestic tasks. It is the stage where an individual is considered sufficiently mature to leave home, provide for him- or herself, engage in sexual activity or marry. In relation to a legal system or customary law, it may signify the age at which a child is regarded as having the same competence as an adult. In most societies the age of majority is specified in law; in the UK it is 18 years of age, in Saudi Arabia it is 15 at which point a child becomes an adult and holds all their rights. Some societies leave the age of majority unspecified as it depends on the individual's physical maturity. In some cultures the onset of menarche is when girl is considered to be a woman, an event often accompanied by rites of passage to mark the transition from being a child to being an adult. For societies which consider puberty the boundary marker, being a child ends around the age of 8–10 years for girls and around 10–12 years for boys. So the chronological age which demarcates the end of being a child can be different across societies. Some parents or guardians may expect children at puberty or in their early teens to take on what would be considered adult roles in Anglocentric cultures, such as working in the family business, cooking meals for the household, taking care of younger siblings or marrying.

The second component of childhood identified by Archard (2015) is *dimensions*, which concerns how a society regards childhood as different from adulthood. In the UK and US, cognitive ability and moral reasoning are vital elements of maturation, alongside physiological maturity, because education, pro-social behaviour and abiding by the law are essential aspects of participation in a democratic post-industrial country. Other societies may place a different emphasis on these aspects and may consider additional aspects important, such as learning about and internalising religious beliefs, values and obligations. Many societies expect children to contribute to the welfare of the family through domestic or productive labour. In many developing countries, due to high levels of poverty and environmental hazards, children are typically expected to master self-care tasks at an early age and often manage without close adult supervision (Twum-Danso Imoh & Ame, 2012). Work and play for children may not be deemed entirely separate activities, as they are in Anglocentric cultures, but instead comprise rehearsal for domestic or productive tasks. Such tasks are likely to consist in a graduation of complexity and challenge corresponding to the physical and cognitive capabilities of the child as he or she grows older (Archard, 2015, p. 42). Societies can differ as to what are considered the significant distinctions between childhood and adulthood. Parents and guardians from minority ethnic communities may be influenced by cultural beliefs and practices from the family's country of origin concerning perceptions of a good childhood and what are appropriate activities for children.

Divisions are the third element of Archard's (2015, p. 37) scheme and relate to how childhood can be divided up into distinctive periods, associated with different expectations. In the first instance, virtually every culture differentiates out a period of infancy characterised by extreme vulnerability and dependency on adult care. In a number of societies weaning or the acquisition of language marks the end of this period. From this point to puberty often constitutes another distinctive phase of childhood recognised by many cultures. As already observed, among some societies this may mark the transition directly to adulthood, while for others it is followed by another period of childhood, known as adolescence in the UK, US and Australia where the emphasis is placed on education, identity development and individuation. In other cultures, such as those of Nigeria and Ghana, the period of youth wedged between puberty and adulthood is closely associated with apprenticeship and acquiring practical skills, although more particularly for males. Each period of childhood is characterised in various societies by similar and/or dissimilar sets of expectations.

Recognising that minority ethnic families sometimes hold different conceptions of childhood, periods of childhood, or the boundary between childhood and adulthood, can help social workers to explore how these might be influenced by culture or religion. These influences may in turn underpin parental motivation and shape their behaviour towards children, explaining such parental choices as children being left home alone or young children caring for even younger children. Equally, it is vital to remember that generations of many minority families have been long established in the UK and are likely to subscribe to Anglocentric conceptions of childhood. Recent migrant families may have acculturated since arriving in the UK. For some of these families leaving children home alone or children in charge of their siblings may be driven by a combination of poverty and the necessity of working to earn money. Often parents in this situation are on or below the minimum wage. Conversely, some parents or guardians may hold idiosyncratic notions about childhood and expectations of children, which they misleadingly attribute to culture or religion. It is for practitioners to explore the underlying reasons for a particular parental behaviour as opposed to condemning the practice and exhorting parents to change. Understanding more about how parents conceptualise childhood can assist social workers to more effectively address with family members childrearing practices which are harmful.

Reflective exercise

Reflect on your own immediate and extended family.

What abilities or tasks are children in your family expected to develop or undertake and broadly at what ages?

How are these abilities or tasks similar to or different from those of adults?

How do aspects of gender, class, disability and family income shape these expectations?

Marriage and harmful practices

Health and social care professionals are increasingly coming across situations in which children, most particularly girls, are at risk of significant harm arising from *forced marriage* or *child marriage*. The nature of *arranged marriage* and *forced marriage* need to be distinguished as they are frequently conflated. *Arranged marriages* have existed for centuries in many parts of the world, particularly Africa, the Middle East, Latin America and South East Asia. It is a form of marriage in which parents and the wider family facilitate the introduction between prospective partners. *Arranged marriages* take place only with full agreement and consent from both partners and can involve the exchange of dowry between families. The families have the opportunity to explore each other's backgrounds, behaviours, attitudes and educational abilities and to make a decision on compatibility. Prospective partners are allowed to spend some time with each other and there is no duress involved. While some view *arranged marriages* as an opportunity to preserve cultural identity and strengthen the bond between families, sometimes marital partners in apparently *arranged marriages* admit to having felt pressured into them.

By contrast *forced marriage* has been described as a form of violence against women and has been found to be prevalent in the age group 13 to 18 years. *Forced marriage* does not give the couple a voice in deciding who they wish to marry and consequently coercion is used and victimisation occurs if the couple oppose the family's plans. There is also evidence to suggest that males can be victims of these forms of abuse. In the UK, the majority of cases of *forced marriage* have been found to exist among South Asian minority communities (Gangoli et al., 2009). Where a *forced marriage* involves a person under the age of 18 years, bearing in mind that the minimum age for marriage with parental consent in the UK is 16 years of age, then this could give rise to a child protection concern. Such a situation would plainly violate the rights of the child under the Convention on the Rights of the Child.

Child marriage is practised by some sections of the population in a number of societies in Africa, Latin America and South Asia, and while it can involve children of both sexes, it predominantly affects girls. This is an area of cultural variation which revolves around Archard's (2015, pp. 35–38) notion of *boundaries* and concerns the age at which boys and girls are deemed adults. Most countries have adopted a legal minimum age for marriage, typically around 16–18 years, but strong cultural norms sanctioning much lower ages can mean widespread violation of the law and poor enforcement in some countries.

Globally *child marriage* has been in decline for many decades and there is considerable diversity of views and often opposition to it in those communities where there is residual practice. In Europe some sections of the Roma minorities in Bulgaria and Romania and Traveller communities in the UK may endorse it. Many people from these groups are actively opposed to such early marriages and there is often considerable disagreement about such practices in local ethnic communities (ERTF & Phenjalipe, 2013; South East Wales Women's Aid Consortium, 2010). As these marriages are not legally recognised, they are essentially informal sexual unions, sometimes between underage children or between an underage child and an adult. Among those families still practising *child marriage,* girls and boys can be considered marriageable on reaching puberty at which point the marriage is agreed on by parents, guardians or other decision-makers in the family. Other families may arrange early marriages as soon as children are aged 16 and therefore can be legally married with parental consent.

Child marriage has adverse implications for the welfare of children, particularly girls, who are often denied choice, withdrawn from education, vulnerable to domestic violence, and can become pregnant before their bodies have physically matured. Children in this situation are plainly likely to be pressured or coerced. In sections of ethnic communities where a girl's virginity prior to marriage is perceived as paramount, *child marriage* may be understood as a means of preserving this. Where collectivist norms prevail, pressure on families to ensure this is the case, or that they observe tradition in order to preserve ethnic group identity, can be intense. While cultural norms are one driver of this practice, so is poverty as families may feel unable to look after their children and early marriage is one strategy of managing this. The customary payment of a dowry (in cash or kind) to the child bride's family can also influence such decisions. Claims of *child marriage* may sometimes be used to disguise a previous rape or sexual abuse.

For social workers seeking to work in culturally sensitive ways with families for whom early, *arranged* or *forced marriages* are possibilities, ensuring they are conversant with the differences between these and being mindful of any nuanced communication from family members will be an important first step. It is entirely possible that poverty and socio-economic disadvantage can be a motivator for any of these forms of marriage; consequently any assessment must adequately explore motivations and feelings from the perspective of the child or young people involved. Social workers should also carefully consider whether an early marriage results in the withdrawal of a young person from education. Tower Hamlets Safeguarding Children Board (2014) *'Jamilla' Serious Case Review* examines the inter-relationships between early marriage, *forced marriage*, dual heritage, interrupted education, transnational families and the role of the extended family.

Tower Hamlets Safeguarding Children Board (2014) *'Jamilla' Serious Case Review*

The mother was of dual heritage born in the UK to a Somali mother and White British father. Her school attendance was poor and she experienced bullying when at school from Somali peers due to her dual heritage. Aged 12 years the mother was taken by the maternal grandmother to Somaliland, from which the maternal side of the family originated and where many relatives remained. While there the mother was subject to *child marriage* and *forced marriage* at the age of 13 years and suffered years of domestic violence from her Somali husband before escaping back to the UK. She was then aged 17 years, had two young children and was pregnant with a third. The Forced Marriage Unit initially referred the family to Children's Social Care due to the mother's perceived vulnerability. But Children's Social Care did not treat this as a referral and merely checked that the family appeared settled in the UK via a telephone call to a relative. The mother was

▶

◄

allocated social housing, which she moved into with her children. She told health professionals that she was receiving support from extended family. Later she informed police that some of her husband's relatives living locally were threatening to take her children back to Somaliland unless she arranged for her husband to join her in the UK. The police made a referral to Children's Social Care and a practitioner telephoned the mother who said she was fine. There was no follow-up and the case was closed. During this time the mother had minimal social interaction with people outside of her maternal family.

Contact by health professionals ceased after the birth of her third child, because the mother presented as cheerful, resilient and loving while appearing to be coping well. Routine monitoring of infants' health normally ceases after six weeks unless parents request developmental checks thereafter. Shortly after the baby's birth the mother ceased her regular attendance at a Young Parents' Group and the local Children's Centre and missed a number of antenatal appointments. No referral was made to Children's Social Care as health care professionals did not observe anything to raise child protection concerns. The mother gave the impression to professionals that she was receiving help from the maternal great-grandmother, who had at this point returned to Somaliland. Unknown to health care agencies the extended family had actually ceased to provide support. The mother, however, was receiving threatening telephone calls from the father after the maternal great-grandmother gave him the mother's telephone number.

The baby aged four months died from cardiac arrest caused by malnutrition at the family home, where the two older siblings were found to be suffering from severe neglect. The mother was charged with causing or allowing the death of a child and with the neglect of all three children. The mother, aged just 18 years, pleaded guilty to cruelty and manslaughter.

Here was a young single mother looking after three children under the age of four years; a task which would have been demanding and tiring for any parent. In addition she had been subject to the traumatic experience of *child marriage* and *forced marriage* in Somaliland, where she had also been the victim of domestic violence that caused two miscarriages. She only escaped back to the UK with assistance from the Forced Marriage Unit, suggesting that there was likely to remain conflict with members of the maternal family both in the UK and Somaliland. Moreover as a mother of dual heritage she may have been vulnerable to harassment or isolation by disapproving family members or people from the local community. All these factors could potentially undermine the parenting capacity even of an essentially loving mother filled with good intentions. These were, according to the Serious Case Review, either 'known or knowable'. As Tower Hamlets Safeguarding Children Board (2014, para.1.3.17) observed,

The assessments undertaken did not adequately seek to understand the implications for mother being of dual heritage and how this affected her experiences both currently and in the past; in particular what this may have meant within her extended maternal family. Given that she had fled a forced marriage arranged by her family this was a relevant area to explore, especially given mother's reliance on these relatives for frequent and regular support.

Reflective exercise

Consider the family circumstances in Tower Hamlets Safeguarding Children Board (2014)

How might the positionality of social workers involved with this family in relation to their race, ethnicity and religious or secular beliefs have affected two-way cultural encounter with different family members?

How might cultural safety have been achieved with the mother given her circumstances?

Black and ethnic minority children and education

Education comprises a huge chunk of childhood and constitutes a formative experience for nearly all children; it can have a pivotal influence on development. Therefore it is crucial to consider its implications for children and young people from racial and ethnic minority backgrounds. Schools and educational establishments do not operate in a vacuum; they are institutions which, regardless of their good intentions and their goal of educating children and young people, appear to be condoning institutional racism and oppression of many minority groups. A report by the Department for Education (2017) found that a higher and disproportionate number of children from some ethnic minority backgrounds were excluded from school for fixed periods of time. The highest is White Gypsy/ Roma at 22%, followed by White Irish Traveller 18%, Black Caribbean 11%; and Mixed White and Black Caribbean 10%. This is in comparison to White British children at 5%. In terms of educational achievement, on average pupils from 'White Other', Pakistani, Black Caribbean, Mixed White and Black Caribbean backgrounds continue to do significantly less well than their White British peers (Stokes et al., 2015). Conversely, pupils of Indian and Chinese heritage generally experience fewer school exclusions and reach higher attainment levels than those from White majority family backgrounds.

It is unfair to conclude that parents of Black children have a poor attitude to education which has been adopted by their children. Graham & Robinson (2004) found that male pupils of African descent are often working with teachers who have no confidence in their abilities and therefore have lowered expectations. Indeed, research by Vincent et al. (2013) corroborates the importance of education in the lives of African Caribbean parents in the UK and the support they offer their children in order for them to succeed. Similarly, children from Asian backgrounds were assumed by many teachers to lack English language skills and therefore the ability to succeed academically, feeding into lowered expectations (Robinson, 2007). Evidence collated by Stokes et al. (2015, p. 15) on deprived children (defined as those entitled to free school meals) found that White British pupils from poor families actually did worse in terms of educational attainment than any other ethnic group. The study concluded that parental and pupil aspiration were significant factors in creating resilience to deprivation and encouraging children from ethnic minority backgrounds to progress at school and achieve academically to a greater extent than working-class White pupils.

Gypsy, Roma and Traveller communities are an ethnic minority group whose children are among the lowest performing academically in the UK. They are also more likely to be identified as having special educational needs and four times more likely than other groups to be permanently excluded from school due to anti-social behaviour. In addition they were identified as more likely to be in receipt of free school meals, thus highlighting the link between poverty and educational disadvantage (Wilkin et al., 2010). The TARGET model proposed to improve educational outcomes for Gypsy, Roma and Traveller children recognises contextual factors which include socio-economic circumstances; wider family and community influences; social identity; past educational experiences; and education policy. The constructive conditions are: respect; trust and safety; partnership; high expectations; flexibility; and access and inclusion (Wilkin et al., 2010).

Parental and community attitudes to learning have been cited by schools as contributing to poorer attainment outcomes for Gypsy and Traveller children. Schools argue that parents collude and sabotage their children's aspirations in that they support them to withdraw from school as soon as they reach an age where they can seek employment and contribute to the family's income. This, in addition to frequent moves, has been found to disadvantage children because stability is seen as a key requirement for achievement and educational progress. Negative stereotypes informing low teacher expectations may also be inadvertently feeding the status quo. Home–school links have been found to be a successful strategy in improving the attendance of children at school, as have regular parent–teacher consultations. Many schools in the UK have targeted support for Gypsy and Traveller children, which can include employing teaching assistants or other members of staff from these communities (Wilkin et al., 2010).

There have been growing concerns about the risks to girls from minority ethnic backgrounds who are missing from education or who have been withdrawn by their parents and carers. It is known that these circumstances result in girls becoming vulnerable to a range of risks including *child marriage, forced marriage* and *female genital mutilation*. Myers & Bhopal (2018) suggest that the numbers of home-schooled children in the UK has increased significantly in the last decade, and while this is not necessarily a concern, it is unfortunate that many parents believe they can provide better education than can schools. Their research about reasons why Muslim parents were attracted to home schooling found that this was due to the experiences of their children in mainstream schools. One participant stated that his son was experiencing Islamophobia, and for another family the desire to have their child in a school which reflected their community meant that home schooling was the only choice available to them.

The view among sections of some communities that education for girls is unimportant can contribute towards girls being withdrawn from education and put forward instead for early or *forced marriages*. This introduces a gendered aspect related to ethnicity into education which is a further intersectional consideration that social workers need to be aware of in their work with some minority ethnic families. Safeguarding children in these circumstances can be difficult, as in the case of Khyra Ishaq where the mother, a devout Muslim, withdrew her and siblings from school under the pretext of home educating them. Instead they were subjected to a regime of harsh punishment and starvation within the closed environment of their home. The mother was able to avoid close scrutiny because parents are entitled to home educate their children and regulations in this area are relatively weak (Birmingham Safeguarding Children Board, 2010).

Child discipline

African Caribbean and South Asian parents can perceive themselves as trying to bring up children in a permissive Anglocentric society, which is eroding the authority of parents over children through an emphasis on *individualism, low power distance* and *indulgence* (see *dimensions of culture* explored in Chapter 1). Phoenix & Husain (2007, p. 24) in their literature review found that Black and minority ethnic parents generally thought that parents from the White majority 'lacked a commitment to parenting, with the result that White children were undisciplined and lacking in respect for their parents and elders'. Chand (2000) and Laird (2008) criticise racist portrayals of African, African Caribbean and South Asian parents as disciplinarians who quickly resort to physical violence to manage their children's behaviour. Despite this pervasive stereotype there is no evidence to suggest that parents of African Caribbean heritage physically chastise their children any more that those from the ethnic majority, while parents of South Asian heritage have been shown to share broadly similar views about child discipline as those from the ethnic majority (Cawson et al., 2000; Maiter et al., 2004).

Research does indicate that parents of Asian, African or African Caribbean heritage are more likely to be referred to Children's Social Care for using an implement, such as a belt or shoe, to physically punish their children compared to the ethnic majority. Yet in these instances, injury was no greater than if inflicted directly by a hand (Gibbons et al., 1995). There is also evidence to suggest that White majority parents tend to use physical punishment when they have lost control, while among Black and minority ethnic parents physical punishment is often administered judiciously rather than in a fit of anger (Phoenix & Husain, 2007). It appears that social workers tend to be more interventionist if an implement is used and to regard it with greater seriousness (Chand, 2000). This may explain why Black children are over-represented in referrals to Children's Social Care for physical abuse compared to White children (Barn et al., 1997). Processes of acculturation also mean that many parents from minority heritage backgrounds have adopted parenting styles more akin to those of the ethnic majority in the UK and US (Nzira, 2011; Robinson, 2007). It is crucial that practitioners explore parental attitudes to discipline and focus on the degree of harm actually caused to the child rather than rely on preconceived notions that Black and minority ethnic parents or carers engage in harsher discipline of their children than those from the ethnic majority.

Greenfields et al. (2010) have argued that despite the questionable evidence suggesting that Black and minority ethnic families are more likely to engage in punitive and harsher disciplinary strategies towards their children, there is a growing body of evidence to suggest that this may indeed be the case with recently migrated parents from specific African and Asian countries. This may be attributable to a combination of cultural norms around childrearing and the additional pressures brought to bear on families through the processes of migration, which are explored in Chapter 7. Additionally, there are many parents who lack the skills and creativity to discipline their children in effective ways, and this may in part explain why the approaches appear to be harsher and more punitive. While children must be protected from significant harm, it is vital to explore with parents and carers what pressures they are under and their range of disciplinary strategies under normal circumstances. According to Nzira (2011), discipline amongst some ethnic minorities goes beyond the nuclear family to include relatives in the extended family network. In some sections of ethnic or faith communities with close social bonds, friends and members of the same religious congregation often feel a sense of duty to assist in the disciplining of children. Therefore the involvement or influence of kin and community members in disciplining children needs to be explored with families.

It is commonly assumed that parents with a strong religious faith are more likely to engage in authoritarian parenting styles, which tend to demand obedience and conformity from children while exhibiting low warmth towards them. A systematic literature review undertaken by Petro et al. (2018) suggests that evidence of this is equivocal, with research indicating that biblically conservative parents are not necessarily harsher in their approach to child discipline. It seems that the strength of religiosity and/or the nature of religious beliefs alone are unlikely to be determinant of an authoritarian parenting style. Other factors such as individual differences or structural inequalities in combination with religious belief are more likely to account for parenting styles. Horwath et al. (2008, p. 50) found considerable agreement between parents of Muslim, Hindu and Christian faiths that the 'core components of good parenting [are]: warmth (love and nurture), structure (expectations, rules) and autonomy support (encouraging individuality)'. In their study many devout parents and adolescents recognised a need for young people to negotiate some values and elements of conduct in a predominantly Western secular society, while meeting the expectations of a religious family. Nevertheless, sometimes parents cite religious teachings and scripture to justify harsh discipline, which has been found to place some children at greater risk of physical abuse than others. However, as Fortune et al. (2010) demonstrate, close reading of the Old Testament, New Testament and the Quran indicates that parents have obligations to guide, cherish and respect their children. While the expectation of a child's obedience to parents and elders may be underpinned by spiritual beliefs, religious teachings often oblige parents to avoid placing unreasonable demands upon their children.

Reflective exercise

Consider your practice with three families from a range of minority ethnic backgrounds which involved concerns about disciplining children.

What are your own personal beliefs about child discipline and how are these informed by your family's cultural heritage?

When you work with families where child discipline is a concern, to what extent do you explore the cultural and socio-economic influences that might shape these disciplinary practices and to what extent are these incorporated into assessment and care planning?

In what ways could you change your practice to pay greater attention to the motivations behind the approach of parents or guardians to child discipline?

Child abuse linked to faith or belief

Religion occupies a central role in the lives of many Black and minority ethnic families, and this has been found to have positive and supportive value for families. There is growing concern that interpretations of religious beliefs and texts have resulted in parenting and disciplinary practices which are abusive to children and unwelcome. There is nothing wrong per se with holding a belief; however, what that belief leads you to *do* may be what could be perceived as posing a risk of harm. A number of children from Black and minority ethnic backgrounds have been maltreated due to their parents' or carers' belief that they are somehow spiritually possessed. Many religions including Christianity, Judaism, Islam and Hinduism allow for the possibility of spirit possession. While some people who believe in possession by malevolent spirits, known as *jinns*, are Muslim, this is actually more strongly associated with cultural rather than religious beliefs. Birmingham Safeguarding Children Board (2010) *Working Together to Safeguard Children in respect of the Death of a Child: Case Number 14* links together many interrelated aspects of parental behaviours around age appropriate expectations, discipline, religious beliefs and spirit possession.

Birmingham Safeguarding Children Board (2010) *Working Together to Safeguard Children in respect of the Death of a Child: Case Number 14*

The father of the children was from an African Caribbean background, but was divorced from the mother and no longer lived with her and the six children. Later the mother's subsequent male partner moved into the family home. The mother was overweight and often dieted, adopting her male partner's ideas about healthy foods for the family as a whole. The mother's partner had experienced extreme punishments as a child involving regular beatings, deprivation of food and the death of his sister when his own father beat her to death for failing to flush the toilet. The couple were described variously as African, African Caribbean and Black British. The mother and her partner were Muslims, while he held a strong belief in evil spirits. They both had extended family living in the UK who often visited the home, including the birth father, although this became infrequent as the couple withdrew their children from school and reduced contact with kin.

In accordance with her understanding of being an observant Muslim woman, the mother adhered to her male partner's interpretation of Islam and was deferential. His beliefs were used to justify increasingly severe punishments for the children involving beatings; starvation; dousing with cold water; removal of toys; and confinement to one room. Punishments were dealt out for, among other things, young children bedwetting and asking questions. His interpretation of Islam became idiosyncratic and was increasingly shaped by his deteriorating mental health. He came to believe that one of the children was possessed by jinns, but failed to consult with an imam or specialist exorcist concerning his views, as might be expected given the family's religious beliefs. Instead he pursued his own practices around exorcism. By the time the children were removed from their carers one child had already died of malnutrition and several were close to death. The Serious Case Review concluded that the mother's partner became completely self-directed in his religious convictions. The lack of social workers' knowledge and engagement with the family's faith and their cultural heritage meant that vital aspects of risk were missed during assessment.

In Birmingham Safeguarding Children Board (2010) the personal biographies of the mother's preoccupation with weight and eating, alongside her male's partner's experience of a harsh disciplinary regime as a child and mental health problems combined with aspects of religion to distort beliefs in ways unrecognisable to devout Muslims and which posed high risks to their children's health. Notably there were many extended family members involved in this family who were becoming increasingly concerned about the children and worried about their own exclusion from the household. There is little evidence that social workers at the time tried to contact them or explore their perspectives. As in other cases this may be due to the focus on the nuclear family form in Anglocentric societies and the influence of *individualism*, which can have an atomising effect on social work practice with family members. In other words there is a professional tendency to intervene with family members on a one-to-one basis rather than as a whole family, reflected both in direct work by practitioners and their pattern of referrals to other support services (Laird et al., 2017).

Reflective exercise

Consider the circumstances in Birmingham Safeguarding Children Board (2010)

How might Anglocentric norms and professional culture have impaired social work practice with different family members?

How might *cultural awareness* and *cultural knowledge* support your practice with families in similar circumstances?

Another manifestation of spiritual possession is *witchcraft labelling*, found to exist among some recent migrants and some long-established ethnic minority communities. While the exact number of children at risk of this form of abuse is not clear, it is acknowledged that this phenomenon is growing in the UK. A *'witch'* is believed to be a person possessed with evil power which is used to harm others. Tedam & Adjoa (2017) concluded that there appeared to be a pattern whereby a church elder, leader or pastor would have to provide confirmation to the family as part of the cycle of abuse. This pastor or church leader is often a highly regarded member of the community whose word is sacrosanct and highly valued. *Witchcraft labelling* is a form of abuse that can have serious and long-lasting consequences for the health and wellbeing of children. Children accused of *witchcraft* are likely to feel traumatised and withdrawn. Children of all ages are at risk of this form of abuse although it appears to be more prevalent among children in the 0–13 age range. Tedam (2016, p. 185) identifies the risk factors associated with witchcraft labelling as:

➢ Children with disabilities or long term ill health

➢ Children in families who are experiencing multiple or enduring difficulties

➢ Children who may be bedwetting

➢ Children who are 'different' for example have birth marks, albinism, skin discolouration

➢ An only child where the mother may be experiencing secondary infertility or multiple miscarriages

➢ Families where there is unemployment and financial difficulties

Children at risk from *witchcraft labelling* may subsequently experience varying forms and severity of abuse, commonly explained away by parents as the process of casting out or ridding the child of the witchcraft. Tedam & Adjoa (2017) found that children are likely to bear longer-term effects of *witchcraft labelling* as a result of related abuse including: hitting; biting; scalding and burning; depriving of sleep; starvation; isolation and exclusion; and sending away to live with relatives. Tedam & Adjoa (2017) developed a Witchcraft Labelling Assessment Framework to aid social workers in their work with children and families where *witchcraft labelling* may be a risk. This framework identifies areas which should be carefully considered by social workers when dealing with cases where children may be at risk of this form of abuse. In the UK, this form of abuse disproportionately affects ethnic minority children and the reasons for this have been attributed to the growth of Pentecostal churches which serve as social support for many isolated families from minority backgrounds, some of which have been found to be complicit in perpetuating *witchcraft labelling* through 'requirements for secrecy and silence as well as pressure to conform' (Oakley & Kinmond, 2014, p. 87).

Female genital mutilation

Female genital mutilation (FGM) is another form of harmful traditional practice. It is illegal in the UK to conduct FGM, to fail to protect a child against it and to take a child abroad in order to conduct it. Healthcare professionals, social workers and teachers are required to notify the police where there is a belief that a girl might be at risk of FGM. Girls are most likely to be at risk around school holidays, as often FGM is planned to take place abroad. Globally, over 200 million girls and women are said to be living with the effects of FGM. Akilapa & Simkiss (2012) estimate that there are over 20,000 girls under the age of 15 living in the UK who are at risk of FGM and an estimated 66,000 adult women living with the consequences of this practice. In the UK, the communities most at risk of FGM are those originally from countries in West and North East Africa and some countries of the Middle East such as Egypt and Yemen. The World Health Organization (2008, p. 1) describes FGM as 'all procedures involving the partial or total removal of the external genitalia or other injury to the female genital organs for non-medical reasons'. The physical and psychological short- and long-term effects of FGM have been widely examined and include (World Health Organization 2008, p. 11):

> ➢ Trauma

> ➢ Pain

> ➢ Excessive bleeding

> ➢ Adverse psychological consequences

> ➢ Infection and transmission of HIV and hepatitis

> ➢ Kidney disease

> ➢ Incontinence

> ➢ Decreased quality of sexual life

Cultural and religious pressures have been found to be the reasons cited for the ongoing practice of FGM. There is also evidence to suggest that families who practise FGM do so from a perspective of care and affection as they feel it is in their daughter's best interest. This makes it a complex practice to eradicate as there may be family members who approve of the practice and may continue to discuss the alleged *'benefits'* of it. Cook (2016) has also argued that it can feel difficult for professionals to approach this as a criminal offence while at the same time trying to respect and value the realities of the population who continue this practice. Conversely, as discussed in Chapter 6 on working with communities, often customs are contested within ethnic communities, particularly where these are oppressive or harmful to women and children. It would be a mistake for social workers to assume that simply because something is called a *'cultural practice'* this makes it a widely accepted practice within a given ethnic group. This calls into question what it actually means to respect cultural and religious beliefs which can play into assumptions that cultures and faiths are fixed and minority ethnic families uniform in their adherence to these when demonstrably huge variations actually exist.

Penny & Kingwill (2018) have suggested that a link between lack of English language competency and high FGM rates exist in diaspora, where there is a greater likelihood that cultural traditions will be preserved, partly owing to the limited effects of preventative messages from public services. Social workers are required to work with families where FGM may be being considered. Their work will have to be extended to the minority communities in which this happens. This will require a good level of culturally sensitive collaborative working with statutory and voluntary sector organisations to directly protect children while encouraging a wider re-evaluation of such harmful traditional practices. Some of these community oriented approaches are considered in more detail in Chapter 6.

Reflective exercise

Social workers are required to respect a diversity of cultural and religious values, beliefs and observances.

What does respecting diverse cultural and religious values, beliefs and observances mean to you and how do you demonstrate this in your practice with families and children?

How do you reconcile this requirement of respect with protecting children subject to harmful traditional practices or child abuse linked to faith or belief?

How have you managed, or would you manage, accusations from a minority ethnic family of racism or being disrespectful towards their cultural and/or religious obligations?

Case study for practitioners

Jane is a Black African female of Nigerian heritage who was born and raised in the UK. She married Didjo, who is of Congolese heritage and who arrived in the UK 10 years ago on a student visa. They are both 34 years old. Together they have a daughter Drekka who is three years old and has been found to be experiencing global developmental delay. Didjo has informed his friends that his daughter has a disability the exact nature of which is still unknown and so he is planning to take her to the Democratic Republic of Congo to seek traditional health care and healing. Jane is concerned that Didjo may be planning something but is unsure of exactly what. Her concerns are heightened when she finds a bottle with an unidentifiable liquid which Didjo claims to have been giving to Drekka to aid her speech and cognition. Jane becomes very concerned and mentions this to another parent at the children's nursery and this parent is sufficiently concerned that she discusses her concerns with the headteacher. The headteacher invites Jane and Didjo into school to discuss Drekka and becomes concerned about Jane's passiveness and Didjo's angry demeanour. The following week Drekka is absent from school and all efforts to reach her parents by phone prove

futile. The headteacher makes a referral to the Local Children and Families' Service, who visit the family and find no one is home. They leave a calling card and Jane rings almost two weeks later, saying Didjo and Drekka are still in Democratic Republic of Congo and will be returning in a couple of weeks. As the social worker, you arrange a visit to the family on their return.

This case study lends itself to a number of cultural competence models in Chapter 4, however, the use of the social GGGRAAACCCEEESSS would be a useful non-oppressive and empowering process to undertake work with Didjo and Jane. This is set out as a series of questions for exploration.

Gender: Drekka is a three-year-old girl. How might Drekka's gender influence the care she is receiving and how are females perceived in the Congolese and Nigerian cultures? What role does Jane have in the family? Are her views and feelings taken into account in all decision-making processes? Consider the referral which described Jane as *'passive'* and Didjo as *'angry'*.

Geography: Where does the family come from? Consideration must be given to their heritage of Nigeria and DRC. Where do they live in the UK? How might that influence their decision-making and care of Drekka?

Race: How diverse is the area where the family lives? What, if any, are their experiences of being Black in that context?

Religion: Does the family practise a faith? What is it and how do they observe religious and other celebrations?

Age: Drekka is three years old and experiencing delayed speech. What are the implications of Jane and Didjo's ages?

Ability: Aim to understand whether there are other persons with disabilities on either side of the family. What is Drekka able to do? What are the family's views about disabilities? What are her strengths and the strengths of her parents?

Appearance: How does Drekka present in nursery? Are there any concerns about her presentation?

Class: How does the family describe themselves in terms of class, both in the UK and in their countries of origin?

Culture: What is the family's culture? How do they describe it? How do they practise their cultural values?

Education: Recap the parents' educational achievements. How much do they value education and consider whether this might be influencing their hopes and aspirations for Drekka.

Ethnicity: How does the family describe their ethnicity? What do you know about Congolese and Nigerian parenting and cultural practices?

Spirituality: Consider Didjo's links with Congo, particularly the suggestion of going to seek *'traditional healthcare and healing'*. What did he mean? What *'treatment'* was offered to Drekka on their recent trip to DRC? How might this be affecting Drekka's health and wellbeing?

Sexuality: Examine this within the context of their marriage relationship.

Conclusion

Families are a primary source of socialisation for children and young people. There are different family forms, each with their unique makeup, advantages and challenges. It is important for social workers to take this into consideration when working with children and their families. It is most certainly the case that the majority of people hold their families in high esteem and value their contribution towards individual and collective success. Practitioners often fail to explore or acknowledge the strengths of Black and minority ethnic families, particularly in relation to *social capital* and developing resilience in their children; but also for many in relation to faith communities and spiritual beliefs. As clearly demonstrated in this chapter, professionals working with families from across different cultural backgrounds need to be aware of diverse approaches to childrearing and be able to distinguish between practices which cause harm and those which positively enhance cultural identity.

6
Practice with Ethnic Communities

Introduction

There is good evidence that child protection social work typically over-focuses on the mother–child dyad at the expense of partnership working with fathers and other significant kin in the child's life (Laird et al., 2017). This narrowness of concern is even more pronounced set against the demise of community and patch social work, which means that practitioners often have little knowledge of the localities where families live (Pierson, 2011). Despite *'family and environmental factors'* constituting one of the three dimensions of *The Framework for the Assessment of Children in Need*, in practice typically relatively little time is devoted to exploring a *'family's social integration'* or *'community resources'* (both sub-elements) beyond rather superficial enquiries about friends and a list of services (Laird et al., 2017). While the family's finances are assessed, its socio-economic positioning and the impact of living in a disadvantaged community are often not (Parrott, 2013; Cummins, 2018). The ecological approach to assessing families which involves exploring and analysing their dynamics and functioning within the context of both the wider family and their community is largely absent from social work assessments (Laird et al., 2017; Morris et al., 2017). This is a particularly crucial oversight when families live in a disadvantaged area and have dynamic relationships with localised minority ethnic communities. Therefore this chapter examines the influence and significance of community in the lives of family members.

Hybrid identities and ethnic communities

Migrant communities, as they become established in their adopted country, encounter new circumstances typically prompting change and adaptation. Attesting to this development, Modood et al. (1997, pp. 332–37) found that second-generation migrants tended to adopt lifestyles and practices influenced by those of the ethnic majority, but which still reflected many of the values and traditions of their parents' generation. Modood et al. (1997, pp. 332–37) also discovered that what determines self-identification with a particular ethnic or faith community is a general sense of belonging to that group rather than necessarily engaging in traditional practices or regular participation in cultural or devotional activities. This evidence again points to the fluidity of culture and religious observance as migrants settle in new countries, adapt to new social and economic circumstances, and are influenced by the norms of the host population.

Globalisation has also spawned hybrid identities as a result of innumerable international exchanges through the internet, low-cost travel and increased migration between countries. Ethnic identities are increasingly transnational and transcultural as they incorporate and transform multiple traditions. The forging of hybrid identities in the UK, as in other countries of Europe and in North America, revolve around the music scene, social networking and the globalisation of the media; resulting in much greater cross-national communication. These add yet another layer of fluidity to the cultural influences and sources of ethnic identification, most particularly for young people. New transatlantic cultural forms are being created, based on the shared African roots of Black British youth and Black American youth. These draw on notions of 'Black pride' propagated by the Black Power Movement in America and Rastafarianism, which originated in Jamaica together with the adoption of Black English and the popularity of rap and 'slack' music (Gilroy, 1987; Sewell, 1997; Bhui et al., 2005).

Modood et al. (1997, p. 291) reveals the increasingly hybrid nature of ethnic identification among South Asian young people, which tends to revolve around a broader youth culture rather than an exclusive identification with their family's country of origin. Many who trace their family roots to the Indian subcontinent increasingly identify as belonging to a common South Asian and Muslim community, rather than the Gujarati, Punjabi, Kashmiri or Sylhet community. The emergence of media such as the BBC Asian Network and the popularisation of music forms derived from Bhangra have also helped to create a wider hybrid identity among many South Asian youths. This is partly a response to Islamophobia, but it also reflects a sense of solidarity with the *ummah*, the worldwide Islamic community, which for many British Muslims can be an important aspect of their ethnic identity (Runnymede Trust, 1997, p. 16; Jacobson, 1997). Information and communication technology has brought about instantaneous news from, and contact with, relatives in countries of origin, resulting in new forms of transnational identification.

Individuals of mixed heritage may draw on a number of cultural influences from their parents and possibly grandparents or other relatives. Those having a parent from the White ethnic majority community and another parent who is Black or Asian may identify or be identified as belonging to a Black and minority ethnic community. For many adults and young people their dual heritage remains important and they may also identify strongly with the cultural values of their White parent (Goldstein, 1999, p. 291). In Leicester Safeguarding Children Board (2011) *Serious Case Review in Respect of the Deaths of Children known as Child 1 and Child 2: Case 'A'* police were called to a number of domestic violence incidents between the White British born care leaver mother and the Middle Eastern born Muslim asylum seeking father. The parents subsequently admitted to social workers that they were experiencing conflict in their relationship due to cultural and language issues, including disagreements over money and migration matters. There was no exploration by social workers as to what this meant in relation to the upbringing of their two children: for example gender expectations; what languages they would speak; or their religion. Indeed the Serious Case Review was critical that Children's Social Care had not clearly recorded the father's ethnicity, religion, immigration status, first language and preferred language of communication. This would have been a crucial starting point to understanding the children's cultural heritage and the points of disagreement between the couple which appeared to be contributing to incidents of domestic violence. Increasingly relationships and unions between people from a range of ethnic backgrounds are leading to young people with multiple heritages and not merely two.

People from different minority ethnic communities, like those from the ethnic majority, hold personal views about the values and beliefs transmitted to them by relatives, friends and the wider community. They exercise choice about many aspects of culture and faith and how they wish to observe them. Additionally, individuals are differently situated by virtue of their class, gender, age, sexuality, marital status or disability. This is likely to mean that they are subject to different expectations regarding their behaviour. Whether a person is: working class or middle class; a man or woman; older or younger; homosexual or heterosexual; married or unmarried; and disabled or able-bodied will mediate how they understand, view and articulate aspects of their cultural heritage. The intersection of these other aspects of identity with that of ethnicity will shape how a person's ethnic identity is realised and expressed. This is yet another instance of how individual circumstances give expression to unique rather than homogeneous forms of cultural and spiritual values and practices.

For very many people their ethnic identity is marginal and they do not conceive of themselves as having a definable culture, while for others religion plays little or no part in their lives. Others identify more strongly with their social class, occupation or political affiliation than with their ethnic background (Cantle, 2008, p. 95). For an increasing number of people their group identity is shaped by several different cultural heritages as a result of unions across ethnic boundaries. Inevitably these children will draw on a range of cultural influences which will result in more diffuse forms of ethnic self-identification.

Reflective exercise

Consider your own ethnic and religious identity.

To what extent do you identify with your ethnic or faith community and why?

How have cultural norms or religious observances within your ethnic or faith community changed over time?

Within your family, to what extent do cultural norms or religious observances differ, as between the different generations?

Power relationships within ethnic communities

When ethnicity or religion is being deployed as an organising strategy by a social group to gain specific political or economic rights or other advantages, then some sections of that ethnic or religious community may have a vested interest in maintaining strict boundaries as to who is accepted as a member. This approach perpetuates a fixed notion of culture and faith to prevent or discourage members from deviation or defection (Barth, 1969). Some opinion leaders within ethnic or faith communities may fear dilution or diffusion of its membership in ways which undercut the political clout which a cohesive, widely recognised minority ethnic or religious group can wield; albeit that this may be wielded to bring to public attention discrimination and disadvantage, in an endeavour to gain basic protections or rights for the group. For example, a faith or ethnic group may insist that halal or kosher food (as prescribed by Islam and Judaism respectively) is available at a day centre for disabled children or that information regarding child protection procedures be available in heritage languages. Nevertheless, in-group power dynamics can determine which religious or cultural beliefs, values or practices are significant markers of group membership, for example the expectation that children are educated in a faith school, or the adoption of customary forms of dress. This leads to a further criticism of multiculturalism articulated by Hasan (2010), who argues that as both policy and practice, it ignores power structures within ethnic and faith communities alongside the oppressions they can perpetuate.

Powerful community or religious leaders or other vocal sections of an ethnic or faith minority can promote particular versions of culture and faith, demanding adherence to them by group members and censure for those who deviate. Here, according to Donnelly (2002, p. 102), culture is being 'constructed through selective appropriations from a diverse and contested past and present. Those appropriations are rarely neutral in process, intent, or consequences.' He observes that vocal sections of a minority can seek to monopolise the definition of the group's culture, or indeed religion, by appealing to a distant past which either never existed or has been idealised and embellished; for example the contention by opinion leaders within a minority group that premarital sex rarely or never occurred in the past, but is now happening due to the influence of permissive norms among the ethnic majority. Negative stereotypes held by people from the White majority, alongside efforts by sections of ethnic minorities to make their community ever more homogeneous, tend to essentialise aspects of culture and faith, turning them into a restricted set of fixed precepts and behaviours. This constructs ethnicity as internally uniform and discrete from other social influences or appropriations from other cultures and ideas. Most cultures in fact offer multiple choices to individuals within a range of possibilities, while many norms are ambiguous and permit a degree of interpretation further extending individual options (An-Na'im, 2009, p. 74). Similarly in relation to faith, beliefs and practices may vary widely as, for example, among the Jewish community ranging from Ultra-Orthodox, to conservative, to reform versions of Judaism.

Conservative forces within minority ethnic or faith communities tend to be facilitated at the expense of more progressive pressures culminating in rigid constructions of ethnicity or religious observance and inflexible boundaries. In these circumstances beliefs and practices can become prescriptive, diminishing individual choice. An acknowledgement of this should not detract from the authentic endeavour by many minority community members to preserve cherished traditions and disseminate fundamental values or beliefs. Nevertheless in Hasan's (2010) view those adopting a multicultural approach can fail to challenge oppressive attitudes and practices within minority communities which disproportionately affect women and children, such as obedience to adult males in the household. He contends that while anti-racism is focused on obtaining equal rights for non-White people, conversely multiculturalism seeks to establish separate entitlements and legal exemptions for minorities, resulting in potentially less equality for some sections within those minority communities. Some sections of the Roma and Bangladeshi communities see little point in female education, as girls are expected to marry and undertake domestic responsibilities rather than enter the workforce. This clearly has implications for parents ensuring that their children receive an education, in tandem with the amount of encouragement (or discouragement) they receive to engage with academic work. Parental attitudes towards education came to the fore in Southampton Local Safeguarding Children Board (2014) *Serious Case Review Family A*.

Southampton Local Safeguarding Children Board (2014)
Serious Case Review Family A

This case involved a White British Traveller family of seven children aged between six and 14 years who lived with both parents on a Travellers' site and later in settled social housing in South East England during the period 2004–11. Three of the children had a statement of Special Educational Needs due to speech and language delays, although neither parent engaged in the assessment process. One child attended a special school and it was anticipated that a second child would also be placed there. A parental separation in 2011 and the father's decision to take all the children to live with him at a Traveller's site on the south coast where he had extended family, meant that neither child attended a special school. The father had a history of mental illness, including at least one suicide attempt, and had been prescribed anti-psychotic medication which he often did not take. He did, however, experience periods of good mental health.

On moving to the Travellers' site with his children in May 2011 the father informed an education welfare officer (who are often qualified social workers) during a visit to the family that he had been and would continue to home educate all his children, even though it was known that he could neither read nor write. The education welfare officer merely documented this, but did not enquire further regarding the education of the children with special needs or the father's mental health, although these were both known about. For Southampton Local Safeguarding Children Board (2014, para.7.3.5) this raised concerns that 'professionals had low expectations of Travelling families'. Notably it is reckoned that 62% of adult Travellers are illiterate, while children from Gypsy, Roma and Travelling communities are six times less likely than others to achieve basic academic qualifications at the age of 16 years (Southampton Local Safeguarding Children Board, 2014, para.8.1.5). Research by Derrington & Kendall (2004) revealed that some Traveller parents fear *'cultural erosion'* through their children attending school and have often themselves had poor experiences of schooling and beyond attaining basic numeracy and literature do not see the point of formal education.

The Serious Case Review noted that while the education service has limited statutory powers to intervene, they do have some powers if they receive evidence that children are not being 'suitably educated' at home. It concluded that the education welfare officers could easily have obtained such evidence and were 'too ready to withdraw from the situation' without making further enquiries to establish the arrangements for the children's education (Southampton Local Safeguarding Children Board, 2014, para.7.3.8). When the extent of the children's neglect and maltreatment by the father was eventually recognised by Children's Social Care services all the children were initially moved to live with their paternal aunt resident on the same Travellers' site. No provision was made for the children's education during this period, partly on the grounds that some practitioners were resistant 'to the idea that the children might be educated outside the family' (Southampton Local Safeguarding Children Board, 2014, para.7.3.12).

It is likely that to a degree the decision by the father to withdraw his children from school and then not educate them at home was being used as a marker of Traveller identity. It was a decision apparently endorsed by many in the local ethnic community who, while expressing concern that the children were being physically neglected, did not complain that they were being denied education. The education welfare officer colluded with this cultural influence by adopting a lower standard of education for Travelling children than for others, possibly informed by a negative stereotype of Travellers as uneducated and nomadic. Even when the children were moved by social workers from their father's care, still no provision was made for their schooling. Social workers seemed reluctant to arrange this on the grounds that respect for Traveller culture meant permitting children to be educated within their community, even though this was not actually happening. Adopting this position ignores the fact that all ethnic communities are heterogeneous and characterised by a diversity of cultural beliefs and practices. What counts as culture or a marker of ethnic identity are typically contested issues within communities. In retrospect, appeal to this cultural norm was used as cover to enable the father to keep his daughters at home where he proceeded to sexually abuse them over a number of years.

Here is a situation in which some sections of an ethnic community are seeking an exemption, that children not receive schooling on the grounds that this is not important to a Traveller way of life. For some Travellers formal education has a *negative valence* (see Chapter 1). This is a contested notion of culture within this ethnic community, with many who value education and committed to good schooling for their children (Le Bas, 2014; Foster & Norton, 2012). In this instance professionals accepted a lower standard of education for Traveller children, than they would have for those from the ethnic majority. Depriving children of education is a form of in-group oppression that denies them life chances. Oppressive cultural norms tend to most detrimentally affect women and children, who in most societies are less economically, politically and socially powerful than men.

Reflective exercise

Consider the circumstances in Southampton Local Safeguarding Children Board (2014).

How did notions of *cultural markers* affect the behaviour of family members, community members and social workers?

What strategies could the social workers involved have adopted to develop an understanding of community power dynamics?

Collectivism in minority ethnic communities

One important underpinning aspect of any society's shared values is the degree to which it is *collectivist* or *individualist* in orientation (see discussion in Chapter 1). These are not mutually exclusive attributes, but operate along a continuum. Drawing on extensive international research Hofstede (2011) established that broadly some societies, predominantly Anglocentric ones such as those of the US, Australia and the UK, abide by norms of behaviour which encourage *individualism*. This prioritises: taking care of oneself and one's immediate family; being independent; having looser ties with other individuals; and expressing one's personal opinions. In such contexts individuals may have fewer social networks and less *social capital* to draw upon in times of need.

Other societies are much more influenced by *collectivism*: those of South Asia, East Asia and Africa place emphasis on integration into extended families and wider social groupings such as clans, tribes, home town inhabitants, members of the same work organisation or faith congregation. Such relationships are regarded as interdependent and reciprocal, but also require loyalty to the group and rely on strong ties between individuals. The welfare of the group commonly takes precedence over the welfare of an individual group member and personal opinions are often subordinated to the needs and goals of the group as a whole, or to maintaining harmony within it. The needs of the family, kin group or community to preserve social status, save face or protect itself against racism may take priority over the needs of victims of abuse or violence. At the same time there may be some vital convergences between the needs of the victim and those of the wider ethnic community, thus presenting a united front to resist racism.

Collectivism and *individualism*, while underpinning cultural orientations, are not mutually exclusive. Particularly in contexts where ethnic groups have left their country of origin, either at some point in the distant past or more recently, to settle in the UK, their values, beliefs and practices may be greatly influenced by those of the Anglocentric ethnic majority. Therefore these concepts should be used tentatively as starting points to explore a family's relationship with their local and wider community, not as a set of fixed stereotypical presumptions about that relationship. Notably there are sub-cultures within the ethnic majority; some sections of the Christian community and Travelling community which can have strong *collectivist* norms.

To take one example of this, Gilligan & Akhtar (2006) in their overview of the literature found that in the UK there is under-reporting of child sexual abuse amongst South Asian heritage communities and a higher rate of withdrawal of allegations compared to the ethnic majority. This is despite other findings which suggest that child sexual abuse is as prevalent among these minorities as among the majority population. In their subsequent research they found that *izzat* (family honour or community standing), which is not an attribute of a single family member but of the kin group as a whole, influences how the family is regarded by others. It concerns the extent to which a family is respected and their dignity or standing within that minority community and can consist of substantial *social capital*. For many households *izzat* remains important, particularly for those living in some of the smaller tight-knit Pakistani and Bangladeshi communities. Its loss can have adverse consequences for all family members, even if only one individual is responsible for damaging *izzat*. It is predominantly bound up with women's behaviour as well as the degree to which a family offers support to others or gives to charity, as these are requirements of the Islamic faith (Wardak, 2000). *Namus* in Kurdish, Turkish and Iranian societies and *ird* in Arab ones also refer to the family's or kin group's honour, related predominantly to women's sexual behaviour. A number of African societies also place emphasis on the importance of honour, which among many newer immigrant communities in the UK has become transformed into notions of community pride and respect (Brandon & Hafez, 2008).

How *izzat* is understood; how important it is; the lengths family members will go to protect it; and the severity of repercussions for those deemed to have incurred *sharam* (shame brought upon the family or community as a whole) will differ from one kin group to another. While notions of honour and shame are influential in some minority ethnic communities, it would be erroneous to surmise that people from these minority groups are equally concerned about how their wider ethnic community views them. For many people ethnic identification and acceptance by the local ethnic community may be less important. This may be because families are geographically distant from other co-ethnics or, as Cantle (2008, p. 95) suggests, simply because family members do not strongly identify with an ethnic group.

Reflective exercise

Consider your own ethnic identification; how strongly do you identify with your local ethnic community?

Describe the different power relationships within your local ethnic community.

How do these community-level power relationships affect you and/or members or your family?

The need for and reliance upon being accepted and assisted by co-ethnics or co-religionists is particularly heightened when minority communities are confronted by racial or sectarian abuse and discrimination from sections of the ethnic majority or when newer immigrant groups face hostility from established minority ethnic or faith communities. Many people in *collectivist* oriented cultures adhere to norms of behaviour centred on relational interdependence and reciprocity between those of the same minority ethnic identity or religious convictions (Laird, 2008). These networks of community-level support can be crucial in enabling impoverished families from ethnic minority backgrounds to meet needs regarding: accommodation; sourcing adequate or customary food; childcare; employment; and access to public services. Among some sections of these minorities the combination of retaining respectability and access to mutual support within their ethnic or faith community, in an otherwise often unwelcoming and intimidating environment, can pose difficult choices for parents. The circumstances in Lambeth Safeguarding Children Board (2014) *Serious Case Review Child H* illustrate some of these dilemmas.

Lambeth Safeguarding Children Board (2014) *Serious Case Review Child H*

This case concerned a Black African Somali father who on escaping civil war in his country joined extended family members in London and lived in their home. His first language was Somali and he later developed a 'workable' level of spoken English. Due to the civil war the parents had been separated for many years and when the mother eventually joined him in 2011 she knew practically no English and thereafter developed only limited knowledge of the English language. Domestic violence quickly erupted in their relationship and Children's Social Care become involved. When the mother was heavily pregnant she was seriously assaulted by the father, who also threatened to kill her and the unborn child. At this point social workers assisted her to leave the family home and she resided in a Women's Refuge for three months. Practitioners, apparently influenced by Anglocentric notions of family form and individualism, did not engage with the extended family; nor did they explore the family's relationship with members of their local ethnic community. This led to a focus on the mother as an individual in isolation from her vital social ties and to the exclusion of the wider family. Soon after the baby's birth the mother returned to live with the father and his relatives. Thereafter the couple denied any history of domestic violence. In view of these circumstances the baby was made the subject of a Child Protection Plan. The domestic violence continued to occur.

The Serious Case Review observed that while women from the ethnic majority often return to violent partners due to emotional ambivalence, financial dependence or fear of losing their children, in some minority communities additional pressure derives from needing to be accepted by community members, access to social networks and to avoid stigma or ostracism by the ethnic community. In situations where a parent speaks little or no English and is wholly dependent on their partner for the right to reside in the UK due to immigration rules on family reunion, then the dependence on kin and community may be all the greater. All these considerations are likely to have influenced the mother's decision to return to the extended family home despite suffering repeated physical assaults by the father.

The impediments mothers encounter when attempting to leave violent partners is salient because it is known that around one in five children in the United Kingdom are exposed to domestic violence, while one third of children witnessing it also suffer maltreatment themselves (Radford et al., 2011). Indeed, domestic violence features in over half of Serious Case Reviews as a contributory factor in child neglect and abuse (Sidebotham et al., 2016). Minoritised women who are considering leaving violent relationships may worry that they will be traced through tight-knit community-based networks or that opprobrium regarding their behaviour may result in penalisation of both themselves and other family members; for example, being refused work by a co-ethnic employer, children being unwelcome in the homes of other community members, or being refused assistance from within the ethnic community (Burman et al., 2004). Social dynamics can operate to pressure women into remaining in violent relationships (putting children at risk) or dissuade them from speaking out about domestic violence to avoid bringing disrepute to their ethnic community or reinforcing racist stereotypes.

Health and social care agencies could exacerbate difficulties for family members by adopting a position of non-interference. Burman et al. (2004) reveal that many women of African Caribbean heritage found themselves unable to obtain effective help in situations of domestic violence because service providers often failed to challenge the prevalence of domestic violence in the local ethnic community for fear of offending community leaders. Survivors of domestic abuse often felt that there was no public forum through which they could articulate their experience. Justifying their position, service providers relied on notions of 'cultural privacy' and respect for minority cultures. Service providers often made assumptions that the minority ethnic communities in their area were closed and looked after their own members, which culminated in a lack of active engagement or outreach. In Lambeth Safeguarding Children Board (2014, p. 12) concerning Somali parents and discussed above, practitioners initially explored the family's cultural background, but then drew back from intervention, as noted by the Review, which commented that:

> The relevance and influence on the family of their specifically Somali experiences (e.g., of their civil war and the long separation of family members, plus the role of the local Somali community in relation to the family and the dominance of male partners) which had initially been explored, was not pursued further – despite the fact that it was reported that 'community elders' had taken a role in mediating between the parents regarding the domestic violence.

The reluctance and hesitancy of social workers to intervene in this instance appears to reflect notions of 'cultural privacy' and the assumption that community members were somehow resolving family problems. This is also an illustration of how power relationships can manifest in more *collectivist* cultural contexts in relations between older and younger people. In sections of some ethnic and faith communities patriarchy is a central organising ideology to the extent that girls and women may internalise oppressive attitudes and values tolerating or assenting to limited freedom and exploitive domestic labour (Hasan, 2010, p. 78). For others it means tolerating high levels of domestic violence. Where there is a cultural influence of *high power distance*, inequality between older and younger people, males and females may be more widely accepted within a kinship group. This should not detract from the recognition that structural factors can greatly amplify power relationships, as in the case of this Somalian mother who had little English, was economically dependent on her husband and his family and was liable to deportation if she separated. If practitioners hold fixed notions of culture and view an ethnic minority as homogeneous, their attitudes and responses can reinforce intra-community power imbalances (Burman et al., 2004). In short, they can permit respect for culture to trump gender oppression or other forms of structural inequality, in turn hazarding children's safety.

Reflective exercise

Consider your practice with families from different heritage backgrounds to you.

To what extent does your practice explore with families their relationships with local ethnic or faith communities?

How have your assumptions or understandings of different local ethnic or faith communities and families' interactions with these influenced your practice?

In the light of these reflections, did you respond any differently to some of these minority ethnic families than you would have to those from the ethnic majority in similar circumstances, and if so why?

Community as a resource

Research by Jayaweera & Choudhury (2008, p. 46) indicates that for many people from ethnic minorities 'rootedness appears to be closely related to family, kin and ethnic and religious community networks in the locality'. When these researchers asked respondents why they preferred to live in areas characterised by the presence of many co-ethnics they identified being near their place of worship; specialist stores and supermarkets catering to their lifestyle needs such as halal food; having the opportunity to converse with others in their first language; being able to spend time with people who shared their culture; and feeling at home in their locality as a consequence. Easy geographic access to amenities, public transport and community resources was also mentioned as important. Many respondents also considered that the diversity in the ethnic makeup of their neighbourhood helped to make them feel accepted and described cordial relations between people of different heritage backgrounds. These positive characterisations of community relations were moderated by descriptions of poor infrastructure, drug dealing, theft, drunkenness, vandalism, violence, noise pollution and lack of safety common to many deprived neighbourhoods where most people from minority ethnic backgrounds live. It is likely that in Lambeth Safeguarding Children Board (2014) the Somali mother placed in a women's refuge with assistance from social workers after repeated physical assaults by her Somali husband found herself isolated from these community resources, which may have been a contributing factor in her decision to return to a violent home situation. Additionally, enculturation experiences growing up in Somalia would have tended to emphasise *familial identity* (see Chapter 1), making this an important source of self-worth for the mother alongside a shared language, heritage and experiences with other co-ethnics. This would have presented challenges to developing a more individualised identity outside of kin and community.

This emphasis on the presence of other co-ethnics or being in a multicultural area alongside accessibility to specialist outlets and a nearby place of worship were not shared by all migrant groups. Polish migrants, who are predominantly Catholic, were seeking to maximise their income and savings in order to return to their country of origin and were more concerned with locating near to employment opportunities and keeping costs down than with the locality in which they lived or the nature of their accommodation. Nevertheless when some of these migrants foresaw themselves as remaining in the UK for the long term with the possibility of being joined by family members, then accommodation and locality often assumed greater significance (Robinson et al., 2007, pp. 56–57). For yet others, such as refugees, their years of insecurity, multiple moves and trauma made it essential for them to remain in a locality or in accommodation which was potentially long term in order to avoid further upheaval, even in the face of racism, poor local facilities and/or relative social isolation. Exploring this attitude further Robinson et al. (2007, p. 58) noted that some refugee-based communities are relatively small and thus often very dispersed not only across the country, but also within a particular town or city. Consequently, there may not be identifiable areas of co-ethnic settlement. As a result according to Robinson et al. (2007, p. 59) such communities can be

organised through a diffuse network of communication, rather than being a community defined by physical co-presence in a particular place. Contact is maintained through word of mouth and internet and mobile phone communication, with particular individuals serving as key nodes within this network through which information flows. Community members come together only periodically, for example at social events, cultural celebrations or religious services.

Accounting for the differential experiences of more recent migrant groups Robinson et al. (2007, p. 59) describe *established contact zones* characterised by multicultural cosmopolitan spaces located in and around inner city areas which have a history of receiving migrants and where those of African and Asian origin do not stand out because of their physical appearance, nor those from continental Europe due to their accent. Therefore they are less vulnerable to racial abuse and often experience living in a peaceable friendly, relatively safe environment where they can avail themselves of assistance from friends, family or community-based organisations. Residents of such zones often positively identified with the multi-ethnic character of their neighbourhood and were more accepting of a plurality of culturally influenced lifestyles. In the study conducted by Robinson et al. (2007, pp. 52–53) a Somali migrant asked to reflect on locality epitomised this, stating, 'now is peaceful, I live in a peaceful area, I have all my neighbours from Somalia, Chinese, Pakistani, Yemeni, multicultural people, so now I feel I am relaxing'. These multi-ethnic areas are often characterised by community cohesion.

Notions of community centre on the nature of social relationships and the extent of social networks. Studies conducted by Robinson et al. (2007) and Markova & Black (2007) have revealed different strategies adopted by groups of recent migrants. Recent migrants from Europe, but also those from Pakistan, tend to use informal networks of kith and kin to obtain information and access accommodation which rely heavily on word of mouth. Polish migrants in some towns had established an 'accommodation circuit' whereby informal networks of co-ethnics informed each other when room vacancies were about to arise and sometimes were able to acquire some priority with Polish landlords. Many Pakistani migrants, who were not joining a spouse, also reported relying on informal networks of family and friends to identify accommodation which could include informal tenancies with landlords of Pakistani ethnicity. These networks proved vital in situations where migrants were impoverished or lacked the necessary documentation to access accommodation or other basic needs.

By contrast recent Somali migrants, many of whom were refugees, were more likely to make use of Somali-led community-based services. These could also act as a bridge to universal or specialist public sector provision. In areas with a longstanding Somali population, public agencies often had translation and interpreting services, which further enhanced access to support services. In all these cases friends and relatives often provided information, advice and assistance while mediating access to different types of provision through their own knowledge and existing network of contacts. Commonly this was aided by their greater fluency in English. In Lambeth Safeguarding Children Board (2014) the Somali father and mother came to live with relatives in England who had already settled in an area where there was an established Somali ethnic community. The extended family engaged local Somali elders to mediate in the violent relationship between the parents, indicating extensive ties to their wider ethnic community.

Community resources are wide ranging and encompass communal spaces including parks and community centres; local outlets; places of worship; faith-based organisations; educational facilities and services; voluntary sector organisations; community-based organisations; community development workers; tenants' associations; libraries; social clubs; special interest and community groups; places of entertainment; transport; credit unions; and cooperatives. Community resources are not necessarily accessible to all members of the locality. An African Caribbean centre or a gurdwara (Sikh temple) may only offer provision to members of that particular ethnic or faith group. Even if they cater for a wider social group, people from other ethnic backgrounds may not know of, or may feel uncomfortable, accessing such facilities. Within an ethnic or religious group there can be sectarian divisions. Because of conflict between clans in Somalia, some Somali-led voluntary organisations in the UK and elsewhere may only cater for particular constituencies within the Somali community. Similarly, Sunni and Shia mosques may exclude Muslims from the other denomination. Indeed, continuing conflict abroad between groups forming part of a larger ethnic or faith community can increase tensions between them in the UK resulting in exclusion of sections of the local minority ethnic population from specialist facilities and services (Laird, 2008).

Practitioners should bear in mind that assuming ethnic communities are by definition composed of tightly knit mutually supportive localised groups of people is also a stereotype, albeit a positive one. As a stereotype it can equally lead to inappropriate and misdirected children protection responses, or possibly lack of response if sources of support within the community are assumed to exist for the family. Central government's imposed austerity in the wake of the 2008 global financial crisis, resulting in the dramatic reduction of funding to the voluntary sector, has greatly diminished community resources. A substantial proportion of the free or low-cost facilities and services provided by not-for-profit organisations have been scaled back or closed (Pemberton et al., 2014). Likewise, community development services and workers have been cut, resulting in much more limited support to communities (Popple, 2015). This has consequences for social work engagement with minority ethnic groups. What community resources are actually available to families must be checked out (rather than presumed) and must form part of any holistic assessment.

Reflective exercise

Consider your practice with families from different heritage backgrounds.

How much do you know about community resources including networks that are available to families from particular ethnic or faith backgrounds?

What strategies could you use to identify and discover more about the community resources and networks that might be available to families from various ethnic or faith backgrounds?

Tensions between ethnic communities

In new contact zones defined as 'white-dominated peripheral estates with little history of accommodating diversity' recent migrants often face hostility, racial abuse and sometimes violence (Robinson et al., 2007, pp. 60–61). Many of them reported feeling they do not belong; vandalism of their homes; being threatened; feeling too frightened to access public transport or services; avoiding being out at night; or walking anywhere alone. Hickman et al. (2008) also observed that in such environments misunderstanding between communities can easily arise. In one example a supplementary school set up by Somali mothers in a district of London to teach their children the Somali language later expanded its function to support educationally underperforming Somali children to acquire literacy in English and improve their maths. The supplementary school continued to be perceived by members of the local ethnic majority as essentially there to reinforce Somali culture and self-chosen segregation. In communal spaces such as the local community centre Somali mothers were viewed as unsociable and unwilling to mix with others, even by long-term residents from other minority backgrounds, while Somali women explained to the researchers how difficult they found it to engage with others due to their poor command of English.

Research conducted by Hickman et al. (2008) revealed that while racism does characterise hostile reactions from people belonging to the majority ethnic community towards those from minorities in *new contact zones*, social dynamics between communities are often more complex. They found that resentment and hostility could arise between long-term settled minority communities and more recently arrived migrants. During the 1990s one English city witnessed the sudden arrival of many Somali refugees who had already claimed asylum while studying in other EU member states and belonged to the educated elite in their country of origin. After settling in the UK these Somali refugees, and later their children, proved quite educationally and economically successful, which caused resentment among youth of the much longer-established African Caribbean community, who were underachieving by comparison. This led to considerable inter-ethnic tensions with outbreaks of violence between young men of both communities as the Somali incomers were believed to be receiving more assistance from government and becoming more successful than members of the settled African-Caribbean population. For many British-born people of African Caribbean background this felt like further marginalisation of an already marginalised community, fuelled by Somali constructions of African Caribbeans as drunkards with low morals and African Caribbean constructions of Somalis as supercilious and in receipt of greater privileges as refugees (Hickman et al., 2008).

Similar problems arise between ethnic communities when recent migrants arrive in already deprived localities and are perceived by the host population to either be adding to existing deprivation (e.g. overcrowded housing) or to be enjoying better access to public provision. Where disadvantaged communities are already coping with structural shortages such as lack of subsidised social housing or access to good schools, there is a high probability that further strain on these public goods will be blamed on more recent incomers to the locality. This same dynamic is also evident when an increasing number of White Eastern European migrants begin to reside in a deprived multicultural area. Such tensions are often fuelled by media reports suggesting that they are coming into the country predominantly to claim welfare benefits or undercut wages in unskilled and semi-skilled occupations, which are disproportionately filled by people from African Caribbean and South Asian minority ethnic backgrounds, thus also taking the jobs of established ethnic communities (The Migration Observatory, 2013). Eastern Europeans can therefore experience hostility in both majority and minority ethnic localities. Many Eastern Europeans from former communist countries with historically low levels of inward migration have not encountered many people of Black or Asian background and consequently can sometimes be deeply racist in turn.

While racial prejudice is clearly implicated in many encounters between established communities and recent migrant populations, it is evident that tensions arise between long-term settled residents and incomers to an area when there is competition for employment or public goods, such as education, housing or health care. This type of conflict, which can transcend racial boundaries, has been termed *settled backlash* by Hickman et al. (2008). It suggests that tensions can arise between settled communities and more recent arrivals regardless of their racial origins, albeit that some of these encounters may encompass a racial dimension, which can in turn amplify such tensions. These dynamics are underpinned by people's understanding of who belongs in a locality and who is an outsider or intruder into it and how that new presence affects access to scarce resources. Hickman et al. (2008, p. 152) succinctly describe this as a context where long-term inadequate social and economic provision fuels resentment against people who are seen as reaping the benefits of current social and economic transformations instead of those who should have priority – 'local people'. In this context, people who are without a job and who would like a car and a house oppose 'migrants' who have a job, a car and a house by arguing that being 'from here' should be the prevailing criterion for the allocation of resources.

Social capital refers to networks of people engaging in reciprocal relationships characterised by cooperation and trust, thus acting as a resource for information sharing and other types of assistance. Building on this concept Putnam (2000, p. 22) differentiates between *bonding,* which involves more inward-looking interactions between members of the same social group that tend to 'reinforce exclusive identities and homogeneous groups', and *bridging,* which is more outward-looking and denotes interactions with people from a range of cultural backgrounds. In localities where large numbers of people engage in *bridging* interactions, relationships between different ethnic and faith groups are likely to be more harmonious and contribute positively to social cohesion. There is evidence that recent migrants in some towns and cities use *bridging social capital* to form webs of mutual assistance with those in a similar situation, but who are not necessarily from the same ethnic or faith group (Robinson & Reeve, 2006). In other places, sections of minority ethnic communities (very recent arrivals, older people and women who are less likely to speak English) may rely on *bonding social capital* characterised by reliance on resources drawn predominantly or exclusively from within their own ethnic or faith community. Notably, many world religions emphasise the importance of charitable giving and supporting others in need (Grant, 2009; Singer, 2008; Weller et al., 2017). While among some sections of faith communities this may extend to people outside that community, other belief systems may emphasise assistance to co-religionists. A large-scale study conducted by Furbey et al. (2006) found that faith organisations constituted key sources of both *bonding* and *bridging social capital* in communities, but that sectarian tensions within faith communities or tensions with other religious or ethnic groups could undercut this potential. Furbey et al. (2006, p. 1) concluded that

> Faith communities can facilitate building bridges and making links with others. They can allow new forms of association, engender trust in shared community initiatives, and motivate particular approaches to questions of social justice and need. But power inequalities within faith communities can also inhibit the development of *social capital,* particularly through the subordination of women and young people.

In localities characterised by high levels of street racism and harassment, it is likely that many people from the ethnic majority are eschewing social engagement, with people from minority communities relying instead on *bonding social capital* with others from their own heritage background – thus reinforcing nationalistic notions of White British identity. In the case covered in Local Safeguarding Children Board (2014) *Serious Care Review Family A*, community tensions erupted in Southampton when a White British Traveller family initially moved from their Traveller site to settled social housing. There followed a succession of referrals to Children's Social Care from health professionals, teachers and neighbours regarding neglect, child maltreatment, children out of control, domestic violence and overcrowded unhygienic home conditions. The parents refused to acknowledge that there were any problems and were frequently unavailable when social care practitioners made visits to the family home. The parents did report that their children were being bullied and there was 'bad feeling' towards the family from other local residents. None of these concerns led to sustained involvement with the family.

Southampton Local Safeguarding Children Board (2014, para.8.1.6) noted that Travellers are 'a group that experiences widespread discrimination … Many of their negative experiences remain unreported and invisible. Feelings of injustice and persecution are understandable.' In this instance a Traveller family had physically moved from their Traveller site into social housing only to encounter hostility from among some of the settled community in the locality. This is not to deny the very real concerns about the children that neighbours and teachers held, and which subsequently proved justified. The father later moved his children back to a Travellers' site in another area where some of his relatives also lived. It is inevitable that when minority families encounter hostility from other ethnic groups they will retreat into their own communities. Mutual distrust will increase reliance on *bonding social capital* rather than *bridging social capital*, thus perpetuating isolation and community tensions.

Reflective exercise

Consider your practice with different racial and ethnic minority communities.

To what extent do you explore with family members their racial or ethnic identification?

How much awareness do you generally have of relationships between different racial, ethnic or faith groups in the localities of the children and families you work with?

What strategies could you employ to increase your *cultural knowledge* in this area of practice?

Economically disadvantaged communities

As minority ethnic families are disproportionately in poverty, living in disadvantaged areas is a significant factor in their experiences of meeting children's care needs (Fisher & Nandi, 2015; Equality and Human Rights

Commission, 2016). In terms of *social capital*, people in poverty are less likely to have ethnically mixed social networks or friends from other neighbourhoods than those who are not in poverty. Those in poverty are more likely to have networks of co-ethnic unemployed friends and therefore have less *social capital* (Finney et al., 2015). Deprivation can also adversely affect cross-community relations, firstly because groups perceive themselves as competing against one another for access to scarce resources and secondly due to reduced public spaces such as those afforded by community centres, leisure facilities and shops which enable people from different backgrounds to meet and interact (Hickman et al., 2008). Resentment by British White residents towards people from an ethnic minority in an area can arise if they are perceived to have access to resources denied to the ethnic majority, such as the setting up of a Pakistani community centre at the same time as the local pub, predominantly frequented by residents from the White ethnic majority, is closed down (Beider, 2011). Despite the adversity of living in deprived areas, Hickman et al. (2008, p. 119) found that such localities

> inspired strong feelings of belonging and loyalty among their residents in spite of the deprivation they experienced. Shared histories and ways of being and belonging were valued. Remaining within and valuing the community was often a protection against its public identity as deprived and dysfunctional. However, powerful desires to escape to safe and harmonious places not afflicted with the burdens of poverty, ill health and bleak futures were also present in deprived neighbourhoods.

Child Poverty Action Group (2017) observes that because families in poverty are less able to participate in social or leisure activities such as visiting the local sports centre, eating at a café or having friends round for a meal, this reduces the contacts that family members have with others in their community, contributing to greater social isolation. Inevitably, children may be unable to engage in activities with peers or feel too ashamed to do so due to lack of appropriate clothing, equipment or funds. Drawing on previous research The Children's Society identified the effects on children of living in poor neighbourhoods, reproduced in the text box below.

The Impact on Children of Living in Economically Disadvantaged Communities

- Economic and material deprivation – anxiety about their family not having enough money for their needs and going without the essentials like food and clothing.

- Social deprivation – poverty restricting their access to attend social events and their ability to maintain friendships.

▶

◀

- School – inability to pay for resources needed e.g. uniform, study guides and not being able to afford to go on school trips.

- Poor quality housing, homelessness and neighbourhoods – affected children sleeping, studying and playing at home, as well as, their mental/physical health. Feeling unsafe and there is nothing to do in their local area.

- Family pressures – tensions between parents due to severe financial pressure and children taking on additional responsibilities in the home.

- Stigma and bullying due to visible signs of poverty and difference.

The Children's Society (2013, p. 3)

Power (2007) studied the challenges for parents of bringing up children in deprived inner city areas which they described as noisy, dirty, polluted, violent, dangerous, congested with fast-moving traffic and characterised by inadequate outdoor spaces or amenities for children.

Lack of supervised community spaces or street patrols by police also made families feel insufficiently safe to take advantage of what amenity there was: parks could be perceived as dangerous rather than a place to enjoy leisure. They also alluded to persistent worry that their children would either become perpetrators or victims of crime, particularly in relation to drugs. This often meant parents endeavouring to keep their children near the home, while recognising that lack of local amenities and opportunities induced boredom and increased the likelihood of them becoming involved in anti-social activities. This in turn discouraged families from using the streets and amenities, thus intensifying the sense of hazard and threat. Low income was a major barrier among parents to enabling children and young people to access amenities and leisure activities.

Inevitably, families who had the chance often moved out of these localities, diminishing stable and mutually supportive social networks and thus creating transient populations in terms of those least able to afford housing, such as asylum seekers, refugees and migrants who moved into these increasingly unpopular and deprived areas. Yet at the same time *social capital* (trust, reciprocity, cooperation and support from social networks) remains vital to parents on low income as they seek to use this to offset their lack of economic capital (property, assets, income), as does access to local public services and facilities, local amenities and community resources. As a result many expressed ambivalence towards the localities in which they lived, on the one hand lamenting and complaining about their physical environment and on the other identifying with other local residents and describing their reliance on established social networks. Manchester Safeguarding Children Board (2016) *Serious Case Review Child B1* considers circumstances surrounding child neglect framed by poverty.

Manchester Safeguarding Children Board (2016) *Serious Case Review Child B1*

The mother, who was of Black British heritage, spoke English as her first and only language, while the British South Asian father spoke both English and Urdu. Both parents had a disrupted education including school exclusions, and had a criminal history for robbery and anti-social behaviour associated with the misuse of alcohol. Although the father was from a Muslim background and celebrated Eid, he did not necessarily adhere to the wider observances of this faith, demonstrating how belief and practice typically vary widely within faith communities. The couple had three children and lived in a two-bedroom property. The mother had worked in a number of casual jobs while the father was long-term unemployed. They were in receipt of a number of welfare benefits including housing benefit to meet rental costs.

The parents lived in the area of a major city ranked in the 10% most deprived areas in England. Compared to the rest of the city their locality experienced a higher crime rate; more adults without qualifications; more children living in poverty; a greater incidence of ill health, and had a concentration of minority ethnic groups. In the schools servicing this area 35% of primary school pupils and 30% of secondary school pupils spoke English as an additional language (Manchester Safeguarding Children Board, 2016, para.45–8). The family were in substantial debt amounting to several thousands of pounds owed to various companies. They were also in rent arrears and their landlord had commenced legal proceedings to evict them from their home.

Police attended multiple incidents of domestic violence, followed by both parents refusing to cooperate. Their relationship was characterised by repeated periods of separation and reconciliation. Children's Social Care had been involved with the family for a decade due to: domestic violence; parental alcohol misuse; non-cooperation of the parents with health, dental and social services; and lack of parental insight into the impact of their behaviour upon the children. Both parents were referred to addiction services to address their heavy drinking, but neither attended. The mother was also referred to, but did not take up, counselling services. The two older children (aged 10 and six years at the time of the Serious Case Review) became the subject of temporary Child Protection Plans on several occasions.

Given this family history a Child Protection Conference agreed to make the mother's third child (to be born shortly) the subject of a Child Protection Plan. At this point it was believed that the father had moved out of the family home. Within a week of being discharged home from hospital the baby was found dead in bed beside the father, who had lain on top of the infant. The father was convicted of neglect and given a suspended custodial sentence. The Serious Case Review concluded that insufficient attention had been given by professionals to the underlying reasons for the domestic violence and its impact on the children.

This Serious Case Review illustrates the intersection between ethnicity, race and poverty. Equality and Human Rights Commission (2016) notes that those from ethnic minority groups are more likely than those from the ethnic majority to be excluded from school; in low-paid work or unemployed; residing in overcrowded housing; and living in poverty. Additionally, the father, although identifying as Muslim, consumed alcohol prohibited by

Islam. He was also in a long-term relationship with someone from outside his ethnic group. Both may have been perceived by others as violating religious injunctions and social norms. As a consequence he may have been estranged from wider kin or sections of his ethnic or faith community who disapproved of these choices. Community resources for this family could therefore have been limited.

These were also parents frequently avoiding health and social services both for their children and themselves. While this was undoubtedly to some extent an effort to evade scrutiny of their care of the children by the authorities, it may also reflect widely shared apprehensions within their ethnic community that many such services discriminate against people with their racial backgrounds and lack sensitivity towards requirements of culture or faith. This is not actually known, because such possible concerns do not appear to have been explored by professionals with this family. In an Anglo-centric society, which prioritises freedom of choice and has a high tolerance for excessive alcohol consumption (see Chapter 2), it may be that these dominant cultural norms influenced social worker perceptions and contributed to a lack of persistent concerted intervention with these parents.

Bywaters et al. (2016) concluded, based on a wide-ranging review of the research, that there was a positive correlation between levels of poverty and levels of child maltreatment and its degree of severity. Bywaters et al. (2016, pp. 28–29) also found that poverty was neither a necessary nor a sufficient condition for acts of child abuse and neglect, but rather a predisposing factor comprising 'either a direct effect through material hardship or lack of money to buy in support, or an indirect effect through parental stress and neighbourhood conditions'. When poverty, which disproportionately affects women and ethnic minorities, is also taken into consideration in situations of domestic violence, the fear of homelessness and material deprivation on leaving the family home or trying to manage as a single parent may be overwhelming (Burman et al., 2004). Where faith communities place a high positive value on family and marriage, single parenthood may also carry additional stigma or the risk of ostracism.

Reflective exercise

Reflect on your practice with families from disadvantaged communities.

To what extent do you consider in your practice the intersection between living in a disadvantaged community and aspects of family life related to race, ethnicity, faith and language?

How do you reflect this consideration in collecting and analysing information, decision-making or in care planning?

What changes could you make to improve your practice in this area?

Black and minority ethnic children have been found to be disproportionately impacted upon by gang culture in some urban geographical areas. This is not to say that children from the ethnic majority are not impacted or do not live in gang-affected areas. The Centre for Social Justice (2009) identified that ethnicity in gang membership typically reflected the communities in which they lived. In Glasgow and Liverpool, for example, gang members were predominantly White, while in Manchester and London membership was prevalent across minority communities, with a growth in gangs from Muslim backgrounds in places like Birmingham. It has been found that there is a link between gang membership and truancy from school as well as a link to deprivation, poverty and living on social housing estates. As Black and minority ethnic children and young people are more likely to grow up in a disadvantaged high-crime area, this can make them more vulnerable. Wood (2010) found that children from ethnic minority backgrounds who came from disadvantaged backgrounds were more likely to be caught in a cycle of violent crime as perpetrators or victims as the next case study illustrates.

Enfield Safeguarding Children Board & Haringey Local Safeguarding Children Board (2015) *Child 'CH'*

The mother arrived in the UK from Jamaica in 2000, with her children, including her younger son referred to as CH. She had a succession of violent relationships and frequently moved home. Later three further children belonging to the mother's female partner joined the household. Both women had a history of criminal offences including shoplifting and acts of violence. The mother's poor health and anxiety around deportation were cited in court to mitigate sentencing. Early on CH told professionals that his home life was unpredictable and violent and that he was subject to harsh physical punishments. For a period CH was subject to a Child Protection Plan, but an application to remove him into public care was rejected by the court. The Youth Offending Service and Children's Social Care tried a variety of unsuccessful interventions.

As Enfield Safeguarding Children Board & Haringey Local Safeguarding Children Board (2015, p. 9) acknowledged, 'Much would have depended however on the cooperation of CH and the ability of professionals to persuade him to separate from his destructive peer group'. CH was later described as 'a troubled, displaced and stressed young man' who had over the years developed a history of anti-social and criminal behaviour often involving guns, knives and drugs. He frequently ran away from home and was known to associate with youths who had a history of violent crime. CH's involvement with gangs started around 2009 and at one stage his mother and her partner were thought to be at risk after arguments with gang members. In 2011 aged 15 years CH who was at the time with a group of teenagers, stabbed to death a 21-year-old Black student in the street. Enfield Safeguarding Children Board & Haringey Local Safeguarding Children Board (2015, p. 18) concluded that at the time of the student's murder 'CH was on a worrying trajectory of violence, offending, disengagement and rootlessness and he was seeking increasingly to identify with gang culture. He was at risk of harming someone or of being harmed.' CH was sentenced to life imprisonment.

This Serious Case Review brings together a series of issues affecting the family and resulting in CH becoming vulnerable to joining gangs. An amalgamation of immigration worries, health difficulties and socio-economic concerns resulted in a family situation which did not appear to be consistent with safe and effective parenting. The family also lived in a disadvantaged neighbourhood with limited amenities and CH may have been drawn to gang membership out of boredom and for thrill seeking as much as a source of social identification away from a family situation characterised by violence and rejection. Intersectionality between economic disadvantage, gender, age and ethnicity is clearly implicated as a Jamaican boy attempts to find his place in a new society. Child protection assessments need to pay attention to the push-pull dynamics of family and social groups within the local community.

Reflective exercise

Consider the circumstances in Enfield Local Safeguarding Children Board (2015).

How might an application of the Social GGRRAAACCEEESSS framework have helped the social workers involved with this family to assess the risk to CH?

In what ways could the use of a *culturagram* have assisted assessment of this family's needs?

Child protection challenges related to communities

There are a range of factors which impair or inhibit intervention in child protection situations which appear to involve an aspect of families in relation to their wider local or ethnic community. Conversely, there are also a number of reasons why people from minority ethnic backgrounds, who are aware of and concerned about child maltreatment, find it difficult to approach Children's Social Care or allied agencies to share this information. This section examines these obstacles to effective child protection in community contexts from the standpoint of both practitioners and community members, who of course may also be a relative of the child. Throughout the next section Southampton Local Safeguarding Children Board (2014) concerning a British White Traveller family, described earlier in this chapter, is used to exemplify a number of community-level considerations in child protection intervention.

Low expectations of families from minority ethnic communities

In Southampton Local Safeguarding Children Board (2014) *Serious Case Review Family A* concerning a single father from the Traveller community with seven children, the *Review* censured police who searched the family's caravan in connection with a reported theft by the children. Despite its being full of dog faeces no referral was made to Children's Social Care. A month later it was found unfit for human habitation. Southampton Local Safeguarding Children Board (2014, para.7.4.5) surmised that professionals 'may have been over-tolerant of matters that should have caused concern – or to put it another way, they had low expectations of the care these children would be receiving'. Summing up their findings Southampton Local Safeguarding Children Board (2014, para.7.5.3, 7.5.5) comment:

> The extent to which the children were unsupervised and neglected, certainly as 2012 drew on, is well evidenced. It is hard to accept that such a situation would go unrecognised and/or unreported if these children did not live on a travellers' site, physically and culturally separate from other local communities…Certainly there is evidence that staff had developed unacceptably low expectations of the care these children were going to receive. It is notable that more than one member of staff contacted police in December 2012 after receiving reports that some of the children might be involved in (low level) criminal activity – yet the more evident continuing neglect of the children went unreported.

Regarding the attitudes and actions of professionals, the Serious Case Review concluded that, 'It seems likely that cultural preconceptions played their part. It is hard to imagine that the evident gross neglect of children from a "settled" community would receive such a muted response from staff' (Southampton Local Safeguarding Children Board, 2014, para.8.5.4). According to the Review, professionals had placed too much emphasises on the family's culture and ethnicity, when they needed to return to first principles; that the child's welfare is the paramount consideration. Practitioners involved in the case 'recognised that they had unconsciously made judgments and subsequent decisions about this family and this case which they would not have made if the family had not been part of the Traveller community' (Southampton Local Safeguarding Children Board, 2014, para.7.5.3, 7.5.5).

The responses of practitioners to this family illustrate how the innate cognitive processes of *concept formation and categorisation* together with *appraisal* can converge to generate and sustain prejudiced stereotypes (see Chapter 1). It is likely that professionals were already under the influence of dominant concepts of Travellers as uneducated, dirty and criminal into which this family was categorised. In terms of *appraisal* this meant that evidence of child neglect was minimised as reflecting Traveller lifestyle habits, while that of criminal activity was highlighted as this affected members of the surrounding settled community. In terms of the process of *selective attention*, police officers and education welfare officers appeared not to notice the dilapidated, filthy home conditions of the children because these coincided with a pervasive negative stereotype which made them unremarkable in this context whereas they would have been interpreted as signs of child neglect if found in a family from the settled community. Therefore in a sense these signs ceased to be seen in the family's caravan or on the Travellers' site. While in this case it was the police and education welfare officers who failed to recognise the extent of neglect, there are clear lessons for social workers too.

Community-based mediators

In Southampton Local Safeguarding Children Board (2014) the Traveller's site warden continued to receive complaints about the children's behaviour, including anti-social behaviour and reports from people out walking their dogs that the children were defecating around the site. While she spoke to the father and aunt about these incidents, she did not report them to the housing officer on grounds 'to do with trust – what they would do with the information and how this might affect her safety on the site and her relationships with the site residents' (Southampton Local Safeguarding Children Board, 2014, para.7.7.5). This meant that information about the family's conditions was not escalated up line management, thus increasing the likelihood that they would culminate in a referral to Children's Care Services. Southampton Local Safeguarding Children Board, 2014, para. 8.1.14) quoting from the conclusions of an agency's report to the Review agreed that from the perspective of social workers, 'staff working on the site were perceived to have considerable expertise and knowledge in working with this community... Their advice was... not robustly challenged in relation to the outstanding child protection issues'.

Social workers from the ethnic majority who in terms of identity development remain located in statuses which mean they predominantly interact with other British White people may find it particularly challenging to relate to people from minority communities. With the exception of practitioners who have reached either *immersion/emersion* or *autonomy* identity statuses (see Chapter 4), most will be highly reliant on community mediators to help them negotiate relationships with members of the wider ethnic group. As this case demonstrates, sometimes these mediators while often very effective conduits of communication can themselves experience divided loyalties as they endeavour to maintain the trust of local community members while interacting with state agencies. Social workers whose identity development is framed by *contact, disintegration* or *reintegration* statuses can lack sufficient insight or self-confidence to identify or challenge the perspectives of community mediators who are conflicted in this way. They may also be unable to recognise when a community worker over-identifies with one particular constituency within a local ethnic community such as a group of male elders or a faith leader.

Threat and safety

Laird (2013) and Stanley & Goddard (2002) in their research provide detailed descriptions of the detrimental psychological and emotional impacts on practitioners of being in unsafe situations or experiencing threats of violence and other forms of intimidation. Frequently, this leads to *flight* responses resulting in minimisation of the level of risk of significant harm posed to the child; deferential and collusive practice; or avoidance of the family, typically by reducing or shortening home visits. Southampton Local Safeguarding Children Board (2014) *Serious Case Review Family A* provides insight into how not just family members, but also community members, can create hostile and threatening environments, which detrimentally impact on social work practice.

Southampton Local Safeguarding Children Board (2014) *Serious Case Review Family A* [continued]

When Children's Social Care received two referrals regarding neglect and abuse of seven Traveller children by their father a social worker went alone to conduct an initial assessment, but was intimated by men with dogs who chased her from the site. Her manager sent her a second time, again alone, when she was again approached by men with dogs and again left fearing for her own safety. A month after these referrals were received, a social worker made a visit, but did not see any of the children and relied on the father's assertion that there were no problems. Later a meeting was held with the father, the aunt living at the site and other agencies, but this focused on arrangements for the children's education and their being unsupervised. The issues raised by the referrals from the education welfare officers and the site warden indicating possible child neglect were not addressed. The Serious Case Review Panel commented that it was 'as if the situation had been re-defined into something that was easier to deal with' while the social worker involved told the Review that the meeting was satisfactory and her 'priority was to engage [the father] and enable him to work with agencies rather than confront him and have a further risk of disengagement and possible flight' (Southampton Local Safeguarding Children Board, 2014, para.7.2.11). Although two social workers later visited the Travellers' site they only spoke to the father and two of his daughters in his presence in the site office and did not gain access to the family caravan. Thereafter the case was closed by Children's Social Care.

The case was eventually re-opened in response to multiple concerns expressed by neighbours and residents of the site that the father was grossly neglecting his children, and a joint visit was made by two social workers accompanied by police officers. A group of Travellers gathered round the family's caravan which, like others on the site, was surrounded by a fence forming a compound, and the situation became increasingly hostile. The site residents refused to permit the social workers and police to enter the compound through the compound gate. After some negotiation they permitted the social

▶

◄

workers to climb the fence and enter the caravan. The Serious Case Review described this as community members demonstrating that they were in charge. The social workers duly climbed the fence and found that 'there was no bedding, no clothes and no toys...The walls were covered in faeces and urine' (Southampton Local Safeguarding Children Board, 2014, para.7.2.20). However, the situation became 'increasingly volatile, with residents threatening to start fires and, in any way they could, prevent the removal of the children – even though [the father] asked the social workers to take them into care' (Southampton Local Safeguarding Children Board, 2014, para.7.2.20).

In the circumstances the police refused to exercise their statutory powers to temporarily remove the children from their home and instead the social workers negotiated with their aunt and another resident to take care of the children on the Travellers' site. Although social workers recognised this was not necessarily in the best interests of the children, it was thought to be an acceptable compromise given the hostile circumstances in which practitioners found themselves and the unwillingness of the police to intervene at the time. The eventual removal of the children from the Travellers' site occurred only after they had made disclosures of sexual abuse by their father shortly thereafter. This was only achieved when police planned their intervention and involved a number of different teams including officers trained to deal with volatile situations. An armed response unit was also in attendance at the site. According to the Serious Case Review police then went in and removed the children safely from the site without community tensions arising.

The female social worker was confronted by members of the community who were clearly intent on running her off the Travellers' site by intimidating her with dogs and their belligerence. It seems likely that this subsequently influenced the redefining of the problem from the more serious one of child abuse and neglect to a matter of the children's education and inadequate supervision. Social workers subsequently settled for a meeting with a few of the children in the presence of the father in the site office and did not insist on visiting the family home. This may also be an example of *flight* by the practitioner, because trying to access the caravan had previously proved so fraught due to opposition from some members of the local ethnic community. Maintaining some semblance of friendly cooperation with the father then became the aim of subsequent interactions rather than pursuing actions, in the face of parental and community opposition, to protect children from maltreatment. This inadequate engagement with family and community culminated in the premature closure of the case at this point.

Here was a paradoxical situation whereby even though the father had agreed to the removal of his children into public care on a voluntary basis, members of the local community appeared determined to thwart this child protection intervention. There was clearly hostility towards the police and social workers and a sense that they were violating community territory and breaching both the community's physical and social boundaries. The ostensibly absurd insistence by community members that the social workers climb over the fence rather than walk through the gate to access the family's compound, was from the community's perspective an exercise in reasserting control in a situation where *'strangers'* were apparently doing as they pleased in their territory. It may also have been a performance of masculinity as men on the Traveller site sought to demonstrate their ability to protect their families from outside interference and prevent Traveller children from being taken away by the authorities. In the end overwhelming force had to be deployed to remove the children from the family's caravan on the site. For some ethnic communities where there is a collective memory of families being systematically separated, as during slavery or the compelled removal of children from first nation peoples in North America and Australia, then social work intervention can precipitation intense community-level responses.

Preserving community relations

In Southampton Local Safeguarding Children Board (2014), aside from the hostility encountered from other residents on the Travellers' site, some social workers were reluctant to remove the children for other reasons. At a strategy meeting it was agreed that the children now known to be suffering neglect would move to the aunt's caravan on the same Traveller's site, despite the fact that she had two children of her own and there were seven additional children to be accommodated. Her caravan had not been seen by social workers, nor were any of the children seen or interviewed to ascertain their wishes and feelings. While social workers accepted that the threshold for the children's removal had been met they nevertheless decided not to remove them, instead designating them Children in Need. Explaining this paradoxical decision, the Serious Case Review observed that practitioners sought arrangements which permitted the children to be cared for by their family and community. They decided that 'it was appropriate to think about finding a solution that would retain the children within their cultural and family network, but this assumed inappropriate proportions: *"Engagement with the community became the…imperative rather than safeguarding the children"'* Southampton Local Safeguarding Children Board (2014, para.7.2.26).

Such conclusions indicate how professional concerns about preserving good community relations can sometimes supersede the pursuit of children's best interests. They echo the findings of Jay's (2014) independent report into the organised sexual exploitation of girls. Children's Social Care and the police came under heavy criticism for failing to intervene in cases of child sexual exploitation in a town in Northern England, where it was suspected that this was being perpetrated by men of Pakistani heritage. Large numbers of professionals and their managers baulked at taking action for fear of creating tensions between the White ethnic majority population and the local Pakistani ethnic community. They were also frightened of being perceived as racist. Instead incidents were minimised, disregarded or given insufficient priority. As a result it is estimated that 1,400 children were sexually abused over a 15-year period in the area (Jay, 2014). These kinds of inhibited and misdirected professional responses influenced by community relations considerations can plainly leave children and young people exposed to further maltreatment. Such responses are nevertheless recognitions that sections of some local minority communities are influenced by *collectivist* rather than *individualist* cultural norms. Hence some people may feel, ashamed, aggrieved or worried by actions taken against others from their own ethnic or faith background. At the same time, the disproportionate and sensationalist media coverage of the sexual exploitation of girls by men of Pakistani heritage, compared to those from the White ethnic majority, feeds racism and Islamophobia. It can also skew the perceptions of social workers as they intervene with children and families from South Asian backgrounds. Practitioners must therefore develop their *cultural awareness* through engaging in reflexive processes to identify when fear of being perceived as racist; worry about damaging community relations; or their own negative stereotypes are leading to under- or over-involvement in the lives of families from racial or ethnic minority communities.

Cultural respect and relativism in work with minority communities

Barn et al. (1997) reveal the reluctance of some social workers to intervene to protect children because they believe that the abusive behaviour towards them is sanctioned by their culture and wider ethnic community. The emphasis on anti-oppressive theory, working respectfully with diversity and standards of professional practice can make this a confusing area for practitioners. They are required to adopt a non-judgemental approach to other cultures and faiths, while retaining professional judgement regarding the level of risk posed to children, particularly when caregivers and/or community members claim that their childcare practices are informed by culture or religion (Payne, 2014; Thompson, 2016). Analysing the slowness of professional responses to child protection concerns regarding the White British Traveller family discussed above, Southampton Local Safeguarding Children Board (2014, para.7.2.26) agreed with the internal investigation of Children's Social Care which concluded that because social workers 'were being culturally sensitive and wishing to retain the children within their wider family and community network this gave legitimacy to the plan, when in fact they knew that it was not what was in the children's best interests at the time'. The Serious Case Review referred to this disparagingly as 'political correctness'.

Hasan (2010) contends that feelings of post-colonial guilt for the historical oppression of subject peoples around the world among White British proponents of multiculturalism, has muted their criticism of oppressive attitudes and practices within minority ethnic communities. Hasan (2010) suggests that this has resulted in an unquestioning respect for cultural and religious diversity. This hesitation to voice criticism is also motivated by the cognisance that Black and minority ethnic communities suffer a disproportionate degree of deprivation and disadvantage (Equality and Human Rights Commission, 2016). Hence there is a reluctance to exacerbate these difficulties by attacking heritages which often act as bulwarks against racism alongside the close community ties which provide an essential safety net for those in poverty. Practitioners who are genuinely anti-racist can be fearful of being accused of racism if they voice criticism of cultural traditions or religious observances, even when they are oppressive or appear to be harming children. They may sometimes retreat from expressing value judgements about standards of childcare, which parents or community members claim are based on cultural norms or religious observance (Hasan, 2010, p. 58; Laird, 2013, p. 177). Social workers in this situation are unlikely to make appropriate challenges to parents, their partners or community members regarding their attitudes and behaviours towards children and young people.

Closed or tight-knit minority communities

Norms can also operate within minority ethnic and faith communities which make it more difficult for members of those communities to engage with public agencies such as the police, health or social services. Negative reaction from the local ethnic or faith community towards those members who involve outsiders in family affairs could be further exacerbated in the presence of strong cultural norms requiring individuals to seek assistance from within the community and disdain for those taking help from without. Similarly, strong mores regarding family privacy within some minority groups can also discourage relatives from contacting public agencies with concerns relating to child maltreatment. This can present difficult dilemmas for community members and kin, particularly if some cultural norms create oppression for some social groups within the community, such as women or children. Southampton Local Safeguarding Children Board (2014, para.8.1.2) commented that the 'abuse of these [Traveller] children was easier to perpetrate and harder for the agencies to detect and prevent because of the circumstances of the family and the community they lived in. It may also have been easier for members of that community to identify the abuse and neglect, and take protective action of some sort, than for a family living in a less open community.' Assessing the community's response the Serious Case Review stated there was evidence that the children's neglect was tolerated within the community to the extent that even the aunt endeavoured to disguise how appalling their home conditions were and that only the children's disclosure of sexual abuse prompted more direct communication with the authorities. It continued:

8.1.18 When evaluating the delay before any concerns were raised by community members, the Panel was advised of the very hierarchical nature of such a community as this. Leading members of the community would not expect that government agencies would be drawn into a situation without their involvement and approval. It was stressed that within the community there would be an extremely strong pressure against involving oneself or *"interfering"* in the affairs of another family.

8.1.19 So, there were strong societal pressures against concerns being publicly raised. A corollary of that is that the concern felt by those community members who did come forward must have been extremely high for them to do so. A professional evaluating this situation with the benefit of informed advice would have better understood the depth of concern felt by some community members about the treatment of these children by their father.

This suggests that social workers need to take into consideration the cultural norms operating in sections of some minority communities which discourage the involvement of those from outside the community. Dominant markers of ethnic identity or idealised notions of culture, for instance obedience to parents, family harmony or mutual assistance, may also make it exceptionally challenging for relatives or community members to communicate their concerns to professionals. This means that whenever someone from a tight-knit community does approach Children's Social Care indicating that a child might be at risk, the possibility should be explored as to whether the information being communicated actually understates the gravity of the situation. Additionally, it needs to be recognised that the person coming forward with such information may have done so in the face of opposition from sections of their own ethnic community and at hazard of adverse consequences once it is known that he or she involved Children's Social Care.

Reflective exercise

Consider the challenges above in working within community contexts.

Have you encountered any of these challenges and if so how did you respond?

To what extent were your responses influenced by your stereotypes; fears of being racist; wanting to preserve good community relations; or hostility from members of a local racial, ethnic or faith community?

What were the implications for children and family members of your response?

How might greater *cultural awareness* and better *cultural knowledge* of a family's relationship with their local racial, ethnic or faith community have improved your practice?

Case study for practitioners

Children's Social Care receives a referral from a teacher who is the designated safeguarding lead at a local primary school. She states that several children of Pakistani heritage aged 8–9 years of age have been found to have welts and bruising on their arms and legs. On further questioning by a teacher, the children reluctantly explained that these occurred when they were hit with a stick by an imam during evening lessons at a mosque-based madrassah, also located in the area. Imagine yourself as the social worker tasked to address this child protection concern.

Before making any decisions regarding this case study, employing *cultural awareness* consider your initial reactions. What is your perception of the Pakistani community, Islam, madrassahs and the use of corporal punishment to discipline children? Try and identify the assumptions you are relying on in this process. What Anglocentric norms or common stereotypes might be influencing your view of this situation? Where might your initial reactions place you in terms of majority or minority identity statuses?

Now turn to the ASKED model. You have already addressed the first element of *cultural awareness:* now move on to consider *cultural knowledge.* What do you factually know about people of Pakistani heritage, Islam and the religious education of children, as opposed to assuming? What gaps can you identify in your knowledge? Make a list of these.

At a minimum you need to have information about cultural norms which influence relations between children and adults, the role of Islam in family life, community identification together with how mosques and madrassahs are typically organised. How might you go about finding out more regarding these aspects?

The internet is often a good starting point, but *cultural encounter* encourages practitioners to enter into mutual cross-cultural exchanges with people from minority ethnic and faith communities. These are encounters which aid the dispelling of stereotypes and help to develop more accurate understandings of minority families and their communities. If *cultural desire* is also engaged, then this could mean visiting a Pakistani community centre or madrassah, alongside other voluntary or specialist services working with this minority community. It could mean finding out more about the heritage or faith of colleagues or friends from a Pakistani and/or Muslim background. Spending time in discussion with a community worker might also be informative. Such experiences would not only support greater comprehension, but also reveal the diversity of attitudes, values and behaviours which exist in any ethnic community.

As a practitioner applying the ASKED model in this situation, you should take into consideration the following points (among others) in deciding how to respond.

Firstly, regarding Anglocentric norms, while it is illegal to use corporal punishment in schools in the UK, parents and guardians among the ethnic majority are permitted to use *'reasonable punishment'* with their children, including the use of physical force. Younger children in particular are generally expected to obey their parents or guardians. This acknowledgement can act as a counter to simply culturalising and condemning the behaviour of people from a minority, by recognising commonalities across ethnic groups.

Secondly, Anglocentric norms and the professional culture they inform, tend to direct practitioner attention towards individual family members and discrete family units, as opposed to communities of people. The professional culture of social work is also secular and lacks a spiritual dimension, so the tendency of social workers is typically to avoid engagement with faith and religious institutions. These constitute potential culture clashes in any intervention.

Developing *cultural knowledge* could reveal that mosques are run by an organising committee made up of usually prominent community members who are responsible for appointing imams and other personnel in relation to the mosque, often including those who teach in an associated madrassah. Madrassahs deliver Islamic education whilst supporting the moral development and retention of cultural heritage. They are a place for children from different mainstream schools to mix with other friends. They may provide valuable time for parents to work or undertake other important tasks. While many madrassahs have in place safeguarding procedures, some do not. A number of imams may be recent migrants from the Middle East and can lack English languages skills. As most madrassahs rely on voluntary contributions in cash and kind from the local community, they can be overcrowded places due to limited funds. While many of those responsible for appointing teachers require them to be professionally trained, others deem religious faith a more important qualification for work in a madrassah. This means that some teachers will be untrained and in overcrowded conditions likely to resort quickly to physical chastisement. *Cultural encounter* with people from the local Pakistani community might lead you to realise that while some parents agree with the imam's approach to disciplining their children, many others are unhappy about it, but find it difficult to know how to raise the issue with such an authoritative local figure or with the mosque organising committee. Understanding key power dynamics within this local Pakistani community is likely to assist in developing an effective child protection response.

This background does not justify adopting a position of cultural relativity and failing to intervene in a misguided attempt at cultural respect. Nor should it discourage practitioners from intervening so as to avoid adverse community-level reactions towards Children's Social Care. Viewed from a child-centred perspective this is clearly an instance of physical abuse and against the law. But this situation does call for a culturally sensitive approach predicated on what is known about this local ethnic community and the diversity within it.

Culturally sensitive starting points in terms of child protection responses could be engaging with members of the organising committee of the mosque and those responsible for appointing teachers or those charged with the day-to-day running of the madrassah. It could also mean approaching well-regarded organisations within the community, for example a local Pakistani community centre, and exploring routes of mediation with opinion leaders in the locality. It might involve delivering guidance around safeguarding to those responsible for running the madrassah or putting the organising committee in contact with other mosques or madrassahs which have adopted good practice around child safeguarding. It could involve coordinated engagement with a variety of stakeholders within the local ethnic community, including the involvement of parents and children. While many Children's Social Care services are under considerable resource pressures, given that the above situation could potentially generate multiple child protection concerns, engaging at community level could actually be the most efficient use of scare resource.

Conclusion

Power relationships in conjunction with collectivist norms within a local ethnic community can exert influence over the responses of families to child protection concerns. How the family, or individual members of it, are perceived by others from within their ethnic community can be important considerations as to what action to take or how to respond to social work interventions. Ethnic or faith communities are commonly a vital source of support to families from minority heritage backgrounds. Social workers need to develop a greater knowledge of these networks and resources in order to be able to link family members into them or to appreciate the role they play in family life.

It is essential that practitioners explore and understand the interacting relationships between race, ethnicity, faith and language on the one hand and living in a disadvantaged community on the other. These relationships may be further mediated by aspects of gender, sexuality and disability. Integrating a dynamic understanding of these issues into risk assessment and care planning is a vital component of culturally sensitive practice. A number of factors can inhibit social workers from intervening effectively with families from minority communities, such as cultural relativism or fear of undermining community relations. There are also considerations which can deter minority family members from approaching Children's Social Care with concerns, such as adverse reaction from their own ethnic or faith community. Practitioners need to be mindful of these factors and develop strategies through supervision, team meetings and multi-agency forums to counter them.

7

Asylum Seekers, Refugees and Recent Migrants

Introduction

This book adopts a widely used definition of migrants as 'those who enter the UK intending to stay for more than one year, "new" or "recent" migrants are those who have been in the UK for five years or less' (Petch et al., 2015, p. 2). Generally the more recently individuals and families come to live or settle in the UK the fewer rights and entitlements they have compared to British citizens. This is also affected by whether the person is from an EU country or a non-EU country; whether they first came to live in Britain before or after Brexit; or is an asylum seeker; refugee; failed asylum seeker, or other undocumented migrant. The multitude of different immigration statuses, in conjunction with correlative rights and entitlements attaching to them, adds a further layer of complexity to working with recent migrants. As most immigrant statuses attract less rights to benefits and services than for British nationals, practitioners will often be working with families with limited entitlements to health, housing, education, employment and financial provision. Although children are normally entitled to free education, they are not entitled to free school meals. Deprivation caused by immigration rules together with the isolation of family units can contribute to very difficult circumstances for families, which in turn can contribute to child maltreatment. This chapter explores approaches to effective cross-cultural social work and examines the challenges for migrant families and for the practitioners who assist them.

Superdiversity and immigration status

The European Union originally consisted of 15 nations whose citizens were all entitled to study, work and live in any member country. In May 2004, 10 new countries joined the European Union, most of them former communist countries with low wage economies. These were joined by Bulgaria and Romania in 2007 and Croatia in 2013. This meant that people from such countries could study or work in the United Kingdom when unemployment was high in their homeland or in order to obtain a higher income relative to that they could command in their country of origin. Consequently many people from other European countries live in the United Kingdom. By 2016 there were estimated to be 3.5 million people living in the UK who had been born in other EU countries (Vargas-Silva & Markaki, 2016b). Out of the 630,000 people coming to live in the UK in 2015, asylum applicants comprised just 5% of this total (Blinder, 2017). In 2015 police identified around 3,000 victims of human trafficking involved in forced labour or sexual exploitation, representing a three-fold increase on the 1,000 victims identified in 2011 (Townsend, 2016). Of those migrating to the UK in 2015 (excepting asylum seekers) 48% stated they were coming to work, 27% to study and 12% either to accompany or join a family member (Vargas-Silva & Markaki, 2016a). London Borough of Lewisham Local Safeguarding Children Board (2009) *Executive Summary: Serious Case Review 'Child J and Child L'* reflects the complexity of transnational relationships.

London Borough of Lewisham Local Safeguarding Children Board (2009) *Executive Summary: Serious Case Review 'Child J and Child L'*

This case concerned a girl born in Portugal during 2002 to a Black African father and a Black Brazilian mother. Subsequently, the father had a relationship with another woman who was also Black African and became pregnant by him. In 2005 this second mother entered the UK with the first mother's daughter, then three years old, who she claimed to be her own daughter, and within a few months gave birth to that child's half-brother. The second mother settled in London, living in substandard accommodation and appeared to have no entitlement to welfare benefits. Within the first six months of her residency the second mother presented the girl, who she described as vomiting and not eating, to health services on five different occasions. The girl was discovered to be losing weight. At nursery school she was found to be bruised and claimed to have been beaten by the second mother, who later admitted to social workers that she had been hitting the child. In August 2006 both the girl and her half-brother were made the subject of Child Protection Plans due to physical abuse and neglect. By this stage the second mother was being erroneously referred to as the girl's stepmother.

Throughout this period, while it was now known that the second mother was not the birth mother of the girl, there was little recognition by social workers of the need to

▶

◄

establish who actually held *parental responsibility* for this child. While there was agreement by Children's Social Care to complete a full assessment, arrange a family group conference and accommodate the girl, none of these plans came to fruition. For the first time in October 2006 the girl's father, who remained in Europe, was contacted by social workers. In June 2008, soon after arrangements were made by social workers to voluntarily accommodate the girl as she was being maltreated, the second mother told them that she had contacted the girl's birth mother who was coming to collect the child. This was the first time that professionals became aware that the birth mother had in fact been living in the UK throughout the period that Children's Social Services were involved with the family. The birth mother was allocated a Portuguese-speaking parent advocate, which was of great assistance during her initial contact with Children's Social Services when there were doubts regarding her identity and holding of *parental responsibility*. The girl was subsequently reunited with her mother in July 2008 and appeared to settle well with her.

The transnational nature of this family, and movement between countries by the parents, made interrogating and comprehending family organisation challenging for professionals. Not only was it important to identify who held *parental responsibility*, but given that the family was living in impoverished circumstances, it was also vital to establish what the mothers' immigration status actually was as this would determine their entitlements to welfare support and social housing provision. In an era of relatively cheap international travel and ethnic *superdiversity*, this is often a complex professional task.

Superdiversity refers not only to the multiplicity of ethnic and racial groups now living in the UK, but also to the myriad pathways, legal and illegal, into the country. These include arriving from a member state of the European Economic Area (EEA); being a migrant from a non-EU country; travelling on a work permit or a student visa; coming for the purpose of family reunification; being an asylum seeker; or coming as a refugee. These are all legal statuses. A proportion of those arriving from other countries may be illegally present in the country, such as undocumented migrants who have been smuggled into the UK; individuals who have overstayed their student, work or tourist visas; family members who due to relationship breakdowns are no longer being financially supported and would be due for deportation; and failed asylum seekers who may be evading the Border Agency. Some individuals may also have been trafficked into the country, meaning that they have been duped or coerced into coming, typically to work in the sex industry or as forced labour. Such workers are commonly threatened; subject to violence; underpaid; their movements restricted; and their identity papers withheld from them (Skrivankova, 2014). The text box below lists the different possible immigration statuses of family members.

Immigration statuses

- British or Irish citizen
- EEA/EU citizen registered pre-Brexit
- EEA/EU citizen arriving post-Brexit
- Family member of EEA/EU citizen
- Non-EEA/EU citizen
- Refugee
- Asylum seeker
- Refused asylum seeker
- Visa holder (e.g. student or tourist visa)
- Overstayer (e.g. tourist visa has expired)
- Unlawful activity (e.g. working on a student visa)
- Limited *leave to remain* (restricted length of residence in UK)
- Relative joining family in UK under family reunification rules
- Trafficked individuals
- Undocumented migrant

These diverse immigration statuses attract different rights and entitlements, which may vary even between people of the same broad migration status as rules regarding residency, duration of employment or period of study are applied to eligibility for public services and welfare benefits. The miscellany and complexity of immigration statuses inevitably creates confusion around eligibility, making it exceptionally difficult for social workers to assess the entitlements of individual family members. Immigration status has fundamental consequences for a family's access to housing, health, education and social services alongside their rights to welfare benefits and family reunification if kin are living in another country. The impact of differential rights to material and financial support has profound implications for safeguarding children and accounts for why a disproportionate number of migrants are represented in Serious Case Reviews.

These entitlements constantly change as, over time, governments tend to narrow the eligibility for access to public services, benefits and family reunification for both documented and undocumented migrants. Very broadly, refugees have similar rights to British citizens with the exception of family reunification. Citizens of member countries of the European Economic

Area have a set of differential rights related to whether they are working, unemployed or studying, in conjunction with their length of residency in the UK. These range from rights similar to those of British citizens to having *no recourse to public funds*, which excludes certain categories of people from access to public funds by virtue of their immigration status. Workers and students from outside the European Economic Area generally have fewer rights regarding access to public services, welfare benefits and family reunification than those from within it. But again these rights vary depending on whether the person is in work or out of work, and how long they have lived in the UK. Family members born and living abroad joining British citizens, such as EEA nationals or a documented migrant from outside the EEA, will often have fewer entitlements than their British relative habitually resident in the UK. Such is the complexity of immigration statuses and eligibility, that migrants themselves may be unaware of their entitlements to public service provision and welfare benefits resulting in neither accessing nor claiming them. Conversely, even when recent migrants are entitled to similar services and benefits as British citizens, for example those granted refugee status, they may be unable to access them due to delay in processing their new immigration status. Such difficulties are illustrated in the next case study.

Tri-borough Local Safeguarding Children Board (2015) *Serious Case Review Sofia*

The mother was a White European national who probably first arrived in the UK in 2006. She was fluent in both spoken and written English. Soon after her arrival she began a relationship and moved into the flat of her partner, but apparently neither worked nor claimed benefits. She became pregnant by a man of Indian Hindu heritage in 2012 who was in the country on a student visa, which expired that same year. At this point her relationship with her partner broke down and she was compelled to leave the flat in which she had been living. Thereafter she had no permanent address. The mother had also been diagnosed with breast cancer and told all the professionals she came into contact with that the father had returned to his homeland. Although the mother was referred to a public housing agency to arrange accommodation for her, because she was from another European country but was not in employment, or part of a household where someone was working, or a self-funded student, she was ineligible for state assistance with housing. Moreover because she had not worked, she was not entitled to any welfare benefits. Many professionals she came into contact with assumed she was not entitled to any assistance from public funds. This was not in fact the case, but the use of the expression '*not eligible for public funds*' on documentation meant that often practitioners simply assumed she had no access to financial support. Consequently the mother become street homeless when seven months pregnant and after the birth of her daughter Sofia moved between multiple unsuitable properties for infants.

The Serious Case Review acknowledged that working with European nationals adds an additional level of complexity to the legislative framework under which social workers practise. This is particularly so in relation to benefit entitlement of EU citizens. In this instance while the mother was not entitled to any welfare benefit, had she been advised to make herself available for work, she might have been so entitled. Also limited financial support (in the form of voluntary accommodation of the infant or funds to assist in maintaining her) could have been made available to her by Adult Services under the National Assistance Act 1948 on the grounds of destitution, or under the Children Act 1989 if Sofia had been assessed as a child in need. These options are designed to be short term and deployed in an emergency as they involve drawing on very limited public budgets. The Serious Case Review found that because documentation described the mother as having *no recourse to public funds* little attempt was made to actually financially support her. It also recognised that this is an area of such complexity that only specialists are likely to be able to assess the welfare entitlement of an individual given their particular circumstances. Similarly, as a foreign national ineligible for welfare benefits, homeless and destitute and placing the child at risk due to poverty, it was also difficult for professionals to be clear as to what public services mother and child were entitled to access. In the light of these findings this Serious Case Review argued that social workers should be able to access specialist advice for themselves and to refer families on for such advice in this area.

Poverty

Through a combination of discrimination (often heightened towards recent migrants), lower wages in their country of origin or desperation if ineligible for welfare benefits, many migrants work in casual, insecure and low-paid work found predominantly in the hospitality, construction, food processing, agricultural, domestic and social care sectors. They often take up employment significantly below the level of their actual skills and qualifications (Anderson et al., 2006). Commonly migrants in these situations hold down several low-wage jobs simultaneously, sometimes combining night shifts with daytime employment. Some may have access to material benefits, for example living in tied, cheap or free accommodation, such as agricultural workers living in a caravan on a farm or a waitress in a restaurant receiving gratis meals. Many workers may not be able to avail themselves of annual leave or sick pay. For those living in the UK as undocumented migrants, refused asylum seekers, with no right of residence and often liable to deportation, taking any job regardless of how poor the working environment or remuneration from employers not asking too many questions, may be the only option to avoid destitution. This leaves them vulnerable to exploitation, such as pay well below the minimum wage, sexual harassment and physical assault. For others, while their initial immigration status was legal, perhaps coming on a student visa, their decision to work rather than study or to stay on in the UK after the expiry of their visa has made their activity illegal (Anderson et al., 2006). The increasing requirements placed upon property owners, health providers and educational institutions by successive British governments to check the immigration status of tenants, patients and students respectively, has increased the avenues of surveillance and hence the efforts by those living illegally in the UK to hide their presence by avoiding public services.

For many recent migrants their willingness to accept poorer pay and working conditions in the UK because these are still better than those in their country of origin can leave them living in impoverished circumstances in a higher cost of living economy. For others, the linkage of immigration status to public provision and welfare benefits, alongside progressively restrictive eligibility criteria has resulted in many categories of migrants being excluded from state services and funds. It is not surprising therefore to find that recent migrants are over-represented among those who are destitute in the UK. In their study Fitzpatrick et al. (2016, Table 1) found that migrants from the EEA were 1.5 times more likely to be destitute than a British-born citizen, while those from Africa or the Middle East were 2.2 times more liable to be destitute. Among recent migrants who were found to be destitute, 38% were, or had been, asylum seekers, while 33% were EEA nationals. Although the majority of asylum seekers reporting destitution were awaiting a decision on their claim, or their status was unclear, notably over one quarter had actually been granted *leave to remain*. It is evident from these statistics that those experiencing destitution in the UK are over-represented among asylum seekers and migrants from Africa, the Middle East and EEA member states.

Reflective exercise

Consider some of the ethnic and racial minority families you have worked with living in poverty.

How did the family's poverty intersect with aspects of race, ethnicity, religion, English language ability and immigration status?

What were the implications of this for safeguarding children?

To what extent did social work intervention or services address these intersecting aspects of family life?

What else could have been done to address these intersectional aspects?

Fitzpatrick et al. (2016, pp. 35–36) also examined the triggers which tipped different categories of migrants into destitution. For EEA nationals it was commonly restricted access to housing benefit on ceasing to be in work. Among many asylum seekers it was a combination of not being permitted to work, the low level of cash benefit received from the Border Agency while awaiting a decision on their claim, and mandatory dispersal to other parts of the UK resulting in isolation from potential support social networks. For those granted refugee status destitution was often precipitated by the abrupt withdrawal of housing and financial support by the Border Agency before they could arrange alternative accommodation or find employment. Conversely, for some migrants, family reunification meant a spouse and children living off a single wage.

For all categories of recent migrants their lack of knowledge regarding eligibility criteria and the availability of assistance from government and non-government agencies meant an inability to successfully navigate the system to access this. These disadvantages are in addition to the factors affecting destitution for British citizens, which include poor health; unemployment; debt; low benefits, their reduction or withdrawal; relationship breakdown; and the relatively high cost of living (Fitzpatrick et al., 2016, pp. 29–35). Tri-borough Local Safeguarding Children Board (2015) discussed earlier in this chapter concerned a recent migrant mother who was a White EU national entitled to reside and work in the UK. But as she was not in work, nor registered as available for work, she was not eligible for welfare benefits and there was confusion regarding her entitlement for other forms of financial or material assistance from Children's Social Care. The next excerpt from the case examines the implications of this for the care of her baby Sofia, while also illustrating how different immigration statuses among family members can profoundly affect parental behaviours.

Tri-borough Local Safeguarding Children Board (2015) *Serious Case Review Sofia* **[continued]**

After the birth of baby Sofia in 2012 the mother was discharged from hospital to bed and breakfast accommodation identified by social workers, while health and social services worked closely together to provide the mother with clothes and equipment for the baby as she had few possessions. Given the destitute situation of the mother she was advised to return to her country of origin, where it was known she would be entitled to welfare benefits. During this period Children's Social Care also contacted the maternal grandmother in the country of origin and the relevant consulate, confirming that arrangements could be made for the repatriation of mother and baby. The mother refused this offer, stating that she did not wish to leave the UK.

▶

◀

Within nine days of being placed in the bed and breakfast accommodation by Children's Social Care and without notice to any agency, both mother and baby left it. As there had been no child protection concerns at the time there was no concerted attempt to trace the family. She later registered with a general practitioner in another area of London and a health visitor then became concerned about the child's low weight and the mother's lack of income. While a referral was made to Children's Social Care the mother evaded meetings with the social worker and it became clear at this juncture that she was unwilling to cooperate with either the health visitor or social worker. After the possibility of using police powers was raised, the mother agreed to the baby being medically examined. The examining paediatrician concluded that there were no problems with the baby's health and this resulted in child protection concerns being dropped, despite the risks posed by the mother's destitution, transient lifestyle and the lack of material provision for the baby including such basic things as feeding bottles. After this episode the mother again abruptly left her accommodation with her baby and as social workers could not trace her the case was closed. The family was later identified again by a health visitor and attempts were made to make contact with the mother who avoided these. As a result is was not known where Sofia and her mother were living between December 2012 and October 2013, during which time there was no contact by health or social care professionals.

Then in October 2013 the mother contacted emergency services. When paramedics arrived they found Sofia unconscious with evidence of vomiting. She was pronounced dead soon after admission to hospital. The autopsy revealed that the child had asphyxiated on food, was significantly underweight for her age and had a number of historic untreated injuries. During the criminal investigation it transpired that since January 2012 the mother had in fact been living or in close contact with the father who was of Indian nationality on an expired student visa and who was therefore unlawfully present in the UK. It appeared that the mother had deliberately misled professionals and evaded contact with them in order to prevent detection of the father and his possible removal from the country by immigration authorities. As a result there was no contact between professionals and the father.

For most professionals involved with this family neglect meant a deliberate act of commission or omission by the parent which resulted in the child not being given shelter, medical assistance, education or emotional support. But because the mother did not appear to be deliberately depriving Sofia of necessities professionals did not treat this as a child protection case. The Serious Case Review was of the opinion that professionals gave insufficient consideration to how parental choices were impacting on the child in relation to unsuitable and transient accommodation alongside extreme poverty caused by lack of entitlement to welfare benefits. In other words there was not a sufficiently child-centred perspective on the lifestyle choices of the mother. As the Review observed, there can be an over-preoccupation with parental intention regarding neglect to the detriment of recognising the impact of parental circumstances on the child.

In this case the mother was homeless and destitute, unable to afford basic physical necessities, dependent on food from Hindu temples and unable to purchase the formula milk she needed for her baby due to her breast cancer. While the Serious Case Review commended professionals for acting quickly to provide mother and baby with material support when these needs came to their attention, it identified a lack of longer-term consideration as to how the mother's homelessness and destitution posed a child protection risk. Apparently professionals perceived the mother's strong desire to have the child and her commitment to care for it as protective factors in circumstances of extreme poverty and where poor material provision for the child was regarded as unintentional on the mother's part. This culminated in a widely shared professional view that the mother was doing her best for her child in difficult circumstances and should be supported rather than penalised through a child protection approach, particularly when no physical signs of abuse had been detected during the medical examination. Generally in the UK destitution and homelessness are not considered child protection issues unless combined with evidence of child maltreatment, mental illness, domestic violence or addiction. As Horwath (2007) suggests, most definitions of neglect include notions of intentionality on the part of parents. However, Dubowitz et al. (2005) argue that regardless of the reasons for the neglect, it is the impact on the child which should be prioritised in establishing whether neglect is occurring. Tri-borough Local Safeguarding Children Board, 2015, para.4.9.4) summarised the implications:

> This review has shown that professionals may fail to acknowledge the impact of poverty and homelessness on children because they judge risk from the perspective of the intention and motivations of the parent, rather than the experience of the child. This means that apparently unintentional destitution is not considered a safeguarding issue and children may continue to be exposed to the risks this engenders.

In addition to material deprivation, those experiencing destitution report detrimental impacts on their mental and physical health often caused by poor diet and stress; fewer social contacts; lowered social status alongside feelings of shame and stigmatisation which increased isolation; greater strain and conflict in family relationships; guilt due to reliance on family members for assistance; and, among many migrant parents, guilt about exposing their children to impoverished circumstances (Fitzpatrick et al., 2016, pp. 44–48). Precisely because of the greater likelihood of their ineligibility for public services or welfare benefits, destitute migrants are less likely to be claiming welfare benefits than British citizens. Migrants are more likely to rely on aid from friends rather than parents or other relatives compared to their British counterparts (Fitzpatrick et al., 2016, p. 49). Recent migrants, like others in severe poverty, also engage in self-help strategies which involve severe household economising, which can detrimentally affect *parental capacity*.

Housing and homelessness

Persistently high house prices in the United Kingdom have priced out large sections of the British population, who are unable to afford a mortgage and are instead reliant on renting a house or flat from the private sector. The sale of a large proportion of government-owned social housing that commenced in the 1980s has also meant that many more people on low incomes are now entering the private rental market than in the past. Taken together, these pressures force up the price of renting in many areas of the UK and leave recent migrants accessing poorer, cheaper and often substandard housing (Perry, 2012). This is because often they do not have savings for a deposit; are seeking to drastically reduce housing costs; may have poor English language skills; or possess little knowledge of the rental housing market or tenancy contracts. Conversely, many landlords will not rent to people without British citizenship or evidence of their *leave to remain* in the UK (Perry, 2012). Other property owners may refuse to rent to recent migrants due to racism or prejudice.

As a consequence recent migrants and refugees commonly live in the least desirable properties in the most disadvantaged areas. As private organisations are contracted to provide accommodation to asylum seekers at the lowest possible cost, they too can also be found in inadequate dwellings. Many recent migrants live in overcrowded multiple occupation dwellings and sometimes sleep in shifts where space is limited. Some are accommodated in dilapidated unfit properties, with inadequate facilities, little privacy and without a tenancy agreement. For those at this bottom end of the rental market, exploitive landlords may fail to maintain the property and may move tenants from one property to another, or evict at short notice. Many recent migrants are unwilling to complain about their housing conditions, particularly if the accommodation is tied to their employment (Robinson et al., 2007; Joseph Rowntree Foundation, 2013). Nevertheless it is important to recognise that the longer new migrants remain in the UK, particularly if they work, they accumulate more rights and knowledge of the housing and rental sector which often enables them to access improved properties in better locations (Robinson et al., 2007).

While many in the private rented sector are subject to circumstances which may require them to move between properties, recent migrants, asylum seekers and refugees are particularly vulnerable to the forces of mobility. This is due to the greater likelihood of holding an insecure tenancy; living in a high-crime area; family breakdown which often leaves separated foreign spouses or civil partners with fewer rights to vital services and benefits than those of British citizens; family reunification; a variation in immigration status; change of intention to stay or purpose of stay; loss of tied accommodation on losing a job; and racial harassment or discrimination (Robinson et al., 2007). As a result a disproportionately large number of recent migrants, asylum seekers and refugees move frequently between short-term forms of accommodation. Robinson et al. (2007) noted that while many do eventually obtain secure accommodation, levels of housing mobility among this social group remain around twice the national average.

The precarious incomes and disadvantageous immigration status of many recent migrants also exposes them to an increased risk of homelessness. Foreign nationals accounted for 19% of all people accepted as *statutory homeless* in the fourth quarter of 2016, according to government statistics and of these just under half were nationals from EEA countries (Department for Communities and Local Government, 2017). Many recent migrants or refused asylum seekers who are homeless rely on the generosity of kin or members of their ethnic community to provide temporary, often overcrowded accommodation. The less fortunate may sleep in places of worship or squats. Others may resort to sheds or shipping containers sometimes rented from unprincipled property owners, especially to those who are undocumented or unlawfully present in the UK. Indeed, those unlawfully present may only be able to access temporary accommodation at any point in time or may move frequently to avoid detection by the authorities.

These consequences are evident in Tri-borough Local Safeguarding Children Board (2015), discussed above, in which a pregnant migrant mother was initially street homeless, although she found short-term accommodation after her baby's birth. It was later discovered that at the time of the infant's death the family was living in privately rented bed and breakfast accommodation unsuitable for a child and where there was no equipment or toys for her. During Sofia's short life her parents had moved between accommodation in seven different local government areas, making it extremely difficult for Children's Social Care and Health Services to track such a mobile family. While this was partly attributable to avoiding the authorities (as the father was unlawfully present in the UK) it was also a function of the family's impoverishment and inability to meet the costs of adequate housing.

Support services for migrants

Funding cutbacks have resulted in the degrading of public services targeted at recent migrants and asylum seekers, leading to increased hardship among these groups. This has paralleled a gradual reduction of entitlement to public services and welfare benefits granted to recent migrants and asylum seekers (Petch et al., 2015, pp. 22–23). Additionally, there is a conflict between immigration legislation determined by central government designed to exclude adult migrants or asylum seekers from public support and statutory obligations placed upon local government Children's Social Care departments to offer assistance to destitute children. Section 17 of the Children Act 1989 places a duty on local government to 'safeguard and promote the welfare of children within their area who are in need', which is legally defined as a child who is disabled or unlikely to achieve or maintain a reasonable standard of health and development or whose health or development will be significantly impaired without the provision of services. This statute also requires Children's Social Care to maintain the family unit, and assistance should be provided on this basis. In most, but not all, circumstances section 17 of the Children Act 1989 can be used to support children who are destitute where this imperils their health or development, through the provision of accommodation or subsistence support, where their parents' immigration status means they have restricted access to welfare benefits or *no recourse to public funds*. However, Children's Social Care can refuse assistance where a family is unlawfully present in the United Kingdom and refusing section 17 does not infringe their human rights.

Price and Spencer (2015) noted that the increasing trend evident in Border Agency decisions towards granting *leave to remain*, but with *no recourse to public funds* meant that a rising number of destitute families were seeking this type of assistance. While section 17 was envisaged to provide temporary assistance, the nature of parents or carers with *no recourse to public funds* presents Children's Social Care with a permanent rather than a transitory crisis in a family's resources, particularly when parents unlawfully present in the UK are unwilling to return to their country of origin. Many such parents have a strong desire to ensure that their children grow up in the UK despite suffering deprivation themselves (Price & Spencer, 2015). Concomitantly, Children's Social Care has experienced substantial cuts to its funding since 2010. As a consequence, the threshold for a case to be designated *child in need* has risen, thus making it more difficult for migrant families to access this kind of support. Social workers report using section 17 for emergency situations, rather than ongoing support, and rely on the voluntary sector to provide continuing assistance (Petch, 2016). Furthermore, while the children of parents who have *no recourse to public funds* are still entitled to receive an education, they are not entitled to free school meals. This again places additional financial strain on Children's Social Care. Children of recent migrants or refused asylum seekers also have a right of access to primary and secondary health care, depending on their immigration status, but some parents may be liable to pay for their family's non-emergency treatment.

Due to both the funding restraints within the public sector and the exclusion of many categories of migrants from some kinds of state assistance, high numbers of migrants are reliant on small-scale voluntary-sector, faith-based and community organisations. These usually offer a mixture of legal advice, advocacy, material assistance, English language support, cultural events, leisure activities, liaison with public services and signposting to other agencies. For example in Tri-borough Local Safeguarding Children Board (2015) the migrant mother from an EU country and the Indian Hindu father who had overstayed his student visa, as parents without recourse to public funds, relied on free food from Hindu temples. Indeed many religions such as Islam, Buddhism, Hinduism, Sikhism and Christianity promote charitable giving and characterise assisting the needy as virtuous (Grant, 2009; Singer, 2008; Weller et al., 2017). Many faith-based organisations depend upon a large number of unpaid and usually unqualified workers who devote their time out of spiritual and humanitarian concern. Consequently, the often informal nature of such organisations, combined with their dependence on voluntary support and unpredictable funding, means that many are short-lived or cannot cater for the needs of those making demands on them. Moreover, such organisations have often specialised in provision for refugees and asylum seekers, with less support available for other categories of migrants (Dwyer & Brown, 2005; Petch, 2016). While charitable organisations can legally assist recent migrants with *no recourse to public funds*, such as failed asylum seekers and unlawfully present migrants, confusion around the legality of providing assistance to these groups has resulted in reduced services and support to them (Petch et al., 2015).

Precisely because of restricted access to public services and welfare benefits due to immigration status, combined with deep budget cuts to vital services and funds, recent migrants, refugees, asylum seekers and undocumented migrants are heavily reliant on extended family and social networks of friends, acquaintances, co-nationals and co-religionists, sometimes involving complex chains of contacts. Such people can offer mutual assistance, direct material aid, advocacy, or provide information about or facilitate access to accommodation, employment opportunities and sources of assistance (Robinson et al., 2007; Laird, 2008, pp. 147–48). For this reason the location of housing for recently arrived migrants can be crucial to enabling them to network with individuals from their own ethnic or faith backgrounds who are most likely to be sympathetic to their plight in a situation where many foreign nationals face racism and bigotry from sections of the British population. Robinson et al. (2007) noted that many recent migrants had developed their own informal, often ethnically differentiated, networks of support and disengaged almost entirely from formal service provision whether by public, private or voluntary organisations. Often these informal means of accessing accommodation and employment did not require recent migrants to produce or sign formal documentation, but were based on mutual trust, albeit that these could nevertheless sometimes be exploitative relationships.

Reflective exercise

Consider your own practice in relation to recent migrants.

To what extent do you explore and assess the coping strategies and support systems of migrant families?

How could you improve your practice to take greater account of this aspect of migrant families?

What strategies could you use to find out what further assistance and support are available to recent migrants?

Family reunification and transnational families

In 2011 family route migrants made up around 17% of all non-EU migration to the UK. Of these 83% were adults joining partners or spouses, the majority of whom were women. Government figures for the year ending September 2017 show similar trends. Children joining parents already resident in the UK account for 6% of the total and thus a small, though growing, category of family route migration (Oliver & Jayaweera, 2013, p. 29; Office for National Statistics, 2018). There exists a continuum of rights to family reunion across migrant categories, ranging from none for asylum seekers to the same entitlements as British citizens for permanent residents (non-British citizens entitled to remain indefinitely in the UK). Even when there is an entitlement to family reunion in principle, this is often subject to further eligibility criteria; a British citizen or permanent resident, known as a *sponsor* must meet a minimum income level set by the government in order to demonstrate that they can maintain their overseas spouse or partner, who under immigration rules will have *no recourse to public funds* during a probationary period in the UK, presently set at five years. These additional eligibility criteria have increased over time, making it more difficult for those entitled to live and work in the UK to be joined by other members of their family. When they are joined by a family member immigration rules often restrict their access to services or benefits. Generally migrants coming via the family route can access compulsory education, health care and employment, but are more restricted in relation to tertiary education, social housing and welfare benefits. Even when family migrants are entitled to benefits or services, bureaucratic delays; shortages in support service; cultural or language barriers; complexity of regulations; and lack of knowledge about the system make for inferior access (Oliver & Jayaweera, 2013, pp. 52–63).

Most of those joining spouses or partners in the UK are arriving to accommodation provided by their British partner. Among those of Pakistani ethnicity 90% stayed with their in-laws or in a property owned by their spouse or family member. Commonly this provided a stable place of residence, particularly in comparison to other categories of migrants (Robinson et al., 2007, p. 14). Nevertheless many family migrants find themselves in privately rented substandard overcrowded accommodation with exposure to racial harassment (Oliver & Jayaweera, 2013). While adult family members joining their partners in the UK are generally permitted to enter the labour market, cultural norms around women entering the workforce, restricted access to child-related benefits and discrimination against foreign nationals can result in such migrants either being unable to work or to earn an income commensurate with their qualifications and employment experience (Oliver & Jayaweera, 2013).

Recent migrants coming to the UK to join a spouse or partner can be forced to leave their home for similar reasons to vulnerable British citizens, such as domestic violence, mental health problems, racial harassment, debt, overcrowding and family breakdown (Robinson et al., 2007, p. 35). For many non-British partners with *no recourse to public funds*, particularly if they have children, being compelled to leave a family home can expose them to homelessness and destitution. Family migrants who leave a spouse or partner due to domestic violence may be exempted from the *no recourse to public funds* provision under the *'destitution domestic violence concession'*, but in practice it may be difficult to prove that this was their reason for leaving the family home. Even if this concession is made, it only grants the affected partner *limited leave to remain* in the UK, which may be as little as three months although during this period the affected partner may make an application for *indefinite leave to remain* in the UK. Some categories of migrants do not qualify for this exemption, such as those joining someone in the UK on a student visa. As a consequence partners from abroad may be exposed to higher levels of violence or exploitation in situations where leaving an abusive British citizen or permanent resident would result in their destitution or deportation (Oliver & Jayaweera, 2013). These considerations appear to have influenced the decision of the Somali mother in Lambeth Safeguarding Children Board (2014) *Serious Case Review Child H*. She joined her Somali husband in the UK under family unification. Due to constant and severe domestic violence perpetrated by him, the pregnant mother was placed in a women's refuge by social workers. Soon after her baby's birth she returned to live with her husband and father of the child and subsequently denied that domestic violence occurred.

The financial and material resources available to a migrant family can vary widely when one or both parents are subject to immigration control resulting in different legal rights and entitlements. As a consequence some families may have low incomes and little recourse to services, while in others working adults may be focused on cutting costs in order to accumulate sufficient savings and eventually return to their homeland. Many recent family migrants, but most particularly men, may be remitting money back to relatives in their country of origin, especially if they funded that individual's travel to the UK. Alternatively they may be remitting money back to be invested on their behalf in the expectation of eventual return to their country of origin. In some societies found in Africa and South Asia there can be strong expectations that men financially support members of the wider family. Sometimes these obligations can be a source of tension for couples or create financial strain for families living in the UK (Higazi, 2005; Lindley, 2005; Laird, 2008; Charsley et al., 2016).

Many recent migrants to the UK experience dislocation from family and sometimes loss of contact with kin in their country of origin, particularly if they have fled war or persecution. This can mean fragmentation of both the nuclear and extended family, with parents and children split between countries or only a couple and their children living in the UK with the rest of their kin permanently living in other countries. Inevitably for some families this leaves them with few or no relatives in the UK to turn to for support (Laird, 2008). Research shows that when parents leave their children in the country of origin, even if later they are reunited, this can lead to tensions, either because the parent has missed out on crucial stages of the child's development or through recrimination from the child due to the parent's absence (Mazzucato & Schans, 2011). This is evident in Surrey Safeguarding Children Board (2014) *Overview Report on the Serious Case Review Relating to: Young Person: Hiers.*

Surrey Safeguarding Children Board (2014) *Overview Report on the Serious Case Review Relating to: Young Person: Hiers*

The mother arrived in the UK from China in 2008, having left her son in the care of his father to complete primary education in his home country. In 2010 the young person, then aged 14 years, joined his mother in the UK and lived with her in a bedsit in a house of multiple tenants. Although on arrival the young person had little English, through the support of the school he developed a degree of language competence in English and began to do well academically. He was known to enjoy school and worked hard. In 2013 the mother needed to return to China for one month and asked her son to accompany her. He refused and also turned down the offer to stay with a family friend living nearby. Consequently, the mother arranged for the landlord and some other tenants to look in on the young person, leaving him enough money to cover food and expenses. Soon after the mother's departure to China police forced an entry to the family's bedsit and found the young person dead, having committed suicide.

In this case it appeared that the prolonged separation of mother and son had contributed to the mother's lack of insight into her child's state of mind, while the son – having a less strong and secure bond with her – refused to accompany her back to China. As recent migrants, mother and son were isolated from other family members and instead relied on friends and ultimately just their landlord, to take care of the son during the mother's temporary return to China. In this case when the young person was reported to Children's Social Services as home alone, social workers relied on making telephone calls to mother and landlord to confirm that he was provisioned for the duration of his mother's absence. Consequently there was no exploration by practitioners of the nature of the relationship between mother and son.

For other recent migrants, cultural norms and information and communication technology encourages frequent contact with kin remaining in the country of origin. Indeed for some families their kinship networks can be extensive and transnational, with regular interactions between family members, including numerous visits and stays by family members from abroad. These exchanges by telephone, email, social media and face-to-face visits may provide and facilitate vital emotional, social, material and financial support. Consequently what occurs within the nuclear family unit may be of concern to apparently quite distant relatives from an Anglocentric perspective (Laird, 2008).

Reflective exercise

Consider your practice in relation to recent migrants.

How did the immigration status of different family members affect power dynamics within the family?

How have you endeavoured to address power dynamics which adversely affect the welfare or safety of children?

Given the additional knowledge from this chapter how might you improve your practice in this area?

Asylum seekers and refugees

Asylum seekers are individuals escaping war or persecution in their country of origin who apply under the international Refugee Convention 1951 to the government of a safer country for asylum. If their application is successful this results in their being granted humanitarian protection or refugee status permitting them to live temporarily or permanently in that safer host country. Those in the process of seeking asylum will have fewer rights than most other categories of recent migrants and are usually entirely dependent on housing provision and basic subsistence from the UK Border Agency. This will include being told where to live under the government's dispersal policy, which seeks to distribute the resource burden of supporting asylum seekers more evenly across the country and away from concentration in south east England. Where asylum seekers have kin or friends already residing in the UK, they may live with them, receiving only subsistence support from the Border Agency. They are not permitted to work while their asylum application is pending. For those refused asylum they will have *no recourse to public funds* and are only entitled to emergency health treatment; however, children of refused asylum seekers remain eligible for free education. By definition undocumented or unlawfully present migrants do not have access to public services or welfare benefits and are liable to deportation back to their country of origin if discovered by the UK Border Agency. People who are asylum seekers or who have been granted asylum generally differ from other migrants in that they will have been forced to leave their home countries due to war, civil unrest or persecution. The experience of having to flee from their own country and becoming an asylum seeker in a host country can have profound effects, which in turn have implications for the care and safety of children as exemplified in the following two Serious Case Reviews.

Lambeth Safeguarding Children Board (2014) *Serious Case Review Child H*

A Black African Somali father escaping civil war in his country joined extended family members in London and lived in their home. His wife, two older daughters and a young son remained in Somalia. Due to the civil war the couple had been separated for many years and when the mother eventually joined the father in the UK some years later, they did not know where their two eldest children were, while their young son was known to be living with relatives in Ethiopia. Domestic violence quickly erupted in their relationship and Children's Social Care become involved. The mother gave birth to her fourth child after being seriously assaulted by the father. Thereafter the mother shortly became pregnant again and just before their fifth child was due to be born the father brought back their three-year-old son from Ethiopia. The boy could not speak any English and was observed to have injuries to his face and marks on his body when first seen by professionals after being in his father's care for several weeks. No enquiries were made by professionals at the time as to the origin of these injuries. This meant that, just two years after reunification of the parents, their family had grown to three children under four years of age. This also led to significant overcrowding in the extended family home. All the children were put on Child Protection Plans. The parents minimised the father's violence, while he was resistant to being assessed. Consequently no exploration of his history, motivation or perspective was undertaken, which also meant that the risk he posed to his children remained uncertain. Within months of bringing his son to the UK the father had killed him.

In this case the parents had been separated for many years and had doubt-less witnessed traumatic events in war-torn Somalia. Due to ineligibility for many welfare benefits, they lived in overcrowded accommodation. Additionally the father, who had not seen his son since his birth, was sud-denly reunited with him in a context where the parents already had two very young children. Brutalisation during war, multiple stressors caused by poverty and cramped conditions, and unfamiliarity with family mem-bers due to long separations culminated in the father's low thresholds for aggressive behaviour directed toward mother and child. He may have held unreasonable expectations of their behaviour, which while informed by cul-tural norms, may also have been exaggerated by trying to regain control in a situation where as a recent migrant he would have experienced considerable powerlessness. The father's quick resort to violence may have been a per-verse assertion of masculinity fuelled by anger and frustration. In this situa-tion the cultural influence of *high power distance* between males and females, parents and children may have been exaggerated by structural disadvantages and the added stressors these would have created within the family.

Leeds Safeguarding Children Board (2010) *Executive Summary of the Serious Cases Review Panel: Re Child Q*

The mother, a Black African, entered the UK in 2001 with her first child and claimed asylum. At this point she was accommodated in Leeds, a northern city, by the Border Agency, due to the government's policy of dispersing asylum seekers away from the south east of the country. In 2002 the mother was visited by a primary mental health care worker who assessed her as being anxious and low in mood due to isolation from other people of her ethnic and cultural background. Although the mother was invited to further appointments in relation to her mental health, she did not attend. This began a pattern of seeking support from services when she felt angry, suffered persistent headaches and was forgetful, attributed by her to witnessing traumatic events prior to arrival in the UK, but then not engaging with mental health services. By 2002 the mother had begun a relationship with a man, also Black African, who first came to the UK in 1996. Between 2002 and 2006 the police attended 41 domestic incidents between the couple, predominantly violence perpetrated by the mother's partner against her.

Alcohol was a known exacerbating factor in many of these altercations. A number of referrals were made to Children's Social Care due to the mother's intoxication in charge of the older sibling. In 2003 this child started nursery and made five disclosures of physical abuse by the mother or her partner, while also exhibiting challenging behaviour. The response was the development of an Individual Behaviour Plan and the involve-ment of a family resource centre. When the child's behaviour appeared to improve the case was closed to Children's Social Care. It may have been that cultural influences originating in the ethnic majority regarding the widespread acceptance and sometimes

▶

> ◀
>
> encouragement of excessive alcohol consumption meant that the threshold for treating such instances as a child protection matter was raised to an inappropriately high level.
>
> In 2006 the mother's second child was born, fathered by her partner. When the Border Agency withdrew financial support from the family, putting them at risk of eviction from their home and destitution, Children's Social Care again became involved. As a result of ongoing incidents of domestic violence family outreach workers were assigned to the family in 2008 and frequently visited the couple and their children. Not until April 2008 were both siblings made the subject of Child Protection Plans. In December 2008 aged two years of age the youngest child was admitted to hospital, were he was found to be dead on arrival having been given a lethal dose of drugs by his mother.

The Serious Case Review concluded that throughout there was a failure to engage with the mother's partner and father of her second child, despite the fact that he was a key person within the family. Indeed he was missing from most of the assessments of the family and little was ever discovered about his background. Nor was consideration given to whether or not he held *parental responsibility* for the children. In relation to the mother the Review found that attention had focused on her rather than on the children, who were never interviewed. Leeds Safeguarding Children Board (2010, para.3.2c) commented:

> When professionals had reason to doubt the veracity of the information provided by [the child's] mother they did not always challenge her but instead accepted her version of events. At times she gave the impression that she was working with agencies and in doing so displayed 'disguised compliance' which professionals failed to identify or challenge. There is some evidence that this failure to challenge [the child's] mother was exacerbated by the fact that she was a black African asylum seeker from a minority culture who was quick to point out areas of discrimination, quick to complain about other agencies, constantly demanding of agencies and whose demeanour was intimidating and testing. It appears that a lack of knowledge about [the] mother's background may have contributed to a lack of confidence in challenging her robustly…

It may have been that among some White British practitioners their stage of majority identity development impinged on their ability to challenge this Black African mother. Individuals who achieve *immersion/emersion* status can still feel guilty regarding their *White privilege* and the legacy of colonialism which sustains power relationships between Black and White peoples. While they may be less ethnocentric in their perceptions and more aware of the structural disadvantages experienced by Black families, over-identification with struggling Black parents can distract professional attention away from child-centred responses. Such feelings of guilt or shame can also undermine a practitioner's self-confidence in working with people from a diversity of racial and ethnic backgrounds and consequently inhibit them from using professional authority appropriately to challenge the attitudes or behaviours of parents from minority groups. Conversely, those from the ethnic majority who attain *autonomy* status are able to resolve acute feelings of remorse or blame and are knowledgeable regarding minority issues while being comfortable working with families from ethnically diverse heritages. They are able to use empathy effectively to comprehend different worldviews and the lived experiences of minority family members.

The mother suffered trauma in her country of origin, which was later compounded by some of her experiences of seeking asylum in the UK, particularly being geographically isolated from others sharing her cultural background. As she was not permitted to work and was wholly reliant on the Border Agency for accommodation and subsistence, which was later withdrawn, she lived in very controlled and impoverished circumstances. Anxiety as to whether she was to be granted asylum or ultimately deported back to her country of origin would have been a persistent stressor. These factors were clearly impacting on her mental health and in turn detrimentally affecting her *parental capacity*. She often felt angry and was violent towards her children, while suffering repeated physical assaults from the child's father. He was himself a recent migrant and likely to have many experiences and feelings in common with those of the mother. Both misused alcohol to manage their distress and trauma.

Ager (1999) identifies five phases of forced migration outlined below, each of which can detrimentally affect health and taken together can have a cumulative impact. It is not therefore surprising that forced migrants in the United Kingdom are known to have a much higher incidence of mental illness than the general population (Thompson, 2001), although many report that their health would be best supported by improvements in their material circumstances as opposed to psychiatric care. The application of these five phases of forced migration is explored in the follow-on case study.

Pre-Flight: Forced migrants will have been exposed to trauma through experiencing violent events during conflicts or as a result of persecution including being injured, assaulted or tortured or watching family members suffer these or witnessing their deaths. Addition trauma may be caused by family dispersal, internal displacement, going into hiding and destitution.

Flight: This may involve escaping across national borders or paying people traffickers while enduring transportation in cramped, dangerous or deprived conditions. Women and children may be particularly vulnerable to exploitation and violence during their journey. The decision to flee may mean family separation and the unknown whereabouts of other family members.

Reception: International law requires those fleeing war or persecution to make an asylum claim in the first safe country. Therefore asylum seekers may spend time in refugee camps in a neighbouring country before their claim is processed or they are permitted to continue onward to a third country which will accept them.

Settlement: On arriving in a potential host country, asylum seekers are subject to intensive vetting of their claim and may be placed in a detention facility or accommodated in often substandard housing in the community. It may take months or years for a claim to be processed, creating uncertainty and fear of deportation and exacerbating any health problems.

Resettlement: For those granted *refugee status* or *leave to remain*, hostile attitudes among receiving communities and discrimination engender fear, anger, anxiety, depression and powerlessness. For many, poverty, unemployment, inadequate accommodation, interrupted education, language barriers, disruption to traditional gender roles, loss of status and lack of clarity regarding final immigration status also contribute to poor health.

City of Salford Local Safeguarding Children Board (2007)
Executive Summary Report of the Serious Case Review Panel
into the Death of a Child: C Aged 17 Months

The case concerned a mother aged 16 years who came to the UK from China in 2005 on a student visa, although she did not attend the college at which she was to have studied. She gave birth to her first child aged 17 years and thereafter claimed asylum. She was accommodated by the Asylum Support Service, living at a number of addresses and receiving support from many different agencies. When her child was 10 months old the mother's asylum claim was rejected and at this point she removed herself from contact with agencies. Thereafter the child was placed into the care of several different carers under informal private fostering arrangements which were not registered with the authorities. In January 2007 the child was admitted to hospital in a hypothermic state and died within a few days. At the time of her entry to the UK the mother was herself a child, without anyone acting in *loco parentis*, although there is now a requirement for a local guardian to be nominated for any unaccompanied child entering the UK. Colleges are legally required to inform the Border Agency when a student from overseas does not attend their course as planned.

The Serious Case Review found that professionals had failed to consider the mother as a child in her own right who should have fallen under safeguarding procedures. This meant that there was a lack of enquiry into the possibility that she might have been trafficked in terms of her *flight* experiences. Notably there was no information available in the mother's language to explain regulations around private fostering arrangements which might have better supported *settlement* experiences. Those professionals with whom the mother came into contact also appeared poorly informed about private fostering regulations and therefore were not sufficiently curious, observant or concerned when aware of the caring arrangements made for the child. As the mother, on being refused asylum, became worried about deportation and felt unable to return to China with her child, she inevitably started to compromise his care. The lack of knowledge ascertained by professionals around the mother's *pre-flight* life and what motivated her to leave her country of origin or what her experiences were during flight and therefore what her fears were of being deported might have informed an assessment of her parenting capacity and therefore the risk she posed to her baby.

On commencing to work illegally, she left her infant son with different carers, becoming ambivalent as to whether to leave him permanently with 'friends'. Despite the mother suggesting to some professionals that she might relinquish her child for adoption or leave him in the long-term care of unrelated carers, this did not result in a referral to Children's Social Care. Such a suggestion by a parent clearly indicates that a child's welfare may be at risk and should trigger a full assessment of the parent and child. City of Salford Local Safeguarding Children Board (2007, p. 3) concluded that this 'was the child of a vulnerable young, single immigrant mother who while in the UK lacked support from her family, had been working illegally, had few friends and spoke little English'. Professionals did not consider the migrant mother as a vulnerable unaccompanied asylum seeking child herself, and instead treated her as an adult. This was compounded by failing to explore her experiences and reactions to forced migration and how this impacted on *parental capacity*. In short, lack of professional curiosity regarding the mother's *pre-flight, flight* and *settlement* experiences adversely affected their ability to recognise the potential for child neglect.

Reflective exercise

Consider your practice with forced migrants, asylum seekers and refugees.

To what extent do you explore the pre-flight, flight, reception, settlement and re-settlement experiences of different family members?

How might obtaining more information about these experiences of family members improve your practice in relation to safeguarding children?

Culture shock

When individuals are enculturated in one country or society and then move to another, they are likely to experience a degree of bewilderment and confusion as they encounter beliefs, values and social practices which are alien or incomprehensible to them from their ethnocentric viewpoint. At the same time they may experience loss of or hostility towards their own beliefs and values or diminution of the ability to pursue their customary practices. The disorientation, frustration and misunderstandings this causes gives rise to intense feelings of anxiety. *Culture shock* is therefore the stress occasioned by the challenges of simultaneously coping with the loss of a familiar, often affirming, cultural context while adjusting to a new largely unknown one. It can also be experienced within the same society as individuals move in and out of different micro-cultures; for example, someone from the pre-dominantly secular ethnic majority entering a devout Sikh community (Neuliep, 2018). *Culture shock* can involve profound challenges to identity as fundamental roles are contested or negated by the new cultural context, for example greater sex equality or non-recognition of foreign qualifications within the host society, which undermines social status and traditional male roles in a heritage culture. Ostensibly minor issues may become major stress-ors as tasks which were simple in a person's home country become arduous in the unfamiliarity of the host country. This may be accompanied by suspi-cions that members of the host population are being deliberately obstructive.

There are numerous models of *culture shock* which outline a series of phases through which the individual passes as they adjust to their new coun-try or community. Neuliep (2018, p. 416) draws on the scholarship in this area to suggest that essentially 'culture shock begins with feelings of opti-mism and even elation that eventually give way to frustration, tension and anxiety as individuals are unable to interact effectively with their new envi-ronment. As they develop strategies for resolving conflict, people begin to restore their confidence and eventually recover and reach some level of accul-turation.' It is known that this process can take up to a year, during which it consumes considerable emotional and mental energy. Where individuals are unable to resolve the crisis stage of *culture shock* or to develop effective strate-gies to manage anxiety, they may return to their home countries or retreat into their ethnic minority communities in the host country and minimise interaction with the majority ethnic community and public services. Zapf (1991) identified indicators of *culture shock*, which are listed below and are explored in the next case study involving a parent struggling to cope with *culture shock* which illustrates the impact this can have on family life.

➤ Consuming more alcohol

➤ Avoiding people

➤ Feeling intense uncontrollable emotions

➤ Preoccupation with emailing and texting family in country of origin

➤ Constantly complaining about the host culture

➤ Holding extremely negative attitudes towards members of the host population

➤ Feeling very isolated

➤ Rumination

➤ Conviction of being misunderstood by everyone, including family and friends residing in the country of origin

---

Leicester Safeguarding Children Board (2011) *Serious Case Review in Respect of the Deaths of Children Known as Child 1 and Child 2: Case 'A'*

A White British female care leaver commenced a relationship with a man who was Muslim from a Middle East country who had entered the UK claiming asylum that same year. Police were called to a number of domestic incidents between the mother and the father, who later admitted to Children's Social Care that they were experiencing conflict in their relationship due to cultural and language issues, including disagreements over money and migration matters. At around this time the mother became pregnant with her first child. Shortly thereafter the father confessed to his GP that he was frustrated at not being permitted to work due to his immigration status as an asylum seeker and felt angry all the time. He also reported experiencing trauma while a soldier in his country of origin, a pre-flight experience. The father was prescribed tranquillisers and offered support services, none of which he accepted. The father felt strongly attached to his country of origin, which he often referred to in conversation, and was constantly in contact with his parents and sister who remained there.

Dominant Anglocentric notions of family as essentially nuclear in form and the social construction of adult family members as independent and autonomous would have meant that practitioners were unlikely to have explored with the father his relationships with relatives or the closeness and significance of these kinship bonds. At this time the family were living in a locality which was 97% White British and the nearest mosque was located some distance away. The father also misused alcohol and drugs, both prohibited by his religion, which contributed to the domestic violence. Geographically, the father was remote from other members of his faith community; additionally, by violating central tenets of Islam he was likely to have been socially isolated from observant Muslims. At this point the couple's first child was eight months old.

The father was eventually granted permission to work in the UK and three years *discretionary leave to remain*. By this time the couple had two young children. Nevertheless incidents of domestic violence involving both the mother and father assaulting each other continued and the police informed Children's Social Care. Social workers conducted an assessment and placed both children on the Child Protection Register for physical abuse. Later the mother stated that the father had moved out of their flat and as this separation removed the occurrence of domestic violence and hence reduced the risk of harm to the children, they were removed from the Child Protection Register. Unknown to Children's Social Care at the time, the father moved back into the flat some months later. The mother clearly hid this development from health and social services for fear of their interference in her relationship with the father

▶

◄

Soon after the mother reported a series of incidents to several agencies involving the father threatening variously to kill himself, to kill her, or take the two children back to his homeland. He was also known to have written notes expressing aversion to his children growing up in the UK, a society which he regarded as immoral, particularly in relation to homosexuality. A few months after the father's threats were reported by the mother, his body was found hanged in a local park with a suicide note which led the police to break into the mother's flat where she and the two children were all found dead, apparently killed by the father before taking his own life.

While this case is plainly an extreme example of *culture shock*, it nonetheless foregrounds the challenges for a parent coping with adjustment to a profoundly different society from the one they have left behind. Parenting capacity is clearly impaired. The father was experiencing a deep sense of loss, and disorientation in his new culture, exacerbated by isolation from people of a similar ethnic or faith background in the host country. Not being permitted to work and earn a living for a number of years while being wholly dependent on his relationship with the mother in order to remain in the UK would also have undercut traditional masculine roles to which he would have been enculturated in his country of origin. This situation also most likely challenged cultural norms in his country of origin articulating *high power distance* between males and females. Indeed there is evidence that there was some contestation between the mother and father in this area. He was also given to ruminating both on the country and extended family he had left behind, but also his own hostility towards the norms of the host country which he perceived as permissive and immoral. He managed his confusion, distress, frustration and rage through misusing alcohol and drugs, together with violence against his family and ultimately himself. This meant paradoxically that by violating the religious prohibition on alcohol consumption he also became alienated from his own faith community. Many of the indicators of *culture shock* identified by Zapf (1991) are clearly present in this case and could potentially have been picked up by professionals to produce a more accurate assessment of parenting capacity or risk to children.

Acculturation stress

Acculturation occurs when people from one cultural background enter the culture of another society as a consequence of migrating from one country to another. *Acculturation stress* encompasses the challenges and distress encountered in adjusting to the cultural beliefs, values and social practices of the host society, which may be the product of efforts to both resist and incorporate these. It detrimentally affects physical and mental health and can result in lifelong effects (Neuliep, 2018). The severity of *acculturation stress* varies depending on the degree of similarity or dissimilarity between the culture of a person's country of origin and that of the host country. The cultures of the UK and the US are much more similar than those of the UK and Afghanistan. Consequently a migrant from Afghanistan is likely to experience a much greater degree of *cultural stress*. This type of stress is also mediated by gender, age, education and income (Berry, 1990). So for instance a male university-educated Afghan from Kabul will likely experience less *acculturation stress* than a female from a rural village in Afghanistan with little formal education. Additionally individual differences mean that some people will possess greater resilience and be better able to successfully cope with the stress of acculturation than others. Thomas (1995) identified five key stressors which contribute to *acculturation stress*. These are described below and explored in the follow-on case study.

Language: Lack of competence in the main language of the host country and situations where some family members acquire language competence (usually children) and other family members do not (predominantly older people).

Employment and economic status: Restriction to low paid, menial, casual employment due to poor language competency, disrupted education, unrecognised qualifications obtained in country of origin and/or discrimination.

Education: Limited schooling or disrupted education in country of origin acting as an obstacle to accessing or utilising educational opportunities in host country.

Family life: Disruption to family life as extended kin networks are lost through the process of forced migration and gender roles change in host country in order to adapt to changing circumstances. These may in turn result in generational tensions or conflicts.

Socio-political and immigration status: Forced migration results in longer term stressors as asylum seekers and refugees endeavour to adjust in a host country. Ethnic conflict in the country of origin may affect relationships between those ethnic groups in the host country. Migrants with restricted *leave to remain*, undecided cases or who are undocumented may continue to experience stress related to their immigration status.

Manchester Safeguarding Children Board (2010) *Executive Summary of the Serious Care Review in Respect of Child S*

A teenager was brought to the UK from a EU accession state by his Eastern European father who came to look for work. Within a few months of their arrival the father travelled on to another EU country leaving his son alone in a city in northern England. At that time the young person had the right to free movement in the UK, but did not have *recourse*

▶

◄

to public funds. This meant that at the age of 17 the young person was abandoned by his father in an unfamiliar country, where English was not his first language and without any means of financial support. He was referred to Children's Social Care for the first time after being found living on the streets. The young person had no documentation or means of identity and was provided with bed and breakfast accommodation while a social worker conducted an age assessment to establish if he was legally a child (i.e. a person under the age of 18 years). Using an interpreter, the social worker confirmed that he was 17 years of age – consistent with the date of birth the young person originally gave. While some agencies used an interpreter in their interactions with the young person, others did not and it was never established what his competence was in spoken or written English.

A referral was made by Children's Social Care to the No Recourse to Public Funds Team, which actually arranges repatriation for adults without financial means of support living in the UK. They appeared to take over responsibility for the young person and began paying for his accommodation. They experienced considerable difficulty in arranging transport to his country of origin as the young person said he did not hold a passport, contacting him became difficult and it transpired that he did not wish to be repatriated. Given these circumstances the No Recourse to Public Funds Team ceased financially supporting the young person and both this team and Children's Social Care closed his case, with some ambiguity as to who was responsible for his welfare. Shortly afterwards the young person presented himself at a homeless centre. This precipitated another referral to Children's Social Care who paid for him to stay at bed and breakfast accommodation. Thereafter he was arrested by police for being drunk and disorderly.

For reasons that are unclear Children's Social Care ceased payment for the young person's accommodation and he became street homeless for a second time. He was again arrested while intoxicated for disorderly behaviour, after which he was referred to the Youth Offending Team and again came to the attention of Children's Social Care. The young person continued to be street homeless, although being temporarily accommodated by a charity during the winter. He was again arrested in an intoxicated state and charged with stealing and later criminal damage. On referral to the Youth Offending Team temporary bed and breakfast accommodation was arranged for him.

After he threatened to kill himself he was referred to Child and Adolescent Mental Health Services for an assessment, which then referred him on for a hospital assessment that did not take place as the young person failed to attend it. At around this time the social worker who had originally worked with the young person when he was first abandoned by his father saw him by chance at the bed and breakfast accommodation and noted his emaciated appearance and signs of self-harm. This prompted Children's Social Care to reopen his case and to provide him with alternative bed and breakfast accommodation which included a daily cooked breakfast. Thereafter he was arrested for a fifth time for stealing whilst intoxicated and again appeared in court for sentencing. At around this time he was required to leave the bed and breakfast accommodation he had recently been moved to due to abusing local residents when drunk. A few weeks later the young person was found hanged in his bed and breakfast accommodation, believed to be an act of suicide.

During the 10 months that the young person spent in the UK he received no assessment of his needs by Children's Social Care or other agencies. The Serious Case Review concluded that this was because aged 17 years the young person was perceived to be an adult rather than a child and treated by most agencies as such. The Review noted that once the young person had been assessed as aged 17, he should have been treated as a child in need – a status which acknowledges that a child's development or welfare will deteriorate unless he or she is provided with additional services. In the absence of this designation the young person's needs were never holistically assessed, recognised, or met. Only his need for shelter was addressed, neglecting his education and wider welfare. It is also salient to consider whether Anglocentric social constructions of adolescence as a period of newfound independence, rebelliousness and risky conduct, alongside the normalisation of heavy drinking in British culture, may have diminished the ability of social workers to perceive the young person's behaviour as indicating that he was in acute distress and at risk of significant harm as opposed to normative adolescent expression. Dominant cultural norms in British society, which emphasise individualism and freedom of choice, may have inhibited social workers from pursuing more authoritative interventions with this reluctant young person who could be challenging to engage with.

This young person, although White and from another European country, was nevertheless subject to a range of *acculturation stresses*. In the first instance he did not speak English and was reliant on an interpreter to communicate. This would have been extremely isolating and made even simple daily transactions challenging and time consuming. He would have experienced considerable difficulty in accessing employment, training or education. His immigration status, which denied him recourse to public funds, would have been a persistent source of stress and led to him being street homeless. Additionally he had been abandoned by his father and did not establish any social or support networks in the UK. As a consequence of this situation he turned to alcohol and theft as a means of coping. *Acculturation stress* would also have been caused by the multiplicity of agencies which became involved in his life. Not only would the functions of each have been difficult to comprehend for a foreign national, but as these agencies disagreed over his age and their responsibility for him, they tended to engage and disengage in rapid succession. His unfamiliarity with the welfare system in the UK would have left him bewildered and feeling out of control. The additional complication of agencies treating the teenager as an adult rather than a child meant that his background and vulnerability were never effectively explored, nor his needs assessed.

Reflective exercise

Consider your practice with families who were recent migrants, refugees or asylum seekers.

What acculturation stressors were different family members subject to, and what impact did these have on the welfare and safety of children and young people?

How might you help to reduce acculturation stressors for parents, guardians and children?

Acculturation in families

In some families generational conflict may occur as different family members acculturate at different rates or to different degrees. This may result in tensions between parents and children, parents and grandparents or children and grandparents. Often children become acculturated first through their participation in formal education, which can also mean they acquire language competency more quickly than other family members. Consequently there may be arguments and disagreements between younger and older family members about the cultural beliefs, values and social practices of the ethnic majority as opposed to those embedded in the family's heritage. Tensions about the authority, justification and aptness of customary beliefs and norms may also arise between genders; for example if females enter the workforce in contradistinction to their former roles in the country of origin (Thomas, 1995). Elders within the family may experience diminution of their traditional role of decision-maker as the greater language competence of younger family members enables them to interact with the host population and experience more economic and social autonomy and power.

Acculturation was an issue in Leicester Safeguarding Children Board (2011) *Serious Case Review in Respect of the Deaths of Children known as Child 1 and Child 2* discussed earlier in this chapter involving a White British female care leaver and an asylum seeker of Muslim faith from the Middle East. In this case there was no formal social work assessment of the father and almost nothing was known about his history or parenting capacity. While it was known that there were tensions between the parents concerning culture, there was no exploration by social workers as to what this meant in terms of gender expectations, childrearing, conflicting or shared values and attitudes. However, the maternal grandfather, who occasionally visited, said that the mother appeared subservient as she was expected by the father to be quiet and serve all the meals and drinks. Professionals did not know what childcare roles the father performed and simply accepted the mother's assertion that he was supportive without further investigation. The mother was keen to discourage practitioners from becoming involved in her family and later it transpired she misled them regarding the father's whereabouts. The Review also expressed dissatisfaction at the failure of Children's Social Care to clearly record the father's ethnicity, religion, immigration status, first language and preferred language of communication. Interpreters were used at times by agencies which came into contact with the father, but not routinely. While he was evidently resistant to being assessed by Children's Social Care, the Serious Case Review concluded that no consistent effort was made to engage him or to ascertain whether he was a resource or threat to his children.

The Serious Case Review also expressed concern over inattention to the dual heritage of the children, who were being brought up as Muslims, and how this affected their parenting, experience of pre-school and day-to-day encounters with people in their community. Indeed there was little consideration given by practitioners as to how living in a predominantly White British locality affected the parents. The Serious Case Review observed that while agency procedures require the recording of ethnicity, religion and language, these were not sufficiently embedded in practice to ensure that culturally appropriate services are provided alongside assessing the implications for the safeguarding of children. As a result practically nothing was known by professionals about the acculturation experiences of the father. The arguments and violence between the parents were not considered in relation to culture clashes. The implications of acculturation for the children and how this might affect their day-to-day experiences of family life, schooling or daily encounters with local community members were not explored.

Not everyone from a minority ethnic community in a host country will experience the same degree of acculturation. Berry (1990) suggests that this depends on, firstly, the extent to which an individual endeavours to interact with or avoid people from the host society, which may be influenced by their own cultural norms and/or by hostility encountered from the host community. Secondly, it concerns the degree to which an individual wants to maintain their cultural identity in terms of transmitted beliefs, values and social practices versus adopting those of the ethnic majority or micro-cultures (e.g. gay community, youth culture) in the host country. Problems can arise within kin networks when different family members acculturate to different degrees. Invariably this will lead to some tension or ongoing conflict over beliefs, values, attitudes, roles and social practices. The transmission of religious beliefs and observances can be a particular area of heightened disagreement, although many families find accommodation through recognising that it may not be practicable to retain the exact form of religious practice as performed in their country of origin (Martin & Nakayama, 2010, p. 319). Much of the research in this field indicates that individual differences and social divisions regarding gender and age play a major role in the process of acculturation (Ward, 1996).

Case study for practitioners

Children's Social Care receives an anonymous referral from a neighbour stating that parents are leaving their two primary school aged children together with a 13-year-old home alone and unsupervised. The referral also claims that the children are sometimes locked in their flat for hours at a time. As the social worker tasked to investigate this child protection concern you visit the flat to discover that the father and mother are asylum seekers from Burundi.

Return to the ASKED model of cultural competence in Chapter 4. Focus on the first element of *cultural awareness* and identify your own attitudes regarding childcare and your expectations around adult–child relationships. Consider how these are informed by dominant Anglocentric norms. Now turn to the subheading 'conceptions of childhood' explored in Chapter 5 and consider how the social construction of childhood in British society informs your assumptions regarding age-appropriate behaviours and childcare needs. Examine the extent to which you conceptualise these as superior to other approaches to family care for children and young people. Being conscious of one's own worldview can assist in working dynamically with ethnic diversity, as opposed to simply prescribing to parents or guardians how they should look after their children.

Due to *superdiversity* it is unlikely that you will have encountered a family from Burundi before and so you may possess little specific *cultural knowledge*. However, a broad general *cultural knowledge* of sub-Saharan societies might alert you to the importance of exploring a number of areas. Many people from the sub-Saharan region speak multiple languages, some of which may be common to people from adjacent countries. Collectivist norms and interdependence between generations tend to be culturally influential. With little *cultural knowledge* to rely on, the quality of your *cultural skill* is going to be crucial in eliciting vital information from this family about their experiences and understandings of their children's welfare.

Questions it might be important to ask relate to languages spoken in the household and with what degree of fluency, and to ascertain whether these are shared by people from other countries or regions. In Burundi, Kirunda is the indigenous African language spoken by most of the population and by many people from bordering areas. French is the official language, which tends to be spoken alongside Kirunda in the cities and by the urban elite. Some English is also spoken, as is Swahili, which is a language common to large sections of the populations in the countries of the Great Lakes Region. Knowing the range of languages spoken by family members can assist in identifying suitable interpreters. *Cultural skill* also needs to be employed in sensitively exploring parental understandings of child developmental needs and age-appropriate care and responsibilities. In many African societies there is an expectation that older children will take care of younger children or that younger children will develop self-care abilities at a young age and/or that children will assist parents and guardians in domestic chores or contribute to generating household income. Diversity within ethnic groups means that parents or other adult carers may have views similar to, or diverse from, those of the ethnic majority. You will need to differentiate between childrearing practices that are different to, or indeed superior to, Anglocentric norms, and perhaps expectations of contributing to overall family wellbeing and conversely those which could potentially lead to significant harm.

Now turn to the GGRRAAACCEEESSS intersectional model in Chapter 4 which considers the impact of structural factors on the experiences of family members. As asylum seekers the parents may be excluded from employment, involved in voluntary work or working unlawfully. Geography and ethnicity, the British Government's dispersal policy for asylum seekers, which can isolate families from clusters of people from their ethnic community, may be a factor in arranging adequate childcare or accessing other forms of support. You will want to consider how parental immigration status, education, class and gender mediate their experiences of being asylum seekers. *Cultural skills* will also enable you to find out from family members how their race, religion and appearance are affecting their treatment by local residents. It could be important to explore with the parents how any experiences of prejudice or discrimination affect their ability to provide childcare and the impact on their children's welfare.

Developing *cultural knowledge* of this particular family through the use of *cultural skills* alongside entering into *cultural encounter* will help to uncover the motivations and intent of these parents. Are they parents who are intentionally maltreating their children; parents who are following accepted cultural norms informed by their own heritage background; newly arrived migrants who are unaware of childcare norms and requirements in the United Kingdom; or an isolated and impoverished family who are struggling to manage adequate childcare and are doing their best to keep their children safe in difficult circumstances? Parental behaviour may be due to a combination of these. While the risks of harm posed to children have to be objectively assessed from a child-centred perspective (regardless of cultural or economic considerations) the worldview and motivations of parents are pivotal in deciding how to intervene. A culturally sensitive approach which explores cultural and structural factors in family life without prejudgement is crucial, as opposed to adopting an *ethnocentric* perspective, or assuming that parental behaviour is dictated by cultural or religious considerations.

Conclusion

Superdiversity means that families from a wide range of racial, ethnic and faith minority backgrounds live in the countries of Western Europe and North America. Assisted by the processes of globalisation, there are now multiple routes of migration resulting in a multiplicity of different immigration statuses, which attract different rights and entitlements.

Recent migrants and asylum seekers have fewer rights and entitlements regarding public services and employment. Discrimination and difficulty providing appropriate documentation can further diminish their access to health care, education, employment, housing and welfare benefits. Consequently such families can experience conditions of extreme poverty.

Aspects of family reunification after a period of separation, transnational family relationships and often different immigration statuses among family members, increase the complexity of social work intervention. The disruption caused to relationships through the experiences of migration and settlement can intensify or change family power dynamics. Refugees and asylum seekers, because of the forced nature of their migration, may be more vulnerable to culture shock and a wide range of acculturation stressors. These may in turn detrimentally affect parental capabilities or impair the positive adjustment of children to their new host country, posing safeguarding concerns. Family members will often acculturate in different ways and to different degrees from one another. This may result in tensions within families, frequently along gender or generational lines. However, individuals typically adopt multiple acculturation strategies, which they deploy in different contexts, and this often results in workable compromises within families.

8

Children's Health and Parental Care

Introduction

Health inequalities between the ethnic majority and minority communities in the UK have implications for the care and protection of children. Public Health England (2017), which collated and analysed national-level data, found that premature mortality rates were higher than average among males born in the Accession States to the EU, the majority of which are former Communist countries such as Poland and Romania. The difference in healthy life expectancy at birth (i.e. the length of time a person has good health) between the most deprived and least deprived areas of England is 20 years. As people from ethnic minority backgrounds are more likely to live in deprived areas, this means that on average they are disproportionately more likely to experience poor health earlier in their lives than their counterparts resident in affluent areas. Infant mortality is highest among families of Pakistani, Black African and Black Caribbean heritage, although rates among those of Bangladeshi and Indian background are similar to those among the White English majority. Notably, the infant mortality rate in the most deprived areas of England is twice that of the least deprived areas. While there are higher rates of smoking (a major cause of morbidity) in the most deprived areas compared to the least deprived, religious affiliation is a significant determinant of the probability of being a smoker. Those stating that they had no religion were much more likely to smoke than those who had a religious faith. Those identifying as Jewish, Hindu and Sikh were much less likely to smoke than the English population average.

The number of babies with low birth weights was higher across all major ethnic minorities, apart from Black Africans, compared to those born to White English mothers. The number of low birth weight babies born in the most deprived areas is double that in the least deprived ones. The number of five-year-old children with obvious dental decay was twice the rate among children of Chinese heritage and one-and-a-half times the rate among South Asian minorities compared to White English children. The rates for those of mixed heritage were comparable to those of White English children and significantly lower for those of Black African origins. Among five-year-old children in the least deprived areas around 10% had obvious dental decay compared to 37% in the most deprived areas.

Adults from many minority communities were found to be at greater risk of poor mental health than those from the White majority population. In particular, 28% of women from Pakistani and Bangladeshi backgrounds were found to be at risk of poor mental health compared to 17% of White women. Gypsies, Roma and Travellers suffer the worst mental health out of all ethnic groups (Equality and Human Rights Commission, 2016). However, people from the Accession States to the EU were found to have the highest incidence of suicide, alongside those from Ireland. By comparison those from African, East Asian, South Asian and Middle Eastern backgrounds had a significantly lower incidence of suicide than the White English population. The incidence of self-harm presents a similar picture (Public Health England, 2017). In relation to overall life satisfaction, 12% of people who were unemployed reported low life satisfaction compared to just 3% of those in employment. In terms of racial background 8% of people who identified as Black reported low life satisfaction compared to 5% of White people in England. Taken altogether these figures relating to physical and mental health suggest intersectionality between levels of deprivation, race and ethnicity, but clearly indicate that these do not directly overlap in terms of health outcomes.

Factors contributing to health inequalities

Malek (2004) warns against a simplistic focus on ethnicity as correlated to mental health outcomes and the pathologising of health care beliefs and practices which influence a number of families from minority communities. This leads to victim blaming and culturalising illnesses, rather than analysing how the disadvantaged circumstances of people's lives contribute to mental health problems. Multiple studies identify a range of socio-economic factors which predispose ethnic minority adults, children and young people to poor mental health. These encompass deprivation; substandard or overcrowded housing; high unemployment; belonging to a low income group; isolation, language barriers and racism (Malek, 2004, pp. 39–45; NHS Glasgow and Clyde, 2010; Salway et al., 2014).

The Equality and Human Rights Commission (2016) completed a wide-ranging overview of the research evidence regarding racial inequalities in the UK and it revealed the following findings. People from ethnic minorities are more than twice as likely as those from the ethnic majority to live in poverty: at 36% compared to 17% for the British White population. This ranged from 25% for people of Indian heritage to 40% for African, African Caribbean and people of mixed heritage to 44% of those of Pakistani and Bangladeshi backgrounds. Where children were living with a head of household from an ethnic minority 42% were in poverty compared to 25% of those living with a White British head of household. Nazroo (1997), in a large-scale survey of health among people from ethnic minority backgrounds found that social class within ethnic groups was also positively correlated with health, indicating that the disproportionate exposure of individuals from minorities to deprivation is a major factor in accounting for health disparities.

Housing conditions are positively correlated to levels of poverty, hence households on higher incomes generally enjoy better housing conditions. Out of the total number of Pakistani or Bangladeshi ethnic households 29% of children lived in substandard accommodation compared to 24% in Black households and 19% in White households. Correspondingly, 21% of children in ethnically Indian households lived in overcrowded conditions compared to 31% of those from Pakistani or Bangladeshi heritage and 27% from Black households. This contrasts with just 8% of children from White families living in overcrowded accommodation. Figures for White Polish households indicate that 30% were living in overcrowded conditions, as were 24% of Gypsy/Traveller households.

People from ethnic minorities are twice as likely to be unemployed as White British people. Women of Pakistani and Bangladeshi heritage were less than half as likely to be in employment, as compared to the average employment rate for the female population as a whole. People aged 16–24 years from ethnic minorities are much more likely to experience long-term unemployment than those from the majority population. When people from ethnic minorities were employed they were twice as likely as White British people to be in temporary work and overall experienced much greater job insecurity that those from the ethnic majority. With the exception of those of Indian heritage, people from ethnic minorities were also more likely to be in low-paid work than those from the ethnic majority. Those who possess a degree and are employed on average receive a quarter less in wages than their White British counterparts.

Children from ethnic minorities experienced high levels of racial bullying in school, while African Caribbean and dual heritage White and African Caribbean pupils had three times the rate of permanent school exclusions than the average. Gypsy/Roma and Irish Traveller children had the highest permanent rate of school exclusions of any minority group. These are also the groups attaining the poorest educational qualifications at age 16, while the performance of children from Bangladeshi and Black African backgrounds has substantially improved. Additionally both adults and children from ethnic minority backgrounds have to contend with high levels of racial abuse, which continues to rise year on year. This includes rises in incidents of antisemitism and Islamophobia. In 2010/11 approximately 3% of people reported experiencing harassment in the previous two years on the grounds of their skin colour, ethnicity or religion. This figure was much higher at 17% for those aged 16–24 years. Racially motivated incidents involving White victims have also jumped dramatically as a consequence of increased economic migration from EU countries, negative media coverage and hostile public attitudes. Most racial harassment consists of verbal abuse, which occurs predominantly around transport hubs such as bus stops and in shopping precincts. Data collected by the police indicates that currently 82% of all recorded hate crime is racially motivated. Notably, 37% of Black people and 45% of Asians compared to 29% of White people felt unsafe at home on their own or in their local area (Equality and Human Rights Commission, 2016).

An extensive body of research indicates that experiences of racism are associated with poorer health indices among individuals from minority ethnic communities (Salway et al., 2014, p. 5). Racism alone has various deleterious impacts on children's mental health including depression, low self-esteem; internalised negative self-beliefs; externalised anger and hostility; elevated levels of anxiety; and addiction. Either resisting or accepting negative racial stereotypes will result in additional stress for children from black and minority ethnic backgrounds (Malek, 2004; Holland & Hogg, 2001; Crabtree et al., 2008). In another study individuals from Pakistani and Bangladeshi minorities, while sometimes interpreting psychological distress through a spiritual worldview, often attributed it to their experiences of social and material disadvantage aggravated by regular racist abuse (Kai & Hedges, 1999). Stress caused by 'cultural and value conflicts, and changes in family relationships' was also reported as a common cause of mental distress (NHS Greater Glasgow & Clyde, 2010, p. 13).

Reflective exercise

Consider your practice with families from racial and ethnic minority backgrounds.

To what extent do you explore with family members how past experiences and current living environments affect their mental and physical health?

To what extent do your assessments and care planning incorporate and address structural factors in the lives of these families?

How might you improve your cultural skills in exploring and integrating structural factors with aspects of race, ethnicity and immigration status in relation to health-related issues?

Systems of health care

Biomedical principles and practice underpin the diagnoses, prognoses and treatment of illness and impairment by the National Health Service in the United Kingdom. However this is not the only approach to health care.

Systems in a number of other countries draw on alternative understandings of good and poor health and use different methods to assess and treat conditions to restore wellbeing. Many people, whether from the ethnic majority or minority communities, who experience illness or look after someone who is ill or impaired, actually draw on a range of health care beliefs and practices. The diversity of health care systems underpinning parental understandings of health and illness alongside their implications for children's care and wellbeing are explored in this section.

Biomedicine

Founded on the natural sciences, biomedicine is the dominant approach to dealing with illness in Europe and North America and is sometimes referred to as Western, modern or allopathic medicine. It is based on the use of pharmacological and physical interventions to reduce or eradicate the causes or symptoms of illness. Disease is attributed to biological factors and physical pathogens, which are targeted by curative treatments. Technology plays a central role in diagnosis and treatment. The mind and body are largely regarded as functioning separately and hence mental and physical health constitute distinctive branches of biomedicine. Despite the global dominance of Western medicine there are influential alternative ways of conceiving health, illness and treatment.

Naturalistic health care

Naturalistic forms of health care, also referred to as holistic systems, are widely practised in East and South Asia and are based on maintaining the equilibrium of elements in the human body. Illnesses are attributed to imbalance in these elements caused by the environment, physical conditions such as childbirth or emotional states, for instance grief. These systems are both preventative and curative in orientation Traditional Chinese medicine (encompassing acupuncture and herbalism) and Ayurvedic medicine, widespread in India and Pakistan, are forms of naturalistic health care. So is homeopathy, first developed in Germany and practised in many European countries. The role of the holistic practitioner is to restore bodily balance through physical intervention such as acupuncture or the prescription of remedies or changes in diet. Chinese and Ayurvedic medicine are underpinned by a classification system of hot and cold foods, which relates not to their temperature, but to their effect on the body, and practitioners may prescribe particular foods to restore health. Therefore naturalistic practitioners treat the mind and body as an integral whole and generally do not distinguish between mental and physical illnesses.

For this reason, some people of Indian descent may conceptualise mental health and illness in a different way from the British medical profession, which relies on the categorisation of clearly differentiated pathological mental states as defined in the Diagnostic and Statistical Manual of Mental Disorders (DSM). Within biomedicine the task of the psychiatrist is to recognise symptoms and identify which mental illness they indicate. Treatment, whether with psychotropic drugs or psychotherapy, is then based on this diagnosis. But interdependency between physical and mental states in *Ayurveda* medicine means that psychiatric illnesses are not necessarily conceptualised in this way by people of South Asian backgrounds. Psychological disturbances may be perceived as 'anxiety' or 'sorrow' as opposed to a diagnosable mental illness (Butt & Mirza, 1996, p. 73). This may permit help-seeking behaviour, which leads to family members and friends providing additional practical and emotional support to the individual without the stigmatisation and distress of (possibly inappropriate) psychiatric intervention.

Likewise, while psychiatry based on positivist science interprets abnormal behaviour as indicative of malfunctioning physiological, neurological or psychological processes, many families of Chinese heritage perceive unusual behaviour as indicating some form of social problem. Consequently, a range of behaviours will be interpreted as non-medical and as matters to be addressed by the family rather than referred to a psychiatrist or therapist (Prior et al., 2000, pp. 831–32). In this connection it is significant that people of Chinese descent have the lowest rates of outpatient appointments or consultations with GPs (Smaje & Le Grand, 1997). While this has typically been attributed to fears of 'loss of face', it may actually be due to different interpretations of what constitutes illness (Prior et al., 2000, p. 832).

Personalistic health care

Health care based on *personalistic* (also called *magico-religious*) belief systems attribute illness and disability to supernatural forces like a deity or demon and sometimes to human agents, such as a witch or a jealous person casting the evil eye. Consequently, when a child is born with a disability or a family member falls ill this is regarded as a punishment or act of aggression inflicted by God, a spirit or another person. Particularly in some small rural communities in Africa and the Caribbean, unexplained illnesses can lead to accusations of witchcraft or sorcery, predominantly against women and children. For some Christians and Muslims a congenital impairment or sudden ailment may be understood as a form of divine punishment or as a test of faith or endurance by those affected, which can include parents or other carers. In this system the victim will seek to identify the agent, spiritual or human, who has caused the illness, injury or disability, typically calling upon the assistance of a shaman, priest, Iman or other spiritual advisor. Once the supernatural cause is identified, the spiritual advisor may perform rituals or give instruction to those affected in order to neutralise or appease the divinity or person believed to be inflicting ill health. Such convictions have occasionally led to child abuse linked to faith or belief, as discussed in Chapter 5.

The belief in karma held by many Hindus and Buddhists can mean that a disability or illness is interpreted as a punishment for misdeeds in a past life or earlier actions during one's current life. This governing principle ordains that the sum of a person's actions determines their fate both in their current and future lives. Personalistic health care systems are based on a close connection with the spiritual world typically intertwined with beliefs and traditions passed down through generations of a family and often subscribed to by other members of their faith or ethnic community. Some beliefs, for example those attributing illness or disability to Jinns (evil spirits) held by a minority of individuals from South Asian backgrounds, are cultural rather than religious in origin as Islam does not sanction them (Crabtree et al., 2008, p. 136).

Many religious faiths also have a long historical tradition of spiritual healing for disabilities, mental health problems and physical illness. The use of prayer and supplication to the divine to heal family members is common across major world religions. Christianity has a long tradition of the *laying-on of hands* by a minister to channel the healing powers of the divine, a practice common among Pentecostal Christians. Some Roman Catholics seek healing through spiritual intervention by visiting shrines such as that at Lourdes in France renowned for miraculous cures. Similarly among many devout Hindus it is believed that visiting a holy place associated with cures may alleviate or remedy a disability or illness; many of these temples and shrines are in India. Conversely amulets, lucky charms, sections of holy script or representations of saints may be worn by people holding spiritual beliefs to protect the wearer against evil or misfortune.

Folk health care

This approach to health care is practised in many developing countries, particularly in more rural regions or where formal health services are inaccessible. This approach relies on healers from within the community who are identified as having a particular gift for healing or where this occupation has been passed down generations of their family. They draw on a predominantly oral knowledge base accumulated sometimes over centuries through trial and error in the application of different treatments. Some may have received an apprenticeship from another healer or practising family members while others may have little training. Generally they adopt a holistic approach without differentiating between physical, cognitive or behavioural malady, but treat these as an integrated whole. Their assessment of the person's illness may also involve investigating a patient's social relationships and interactions with their environment.

Lay health care

Lay medicine (or the popular sector) is commonly the first medical system people refer to regardless of culture or faith. Many people who fall sick initially self-medicate, often based on the advice of friends or family or on the basis of practices passed down through generations, predominantly via women. To take a typical example, nursing mothers frequently consult their own mothers about infant care or apparently minor ailments. Among the ethnic majority treatment of a cold includes remedies such as drinking honey mixed with lemon or going to bed with a hot-water bottle, although none of these are grounded in the principles of Western medicine. Other home treatments to ward off ill health included bananas for good digestion, carrots to improve night vision and avoiding sexual intercourse during pregnancy to prevent damage to the baby's head – none of which are supported by scientific evidence (Holland & Hogg, 2001, pp. 26–27).

Reflective exercise

Consider your own health care practices and those of your immediate and extended family.

Which systems of health care do you draw on and in what circumstances? Why do you make these choices?

Which systems of health care do different members of your family draw on and for what kinds of health problems? Why do they make these choices?

Do you notice any gender or generational differences or patterns in these choices?

Health care systems and child protection

The case study in the text box below examines how parental health care beliefs can put children at risk. It also examines how such beliefs are transmitted through families and the importance of understanding family forms outside of a narrow Anglocentric conception of the family unit as comprising primarily parents and children. This case study clearly underlines the importance of understanding the dynamics of transnational families.

London Borough of Waltham Forest Safeguarding Children Board (2011) *Serious Case Review: Child W*

The mother and father moved from Ghana to live in the United Kingdom in 2000 and had four children. English was the couple's second language and although both spoke it fluently the father's English was difficult to understand. The mother was a qualified nurse. There had been previous child protection concerns regarding the force-feeding of an elder sibling, although this was believed to have been performed by the child's grandmother. All of the children displayed signs of inappropriate feeding. In 2009 the mother expressed anxiety to health practitioners regarding her new baby's feeding within the first few months of her birth. Although advice and guidance was provided, the baby was not seen by professionals again until the day of her death in March 2010 when she died aged 10 months of pneumonia caused by solid food in her lungs. The mother was jailed for three years for force-feeding her baby. During the trial it emerged that the mother held a jug full of liquidised meat and cereals to the baby's mouth to prevent the baby from closing her mouth, causing her to choke and aspirate food. The mother told the court that 'she and her siblings had been fed the same way by her mother in Ghana when they were weaned onto solid food'. She added in evidence 'I didn't do anything at all to hurt her'. The police who investigated the crime described the mother as 'obsessed' with the baby's weight while the mother's partner told police that 'to feed the Ghanaian way is to pour it into your mouth' (Guardian Online, 2011).

The Serious Case Review concluded that 'practitioners were insufficiently sensitive to obtaining an understanding of the significance of cultural and/ or individual values with regard to weigh, body image and feeding practices' (London Borough of Waltham Forest Safeguarding Children Board, 2011, para.4.1.3). This meant that social workers held inadequate information to accurately assess the risk of significant harm posed to the children of the family. The Serious Case Review noted that 'practitioners completing assessments need to sensitively consider the culture of a family and their immigrant status', including the 'reasons for parenting practices and the impact on the child' alongside the 'potential for change should it be judged that behaviour is potentially harmful' (London Borough of Waltham Forest Safeguarding Children Board, 2011, para.5.1.6). The report of the investigation into the baby's death also observed that there was 'insufficient forensic focus on the investigation because professional concerns were mistakenly diluted when maltreatment within the family was perceived to be motivated primarily by carers' concern for a child's welfare' and intended to give the baby nutrition (London Borough of Waltham Forest Safeguarding Children Board, 2011, para.4.1.6).

LeVine & LeVine (1983) in their overview of child care practices in sub-Saharan Africa note that during the 1950s and 1960s anthropologists recorded the force-feeding of infants in Kenya and Nigeria, as well as in

Ghana. The historically high infant mortality rates in all these countries, often as a direct or indirect result of dehydration or malnutrition, has created a folk medical practice of force-feeding babies who appear reluctant to take nourishment, often by holding their nose so that they have to open their mouth to breathe, at which point food is administered to them as they try to breathe. This technique is also used when introducing infants to solid food, which can sometimes be done abruptly rather than gradually, due to culturally embedded concerns about child starvation. This means that an apparently thin infant or one slow to feed can be a cause of considerable parental anxiety. While public health programmes in West and East Africa seek to discourage the force-feeding of young children due to the danger of their aspirating food and choking to death, nevertheless this remains a quite common practice. In the above case, the Ghanaian mother, heavily influenced by her own enculturation experiences applied a *folk medical practice*. But it is important to recognise that this practice is subject to considerable controversy in present-day Ghana. It represents both a cultural practice that is maladaptive in the different socio-economic environment of a post-industrial country, but is also subject to increasing condemnation in Ghana as changes in culture over time challenge previously sanctioned practices (Boamah, 2014). This also highlights the fluidity of culture and its contested nature.

While this particular example concerned a *folk medical system*, the very strong influence of the grandmother in this case indicates the pathway for *lay medical practices* in child health care to be passed down through the generations. It also demonstrates how enculturation in countries of origin can continue to influence the beliefs and practices of adults who subsequently move and settle in another country such as the UK. The grandmother as an elder was a transmitter of cultural norms, coming from a society which tended towards *high power distance* between older and younger people. In comparison to dominant relationships in British society, this also meant that her worldview and opinion carried considerable weight with her daughter. However, these cultural norms were nevertheless highly contested in the country of origin. Social work practice in this case also appears to have been focused on the mother–child dyad, illustrating yet again an Anglocentric conception of the family as being essentially nuclear rather than extended and therefore lacking attention to the wider kinship relationships and influences.

Health care delivery and child protection

Having considered beliefs about health and illness, the next case study focuses on parental understandings of health care delivery. It involves the intersection of nationality, race, social class and education with health care considerations and examines how these can pose risks to children.

Kingston Local Safeguarding Children Board (2015) *Serious Case Review Family A*

An affluent professional White middle-class couple moved from South Africa to the UK where they had four children, all of whom were British nationals. The children were observed by professionals to have good relationships with one another and with their parents. The three youngest children aged three and four years old had spinal muscular atrophy, a life-shortening condition, which causes severe muscle weakness resulting in difficulties moving, breathing and swallowing. The eldest child was eight years old. All four children attended mainstream schooling and were described as intelligent and happy. It was acknowledged by professionals that the parents often provided outstanding care to their children.

However, there were fundamental disagreements between medical staff and the parents about medical interventions which doctors maintained would reduce the children's discomfort and maximise their potential. The parents stated that they wanted services, not assessments. The parents were very assertive and often subjected professionals to close questioning. The father was a company director and lawyer. Throughout the father acted as an intermediary in discussions regarding medical intervention and practitioners were frequently prevented from discussing this directly with the mother. The father was often abroad in connection with his employment and the mother smothered to death the three youngest children while her husband was away on one of these trips. She was given a Hospital Order after admitting manslaughter on the grounds of diminished responsibility.

The Serious Case Review criticised social workers for not exploring with the parents their experience of health services in their country of origin, where the couple had been used to selecting whichever services they wanted and paying for them. They were unused to, and resented, receiving advice from social workers and health care professionals as to what support their children required, which is the norm in the UK. Professionals were in turn confounded by these parents, who appeared to have little respect for their advice or deference to their expertise. This led to a situation of mutual incomprehension as parents and professionals contested each other's different conceptions of health care delivery. The Serious Case Review also surmised that 'another factor at play with this family may have been their comparative wealth and power, and lack of automatic respect of professional advice, including that given by experts. This attitude is unusual and practitioners were wary' (Kingston Local Safeguarding Children Board, 2015, para.5.12.7). This meant that professionals adopted an overly cautious approach to triggering child protection procedures despite concerns about parental medical neglect.

In this case South African parents' unfamiliarity with the British health care system and the authority it invests in medical opinion resulted in constant conflict over the children's treatment. Additionally, the parents were racially White and from a high socio-economic group, which appears to have hindered the responses of social workers when the threshold for initiating child protection procedures had been met. The intersection of class, race and ethnicity accounts for parental enculturation experiences in their country of origin alongside their racial and class-related sense of superiority and the self-confident authority which they adopted towards medical staff and social workers. At the same time social workers were also confused by the contradiction of parents who provided a high standard of care to their children with whom they had very positive relationships, but who simultaneously acted in ways which undermined their children's wellbeing. When parents are acting in ways consistent with their own cultural or faith beliefs they can indeed love their children greatly and otherwise act as good carers because they are so convinced of the rightness of their choices.

Reflective exercise

Consider Kingston Local Safeguarding Children Board (2015).

Reflect on your own majority or minority identity status. If you were working with a White South African middle-class professional father who constantly disagreed with you and subjected every social work decision to intensive questioning, how would you feel, think and react?

How might application of the GGRRAAACCEEESSS framework assist you in this situation?

Pluralism in health care choices

In both China and India the state supports the practice of indigenous health care systems and many patients make use of biomedical interventions alongside traditional Chinese or Ayurvedic medicine depending on their symptoms. A plurality of approaches to health care, disease prevention and curative treatment is therefore typical of how people in these countries approach managing health and illness. By contrast biomedical practice in Europe and North America has generally been hostile to, or minimised the contribution of, other health care systems to disease prevention or the treatment of illness (The Economist, 2017). Therefore people from some minority ethnic communities may be more used to availing simultaneously of several distinct sources of health care than are those from the ethnic majority (Gervais & Jovchelovitch, 1998; Holland & Hogg, 2001). Nevertheless, in the United Kingdom up to one third of the population, thus including a high proportion of people from the ethnic majority, use complementary and alternative medicine to take care of health problems ranging from minor aliments to major diseases (Harris & Rees, 2000). Among any ethnic minority, as among the ethnic majority, there will be a wide variety of views and behaviours regarding the use of alternative health care systems. This will be influenced by gender, age and country of birth, alongside the health beliefs subscribed to by other family members. Older Chinese people, particularly if they have spent their formative years in China, may prefer to consult with a practitioner of Chinese traditional medicine rather than a general practitioner (Wah et al., 1996, p. 109; Prior et al., 2000, p. 825).

In practice people living in the UK tend to draw on multiple systems of health care. For those belonging to the ethnic majority the use of alternative and complementary medicine is increasingly common with individuals using, for instance, acupuncture for backache while still taking analgesic drugs prescribed by their general practitioner. A person of South Asian heritage may alter their diet to reflect the need to take cold foods for a fever, but still visit a family doctor employed by the National Health Service. Others may make use of the services of Hakims or Vaidyas for minor aliments or mental health concerns, but refer themselves to a primary care doctor or the Accident and Emergency Unit of a hospital for more major illnesses. Someone of Chinese heritage may use acupuncture and medicinal herbs to recover from an operation performed by a surgeon practising biomedicine. Homeopathy may be sought out by people from the ethnic majority or ethnic minorities to treat a chronic asthmatic or skin condition which biomedicine has been unable to resolve. A White British mother may rely on lay medicine and the formula for a drink passed down to her by a grandmother to treat a child's diarrhoea, before later taking her to a GP's surgery. Someone of African heritage may turn to a traditional practitioner for spiritual advice while also attending hospital for tests to identify the cause of their painful symptoms. Muslim or Christian parents may pray for their son with leukaemia to be healed while still taking him for regular chemotherapy predicated on a biomedical approach. This pluralism of health care based on a pick-and-mix approach to beliefs and treatments in order to avail of the optimum advice and intervention is extremely common in the United Kingdom. Furthermore, many practitioners of alternative medicine and complementary therapies will refer their patients on to biomedical physicians if an illness appears grave or their health care approach is known to be less effective for that condition (Laird, 2008).

Health, diet and fasting

People will probably be influenced by the health care systems that relatives utilise or the pluralist choices they make. But they can also be influenced by some of the underpinning principles of these systems even when the original meaning is no longer known or understood. Many Asian families continue to utilise notions of 'hot' and 'cold' foods in the preservation of health and treatment of ailments, alongside traditional cooking practices, even though the precepts of Ayurvedic and traditional Chinese medicine may be unfamiliar. Many families of Chinese, Indian, Pakistani and Bangladeshi ethnicity place importance upon food in relation to their health. While people from the ethnic majority generally tend to perceive fewer links between different kinds of food and related health outcomes, evidence is emerging of links between diet and disability. Autism and epileptic seizures appear to reduce in severity in children treated with prescribed diets for both these conditions (Pulsifer et al., 2001; Whiteley et al., 1999). Overall diet can assume a more central role in health promotion for many ethnic minority families, than is usually the case among the ethnic majority. However, it needs to be recognised that second-generation migrants often adopt the eating habits of the White British population through acculturation in the host country (Smith et al., 2011).

Cultural influences regarding the relationship between food and health are overlaid by religious requirements and taboos. For instance devout Buddhists are vegetarian as all meat is prohibited; for both Jews and Muslims pork and its derivatives are proscribed. For observant Jews and Muslims animals for consumption must have been slaughtered in the prescribed manner, while for devout Hindus the way food is prepared and cooked must conform to religious precepts. Practising Sikhs are required to abstain from alcohol, as are Muslims. These religious restrictions may have implications for taking prescribed medication, for example pills with a gelatine coating or an alcohol-based solution. In other faiths certain foods can be forbidden on certain days, for example the practice among strictly observant Catholics of eating fish rather than meat on Fridays or of abstaining from meat and alcohol on certain holy days. Fasting is also widely practised in many religions; during Ramadan among Muslims as an act of worship, and among some Pentecostal Christians who abstain from food to supplicate God on behalf of person suffering illness. Similarly, devout Hindus may observe fasting during certain religious festivals, as a spiritual discipline, to bring good fortune to the family or to beseech the divine to relieve another person's suffering (Henley & Schott, 1999).

Health and faith

The majority of Western Europeans view illness as caused by a combination of misfortune, heredity, individual behaviour and environmental factors (Henley & Schott, 1999). Those of other cultural backgrounds may draw on a wider range of explanations. To take one example, many people of Indian heritage living in the United Kingdom, regardless of age, hold a variety of beliefs as to the cause of an impairment or illness. These include physiological, psychosocial and supernatural explanations. The range of factors causing ill health is similar to those identified by members of the ethnic majority, with the exception that more emphasis is sometimes placed on spiritual causes by those of Indian ethnicity (Jobanputra & Furnham, 2005). In some African societies while bacteria or viruses may be believed to be the mechanism of infection there is greater emphasis on why the person has become ill or impaired, which may be attributed to supernatural causes (Henley & Schott, 1999, p. 24). Such interpretations may continue to be significant for some families settled in the UK.

A family's religious convictions can also shape understandings of the cause of an illness or its meaning, though most people actually draw on a range of beliefs regarding both the origin and treatment of disability and disease. Mainstream religious beliefs across faiths do not preclude medical intervention or aid for those who are sick or impaired, although there may be some limited prohibitions – for example treatment using blood products among Jehovah's Witnesses, a Christian denomination (Andrews & Boyle, 1999). Nevertheless stereotypes abound. Muslims are thought to either believe that their child's disability is a punishment from Allah or to adopt a fatalistic attitude which frustrates any action to improve their child's condition (Ali et al., 2001, pp. 962–63). Qur'anic teaching actually encourages individuals to take care of their health and seek medical treatment to that end (Ahmed, 2000, pp. 31–32). While some people do draw on religious accounts of illness or disability, more often than not these are combined with physiological explanations. They very rarely inhibit individuals from seeking medical assistance (Bywaters et al., 2003, p. 508). Indeed, lack of information and the language barrier are perceived by those of Pakistani and Bangladeshi descent, who are predominantly Muslim, as much more prohibitive in accessing health service provision (Ismail et al., 2005, p. 501).

Equally, many of South Asian descent perceive little connection between illness and disability on the one hand and spirituality on the other. Their views tend to be similar to those of the ethnic majority and for them cure is a matter of seeking out the right medical treatment. Typically the adherents of any organised religion will hold a gamut of beliefs ranging from the strictly observant devotee with orthodox views to those who are mostly unfamiliar with the sacred texts of their faith, largely non-practising, but nonetheless identify themselves as belonging to a particular religion (Laird, 2008). Commonly, members of the same kinship group do not share the same spiritual beliefs or observe the same practices. They may differ in their level of devotion to a particular faith or belong to different religions entirely. The existence of a variety of religious perspectives and observances within a family will inevitably influence the degree of consensus or conflict over how an illness or impairment is understood and the appropriate health care for it.

Religious beliefs are for many people a source of guidance, reassurance, support and resilience (Holloway & Moss, 2010). For instance, the Quran offers an explanation of illness and disability, interpreting them as a test or opportunity sent by Allah to improve oneself through patience, commitment and effort in the face of difficulty (Ahmed, 2000, pp. 31–32; Yamey & Greenwood, 2004, pp. 457–58). Similar spiritual interpretations abound in other world religions, which may place emphasis on acceptance of an illness or pain as divine will and the recognition that suffering has a moral and spiritual dimension, sometimes designed to teach a lesson or strengthen character (Henley & Schott, 1999). Having a faith and adhering to religious practices such as congregational worship, meditation or prayer has been found to reduce anxiety and depression while improving the ability to manage or recover from sickness and debility (Cinnirella & Loewenthal, 1999; Koenig et al., 2001). Illness and disability affecting a family member may therefore be comprehended as an opportunity to re-focus on the spiritual aspect of living and relinquish material or petty concerns. Nevertheless some devout believers, whether Christian, Jewish, Muslim, Hindu or Buddhist, may become convinced that their illness or disability is a form of divine punishment, affliction by evil spirits or due to past misdeeds. This does not necessarily prevent them from accessing medical care, but it can mean considerable attention given to spiritual intervention (Laird, 2008).

Health beliefs and child protection

The circumstances in Bexley Safeguarding Children Board (2013) *Serious Case Review Baby F D.O.B. 01.01.2012: D.O.D. 14/06/2012*, which is discussed next, brings together issues of diet, medical treatment and faith. The case examines how parents with strong religious convictions can persist in these despite the significant risks they pose to their children. It also analyses the ethical dilemmas this presents for practitioners endeavouring to respect cultural and spiritual beliefs while at the same time protecting children from harm.

Bexley Safeguarding Children Board (2013) *Serious Case Review Baby F D.O.B. 01.01.2012: D.O.D. 14/06/2012*

In January 2012 a baby boy was born to parents of Black African origin with strongly held religious beliefs which included adherence to veganism. The mother was a

▶

◀

housewife and the father an adult respiratory nurse and both were involved with their church congregation. Many Seventh Day Adventists (a Christian denomination) are vegan and regard the body as the temple of the Holy Spirit which must therefore be kept pure. During the antenatal period the mother refused on religious grounds an ultrasound scan and nutritional supplements which she was advised to take during pregnancy to ensure mother and foetus received appropriate nourishment given the mother's strict vegan diet. The mother also told an obstetrician that she would not be accepting ante-natal care, or seeking medical help for illness, on religious grounds. Shortly after birth the baby required treatment for jaundice, respiratory problems, hypoglycaemia and bleeding in the brain. The parents refused their consent for medical treatment including the administration of antibiotics and vitamin K on religious grounds, resulting in a Child Protection Referral being made by medical staff to Children's Social Care. At this point the parents gave their consent for treatment and stated that if their baby became ill in future they would seek medical treatment for him. The baby's health quickly improved and he was discharged home from hospital within the week.

A joint home visit by a health visitor and a social worker took place a month later, dur-ing which the parents claimed that they had not refused the vitamin K for their child on religious grounds, but due to not understanding its importance for their baby. This contradicted the version of events recorded by hospital staff, but was not challenged by the social worker. At the time the parents stated that hospital staff had harassed them into accepting treatments for their child and they had considered making a complaint. The Serious Case Review panel surmised that rather than this parental attitude raising safeguarding concerns and therefore deeper questioning and greater challenge of the parents, the practitioners backed off – anxious not to be seen as disrespecting the par-ents' faith or appearing judgemental, and possibly intimidated by the prospect of the parents making a complaint about them. Consequently no Child Protection investiga-tion was initiated. The parents also reiterated that they did not take food supplements due to their religious beliefs and had not decided on whether or not to have their baby vaccinated. Thereafter the parents failed to attend follow-up hospital appointments or have their baby immunised. Police were called to the family home almost four months later when the baby was found dead due to Florid Rickets caused by severe vitamin D deficiency. The parents told police that while they were aware their baby was becoming ill due to not feeding and swelling around his eyes and arms; they were awaiting 'a sign from God' as to seeking assistance or treatment for him. The parents were later found guilty of child neglect and manslaughter.

The Serious Case Review was concerned that professionals did not chal-lenge the extreme expression of religious faith which resulted in refusing antenatal tests, food supplements or medical treatment for illness. The risk which these posed to the baby was given insufficient consideration. Instead, once the parents consented to initial medical intervention for their very sick baby (though only after the prospect of child protection involvement) the ongoing risk posed by these religious beliefs and obser-vances was minimised by professionals. They did not seek to explore and ascertain a deeper understanding of the parents' motives and behaviours. Consequently the parents' assertion soon after this episode that they would in future always seek medical assistance for their child was simply accepted at face value. The Serious Case Review found that health care professionals tended to focus on parental choice at the expense of considering its impact on the child. The disproportionate attention given to parental choice also reflects dominant majority ethnic values in relation to individualism and autonomy and illustrates how professional responses are often influenced by these. Bexley Safeguarding Children Board (2013, para.6.9–6.10) concluded that 'Litigation and or complaints against staff in relation to recognising the legal rights of the mother and the ethnic, cultural, religious rights of parents are likely to be influencing professionals' behaviour and in turn losing the voice of the child.' If social workers are to have the confidence to challenge ethnic minority family members who use accusations of racism to fend them off, then aside from developing a secure ethnic identity themselves, practitioners need to be confident that they will be backed up by management. Evidence from research indicates that this is not always the case, with some team leaders apparently lacking the insight, confidence or resolve to confront this type of parental strategy (Laird, 2013).

The parents' attempt to deny their child life-saving medical treatment and essential nutrition constituted neglect, but it was framed within a set of religious precepts and in the absence of other abusive behaviour towards the child. Because of the endeavour of professionals to demonstrate respect for the family's religious values and beliefs, and the fact that they were anxious to avoid prejudice or an accusation of discrimination, attention focused on parental rights rather than the risk possessed to the infant. There was a professional reluctance to question the extreme expression of religious practices which precluded fairly standard medical treatments to save a baby's life or protect against preventative diseases. The mother's refusal to take vitamin supplements, commonly accepted among vegans to ensure the nutritional health of pregnant women or very young children, was also a matter of concern. This aspect highlights the absence of a spiritual dimension from social work and the discomfort many practitioners experience in relation to matters of faith, as a result of which they often fail to explore with family members their religious beliefs and the implications these have for children's wellbeing. By not passing professional judgement on such parental health care choices social workers adopted a position of cultural relativism in which practices regarded as normative by a particular social group are permitted, regardless of the detriment they cause to other members of that group. In this case the withholding by one member of the group, a parent, of vital nutrition and medical treatment from another member of the group, an infant, resulted in their death.

Reflective exercise

Consider the circumstances in Bexley Safeguarding Children Board (2013).

Practitioners in this case were struggling with dilemmas around respecting parental religious beliefs and parental autonomy while at the same time protecting a child from significant harm as a consequence of parental religious convictions and observances. The parents intimated that they were being harassed by professionals to accept treatments for their child in contravention of their religious beliefs. They appeared to be considering making a complaint about the lack of respect for their faith-based beliefs and observances.

How might the majority or minority identity development statuses of the health professionals and social workers involved in this case have influenced their thoughts, feelings and responses to the parents?

How might the complaints procedure of Children's Social Care and the attitudes of frontline or middle managers have influenced the decisions or behaviours of the social workers involved?

Personal beliefs and the good life

Beliefs about health care are not necessarily informed by religious convictions, and many people with a secular worldview can nevertheless hold strong views regarding health care treatment for themselves and their children. Holloway & Moss (2010) identify what they term 'secular spirituality', which refers to the belief systems of a proportion of people who declare themselves atheist, agnostic or not members of any organised religion, but nonetheless hold convictions concerning the meaning of life and the nature of death. Many people draw on an assortment of spiritual beliefs – some religious in origin, others drawn from cultural sources or prompted by their life experiences. These necessarily highly personalised belief systems about what constitutes a 'good life' or quality of life can have implications for people's attitudes towards health, illness and disability.

In Kingston Local Safeguarding Children Board (2015) *Serious Case Review Family A* concerning an affluent professional white middle-class couple who moved from South Africa to the UK (discussed earlier in this chapter) a number of health care beliefs influenced their decisions. The mother, formerly a designer, was resistant to accepting adaptations or equipment in the home, which were visually unattractive or created an institutional ethos. From the parents' viewpoint this was also an endeavour to maintain 'normality' for their severely disabled children. This led to a number of disagreements with professionals seeking to introduce aids into the home to assist the children to eat and avoid choking. Doctors sought to introduce medical interventions which would reduce the children's discomfort and maximise their potential. Conversely the parents wanted their children primarily to have quality of life by refusing them painful procedures, even if this meant shortening their lives. The mother also became extremely distressed on witnessing her children experience discomfort or pain as a result of medical intervention. Both parents indicated that they wanted health care professionals to deliver a palliative approach to their children's care rather than a focus on longevity. When one of the children was admitted to hospital, on several occasions the mother objected to nursing staff giving the child oral feeds and interfered with medical equipment providing oxygen. A number of practitioners also concluded that advice being given to the mother about feeding, physiotherapy, language therapy and the use of aids for the children was not being followed. Yet in all other respects the parents were observed by professionals to provide outstanding care to their children, all of whom had positive relationships with their mother and father.

When professionals became aware of possible medical neglect they were caught between endeavouring to explain, and persuade the parents to accept, medical interventions which would enhance the quality of their children's lives or invoking child protection procedures leading to a more confrontational response. Faced with this dilemma, professionals worried that even when the threshold for commencing child protection procedures had been met, invoking them would place such pressure on the parents that the family would break down. Instead, social workers relied on the medical doctors involved arriving at a consensus as to the level of risk posed to the children's health. But this consensus was not reached, and consequently there was no resort to child protection procedures. This meant that the parents received mixed messages regarding the seriousness of the conflict between the parents' beliefs and the views of professionals concerning their children's medical care.

In this case the parents, who demonstrably cared greatly for their children, wanted to protect them from discomfort and pain, thus increasing their quality of life, even if that ultimately shortened it. They also sought to make their home as normal an environment as possible for their children, although the rejection of some equipment may also have been driven by the aesthetic concerns of the mother in relation to home decor. On the other hand medical staff viewed increasing the children's potential to do more for themselves through the provision of equipment and surgical intervention as enhancing their quality of life. These are conflicting conceptions of the 'good life' and what the desired ends should be of health care interventions. The only way of resolving this kind of impasse between professionals and parents is to focus on the impact of medical intervention, or its absence, on the child and consider whether parental choices pose a risk of significant harm.

Reflective exercise

Consider your practice with families from racial and ethnic minority backgrounds.

How thoroughly do you explore the religious or spiritual worldview and observances of family members in relation to children's health and health care?

If you have not explored these thoroughly with some families you have worked with, identify the reasons why.

How might you develop greater *cultural skill* in this area of practice?

Family care

For both the ethnic majority and those belonging to minorities family members are an essential source of advice, assistance and direct care for someone who is ill or severely disabled. While families of the ethnic majority are generally assumed to be essentially nuclear or single-parent, thus requiring support to care for a disabled or ill child, stereotypes abound regarding the family arrangements and provision of care by those from minority ethnic backgrounds. The stereotype of a South Asian household consisting of a closely knit extended family bound by mutual obligations hinders effective service provision by health and social care professionals. In reality the extended family unit is usually curtailed by strict immigration control; the growing preference for nuclear households; the fragmentation of social networks due to geographical mobility; the participation of women in the workforce; and family breakdown (Katbamna et al., 2004, p. 399). As among the ethnic majority, the amount and quality of informal care available may be adversely affected by the stigma attached to mental illness or such conditions as Down's Syndrome and cerebral palsy.

There is also a widespread assumption among service providers that families from minority ethnic communities *'look after their own'*. This is powerfully reinforced by the perceived concentration of different ethnic communities in relatively few cities or in particular localities of towns and cities. Many households do indeed comprise extended families, live in the same locality as other relatives and enjoy a close and mutually supportive affiliation with other kin. But many other households do not. The established Chinese community in the UK is widely dispersed, as are also groups of recent migrants from Eastern European countries. In England over half of ethnic Chinese respondents to a large-scale study reported having no relatives living in their area (Sproston et al., 1999). Moreover, immigration to Britain may separate close kin; adult children may move elsewhere; family disputes may result in young parents being cut off from relatives;

family disagreements may weaken once strong kinship bonds; or economic necessity may force a parent to live at a distance from their extended families. Racism and substandard housing in deprived localities, which disproportionately affect people from minority ethnic backgrounds, may further isolate individuals and households from wider social networks and amenities. Low income, lack of knowledge regarding benefit entitlement and the language barrier are likely to increase the difficulties of families caring for an ill or disabled relative (Laird, 2008).

Despite racial stereotypes which assume that people from ethnic minorities live in multi-generational extended family units, the reality is that most are caring in much the same way as are those from the ethnic majority. In other words, informal care is chiefly provided by female kin, often with little aid from other family members (Laird, 2008). The amount of care which relatives are expected to provide to an ill or disabled child can also vary. In families influenced by cultural values which emphasise interdependence over independence, less demand may be placed on an individual's self-care as other family members, predominantly women, undertake these tasks for them, such as dressing and feeding (Galanti, 2008, pp. 102–103). For example the concept of *amaeru* in Japanese culture, meaning to accept dependence on another's generosity and kindness, still influences some family members in choosing to care for those who are ill or debilitated, and may be preferred at times to making use of health or social services (Leininger & McFarland, 2002, p. 457). For families influenced by the cultural norms of more collectivist societies, such as some people with roots in the Philippines, there may be less emphasis on a child reaching their full potential in terms of self-care or autonomy as opposed to achieving a balanced interdependence between carer and child. Conversely in some societies the notion of disability as a social category is not widely recognised. While there is an acknowledgement that the individual has an impairment due to, say, blindness, a physical injury or a learning difficulty, they are nevertheless expected and encouraged to follow customary life cycle patterns, such as schooling, working, marrying and parenting, as for example in a number of South American cultures (Lattanzi & Purnell, 2006, pp. 148, 292).

Religious belief and the degree of spiritual devotion among family members may also affect care for family members. As Patterson (2013, p. 204) found, 'Often, religious beliefs and practices are deeply compatible with those of the health care system – the relief of suffering and pain and helping those who are ill or in need, for example, is supported by most major religions'. Research also reveals that religious beliefs inform caregiving in kin groups where children and young people are disabled or family members have mental health problems. These beliefs are manifest both in the commitment to provide ongoing care and also in positive coping strategies adopted by family caregivers (Marshall et al., 2003; Pearce et al., 2016; Smolak et al., 2013). Religious beliefs may therefore tend to reinforce care of ill or disabled parents or children within the nuclear family, kin group or wider faith community. The latter may be, for example, through the assistance of the congregation of a local church, mosque or synagogue to which the family or relatives are affiliated.

Decision-making and consent in health and social care

Decision-making affects not only issues of consent to treatment, but whether professional recommendations around self-care, health care and social support are complied with by the ill or disabled child/parent and other key members of their family. In Anglocentric cultures the individual is the primary decision-maker and even children of sufficient age and understanding may be permitted to make health-related decisions on their own behalf, even when they contradict the opinions or desires of their parents or guardians. In other cultures the family is the primary site of decision-making, because the good of the family takes precedence over the wellbeing of any single family member. For this reason many adults and older children may wish to consult widely with kin before deciding on health care treatment or inputs from Children's Social Care. For some families traditional social hierarchies may dominate the decision-making processes; for example, elders, males or the recognised head of family (e.g. an eldest brother after a father's death) can have a disproportion influence on the outcome. Authority figures in families can vary greatly depending on cultural influences, the opinion of a mother-in-law or grandfather in a multi-generational household of Pakistani heritage may hold considerable sway. Similarly, male kin in a Roma family originating from Hungary may assume the dominant role in decision-making while women of the family are expected to acquiesce. In many cultures, who makes the decision depends on what the decision relates to, so women within the family may be more influential in matters concerning children's health. These varied patterns of decision-making may result in *deferred* (so that family members can consult) rather than *refused* acceptance of health treatments or social care interventions (Galanti, 2008).

In Waltham Forest Safeguarding Children Board (2011) *Serious Case Review: Child W – Executive Summary* (first discussed in Chapter 7) a Ghanaian mother force-fed her children as infants, eventually resulting in the death of her baby daughter. The ensuing investigation established that insufficient account was taken of the influence wielded by the grandmother. Indeed, there had been previous child protection concerns regarding the force-feeding of an elder child, which was believed to have been perpetrated by the grandmother. It emerged from the investigation conducted by the Serious Case Review that the grandmother continued to be an influential figure in the family, particularly in relation to infant care, despite remaining in Ghana for most of the period the father and mother lived in the United

Kingdom, where they had moved as adults. The mother also told social workers that she had been fed in the same way by the grandmother when she was a child. While the father argued that this was a widespread practice in Ghana, it was the grandmother who was extremely influential within the family in maintaining this after the parents moved to the United Kingdom. Unfortunately this dynamic was not fully understood by social workers at the time. This lack of insight could be partly attributable to the dominance of Anglocentric notions of the family unit as nuclear, which resulted in a lack of comprehension or exploration of other family forms, in this case a transnational family whose bonds of close kinship spanned two countries. Assumptions appear to have been made by practitioners predicated on *low power distance* norms between older people and adults predicated on Anglocentric norms. This fails to consider how processes of enculturation in a country of origin may result in *high power distance* norms operating within families. Professionals need to adopt an open mind as to the balance between enculturation experiences derived from a country of origin and how these may have been modified by acculturation experiences in a host country. This requires practitioners to explore social dynamics, roles and decision-making processes within families through discussion with family members as opposed to relying on conjectures and stereotypes.

The degree to which historical immigration and settlement or more recent migration has dispersed the kin group will affect to what extent traditional authority structures are replicated in the UK. How long the family has resided in Britain and experiences of acculturation will inevitably influence how decisions are arrived at. Among some families these may more closely reflect the *individualism* common among the ethnic majority, than customary *collective* patterns of decision-making still predominant in countries of origin. Conversely, for some asylum seekers, refugees or recent economic migrants, to counteract trauma, disorientation, vulnerability or threatened loss of cultural identity some may exaggerate the power distance between men and women or adults and children, resulting in an accentuation of that typical in the family's country of origin (Galanti, 2008; Laird, 2008). Furthermore, the public performance of masculinity by men, portraying themselves as authoritative figures, while women perform femininity through apparent deference, may not reflect the reality of day-to-day family dynamics. Sometimes such public performances can be essential to maintaining self-esteem or preserving pride regarding ethnic *group identification*. Influential decision-makers may simply emerge from within kinship groups regardless of cultural norms by virtue of force of character or because they possess a significant attribute, such as being the only family member who speaks English, earns an income or has a health care background. Decision-making by family members in Walsall Safeguarding Children Board (2014) *Serious Case Review Child W3* challenged stereotypical expectations of women's subservient role in South Asian families.

Walsall Safeguarding Children Board (2014) *Serious Case Review Child W3*

The mother was British born and of Bangladeshi heritage in an arranged marriage with a man from Bangladesh who migrated to the United Kingdom to join her. They were both practising Muslims. The mother was bilingual in Bengali and English and very fluent in written and spoken English. She was described by Walsall Safeguarding Children Board (2014, para.1.4.6) as 'intelligent, demanding and articulate, while the father possessed only a little spoken English'. Together the couple had six children, of which three had disabilities. The mother, due to her much greater English language competence, knowledge of public services as a native of the country and forceful character, dominated both father and children and took all child care related decisions. Hence she mediated all contact between health and social care professionals and the family, and her perspective was the one accepted as the authentic account of happenings within the household. Over an eight-year-period multiple domestic violence incidents, many clearly instigated by the mother, were reported to the police or Children's Social Care. The mother consistently blamed the father for these incidents and portrayed herself as the victim, which was accepted at face value by professionals.

The Serious Case Review remarked on the mother's ability to evoke sympathy in professionals on the basis of assertions which were not checked or verified. Information that the eldest son undertook most of the housework and had substantial childcare responsibilities was overlooked. It later transpired that he was effectively a young carer. Similarly, the father claimed that he took on most of the childcare, while the mother largely neglected the children's care. This information did not lead to any revision of perceptions of the family by professionals. This meant that social workers had a poor comprehension of the actual as opposed to stereotypical gender roles and consequently lacked an understanding of family dynamics. The father's and children's viewpoint was completely lost from assessments and with it the maltreatment perpetrated by the mother.

It is probable in this case that negative stereotypes of South Asian women as passive and men as highly patriarchal and oppressive may have predisposed practitioners to assume the father was the primary decision-maker in the family when in fact it was the mother. Social work responses in this case perhaps illustrate the cognitive process of *selective attention*, whereby information that was known – for example that the father cooked or that the mother appeared extremely forceful – was either unconsciously edited out of perception or minimised by practitioners maintaining the pervasive stereotype of South Asian women as passive and men as oppressive. The processes of *memory* may also have led to social workers inadvertently forgetting observations or information that contradicted the notion of South Asian women as passive.

The expectation or requirement that health-related decisions are made by the family, or authority figures within it, has implications for confidentiality. The professional cultures of health care staff and social workers place importance on sharing information about the health status, impairment or treatment of a family member with as few people as possible (Holland & Hogg, 2001; Laird, 2008). Where families are multi-generational, conjoined households or, as among some Roma or Travellers, include a large network of relatives (often called a clan) this can present considerable challenges in terms of maintaining privacy and supporting notions of individual autonomy which are deeply embedded in Western societies and hence in social work values. Greater emphasis upon reciprocal family bonds can also make for much greater interdependency than is usual within the ethnic majority. Some South Asian parents and grandparents may continue to be very involved in the lives of adult children or grandchildren even if they live elsewhere. Similarly, the cultural norm of *familismo*, influencing interpersonal relationships in many families of Hispanic heritage, places great importance upon social bonds with extended kin. Among some families of Chinese and Japanese heritage deference to the opinions of older relatives, particularly fathers, may remain important (Laird, 2008; Leininger & McFarland, 2002, pp. 277–78).

Reflective exercise

Consider your own practice with families from racial or ethnic minority backgrounds.

How thoroughly do you explore the decision-making processes within these families and how well do you think you understand them?

If sometimes you do not explore these thoroughly or sufficiently comprehend them, identify the reasons why not.

What strategies could you employ to improve your *cultural skill* in this area of practice?

Take-up of mental health services

Many minority ethnic communities report that mental health within the family results in a *collective stigma* which means that the shamefulness of mental illness adversely affects not only the individual who is unwell, but their whole family. According to NHS Greater Glasgow & Clyde (2010, p. 14) 'This was frequently connected to aspects of culture and community such as strong family bonds and extended family structures, and with some of the underlying explanatory causes such as inheritability and blame'. In turn this could detrimentally impact on the marriage prospects of family members experiencing mental ill health, especially among those from

Muslim, Sikh, Hindu and African Caribbean communities. The concept of *collective stigma* could also mean other family members being shunned. Many participants in the research conducted by NHS Greater Glasgow & Clyde (2010, p. 14) reported that this was a major reason why families concealed any mental illness and that, ultimately, 'the value placed on family reputation and marriage may lead family members to refuse support and keep the individual in isolation'.

In a number of faith communities – Islam, Sikhism and Hinduism and some Christian denominations – the imbibing of alcohol is forbidden. Consequently among more religiously conservative families, the alcoholism of a family member may be denied or hidden, or that person shunned by relatives. Lack of cultural appropriateness is also cited by people from across ethnic minorities for not accessing mainstream addiction services (Hurcombe et al., 2010). More generally, Salway et al. (2014, p. 5), drawing on multiple studies, conclude that 'low levels of cultural competence within healthcare interventions contribute to low uptake, negative experiences and poor outcomes among minority ethnic groups'.

Negative experiences of service provision and institutional racism also affect the degree to which people from a particular minority community are willing to engage with health and social care professionals. Compared to members of the White majority population those of African Caribbean descent experience higher rates of compulsory placement in secure psychiatric units; are up to 12 times more likely to be diagnosed with schizophrenia; are less likely to receive psychotherapy or counselling; and are more liable to police involvement in their detainment (Laird, 2008; Equality and Human Rights Commission, 2016). Consequently many from the British African Caribbean community express fear of discrimination by mental health services (Keating & Robertson, 2004). It is therefore unsurprising that people of African Caribbean heritage under-utilise mental health support services and repeated contact with them actually tends to decrease service use (Mclean et al., 2003, p. 658). They also report lower satisfaction scores than White British mental health patients and express interest in accessing specialist voluntary sector services tailored to their cultural needs (Mclean et al., 2003, p. 658; Secker & Harding, 2002; Campbell et al., 2004).

The distrust and unease felt by many people from minority backgrounds towards White-led publicly funded health care inevitably means that some families choose to look after ill or disabled family members rather than engage with public services. Right across minority ethnic groups a substantial proportion of individuals describe experiencing mental health services as alien to their culture or faith, both in terms of its individualist focus and its lack of holistic assessment and care (Faulker, 2014). People with a strong religious faith may seek guidance from a spiritual advisor in preference to accessing health care services (Galanti, 2008, pp. 98–99). These perspectives appear at work in Leicester Safeguarding Children Board (2011) *Serious Case Review in Respect of the Deaths of Children Known as Child 1 and Child 2: Case 'A'* involving domestic violence between an asylum seeking Middle Eastern father and a White British care leaver mother who had two young children, which the father subsequently murdered (first discussed in Chapter 7).

Leicester Safeguarding Children Board (2011) *Serious Case Review in Respect of the Deaths of Children Known as Child 1 and Child 2: Case 'A'* [continued]

The father told his GP that he felt angry all the time. He also reported experiencing trauma while a soldier in his country of origin. His doctor prescribed tranquillisers, gave him information about domestic violence and post-traumatic stress disorder and referred the father to other agencies for anger management and counselling. The father did not make contact with any of these agencies and no referral was made to Children's Social Care. At a later appointment the father again reported to his GP feeling angry and stressed and was advised to see the practice therapist, but he did not do so. He was also known to use alcohol and drugs, although this does not appear to have been shared with the doctor as no referral was made for addiction services. In this case a man recognised as having mental health problems was referred to apparently appropriate services, yet failed to avail himself of any despite experiencing considerable suffering.

While gender could have played a role in the father's refusal of services, as the performance of masculinity in most societies requires men to appear strong, the fact that he had already admitted having poor mental health to his doctor suggests that something else was going on. As a Muslim from the Middle East the father may have found the notion of mental illness alien or stigmatising due to his enculturation experiences. He is likely to have come from a cultural background where addressing such difficulties takes place within the family. But he was isolated from his family due to living in the UK. The idea of consulting with a therapist may have felt bewildering or in his view only for people who are 'crazy'. Moreover, he identified as a Muslim, and consuming alcohol was forbidden by his faith as were drugs. Admitting to this addiction would have been profoundly shaming and deeply stigmatising for him within the local Muslim community. It is notable that the parents appeared quite isolated from social networks. This meant that the father did not take advantage of any assistance for his mental health problems, which eventually culminated in him murdering his family and then committing suicide. Little was ever known by social workers about the father's cultural heritage or faith beliefs and hence they had minimal understanding of his conception of mental illness or treatment.

Reflective exercise

Consider the circumstances in Leicester Safeguarding Children Board (2011).

How could a practitioner create *cultural safety* in work with a father in similar circumstances?

How would a culturally competent organisation deliver mental health services to a father in similar circumstances?

Case study for practitioners

Children's Social Care receives a referral from a consultant paediatrician at a local hospital who is treating an eight-year-old boy for tuberculosis. The consultant is worried by the attitudes expressed and some of the behaviours of the mother and father, who are of Indian ethnicity and also practising Hindus. The parents have told the consultant of their intention to treat their son at home with 'cold foods' and to consult with a sadhu (holy man) to understand why he is ill. Successful biomedical curative treatment for tuberculosis involves adherence to a strict drug regime. The couple have two other children living at home. You are the social worker tasked to conduct an initial assessment with this family.

Consider the CCAM model in Chapter 4. Developing *enlightened consciousness* involves as a first step recognising one's own sense of superiority regarding the heritage beliefs, values and practices which may influence the lives of people from other ethnic or faith groups. The second step requires practitioners to counter any automatic tendency to denigrate or devalue these, by ceasing to rely on stereotypes based on minimal information. Instead what is needed is the accumulation over time of a *grounded knowledge base* about other worldviews. Having a broad-based familiarity with the variety of ways in which religious and spiritual views can contribute to people's understanding of health, illness and disability would help inform a culturally sensitive approach to assessing this family. This *grounded knowledge base* needs to include an appreciation of the range of reasons why some families from racial and ethnic minorities may be reluctant to engage with health and social services. It will be vital to explore with family members what their previous experiences are of health and social care services, or any concerns they have based on knowing about the experiences of other people from their ethnic or faith community.

Cumulative skill proficiency is achieved through reflexively engaging with many families from different racial, ethnic and faith backgrounds over a period of time. Developing this enables you to sensitively explore family structure and decision-making processes. So, for example, is this a nuclear family or part of a larger *ghar* living across several different dwellings in the same vicinity? Is the family practising a traditional form of virilocal residence whereby wives move to live with their husband's family? Conversely, is the nuclear family unit isolated from the rest of their kin group due to geography or interpersonal conflict? Are there transnational aspects of family relationships? What are the implications of these various family arrangements in terms of influences and decision-making about children's health care?

The growing capacity to avoid making stereotypical assumptions or adopting ethnocentric perspectives would facilitate an open-minded discussion of the family's religious beliefs in relation to their children's health. This is only likely to occur if family members feel *culturally safe* and that they are not being judged by the practitioner regarding their spiritual beliefs. *Cumulative skill proficiency* could be deployed to gather information on the parents' religious convictions and what influence they might have on whether the drug regime advised by the consultant paediatrician is likely to be followed. Karma, the Hindu belief that actions in this life or a previous life have adverse consequences at a later point in time, means that these parents need to understand why their son became ill. This is a search for the spiritual cause and does not necessarily mean that the parents are unaccepting of the medical diagnosis. Given that devout Hindus are vegetarian and abstain from alcohol, it is also important to understand if these observances raise concerns for the parents regarding the use of animal products or alcohol in medications.

It also needs to be borne in mind that there is not necessarily a conflict between different health beliefs and practices. For example 'cold foods', which include fruit, if eaten in more quantity would probably help boost their son's physical health. Aside from this, for many families using the preventative or curative treatments of several different health care systems at the same time is not regarded as unusual. These are of course all aspects that need to be explored with family members through *cumulative skill proficiency*. This is a skills set which enables practitioners to work from a *grounded knowledge base* that enables them to identify relevant cultural and spiritual areas for exploration, while doing so with information-gathering approaches which are culturally sensitive and respectful.

Conclusion

Research evidences widespread health inequalities between the ethnic majority population and those from minority ethnic communities. These inequalities are correlated to racism, poverty, unemployment, substandard housing and immigration statuses which reduce the rights and entitlements of family members. The Western system of health care, which is predicated on biomedicine, is generally hostile to alternative approaches to maintaining health. However, many people from a number of minority heritage backgrounds draw on principles and understandings of health and illness underpinning other systems of medical treatment. Family members often utilise multiple health systems in identifying the cause and obtaining remedy for illnesses.

Religious, spiritual and secular understandings of what constitutes the 'good life' can influence parents' and children's views of illness and impairment. These can have adverse implications for children's health care. Equality, spiritual beliefs, religious observances and ideas about quality of life may have beneficial effects on a family's care of a sick or disabled child or young person. Additionally, decision-making processes within families can have far-reaching implications for safeguarding in the context of health and social care provision for children or young people who are ill or disabled. Anglocentric, and often stereotypical, perceptions of gender and inter-generational power relationships can obscure the realities of decision-making in families and hinder culturally sensitive practice.

9
Communication and Families from Ethnic Minorities

Introduction

Effective communication is foundational to social work practice. Sending and receiving information are complex processes involving interdependent cognitive, emotional and behavioural elements. Theories of communication provide insight into how people both formulate the information they want to impart and comprehend the information being sent to them by others. Interactions are complicated by the fact that people often convey unconscious messages about their feelings, attitudes and worldviews. As understanding what someone else means by their words and/or gestures requires some degree of interpretation, this adds another set of cognitive and affective processes. Cross-cultural encounters can pose additional communication challenges as people from different ethnic backgrounds frequently bring to bear different assumptions and perceptions regarding the social world. This chapter explores the complexity of cross-cultural communication with family members and its implications for safeguarding children, while suggesting strategies for improving practice.

Communication theory

Through the processes of socialisation and enculturation children learn how to communicate with others. Even between two people from the same ethnic group, communication is not an instantaneous act. Rather it relies on the sender of a message encoding their intended meaning to produce communication. The verbal component of this is language, which will reflect the sender's choice of grammar, vocabulary and sounds while the non-verbal element comprises their behaviour in terms of facial expression and hand gestures. Once sent, the message embedded in both verbal and non-verbal channels has to be decoded by the receiver. This is a process which involves interpretation and therefore is open to *mis*interpretation of the meanings the sender intended the message to convey. The receiver of the message then encodes a response based on their interpretation of what they think they heard and observed imparted by the sender. Once this response is sent the original sender of a communication now becomes the receiver of the reply to it and in turn decodes this through a process of inter-pretation, encodes a further message to send and so on, creating a feedback loop between the two communicators. These exchanges can occur rapidly, overlap or be simultaneous and contain both conscious and unconscious interpretative elements. When multiple communicators are interacting, the web of encoding and decoding messages can become exceptionally complex and misunderstandings easily proliferate.

As people encode and decode messages they apply cultural filters which comprise mostly unconscious rules concerning how to convey and interpret messages. These form a set of expectations regarding the communication process and prompt emotional responses, which are in turn related to value judgements. A practitioner from the ethnic majority is likely to expect to shake hands during a greeting, as is the norm in Anglocentric societies. However if this is met instead by a slight bow from a mother of Thai heritage, as this is the traditional greeting in Thailand, the practitioner's frustrated expectation may initially elicit surprise and confusion perhaps followed by assumptions that the mother is servile or oppressed, as these tend to be the connotations associ-ated with bowing in Western societies. In a child protection context such an assumption can distort professional judgement around risks posed to a child, in this instance by construing the mother as disempowered and dominated by others. Ethnocentrism in the context of communication means that people tend to interpret messages from their own culture-bound worldview and usually lack the insight to recognise that some verbal and non-verbal commu-nications are assigned different meanings within other cultural contexts.

While encoding and decoding are essentially cognitive processes they invariably reflect how a particular sender of a message is feeling and may also involve emotional reactions to other communicators. Such emotional states and affective responses to others create 'noise' which influences how a message is interpreted. If a social worker is hurrying between home visits to families and is anxious about making the next visit on time, he may be more abrasive or short in his delivery when speaking to the child in the household. As a result the child decodes this as irritation with them, feels anger towards the social worker in return and encodes a message incorpo-rating this unstated feeling. The social worker is confused on decoding the child's ambiguous message and so on. Inevitably considerable emotional 'noise' is created in this type of exchange.

Stereotypes or assumptions regarding a person's motives can also create 'noise' which interferes with the interpretation of a message. Many of these stereotypes and assumptions can operate at an unconscious level, making it particularly difficult for practitioners to recognise how their decoding of a parent's or child's message is being warped. If a social worker holds the stereotype that males from a Pakistani heritage background are highly patriarchal and females subservient, and a father says 'my daughter is respectful' the practitioner is likely to decode that assertion along the lines of 'my daughter does what she is told to by me'. Yet respectfulness of itself is generally a positively valenced value across cultures, including in Anglocentric societies. The father could simply have encoded the message to mean his daughter is considerate of other family members. But in this instance *'noise'* created by a stereotype interferes with accurate decoding and the practitioner hears a message that was not actually sent. When communication is between people of different racial backgrounds or ethnicities, particularly if they have different first languages, the scope for misunderstandings is magnified (Matsumoto & Juang, 2004). The enormous potential for inadvertent and unrecognised misunderstandings between people from different cultural and faith backgrounds makes it imperative to take additional time to build rapport with parents, guardians, partners and children.

Rapport building

When people meet they typically engage in some small talk or casual conversation. Linguistically this is referred to as non-task oriented conversation which has no explicit transactional goals. In other words neither party is overtly trying to achieve anything specific through the communicative exchange at this point. Often such conversations revolve around superficial family activities, holidays, leisure or in the UK comment on the weather. This aids the creation of positivity and cooperativeness between the parties, while contributing to rapport in preparation for the ensuing discussion around substantive matters. There can be cultural variation in norms regarding how long non-task oriented conversation ought to, or is expected to, last for before turning to address the purpose and substance of the interaction. In Germany people tend to settle down to business within a few minutes whereas in Spain and Italy it can be almost half an hour before the actual subject matter is broached and for which the meeting was arranged (Hua, 2014, p. 25). Different norms about small talk can lead to misunderstanding in cross-cultural encounters. A person influenced by cultural norms which emphasise extended small talk as a conveyor of sociability, respect and politeness is likely to feel snubbed, disliked or bewildered by an individual from a different ethnic background who cuts short this element of their interaction. Social status and other forms of power relationship between social groups can affect how small talk is performed. For example in most societies it is the person who holds the superior position, due to perhaps being older or more educated, who usually determines how long small talk lasts before shifting into goal-oriented conversation (Hua, 2014).

While the name *'small talk'* conjures up a dialogue of mundanities, the divide between this and purposeful discussion exists on a continuum and they are not separated into discrete conversational categories. So casual enquiries as to how family members are getting along, or how someone enjoyed their recent holiday, can be at one and the same time superficial in terms of content, but substantive in relation to the social messages being conveyed. Of course communication that is apparently *small talk*, such as a practitioner's casual question about a family member, can also be subtly part of the business of the meeting, that of completing a needs assessment. Hence task-oriented conversation can be embedded in *small talk*. While *small talk* most often occurs at the commencement of an interaction it can also be important at the end of a task-oriented meeting as the parties endeavour to wind down the meeting, affirm one another's value and inclusion and prepare to take their leave (Hua, 2014).

Precisely because racial and ethnic differences often generate an additional layer of potential misinterpretations and misunderstandings, rapport building during initial encounters with individuals from diverse cultural backgrounds becomes crucial. As Leigh (1998, p. 60) observes, 'in most situations the natural conversation openers are regarded by social workers as preliminaries that ought to be focused quickly on the reasons why the person is at the interview. Prolonged conversation is viewed as the behaviour of a person who is attempting either to avoid the problem or to deal with anxiety.' Consequently, in most encounters informal conversation is cut short as the interaction moves fairly quickly to the matter which prompted the practitioner to meet with family members or their close friends and neighbours. This is perpetuated by the conception of time embedded in Anglocentric cultures which segments time for specific tasks, and it is accentuated for social workers by performance management through online software systems of surveillance (Broadhurst et al., 2010; Munro, 2011). Despite the time pressures under which practitioners operate there is an additional imperative in cross-cultural encounters to use social chat, frequently treated as of minor importance, as an opportunity to explore the cultural context of people's lives.

Small talk is often used to help create a friendly and non-threatening atmosphere prior to commencing the work phase of the practitioner–service user interaction. In cross-cultural interactions Leigh (1998) suggests extending this into a more prolonged endeavour to understand the affiliations, lifestyle and worldview of family members. In part this requires an acknowledgement by practitioners that the family can act as a resource to help educate the practitioner about the family's ethnic heritage. Casual friendly conversation with family members or other significant individuals from within their ethnic group, can be vital in helping practitioners demonstrate a genuine open-minded interest in the family's background and enabling family members to evaluate the social worker and judge their trustworthiness, approachableness and capacity for comprehending the family's circumstances and difficulties. Without making time to create this opportunity, it is immensely difficult for the practitioner to then draw out from parents, children and their relatives key social norms, beliefs and behaviours shaped by culture and faith which are relevant to safeguarding children.

Extending the period of social informality is crucial to building sufficient trust to be positioned to conduct an *ethnographic interview* (Leigh, 1998). This sensitively explores with kin the role of culture and religion in their lives and the degree to which enculturation, acculturation, hybridity, transnationalism and for some migration, affects their ethnic identification, lifestyle, outlook and experiences of racial or sectarian abuse and discrimination. The vital need to build rapport with parents and children from a different heritage background is borne out in Gloucestershire Safeguarding Children Board (2011) *Serious Case Review: Redacted Overview Report Re SCR 0310.*

Gloucestershire Safeguarding Children Board (2011) *Serious Case Review: Redacted Overview Report Re SCR 0310*

A single mother and her four children (three of whom were school age and the youngest aged two years) migrated from their country of origin to the UK in 2009. They immediately moved into a two-bedroom dwelling with relatives who had migrated a month earlier. None of the children could speak English, while the mother was described as having 'very basic English'. Due to her immigration status she had *no recourse to public funds* although she did have the right to undertake paid work. Within days of her arrival the mother registered her children with a GP and contacted Education Services to arrange for their schooling. During their initial introduction to the school the children were described by teachers as malnourished, poorly dressed and destitute. They were also very unsettled, which was exacerbated when the mother physically pushed one of the children who soon afterwards bit a teacher.

The mother was asked to withdraw two of the children temporarily in order to protect other pupils and until a reintegration plan could be put in place. This left just the eldest child attending school. It later transpired that some of the children had probably not attended formal education in their country of origin. Invariably the children in this unfamiliar situation would have felt very disoriented and confused, particularly given that they had recently moved to a new country and did not know the language. When a month later the children again attended (although no reintegration plan was developed) the mother was seen to slap one of the children. The Serious Case Review surmised that the mother would have experienced feelings of disempowerment and confusion in this new environment, impairing her *parental capacity* and resulting in impatient responses to her children's behaviour.

Later the mother also failed several times to pick up one of the children in order to provide them with lunch, as they were not entitled to free school meals. It later transpired

▶

◀

that in fact the mother was often away from the home looking for work or in casual employment, leaving the children for long periods in the care of other adults in the household. Many professionals who interacted with the mother were unsure of her ethnicity, language or culture. Moreover, some practitioners made the mistaken assumption that she spoke a dialect of her language for which it would be difficult to find an appropriate interpreter. Similarly, teaching staff failed to sufficiently engage with the eldest child at school to ascertain her first language and she remained socially isolated, communicating little with other pupils. Within three months of the family's arrival in the UK the emergency services received a telephone call stating that the two-year-old daughter was unconscious at home. She was resuscitated by paramedics and admitted to hospital where she was discovered to have hypothermia and multiple old injuries.

What is evident from this account is that quite basic information about the mother's native language, her impoverished circumstances and her experience of being a recent migrant were not known. Likewise, it was not known that some of the children had little experience of schooling, nor what native language they spoke. It also remained unknown whether the children were being left in the care of kin due to a cultural practice or as the result of the mother's straitened circumstances, which forced her to be away from them most of the time, working long hours for low pay. Similarly, because nothing was known of the mother's cultural heritage, it was not clear whether the harsh disciplining of her children and unrealistic expectations of their behaviour was due to cultural factors or acculturation stressors resulting from being a new arrival in a foreign country. Yet this was a mother who had brought her children to the UK seeking a better life, had quickly arranged their access to health and education services and was working extremely hard to earn an income.

Rapport can also be promoted by using *cultural knowledge* – a component of several models of cultural competence described in Chapter 4. While it may take an initial interview or introductory home visit to establish the ethnicity and languages spoken by family members, once this is done rapport can be facilitated by learning a few words of greeting and courtesy. Using customary honorifics when addressing family members and checking that your pronunciation of people's names is correct is essential to building working relationships with those who have little or no knowledge of English. Understanding different naming systems is also imperative, both in terms of getting right people's names and their relationships to each other and regarding accurate recording. In the traditional Chinese naming system the family name comes first, followed by a two-part personal name normally said together. Typically among South Asian Muslim families, wives do not share the family name and instead have a two-part name comprising a personal name and a title or sometimes a second personal name. South Asian Muslim males customarily have a two-part name consisting of a sacred name followed by a personal name, with the sacred name never being used on its own. In the traditional Somali naming system both males and females have a personal name followed by their father's and then paternal grandfather's personal name. Here again husbands and wives do not share a surname as is usual among the ethnic majority (Henley & Schott, 1999). While practitioners need to take time to accumulate knowledge about common naming systems, it needs to be borne in mind that not all families from a particular ethnic group will adhere to a traditional naming system and many may have adopted an Anglicised version.

Reflective exercise

Consider the circumstances in Gloucestershire Safeguarding Children Board (2011).

How would you engage in social chitchat to build initial rapport with a mother in similar circumstances to those in this case?

What *cultural skills* could you employ to facilitate such a discussion bearing in mind that this is *small talk* to build rapport?

How might working with families from a similar or dissimilar racial, ethnic or faith background to you influence your initial encounter and how would you go about building rapport in these circumstances?

Verbal communication in an additional language

Many migrants who arrive in the UK do not have English language competence. In Gloucestershire Safeguarding Children Board (2011) the mother was described as having 'very basic English'. While initially none of the children could speak English, within a few months the eldest child (the only one to attend school consistently) was described as developing English language skills. At this point, where the family had only been in the UK a few months and English was a new language for them all, the potential for misunderstanding when conversing with professionals in English was high. This is due to the syntax, semantics and pronunciation differing so widely between languages as to make it extremely challenging to achieve high accuracy in an additional language. Indeed some migrants may be conversing in a third or fourth language. A Senegalese father may speak Wolof, an African language and the *lingua franca* of his country of origin, French the official language, Arabic as he is a Muslim and English to communicate in the UK.

Researchers generally agree that children up to around the age of 12 have the greatest potential to acquire an additional language to a high degree of competence. After this age language acquisition tends to become more difficult and often the grammar and phonology of additional languages is not fully assimilated. It is for this reason that people speaking or writing in a second, third or sometimes fourth language commonly make grammatical errors or sometimes converse with a strong accent (Lustig & Koester, 2013). Such situations can create multiple communication challenges for social workers and other professionals involved in safeguarding children.

Some languages, such as Mandarin and Japanese, do not use verbs to convey tense whereas in English the form of the verb is essential to indicating whether an action takes place in the past, present or future. Misunderstandings can result when a second or third language speaker of English mistakenly uses the past tense rather than the present tense, thus misleading a social worker into thinking that a visit back to the home by a violent father occurred in the past rather than in the present. If the incorrect pronouns are used this can mislead practitioners as to who has done what. In some languages, for example Estonian, Hungarian, Yoruba and Malay, pronouns are gender neutral. If this rule is carried over into conversing in English then 'he', 'she' and 'it' may be used interchangeably without attention to the actual gender of the person who is being referred to. So for example a recent Estonian migrant girl might mis-describe the person mistreating her by identifying them with the incorrect gendered pronoun in English. This would clearly mislead any professional trying to conduct a child protection enquiry. Often such language rules are unconscious or taken for granted and are therefore difficult for those speaking English as an additional language to identify or for a native English speaker to recognise.

A strong accent carried over from the phonology of a first language into an adult's or child's spoken English or mispronunciations of words can also result in phrases being misheard by a practitioner, creating unrecognised misunderstandings. Equally, some people speaking English as an additional language may mistake the meaning of some English words and use them incorrectly, leading to misinterpretations of their messages. A Spanish teenager might tell a social worker she is 'embarrassed' meaning she is pregnant, because the Spanish word for this is 'embarazada' which sounds quite similar. Clearly this creates a fundamental misunderstanding about the situation. Professionals can inadvertently cause confusion for non-native English speakers by using everyday colloquialisms such as 'sitting on the fence', 'lost the plot', 'gutted' meaning devastated, or 'wicked' meaning cool. These phrases are likely to be interpreted literally, prompting bewilderment or offence to the person speaking English as an additional language.

Moreover, when people have learnt English as their first language in a different country for example in the US or Nigeria (where English is the official language), semantic differences in the use of words can still persist. Americans refer to the floor at ground level as the first floor while Britons refer to it as the ground floor. This semantic discrepancy, while apparently insignificant, could be crucial in establishing the location of family members, neighbours or events, when conducting a child in need assessment. Likewise in American English *'trousers'* are named *'pants'*, which in British English is an item of underwear. In a child protection enquiry confusion over the meaning of these terms could clearly mislead a social worker. Double-checking if a message has been fully understood is crucial even when a family member's first language is actually English.

Similar effects can sometimes occur in written communications such as letters, emails and texts, when they are composed in English as the author's second or third language with misuse of vocabulary or erroneous grammar giving rise to miscommunication. While purely oral languages are now rare, a number of adults and children may not be able to read or write in their first language due to lack of access to formal schooling. This may make written communication in English even more challenging to learn. It was significant in Walsall Safeguarding Children Board (2014) concerning physical abuse of their children by a British-born mother of Bangladeshi heritage and Bangladeshi-born father who spoke little English. Children's Social Care relied over the years on a series of six formal written agreements with the parents to improve the family situation, which was characterised by domestic abuse and neglect of the children. These were routinely breached by the parents, for which there were no consequences. However, it was not clear if these written agreements were ever translated into Bengali for the father, and even if they were, whether he was literate in his first language, and could have understood them. In Gloucestershire Safeguarding Children Board (2011), although it was known that a single mother recently arrived in the UK only spoke a little English, when she registered her children at a local GP surgery a welcome letter in English was sent to her from the health visiting service containing relevant contact information. A health visitor also left a voicemail message in English for the mother.

Code-switching

Nigerian English is spoken both in a standardised and creolised form and many people code-switch between these two languages. *Code-switching* occurs when a person can speak a number of languages, but chooses different ones depending on the context and who they are speaking to. Someone of Nigerian heritage might use standardised Nigerian English during interactions with professionals, but its creolised form when with kin. Even within the UK native English speakers articulate the language in different ways; patois spoken by many of African Caribbean heritage and derived from Jamaican Creole, is being increasingly adopted by young people from the ethnic majority. Glaswegian English, a Scottish dialect, involves shortened forms of many English words, distinctive phonemes and dissimilar meanings given to some words from their Standard English denotation.

Unsurprisingly many people engage in *code-switching*, a girl of African Caribbean background might use Standard English when addressing a teacher in school, but patois with friends and family. It can also occur across languages and not just dialects. In an ethnically Chinese household, parents might use Cantonese with grandparents and a mixture of English and Cantonese speaking to one another or their children depending on the topic of conversation, while using English in public spaces. *Code-switching* can be used to convey the closeness of a relationship; to exclude others from a conversation or social group; or because one language or dialect feels more comfortable or apt than another relative to the topic of conversation. *Code-switching* can also be used as markers of ethnicity; for example, the use of Gaelic among Irish people and Welsh among those from Wales is often a proud expression of cultural identity and social group affinity. However, *code-switching* can be deployed to obstruct child protection enquiries.

In Cambridgeshire Safeguarding Children Board (2015) a child was compulsorily admitted to hospital under police powers due to suspected sexual abuse. The mother and stepfather engaged in a heated public discussion in their first language incomprehensible to hospital staff, even though both parents were known to speak English. This use of *code-switching* by the parents from English to their heritage language was clearly designed to exclude professionals from their conversation, and possibly to concoct a story to explain the child's injuries at short notice or perhaps for the stepfather (subsequently discovered to be the perpetrator) to threaten the mother.

Code-switching was also used by a parent in Walsall Safeguarding Children Board (2014) to frustrate professionals trying to establish who had assaulted a child admitted to a hospital with knife wounds. This case concerned a British-born mother of Bangladeshi heritage and her British-born children. The injured child was reluctant to speak while his older brother, who was also present, began to disclose that the mother had used a knife. She spoke firmly to him in Bengali and thereafter he said nothing further. This was despite the fact that mother and sons spoke good English. Conversing in her heritage language was being used by the mother to issue a threat to silence her elder child. Lack of language competence in Bengali meant that the professionals present could not prove this. Clearly the use of a heritage language by a parent, when all present speak fluent English, is probably being deployed to thwart comprehension by practitioners.

Dialects and accents

A person's accent comprises distinctive pronunciations of English words due to their: speaking in an additional language; being from another English-speaking country; or from a region of the UK. Some native English speakers use dialects, which are versions of English but with distinctive vocabularies, grammars and phonology and use many words and phrases not found in

Standard English while generally being mutually intelligible among English speakers. Many English dialects are spoken in the UK including Black English, Broad Yorkshire, Scots and Cant (among Irish Travellers). Each accent or dialect attracts a range of assumptions or stereotypes about the speaker. Research studies reveal that people's accents are used by others to make initial judgements about them. Commonly those speaking with an accent because English is their second or third language are assumed to be less intelligent or less competent. In relation to dialects, research reveals that for instance a speaker of Black English will be supposedly less reliable than if they used Standard English, while someone speaking in Broad Yorkshire is likely to be regarded as more trustworthy than people with other regional accents (Lustig & Koester, 2013, pp. 173–74; Workman & Smith, 2008).

Different accents are also associated with class positions in the UK. Accent is therefore a powerful marker of in-group/out-group distinctions for listeners and is a primary social characteristic upon which people are appraised, often resulting in stereotyping, stigmatisation and discrimination for those who have working-class, regional or non-native accents. In Rochdale Borough Safeguarding Children Board (2013) involving the sexual exploitation of girls, the families affected complained that police and social workers dismissed them because they were identified as belonging to the underclass or precariat. It is worth considering whether the accent of these girls and their parents, alongside their use of English, influenced the perception of professionals, perpetuating stereotypes of them as less intelligent or trustworthy.

Reflective exercise

Consider your own practice with families from racial and ethnic minority backgrounds.

What assumptions do you make and what stereotypes are engaged when you hear a family member converse in a foreign language to you or speak English with a foreign-sounding accent?

How do these first impressions influence your initial interactions with family members?

To what extent do you explore with different family members what languages they speak?

What are the challenges of finding out more about what languages family members speak and how could you address these?

The foreign language effect

When individuals are speaking English as their second or sometimes third or fourth language this can plainly create challenges for practitioners in decoding their messages. There are also difficulties for additional language English speakers. Researchers have identified a *foreign language effect* by virtue of which those speaking in languages other than their native one experience a decline in cognitive ability, which diminishes their capacity to process information. Encoding and decoding messages are therefore sensitive to a person's affective state. Consequently, they often require more time to decode and encode messages.

In Gloucestershire Safeguarding Children Board (2011) involving a recent migrant mother, the social worker relied on family members (who had only arrived in the UK four months before) to interpret for her during a highly emotionally charged Child Protection Interview regarding her child's injuries. This context would have impaired the ability of family members to effectively process information and verbally communicate in a second language. In Coventry Safeguarding Children Board (2013) the Polish mother initially spoke little English on arriving in the UK, but improved on this over time, although she never become entirely fluent. There were contradictory understandings between agencies and professionals as to the level of the mother's proficiency in English as this was sometimes obscured by her heavy consumption of alcohol.

Of course some speakers of English as an additional language may achieve a very high degree of proficiency, especially if they started learning it in childhood, and may be largely impervious to the *foreign language effect*. Nevertheless, it is imperative that practitioners take time to develop self-awareness in relation to their own experiences of trying to get by in a country where they do not speak the language or have only a little knowledge of it. People may also behave differently from normal when attempting to communicate in their non-native language. Reproduced in the text box below from NEC (1990, p. 16) are a number of common coping behaviours in this situation which can clearly be at odds with much of a person's usual conduct. Practitioners need to consider how these effects might create misleading impressions during interactions with a parent, guardian or child communicating with a limited knowledge of English.

Communicating in a foreign language

When communicating in foreign language you may:

- Smile a lot and make friendly gestures to show that although you cannot communicate you want to be helpful.

- Become very tired, even during a short conversation, and switch off.

- Go ahead and do things you are not sure about without checking or asking advice.

- Remain passive and silent, in case you get out of your depth.

- Settle for a simple, though inaccurate, explanation, and give up the attempt to express the complete truth because it requires more complicated language than you can manage.

▶

◄
- Pretend that you understand to avoid exasperating the other person and forcing them to repeat the whole thing again.

- Feel that everyone is talking about you.

- Become more sensitive to non-verbal signals, for example, body language, tone of voice.

Inter-cultural competence in conversation

Communication Accommodation Theory concerns the way in which people from different backgrounds endeavour to converge towards each other in their communication styles in order to convey affinity or increase mutual understanding of messages. Coupland et al. (1988) argue that this does not necessarily mean that individuals participating in a conversation adopt the same speech characteristics as each other, but rather that they adapt their typical modes of communication to develop a fit between their different ways of communicating. Coupland et al. (1988) also theorised four accommodative strategies used to achieve this which are particularly crucial when individuals have different linguistic proficiency in the language they are using to communicate. These are outlined below and can be deployed by practitioners when working with non-native English speakers.

Approximation strategies: involve convergence towards the other individual's performance in terms of accent, speech rate; modifying one's own accent to be more comprehensible to someone unfamiliar with it or slowing down one's rate of verbal delivery.

Interpretability strategies: refer to a sender's modification of the complexity of their message in order to improve its clarity for the receiver. This is also a function of the sender's perception of the capacity of the receiver to comprehend their messages.

Discourse management strategies: encompass the adaptive use of turn-taking, topic-selection and acknowledging *face* needs by individuals during an exchange in order to facilitate the conversation.

Interpersonal control strategies: involve the individual permitting those they are endeavouring to communicate with to have more control over the interpersonal exchange; by encouraging the other person to initiate topics of conversation, asking open questions.

As Hua (2014) observes, while accommodation strategies are usually well intentioned, they can easily result in over-accommodation as in the case of what is commonly referred to as *'foreigner talk'*. This often occurs when native speakers of a language greatly under-estimate the linguistic competence of non-native speakers. Typically during such an encounter the non-native speaker is perceived as possessing low linguistic proficiency and as a result the native speaker proceeds to drastically simplify their speech register, which becomes 'characterised by high frequency words, reduced syntactical complexity, clearer and exaggerated articulation, slower speech rate' (Hua, 2014, p. 134). Patently this kind of behaviour can come across as patronising and disrespectful. Moreover, health and social care professionals are known to be reluctant at times to clarify confusing verbal messages or double-check their comprehension when interacting with an additional language English speaker for fear of offending them.

When a misunderstanding does occur during communication this can be signalled using interjections such as 'pardon', 'could you repeat that please' or more explicitly in terms of meta-linguistic enquiries such as 'I'm not sure what you mean' or 'could you explain that again, I did not fully understand'. Other less constructive ways of managing misunderstandings include ignoring the messages that are not understood as opposed to indicating to the sender that their message has not been comprehended. Some receivers of messages they find confusing respond through the use of silence during these parts of the conversation or with non-committal or token vocalisations such as 'um' and 'yeah' (Hua, 2014, p. 138). Therefore effective communication involves a practitioner being able to pick up on the verbal and non-verbal clues from a parent or child indicating that they have not understood the message, while engaging in further communication to clarify and rectify the misunderstanding. Drawing on the literature Hua (2014, p. 139) suggests a set of strategies, described in the text box below.

Clarifying meaning during communication

Confirmation checks: these include asking direct questions about a message that has been sent, such as 'did you understand that?', 'would you like me to explain that again?', 'have I understood what you meant?'

Self-repair: refers to the sender rephrasing a message or elaborating further on it to provide clearer articulation of content or more clarity.

Interactive-repair: involves a degree of mutual acknowledgement of a misunderstanding between the sender and receiver and working together to develop shared meanings and understandings.

Letting it pass: means ignoring ambiguities in some messages in order to focus on the key content of the conversation.

Communication without an interpreter when English is a speaker's additional language

In Gloucestershire Safeguarding Children Board (2011) the eldest child had come to the UK unable to speak English, but within three months of regularly attending school was developing English language skills. Teachers and social workers spent insufficient time with her to establish what her language competence was in English. This contributed to a lack of communication with the child and hence difficulty obtaining information about what was really happening in the home. Social workers communicating with people speaking English as an additional language need to appreciate that their competence may change over time. Therefore it is crucial to devote time to casual conversation to build rapport in order to establish what a parent's or child's level of fluency in English actually is before moving on to child protection related matters. It is also vital to be mindful that English language competence is greatly diminished for a non-native speaker when intoxicated or if they are in a highly emotional state.

Practitioners also need to be alert to the possibility of being misled by family members as to the English language competence of children, particularly when native speakers of a language can be predisposed to considerably under-estimate the linguistic competence of non-native speakers. In Cambridgeshire Safeguarding Children Board (2015) the mother, who was from an EU country, presented her daughter at the GP surgery with bleeding around the genital area and difficulty passing urine or defecating. On examination by the doctor bruising to the child's body was also seen. The mother told the doctor that her daughter could not speak English and only spoke another EU language, and as a consequence the child's history was taken from the mother. The child was only seen in the mother's presence and she reported that her daughter told her she had fallen out of bed that morning. The doctor described the child as 'quiet and shy' during this meeting. Just a few hours later after the GP's referral the mother took her daughter to a hospital's paediatric emergency department where the child was spoken to directly in English by a nurse. Contrary to the mother's assertion, the child could communicate in what the nurse described as an 'understandable' level of spoken English. On examination the child was found to have blood in her urine, extensive bruising and a human bite mark on her neck. Children's Social Care and police were immediately alerted and police protection powers triggered.

In Coventry Safeguarding Children Board (2013) the Polish mother, who on first arrival in the UK spoke little English, tried to discourage professionals from interacting directly with her four-year-old son by telling them that he was 'retarded'. She also pressurised his seven-year-old sister into corroborating this assertion. While it was known to professionals that the four-year-old could speak a little English, social workers increasingly relied on his sister to interpret for him and his teachers communicated with him through gestures. The sister was frequently used by professionals as an interpreter for her mother and brother. This included at one point being asked by two police officers to explain an earlier injury to her four-year-old sibling, potentially caused by an adult in the household. When the toddler was referred to a paediatrician because of concerns about his weight loss and unkempt appearance, the paediatrician described him as not articulating any intelligible words and speculated this could be due to a speech delay. In school he was observed to be socially withdrawn. Native English speakers, predisposed to think that speakers of English as an additional language are less able, failed to realise that here was a young, shy, unconfident child with limited English language skills. He desperately needed the commitment of practitioner time to build rapport and establish his language competency to enable him to describe his experiences of extreme maltreatment by his mother and her partner. In situations where the practitioner is communicating with someone who can speak a little English, but is not fluent, NEC (1990, p. 15) offers advice reproduced in the text box below (adapted for use by any health or social care practitioner).

Communicating without an interpreter

- Avoid jargon, long words and difficult idioms

- Speak slowly and try not to get louder

- Listen for the words the person knows, and try to use them

- Plan what to say before you start

- Stick to one subject at a time

- If you give instructions, say them in the order you want the person to do them

- Pause between subjects and signal. Say, for example 'Now I want to ask you about...'

- Use active tenses, not passive. For example, 'the doctor will see you', not, 'You will be seen by the doctor'.

- Try to avoid questions that can be answered with 'yes', for example, 'Do you understand?' 'Yes' is one of the first words anyone learns in a foreign language, but it does not necessarily mean they understand. 'Yes' can also mean:

  o 'Yes I'm listening but I don't understand.'

  o 'Yes I want to be helpful but I don't understand.'

  o 'Yes, I'm listening but I'm too tired and confused to take in what you are saying even though I know you mean well.'

  o 'Yes I'm listening and I feel under great pressure and if I say "yes" you might go away.'

Conversely, NEC (1990) also warn against overestimating the amount of English a person understands. Often people speaking in their second or their language seem to easily manage conversation comprising social chitchat and familiar subjects, for example what things they did during the previous week. This can convey the impression of greater competence in English than they actually command, when in fact once the discussion moves from small talk and current events to the past, future and abstract matters they are left struggling with comprehension of spoken English. Conversing in an additional language is effortful and often demands immense concentration for the speaker, which will affect their ability to remember all that was discussed. Hence even short or ostensibly straightforward communications ought to be backed up with a synopsis in a written or oral format comprehensible to the family member. Precisely because communicating in a second or third language requires effort and focus from a family member, stressors in the environment or stress caused by the topic of conversation can easily degrade their language competence. Social workers need to be aware of, and listen out for, the fluctuation in the ability of family members to understand and speak English. Reducing stressors should be a prime consideration in any interaction for this reason. Practitioners also need to be mindful of the extent to which child protection work of itself is stressful for parents and children alike and how this might degrade their English language competence.

Reflective exercise

Consider your practice with families from ethnic minority backgrounds.

What strategies could you employ to better assess their verbal and literacy skills in their first language and any additional languages including English?

What strategies could you use to distinguish between levels of proficiency in speaking and comprehending additional languages?

Pragmatics of language in cross-cultural communication

Regardless of a person's proficiency in English, the *pragmatics* of different languages can still produce fundamental misunderstandings. *Pragmatics* refers to how language is actually used by people in different contexts, and the meanings given to particular phrases. This aspect of language is highly influenced by cultural ideas and practices. Societies differ in the degree to which asking direct questions or making direct refusals is acceptable behaviour. In Anglocentric cultures such as those of North America, Australia and the UK asking direct questions or 'clearing the air' is commonplace. In countries such as Japan and China the preference is for face-saving approaches to addressing problems between people. Therefore, even when adults and children have a good command of English, misunderstandings may arise where for instance an ethnic majority social worker conducting a child protection investigation poses direct questions to family members who are first-generation Chinese migrants. To the family, the social worker appears aggressive and careless of their reputation which is likely to undermine rapport building and partnership working. Similarly, some languages have polite or formal modes of address and/or grammatical constructions which reflect social hierarchy and thus the status of the person being spoken to. When these are violated, for example by a social worker using the *pragmatics* of English rather than the *pragmatics* of Spanish while working with parents born in Mexico, then the practitioner's manner can appear impertinent or disrespectful. How language is deployed in cross-cultural contexts can be crucial even when all the parties to the interaction can communicate in English. This is because each language has a unique set of *pragmatic rules* which often correspond to the related culture.

Due to the fact that people speaking any second or third language frequently carry over the *pragmatics* and intonations of their first language, practitioners need to be wary of making judgements about a family member's attitudes towards the content of verbal communication without fully checking this out through further discussion. In Mandarin, the most widely spoken Chinese language, politeness is conveyed through the deployment of different pronouns and verbs, rather than through discrete words such as 'please', 'thank you', 'excuse me', 'sorry', 'could you', etc. When a person leaves these out they can appear abrupt, rude or offhand to a native English speaker. Similarly, in some languages the syllables in a sentence are more consistently stressed than is common in English. When an individual transfers over this kind of intonation from their native language to speaking English they can sound abrasive or angry. Practitioners in these cross-cultural interactions need to avoid jumping to conclusions about the feelings or attitudes of family members that they think are being conveyed through how non-native speakers use English. Instead practitioners should try to suspend judgement and double-check any assumptions through further discussion with family members.

Using an interpreter to communicate

Serious Case Reviews reveal multiple issues arising from the failure to use an interpreter. In Coventry Safeguarding Board (2013), after a referral from the school nurse, a four-year-old was examined by a paediatrician. At this interview, while the Polish mother had declined an interpreter as her spoken English had improved over the six years that she had lived in the UK, the clinician did not think that perhaps an interpreter might be needed to communicate with the child. This meant that it was the mother's perspective alone which was heard as she told this doctor that her son had an excessive appetite, engaged in faecal smearing and behaved aggressively towards other children. Unbeknown to professionals at this time, the mother and her male partner were hitting the child, immersing him in cold water and forcing him to do extreme exercises as punishments. Making a broad point regarding the importance of engaging interpreters appropriately after investigating a similar lapse, Cambridgeshire Safeguarding Children Board (2015, para.5.1.5) concluded:

> It is important for both universal and specialist services to clarify with the family and children at an early stage what languages are spoken, and to what extent they are spoken within the family. This will help to clarify areas where interpreters are needed, and where direct verbal communication with children can take place.

In relation to adults, Coventry Safeguarding Board (2013) found that professionals had taken insufficient account of the excessive consumption of alcohol by the Polish mother and her three successive Polish male partners, together with its impact on the children. As a consequence there was minimum effort to address the misuse of alcohol and the causes of domestic violence; or to involve the mother's male partners/fathers directly in interventions which were instead focused on the mother managing the care of her two children. The Serious Case Review attributed the lack of social work with the fathers and partners partly to the perception that they were transient figures in the household and were perceived as threatening individuals. In fact for periods they had either resided in the family home or remained in contact with the family. The stereotyping of fathers and male partners by social workers as absent parents or risky figures for children is widely known to result in poor partnership working (Morris, 2012; Morris et al., 2017; Featherstone, 2013). The Serious Case Review also concluded this was due to the language barrier as they spoke Polish and had little English, but social workers failed to engage interpreters to enable them to work directly with the fathers and the mother's partners. In this instance gender intersected with ethnicity to exacerbate the lack of direct work with fathers or male partners which characterises social work practice in the UK, the US and Australia (Laird et al., 2017).

Similarly, in Walsall Safeguarding Children Board (2014) a British-born mother of Bangladeshi heritage and bilingual in both English and Bengali was in an arranged marriage with a Bangladeshi father whose first language was Bengali and who spoke little English, although he had lived in the UK for some years. They had six children together. Over a three-year period the family had 236 contacts with health professionals, quite aside from those with social workers due to child protection concerns. Despite this, it was rare for social and health care professionals to meet the father and his poor English exacerbated the evident lack of direct communication with him by professionals. Only occasionally was an interpreter arranged to support interaction with the father, for example at a Child Protection Conference. As a result the mother's consistent claim that the father failed to help with caring for their six children dominated professional comprehension of what was happening in the home. It later transpired that in fact the father undertook all the cooking and the majority of the children's care. Here gendered stereotypes of the parents regarding childcare involvement were overlaid by assumptions about Bangladeshi ethnicity in relation to the nature of arranged marriages and oppressive power relationships between men and women in Bangladeshi culture. This created a bias in the perception of family dynamics and led too easily to accepting the mother's version of the situation and therefore not communicating with the father through the employment of an interpreter.

An interpreter is needed when the family member or someone from their ethnic community does not speak English; has poor fluency in English; it is not clear what fluency they have; or when they attend a crucial meeting with far-reaching consequences, such as a Child in Need assessment, enquiry into a suspicious injury to a child, or a Child Protection Conference. It is important to recognise that employing an interpreter does not of itself resolve problems of failing to hear the voice of a child or family member. For instance in Walsall Safeguarding Children Board (2014), although sometimes an interpreter was arranged for face-to-face meetings with the Bangladeshi father, occasionally the wrong interpreter was requested by staff; for example, one social worker asked for an Urdu interpreter to assist with an assessment when the father's first language was Bengali, albeit that he knew some Urdu. At other times, even when a Bengali interpreter was present, for example at a child protection conference, the father's perspective was lost in a situation where the British-born mother, fluent in English and articulate in expressing her viewpoint, dominated the parental contribution to the conference. In this case gendered understandings of parenting roles in a family of Bangladeshi heritage probably impaired the ability of practitioners to reach for and explore the father's perspective and integrate it into child protection deliberations.

Reflective exercise

In the section above a series of issues arise in Serious Case Reviews in relation to the presence or absence of interpreters.

▶

◀

Identify all the different problems encountered by practitioners in the Serious Case Reviews mentioned above.

Describe how you would use *cultural skills* to practise more effectively in similar circumstances to those described in this set of Serious Case Reviews.

Service user perspective on interpreters

Edwards et al. (2005) explored the views of people from minority ethnic communities regarding the use of interpreters to access services. They found that service users decide what level of English proficiency they think is required for dealing with a particular service and then arrange the interpreter they need, e.g. family member, friend or professional interpreter. A good interpreter was deemed to be someone who explained procedures; demonstrated empathy; advocated for them; and was trustworthy. Many service users preferred to have a family member or friend interpret for them, reporting that they fulfilled all the criteria of a good interpreter. This can plainly create problems in child protection work, as illustrated by the situation which arose in Gloucestershire Safeguarding Children Board (2011). Here professionals were either unsure of a recent migrant mother's native language or were under the mistaken impression that she spoke a dialect of it for which it would be difficult to find an appropriate interpreter. This was not helped by the migrant mother's apparent reluctance to engage with professionals, further exacerbated by her lack of English language skills. Consequently practitioners continually relied on family members or other adults in the household to interpret for the mother. This approach was particularly criticised by the Serious Case Review when a police officer and social worker conducted investigative interviews with the adults living in the family home acting as interpreters following the discovery of the youngest child's injuries. As the social worker involved later admitted, she found it difficult to understand what the many adults present were saying to each other or to prevent them from answering the practitioner's questions on behalf of the mother.

Conversely, a minority of service users said they were less likely to use such informal interpreters due to feelings of embarrassment, concerns about privacy or worry that the family member lacked specialist knowledge. Professional interpreters were often preferred for dealing with important legal or medical issues and their confidentiality valued. However, some service users regarded professional interpreters provided by the service they were trying to access as uncaring, controlling provision, or as simply representing the service. They also reported not understanding the role of the interpreter, which was frequently not explained to them. Nevertheless, getting to know a professional interpreter over time could counter these initial assumptions and some service users reported coming to trust the interpreter when they had the opportunity to develop a working relationship (Edwards et al., 2005).

Reflective exercise

Consider your experiences of using interpreters in your work with families from ethnic minority backgrounds.

What challenges did you encounter and how did you address them?

Make a list of the things you or your agency could do to improve practice with families using interpreters.

Non-verbal communication in cross-cultural practice

Non-verbal communication comprises all behaviours, aside from words, which occur during the sending and receiving of messages. These usually incorporate both conscious and unconscious elements. Professionals in both Cambridgeshire Safeguarding Children Board (2015) and Coventry Safeguarding Children Board (2013) believed that the children concerned could not communicate in English, but did not engage interpreters to compensate, instead relying on the children's non-verbal communication. These observations tended to rely on superficial non-verbal communication such as that the child smiled and appeared happy, therefore indicating that they were not being maltreated. These were professional judgements subsequently disproved. The following section explains multiple aspects of non-verbal communication relevant to cross-cultural encounters and draws on Lustig & Koester (2013) and Neuliep (2018).

Physical appearance

This refers to a person's body shape and height, their skin and eye colour, hair style and facial features alongside characteristics which indicate age, gender, self-care and physical condition. It encompasses body adornments such as attire, jewellery, amulets, makeup, body odours and artificial aromas and body modifications, meaning piercings, tattoos and cosmetic surgery. People commonly use physical appearance to convey information about their identity and affiliations, for example a father dressed in a khamiis or thobe (long-sleeved ankle-length garment); a young person with dreadlocks;

a girl wearing hijab; a teenager with extensive tattoos; or a mother smartly dressed and adorned with expensive jewellery. Some aspects of physical appearance such as skin colour or facial features cannot be changed, while others such as attire can, but both are central to racial and ethnic stereotyping. If a social worker interviews an ethnically Pakistani father who has a beard, the practitioner might assume he is a devout Muslim and, following on from this, imagine that he holds radical Islamist views (Laird, 2008, p. 83).

Conversely, how a social worker dresses will also convey non-verbal messages to family members. While social workers are exhorted to dress professionally, there is often no explicit dress code and practitioners are usually left to fall back on *'practice wisdom'* to direct what clothes they should wear depending on their role and tasks with families and colleagues (Scholar, 2013). Sometimes social workers consciously convey non-verbal messages through dress, by choosing to wear jeans and a T-shirt when meeting a young person in foster care in order to suggest informality and contribute to rapport. Equally, practitioners may be oblivious to the non-verbal messages their choice of attire conveys. Fashion trends among majority ethnic women often encourage plunging necklines, bare legs and arms or exposed midriff. Among men, fashion trends can encourage baggy low slung trousers, scruffy jeans or exposed pants. While dress of this kind may pass as simply fashionable among many families of White British heritage, it can convey very different messages to those from other heritage backgrounds. Among some families of Indian heritage where modesty of dress is important culturally or in relation to faith, among practising Muslims where females are required to cover up bare flesh, such attire can appear to be flaunting sexuality, immodest and disrespectful.

Where male and female social workers adopt more casual attire (even if smart) such as open neck shirts, jumpers and trousers as opposed to skirts and blouses or shirts and ties respectively, professional credibility and gravitas can be undermined with some minority families. A family whose heritage background is rooted in Africa, where people often express authority and social status through the way they dress, may lack confidence in the competence of a casually garbed social worker. Family members may also conclude that such a practitioner regards them of little consequence because they appear to have taken little time over their attire; and/or they may assume that the social worker lacks seniority or decision-making powers. In reality, the practitioner concerned may have deliberately decided not to dress too professionally or 'power dress' because they want service users to see them as 'ordinary and approachable' (Scholar, 2013; Beresford et al., 2008, p. 1402). While these kinds of inadvertent non-verbal mixed messages can of course occur between practitioners and families from majority ethnic backgrounds, there is greater potential for misunderstandings when working in cross-cultural contexts. Self-presentation in relation to dress is therefore a crucial consideration and involves being aware of, and accommodating, such sensitivities.

Paralinguistics

Paralinguistics refers to qualities of the voice and includes its pitch, rate, volume and intonation, which are all used to convey non-verbal messages about the content being spoken, for example using inflection and loudness to indicate irritation or convey sincerity. These non-verbal aspects are often unconscious and can convey information that either the speaker does not realise they are revealing or of which they themselves are unaware, e.g. unconscious anger. *Paralinguistics* also includes non-speech sounds such as laughing, crying, sighing and fillers such as *'uh'* and *'um'*. *Paralinguistics* generally convey the attitude of the speaker towards the content of the communication or their emotional state. There are differences in how quickly or loudly people from different cultural backgrounds speak. People from Ireland tend to speak English more quickly than their British counterparts, giving rise to assumptions that the speaker is excited or agitated. Among many people whose first language is Cantonese, speaking loudly is perceived as demonstrating confidence in what one is saying, but if transferred into speaking English as an additional language, it could be interpreted by a practitioner as angry.

Similarly, patterns of inflection and the meanings they hold varies between languages, but frequently when someone learns a second language such as English they transfer across many of the inflections from their native language. Arabic speakers tend to use a flat intonation for declarative sentences (ones making a statement); hence a mother who migrated from Saudi Arabia to the UK may communicate a narrative account of events concerning her child with little change in intonation, resulting in a native English speaking practitioner interpreting this as an indication of parental detachment or indifference. Conversely, the Saudi mother might construe the practitioner's statements about procedure or service provision as irritated or impatient because they will have a more animated delivery compared to Arabic speakers.

Silence also falls within the parameters of *paralinguistics*, and there is research evidence to demonstrate that it carries different meanings across cultures. In Anglocentric countries silence is generally experienced as the absence of communication and felt to be awkward, except perhaps between kin or close friends; in other cultures silence is actively used to send messages. In Japanese and Chinese society silence is deployed to avoid overt confrontation when people are in dispute, but can signal disagreement or the refusal of a request. It is also frequently used during conversation as a pause for thought (Hasegawa & Gudykunst, 1998). Among Finnish people silence is valued as reflecting thoughtfulness and intelligence, while talkativeness is associated with unreliability and slickness (Carbaugh & Berry, 2001). If a social worker is interviewing parents of Chinese heritage they might present as quieter than a British couple, leading to a misleading assumption that they are being evasive or resistant.

Facial expression

Facial expression, which includes eye contact, is the main site of emotional expression. Researchers have established that across all cultures people use the same facial expressions to convey the primary emotions of happiness, sadness, anger, fear, surprise, disgust, contempt and interest. However, these do differ in frequency, duration and intensity across cultures. People from *collectivist* cultures, such as those of East Asia, tend to express less negative emotion than those from *individualist* cultures predominant in Western Europe and North America. There are cross-cultural differences in relation to eye contact. Among the ethnic majority gazing at someone can convey friendliness or confrontation, depending on context. It also communicates interest when a listener looks at the face of a speaker, or honesty when a speaker looks directly at a listener. Among many people of East Asian descent the gaze is averted when a person of lower social status (e.g. a younger person) interacts with someone of higher social status (e.g. an older person) and among many South Asians when unrelated males and females interact. Violating these social conventions risks offending the higher status individual in the first example, while creating embarrassment or disapproval for both parties in the second. But a social worker might mistakenly assume that the avoidance of eye contact by family members during a child protection related interview means they are disengaged or have something to hide.

Proxemics

Proxemics concerns the use of space during interpersonal communication, which is now known to be culture-specific, meaning that different societies have norms regarding distances between people during interactions which commonly depend on their gender, age, social status and degree of familiarity. People in Sweden generally tend to stand further away from one another during conversation than those from Spain or Italy. Males and females in India, Pakistan and Egypt are expected to stand further away from one another than individuals of the same gender when conversing, otherwise they risk being judged immodest. While acculturation may take place when people migrate to the UK from these countries nevertheless the typically unconscious use of interpersonal distance may continue to frame encounters. This can lead to misunderstanding as when an English social worker stands at a greater distance while interviewing a parent of Latino heritage than is the norm in many South American cultures. To the parent, the social worker can appear aloof, undermining rapport. Likewise, an English male social worker who sits during a home visit at the same proximity he normally would to an English female friend, could make a mother from a South Asian background feel uncomfortable or affronted. Religious observance in terms of modesty between men and women as promoted in Islam may dictate that males and females adopt a greater interpersonal distance than is the norm between those of a British Anglocentric heritage. Conversely an ethnically English or Irish practitioner could feel threatened by a father of Italian heritage who moves closer during conversation simply because this is normative in his culture, because it is typically perceived as confrontational in British and Irish societies.

Kinesics

This refers to all bodily movements and includes head movements, gestures, body posture and any other physical movements used in communication, although *kinesic* messages are primarily conveyed by the face, arms and hands. Emotions, while conveyed primarily through facial expression and eye movements, are usually displayed to some extent through *kinesics*. For example abrupt, vigorous hand gestures convey irritation. Display of emotion may differ across cultures; for example, for many people of Chinese heritage the expression of emotion may be less intense, less often and of shorter duration than is typical among those of White American or British descent. Gesticulation tends to be used more often and more expansively by people from Southern Europe. Obviously these are broad generalisations and there is huge diversity within ethnic groups as well as between them. It means that practitioners working with a family of Chinese ethnicity or Italian heritage need to consider whether cultural norms relating to *kinetics* explain more apparently subdued or animated reactions to issues than anticipated, or if these are in fact individualised responses. Therefore social workers need to verbally double-check any assumptions they are making based solely on observing the *kinesics* of family members.

Haptics

This is the study of physical contact between people during communication which commonly conveys basic information about the nature of their relationship. It can be used to express positive or negative emotions; control a person's behaviour; indicate power or social status as high-status individuals tend to touch more than they are touched; fulfil rituals or formalities such as the handshake or hug on greeting; or in task-related behaviours such as during a medical examination. Cultures vary as to the amount of physical contact that is normative during everyday conversation. In societies of the Middle East, Latin America and Southern Europe individuals tend to touch more than is typical among people of the ethnic majority in the US or the UK or Chinese people. There are also cross-cultural differences as to where it is acceptable to touch. Among many Thais the head is considered the seat of a person's spirituality and has religious significance, so for this reason it should not be touched. Among many African societies the right hand is reserved for greeting and eating food when not using utensils, while offering something or touching with the left hand is considered disrespectful. By contrast English and Irish people regularly pat the heads of their children as a sign of affection and use both hands to touch others. Physical contact between males and females, unless they are close relatives, is forbidden or disapproved of among many Muslims, while among the ethnic majority in the US and UK it is touch between two males which attracts most censure, or the assumption that they are homosexual.

Broadly speaking in *contact cultures* such as those of Southern Europe, the Middle East and Latin America individuals when communicating tend to stand closer together, engage in more direct eye contact, touch more frequently and speak in louder voices than people in non-contact cultures such as those of North America, Britain and the Far East. These social rules are mediated by age and gender; among many people of Arab heritage two men or two women standing close together and touching every so often conforms to social conventions while a man and woman doing this would be deemed improper. Practitioners need to exercise caution in interpreting the non-verbal communication between family members in relation to touch, and drawing conclusions from this about family relationships and dynamics. It also means that they need to consider cross-cultural behaviour in relation to themselves. If a mother's Spanish male partner touches a male social worker, he may simply be observing the norms of friendliness towards other men as opposed to the Anglocentric interpretation of behaving menacingly or making a sexual advance.

Olfactics

Olfactics is the study of smell. Body odour, the use of perfume, the smell of shampoo or the aroma of herbs or spices from cooking in a person's home all convey non-verbal messages. In the UK and the US personal hygiene and particularly disguising natural bodily smells has assumed a moral dimension as Protestants, the majority religion, in both countries historically emphasised that *'cleanliness is next to godliness'* and, as in many other faiths, is related to spiritual purity. While smells in themselves are neutral they are often ascribed social significance. People from discriminated out-groups such as Irish Travellers, Roma and homeless people are commonly stereotyped as smelling. The whiff of alcohol, cigarette smoke or marijuana from one person can convey many social messages to another, including assumptions about lifestyle, addiction and laziness. Anglocentric cultures associate body odour with poverty, poor hygiene and lethargy but other cultures regard body odour as reflecting vitality and do not seek to mask it with perfumes and deodorants (Neuliep, 2018). Practitioners are, of course, not immune from making assumptions about other people based on how they, or their homes, smell. This makes it imperative to be mindful of smell as a form of non-verbal communication and to reflect on what messages smells convey to a practitioner and what stereotypes or assumptions are being triggered.

Environment

The *environment* includes the physical features of the surroundings in which an interpersonal interaction takes place, which can include settings as diverse as the home, office, café, street, day centre, hospital, etc. Objects within these settings such as furniture, lighting, décor and sounds convey non-verbal messages such as formality established by the presence of a desk or impressions regarding social class through choice of furnishings. The degree of privacy, formality, conviviality, familiarity and space in the place where an interaction occurs will also shape interpersonal communication. In situations where individuals can control their environment, such as in their home, then what they place in it and how it is arranged will also convey messages. A social worker making a home visit where in one room he sees a small Buddhist shrine may make assumptions about the family's degree of religiosity, or if Bhangra music is playing on a radio, he may conjecture about their ethnic identification and lifestyle. This can lead to assumptions and judgements regarding the beliefs and habits of family members, without these matters even being discussed. Some of these messages may be intended by the sender (family member), but others may simply be misconstrued by the receiver (practitioner).

Likewise, meetings with family members in offices not only invariably convey formality, but can send messages about ethnic majority culture. For example, small interview rooms with few chairs may give the impression that meetings are always with individuals or nuclear family units rather than kin groups, and they may make it difficult to observe customs around interpersonal distance between males and females. The cultural unfamiliarity of the home for the social worker or the office setting for family members may in itself create constraints in communication as for each party these become liminal spaces in which people feel unsettled, are unsure of accepted norms and become nervous about how to act appropriately.

Chronemics

Chronemics as an area of study examines how people conceptualise time and the rules they apply to its use. *Formal time systems* concern how time is measured in different societies: through units such as days and months, or the passage of seasons. In some cultures such as that of the ethnic majority in the UK and US, time is primarily segmented into hours and minutes which assume huge importance in relation to how it is utilised, particularly in the workplace. There are prescribed timescales for different child protection procedures and managerial expectations as to how many home visits or reviews of children's circumstances a practitioner completes in a week or month. Other cultures may not place such emphasis on the use of time in this very precise and task-oriented way. This can lead to cross-cultural confusion about expectations, for instance as to when the specifics of a Child in Need or Child Protection Plan should be fulfilled by parents, their partners or other family members.

Informal time systems relate to shared understandings between members of the same culture as to how time should be utilised. Different cultures often have time norms around arriving at and leaving events, together with the timings of happenings over the period of an event or how long to wait for something to take place. The cultural norm among the ethnic majority places importance on timekeeping and being late to an agreed meeting or event is considered rude and an inconvenience to others. They also expect decision-making or agreed actions to take place quickly and can be impatient with perceived delays over days, weeks or months. A practitioner from the ethnic majority, or one acculturated to their norms around *informal time systems*, will anticipate a parent arriving approximately on time to an office-based interview or a family appearing within a few minutes for a home visit.

Many societies place less emphasis on such exact timekeeping. In many South American cultures people can arrange to do a number of things at around the same time or are quick to cancel or change the timing of an event if they need to attend to some other matter. As conserving interpersonal relationships is considered more important than timekeeping, responding to a social need is likely to take precedence over the pre-arranged start or end time of an engagement. Here a more flexible approach to time contrasts with that of inflexible fixed times for events common among the ethnic majority. A practitioner who arranges for a child with learning difficulties to meet respite foster carers may be irritated or assume lack of interest from parents of Argentinian heritage when they arrive late. From the parents' worldview they were simply ensuring that a prior family visit finished convivially rather than on time. Conversely, in other cultures, such as that of Korean society, timekeeping can reflect social status. Those having a lower social status are expected to arrive on time to a meeting, while those of higher social status may arrive later, making the former wait. Here different rules relating to time apply to different individuals depending on their relative social positioning or their social relationship to others.

Reflective exercise

Consider your practice with three different families from minority ethnic backgrounds.

What were your initial impressions or assumptions as you walked into their home for the first time and what aspects of the environment influenced these?

What were your first impressions or assumptions based on the appearance of different family members?

Recall the facial expressions, gestures, positioning and movements of different family members in their home and your interpretation of them.

To what extent did you check out these interpretations or assumptions with family members at the time or at a later point?

How could you improve your practice in this area?

Anxiety in inter-cultural encounters

As Gudykunst (2005, p. 287) observes in the context of communication, anxiety 'stems from feeling uneasy, tense, worried, or apprehensive about what might happen...[and] is based on the anticipation of negative consequences'. This social anxiety occurs when a person is motivated to create a certain impression before others in the expectation of receiving desired responses, but is unsure of their ability to do so. The less confident the person is of creating the *'right'* impression, the more anxious they will be. Social anxiety is likely to be heightened in situations involving intergroup (or in this case inter-cultural) interactions because the uncertainty is greater and individuals generally want to avoid being perceived as foolish, prejudiced or incompetent communicators. Individuals also have a maximum and minimum threshold for anxiety. If they are operating above their maximum then managing high anxiety will become the focus of their attention during the interaction, rather than attentiveness to the exchange of messages. Information is likely to be decoded and encoded in a simplistic way by a socially anxious person. This anxiety may also discourage the individual from engaging in interactions with *'strangers'* such as people of a different gender, from a different income group or a dissimilar ethnic background. In this context a *'stranger'* is someone who is simultaneously physically close and relatively socially remote.

As few people belong to exactly the same set of social groups, everyone to some degree experiences others as *'strangers'*. Each will have identities and practices arising from social group memberships with which the other is unfamiliar. Males and females belong to different social groups, as do Christians and Muslims creating diversity of experience. This can lead to avoidance behaviour, which encompasses not only evading interactions with *'strangers'* (i.e. those belonging to a different social group) but terminating interactions with them as early as possible. Such strategies, when adopted by professionals working with families from a different ethnic or racial background to themselves, reinforce incompetent practice, feelings of inadequacy and lack of confidence to act appropriately. These in turn are likely to convey nervousness, indecision or prejudiced attitudes during inter-cultural encounters. The implications of this type of social anxiety are evident in several Serious Case Reviews.

In Leicester Safeguarding Children Board (2011) *Serious Case Review in Respect of the Deaths of Children Known as Child 1 and Child 2: Case 'A'*, which concerned a White British care leaver mother and a Muslim Arab father with limited English, social workers had multiple contacts with the mother, but hardly any with the father. A similar pattern emerged in Walsall Safeguarding Children Board (2014) *Serious Case Review Child W3* which involved a Bangladeshi father with little education and limited English language married to a British-born mother of Bangladeshi heritage who could communicate articulately in English and was well educated. While the inadequate involvement of fathers in child protection practice is known to be widespread (Laird et al., 2017), in this instance gender appeared to combine with ethnicity to exacerbate this tendency. Arguably social workers, who are predominantly White British female and educated to degree level, barely spoke to the fathers, as compared to the mothers. Possibly this was because the fathers were perceived as greater *'strangers'* as they belonged to more social groups which differed from those of the social workers. This meant that probably it was less anxiety-provoking to interact with the mothers, who were female, British and spoke fluent English, in contrast to the fathers. The faith of family members, in this instance Islam, can also increase the sense of others being 'strangers' and correspondingly the degree of anxiety and uncertainty felt by practitioners, particularly if they are atheist, hold a different faith or are largely non-observant in terms of their own religion. This uncertainty and anxiety can be expressed through complete non-engagement with the religious beliefs and observances of family members or result in only superficial knowledge about their faith.

If a practitioner's anxiety levels are below their minimum threshold, then they are likely to treat the encounter routinely, without much reflexivity, and lack curiosity – resulting in an obliviousness or insensitivity to significant communications from family members. If a practitioner assumes that an interaction is predictable, they will have little anxiety about it, but also minimal alertness to novel messages or miscommunications. Plainly levels of anxiety which rise above the maximum threshold or drop below the minimum contribute to ineffective communication. Gudykunst (2005, p. 289) argues that there is a drastic drop-off in communicative effectiveness outside of an individual's range between their maximum and minimum thresholds, as opposed to a gradual decline in effectiveness. The term 'communicative effectiveness' means the extent to which the person receiving the message decodes it in such a way as to derive a similar meaning from it as the one intended and encoded by the person sending the message. The greater the number of shared understandings of messages the more effective is the communication during an interaction.

Reflective exercise

Consider your recent practice with families from racial, ethnic and faith minorities.

To what extent did you meet and discuss matters more with some family members rather than others?

Reflect on whether some of these patterns with different families may be due to feelings of greater anxiety around perceptions of '*strangers*'.

What actions could you take to increase your *cultural desire*?

Stereotyping and inter-cultural communication

In Walsall Safeguarding Children Board (2014) practitioners gender stereo-typed the parental roles of the mother and father and assumed, due to the family's Bangladeshi heritage and Muslim faith, that the father was a power-ful figure in the household. They therefore assumed the father had little role in the children's upbringing while the mother was primarily responsible for looking after the children. As a result the father was largely overlooked by social workers when in fact he was the main carer for the couple's children. In this instance social workers foregrounded the categories of gender and faith as opposed to that of educational background and nationality (as related to English language competence and familiarity with public services in the UK). Even when the father alluded to taking care of the children he was not heard by practitioners. Walsall Safeguarding Children Board (2014, para.5.9.20–5.9.22) concluded that:

> An issue not addressed…is about the power balance between these parents as a function not of their gender or faith (when the father's position would 'out-rank' mother's) but of their background and education. Mother is British-born and educated, extremely articulate and literate, very well-informed about and very successful in, accessing and co-ordinating a wide range of financial support and other services. Father in contrast, is a Bangladeshi-born man of limited education

with very limited command of English, is long-term unemployed and dependent upon his wife and children. The school (and author) noted father's quiet and almost subservient manner.

When a practitioner experiences anxiety below the minimum threshold he or she tends to communicate routinely and simply interprets the *stranger's* messages from his or her own ethnocentric perspective. Being aware when a stereotype has been activated requires both self-awareness of the stereotypes one holds and a conscious effort to counter these through an open-minded engagement with the *'stranger'*. In the above case gender stereotypes in relation to the South Asian parents were triggered, which impaired the ability of the social workers involved to recognise other power relationships in play. Self-awareness enables practitioners to acknowledge which stereotypical perceptions are being triggered, while managing the anxiety produced by the unpredictability felt on suspending them. Successful anxiety/uncertainty management involves maintaining anxiety and uncertainty between an individual's minimum and maximum thresholds in order to make effective communication possible.

Privacy and personal disclosure

While social scientists have established that the need for social interaction and seclusion at times is an innate tendency, the degree to which norms reinforce this varies cross-culturally. The strategies individuals employ to achieve greater social interaction or greater seclusion is also influenced by cultural factors (Neuliep, 2018, p. 131). At a fundamental level many societies have different mores (sometimes backed by legislation) regarding which behaviours should be enacted in private and which are public; for example sexual intercourse, and touching between people of opposite sexes. Westin (1967) identifies four types of privacy which are bound up with autonomy, emotional expression and communicativeness:

Solitude – being alone or unobserved by other people

Intimacy – being able to conduct a social interaction or relationship with another person without interference or observation

Anonymity – being unknown in social situations, including the use of social media and making purchases or having control over personal data when receiving services

Reserve – the ability to deploy psychological barriers to prevent intrusion into one's own thoughts and feelings

A person's need or desire for each of these types of privacy will be a unique fusion of cultural norms, gender identity and individual character traits.

Research indicates that cross-culturally males tend to exhibit a higher inclination towards *solitude* than females, while females display a greater tendency towards *intimacy* with family and friends (Pedersen & Frances, 1990). *Individualist* societies such as those of European countries have enacted legislation to protect people's privacy, but other societies place less emphasis on privacy or may have different concepts of what privacy means. In Gloucestershire Safeguarding Children Board (2011) a single mother and her four children (three of whom were school age and the youngest pre-school) migrated from their country of origin to the UK seeking a better life. They immediately moved into a two-bedroom dwelling to live with relatives who had migrated a month earlier. None of the children could speak English, while the mother spoke very little English. Education welfare officers, social workers and police officers who visited the home to speak to the mother all found themselves interacting with multiple adult family members who were present in the room with the mother and acted as interpreters for her, often speaking on her behalf. These encounters, while acceptable and comfortable for the family, compromised professional confidentiality and an investigation into the youngest child's injuries.

Among a number of Traveller communities in the UK privacy may refer to *intimacy* between (extended) family members, but *solitude* and *reserve* towards people who are not kin. In Southampton Local Safeguarding Children Board (2014) *Serious Care Review Family A* concerning the sexual abuse and neglect of children by their White British father from a Traveller community, there appeared to be high tolerance of his suspicious behaviour and known neglect of his children because there are extremely strong social pressures against residents on the same Travellers' site involving themselves or 'interfering' in the affairs of another family. There are also powerful cultural norms among British and Irish Travellers against involving people from outside their community in their affairs. This meant that other residents on the Traveller caravan site were slow to disclose their concerns about the father's treatment of his children to professionals. Assessing the community's response, the Serious Case Review stated there was evidence that the children's neglect was tolerated within the community to the extent that even the children's aunt endeavoured to disguise how appalling their home conditions were. Southampton Local Safeguarding Children Board (2014, para.8.1.2) revealed that the 'abuse of these children was easier to perpetrate and harder for the agencies to detect and prevent because of the circumstances of the family and the community they lived in'.

Reserve essentially refers to the degree of self-disclosure in relation to the depth of what is divulged; the nature or range of topics divulged; the timing of disclosure relative to the length of the interaction or duration of the relationship; whether what is divulged reflects positively or negatively on the disclosing individual; and the target of the disclosure, meaning who is typically the recipient of disclosures (Lustig & Koester, 2013, pp. 244–45).

Modesty may be a factor regarding what self-disclosures it is appropriate to make in different social contexts. Discussing sexual matters may be considered degrading and shaming among some sections of ethnic minority communities to a much greater extent than is the case for people of White British heritage (Henley & Schott, 1999). For many individuals regardless of their ethnic background this sense of discomfort and transgression can be heightened when disclosures of this nature are made to someone of the opposite sex or if an interpreter of the opposite sex is present.

Haya (modesty) is a religious concept within Islam implying shyness or reserve in sexual matters designed to prevent lust or promiscuity. Discussion about sex may be taboo or the vocabulary lacking in heritage languages spoken in some minority ethnic communities, making it exceptionally difficult for children and young people to disclose sexual abuse to adults in their family or community. At the same time this can make it difficult for parents or relatives to approach public agencies with information if they suspect or are aware of such abuse (Gilligan & Akhtar, 2006). Among strictly observant Catholics, it may be deeply shaming to discuss premarital sex as this is regarded as a sin. Similarly, for Hindus or Sikhs to admit to the consumption of alcohol, which is forbidden by these world religions, may be a source of disgrace. Notwithstanding evident cross-cultural variations, it must be borne in mind that differential acculturation experiences and individual differences also shape what subjects family members are prepared to discuss, and how much they are willing to reveal about themselves. In this respect culture is but one influential factor and not the sole determinant of modest behaviour.

For social workers, faced with this diversity of norms around *reserve*, rather than assume family members are resistant to intervention, aloof or shy because they seem loath to divulge personal information, it is important to explore whether cultural factors are influencing the interaction. If they are, the positionality of the social worker, particularly their ethnicity, gender or age may affect what is disclosed. If the person is from a heritage background where personal issues are predominantly restricted to discussion with kin or close friends rather than as a means to establish new social bonds, then more time building rapport may be necessary. Account also needs to be taken of the fact that some subjects of conversation, such as sexual intimacy or domestic violence, are considered vulgar, offensive or taboo in some cultures, creating a further layer of reserve, which has to be addressed by the practitioner before disclosures from family members are likely to be forthcoming.

Conversely, professionals should be alerted to the urgency and seriousness of a situation if there is disclosure of child maltreatment by family members from heritage backgrounds that generally discourage the sharing of personal information with non-kin or those outside the ethnic community, or where cultural norms restrain discussion of sensitive matters. For example in Southampton Local Safeguarding Children Board (2014) *Serious Care Review Family A* the warden on a Travellers' site made a referral to Children's Social Care after being approached by a number of female site residents who expressed concern for the welfare of the children and obliquely suggested that they were being sexually abused. The social work follow-up was inadequate as insufficient attention was given to the fact that the disclosures had come from members of an ethnic community with cultural norms discouraging such communication with professionals. To a culturally sensitive practitioner the disclosures of maltreatment by other Travellers would have conveyed that the children were at a high level of risk.

Reflective exercise

Consider the various issues relating to privacy and disclosure raised in the section above.

How might your positionality affect disclosures from a: White British father who is a devout Christian; Traveller mother living on a Traveller site; British African Caribbean young person; grandfather who is a practising Muslim; and a recent migrant Polish mother?

How would you use *cultural skills* to encourage and address issues surrounding privacy and disclosure from these different family members?

Case study for practitioners

Children's Social Care receives a referral from the police who picked up a young white male at 3.00am in the city centre who is drunk and confused. The police were unable to find out much about his personal history, as he appeared to have minimal language skills in English. However, they have established that he originally came to the UK from Greece. The young person is currently staying in a hostel for the homeless and you are the social worker tasked with meeting him to conduct an initial assessment.

Return to the cultural competence models and tools in Chapter 4. Without having any background information, it is particularly important to adopt a starting point of *cultural awareness*. This means tuning into one's own cultural and spiritual heritage, while recognising the potential for differences of cultural and religious beliefs, values and practices held by the young person. *Cultural sensitivity* will involve exploring the cultural and spiritual influences for this teenager without assuming that they are inferior to one's own and/or those shaped by dominant Anglocentric norms. If this young person is experiencing high levels of *acculturation stress*, then creating a culturally safe encounter by proactively conveying respect to bolster his dignity will be crucial to encouraging him to communicate about his background.

The culturagram is a useful tool to guide a comprehensive discussion to gather relevant information about this young person's life and experiences. This includes in the first instance finding out what languages he speaks and/ or reads and to what degree of competence. It will involve identifying his immigration status and what the implications are of this regarding access to services and financial support, bearing in mind that he may be unaware of his entitlements. It will also be important to gather information about the significance to him of kin relationships, paying attention to family expectations of this young person relative to his gender and age. Developing a broad-based *cultural knowledge* would include familiarity with the types of cultural and spiritual resources to be found within geographic ethnic communities, as well as internet-based communities of practice which this young person could access. This may be affected by whether other members of his family are also present in the country, elsewhere in Europe or beyond.

The GGRRAAACCEEESSS model is a helpful corrective to the tendency to culturise the beliefs and behaviour of people from racial and ethnic minorities, by assuming that these are always, or typically, dictated by culture or faith. Many aspects of people's experiences and worldviews are shaped by economic, social and political forces, including their positionality within their society, faith community or ethnic group. There is a need to explore with this young person how his age, gender and class or current circumstances influence his beliefs, attitudes and behaviours. His lack of proficiency in English may create further challenges for communication, and determining whether he has a learning disability or health problem impairing his cognitive ability will also be important. These additional considerations of how structural factors and/or personal circumstances shape a person's worldview, actions and responses can only occur if practitioners retain an open mind about the motives for behaviour. This requires you to explicitly explore these with family members rather than relying on attributions from an ethnocentric standpoint.

Conclusion

Casual conversation can have much more social significance in many cultures compared to Anglocentric societies. Consequently building rapport through the extended use of small talk can be more necessary in practice with families from ethnic minority backgrounds, particularly during initial encounters. Otherwise social work interactions can appear rushed or discourteous. People from ethnic minority backgrounds tend to speak additional languages to a much greater extent than those from the ethnic majority. Sometimes meanings and *paralinguistics* from a person's first language are carried over into English, which can lead to misunderstandings. Therefore even when people appear to have English language proficiency, which can change over time, double-checking meanings remains vital.

In situations where family members speak little or no English, practitioners can over-rely on their non-verbal communication to assist with communication. This can be a source of misguided assumptions or stereotypes, particularly when the language barrier or lack of an interpreter means that these are not double-checked through verbal exchanges. Practitioners need to be aware of the diversity in non-verbal communication across different cultures. Cross-cultural encounters for many people elicit a degree of anxiety. This can be used productively when it assists practitioners to recognise that they are unsure of family organisation or the significance of religion in family life. They are then better positioned to ask respectful curious questions. If anxiety is overwhelming it can lead to retreat from genuine encounter and reliance upon preconceived assumptions and stereotypes.

10

Culturally Competent Risk Assessment

Introduction

Previous chapters have examined key dimensions of culture and the nature of ethnic identity. They have also explored the diversity of family forms and considered both the support and pressures that kin can exert upon parents and children. Various conceptions of childhood and approaches to childrearing were explored, alongside discussion as to whether such practices are different rather than detrimental. Black and ethnic minority families and those of mixed heritage clearly face additional challenges bringing up children because of racism and discrimination. Like extended families, ethnic communities can be a source of much-needed identification, safety and support, but they can sometimes exert significant influence over family matters. The relationships between families and their local ethnic communities can have profound implications for social work practice. Families and children who are asylum seekers, refugees or recent migrants not only commonly encounter prejudice and discrimination, but due to having fewer rights may be ineligible to receive many welfare benefits and public services. Caring for a child's health is a primary requirement of parenting and sometimes beliefs and values, often influenced by culture or faith, can impede necessary health care interventions. Working in all these practice situations requires *culturally sensitive* communication skills which avoid stereotyping and facilitate *cultural encounter* with children, young people and families from Black and minority ethnic groups. However this needs to take place in the context of protecting children through the effective assessment of risk. The first half of this chapter investigates how risk assessment can be integrated into *culturally competent* practice with families. The second half comprises an case study for practitioners which combines the principles of risk assessment with models of cultural competence and applies them to a hypothetical ethnic minority family.

Human rights, culture and faith

Human rights are founded on the idea that every individual is entitled to fundamental protections by virtue of being human, such as the right to life and the freedom to hold opinions and express them. Every person is deemed equally entitled to these protections because everyone is adjudged equally human and therefore possesses the same status. Human rights are now codified in the Universal Declaration of Human Rights adopted by the General Assembly of the United Nations in 1948, which sets out the minimum requirements for a dignified life. These are binding all members of the United Nations, requiring them to enact laws in their countries to uphold the 30 human rights adumbrated in the Declaration. Governments must take action to guarantee these rights and prevent their violation either by public bodies or organisations carrying out public functions on behalf of the government. These rights are also inalienable, meaning that since a person cannot cease to be a human being they cannot be dispossessed of their rights regardless of how malevolently or cruelly they behave and regardless of their gender, disability, race, sexuality or other status.

The UN Universal Declaration of Human Rights is foundational to a number of subsequent international treaties concerning fundamental rights including the UN Convention on the Rights of the Child (CRC), adopted in 1989 and translated into domestic law by signatory countries. The CRC provides those under the age of 18 years with additional rights which both complement and extend their entitlements under the UN Declaration. For instance, under article 9 of the Convention the government is obliged to ensure that children are not separated from their parents except where this is in their *best interests* and after consideration by a court of law. Under article 12 children capable of forming a view are given the right to be heard in any judicial process and their opinion given due weight. The CRC also bestows a number of rights upon parents including, under article 14, the right to provide direction to their child 'in a manner consistent with the evolving capacities of the child'. Article 19 obliges the government to take all measures necessary to protect the right of children to be free 'from all forms of physical or mental violence, injury or abuse'.

UN Convention on the Rights of the Child in articles 5, 8, 17, 20, 29 & 31 grants rights to children and parents regarding the transmission of culture and faith and its expression. The exercise of such rights is not boundless, as under article 19 the Convention forbids 'all forms of physical or mental violence, injury or abuse, neglect or negligent treatment, maltreatment or exploitation, including sexual abuse'. The threshold at which a particular behaviour becomes child maltreatment is not defined. While in the UK the legal concept of 'significant harm' attempts to create such a threshold, this nevertheless remains open to professional judgement and is commonly relative to the age, health, maturity and disability status of the child, in conjunction with the intensity and chronicity of the parental behaviour giving concern (Munro, 2008, p. 50).

Some acts, such as starving a child accused of witchcraft, or female genital mutilation, constitute unequivocal and extreme violations of a child's rights under the CRC. But in many other instances when family members engage in a practice influenced by culture or faith, it may not be immediately apparent whether that practice is beneficial, neutral, disadvantageous, hazardous or harmful for the child. Article 3 of the CRC provides guidance to professionals faced with such decisions through the introduction of a legally binding requirement that:

> In all actions concerning children, whether undertaken by public or private social welfare institutions, courts of law, administrative authorities or legislative bodies, the best interests of the child shall be a primary consideration.

In the UK the *best interests* of the child are actually *the* paramount consideration for a court under domestic law implementing the UN Convention on the Rights of the Child. However, as neither the CRC nor domestic law actually defines what is in a child's *best interests*, this is left to the deliberation of the court. The indeterminacy of what constitutes a child's *best interests* can therefore become a matter of disagreement between families and social workers when considered from different cultural and religious viewpoints. It is the simultaneous requirement for practitioners to both respect and accept diverse expressions of culture and faith while at the same time protecting children from harm enshrined in the CRC and underpinning social work professional values which creates ethical dilemmas for practitioners intervening in the lives of families from a diversity of ethnic backgrounds. This becomes even more complex when conceptions of what constitutes a child's *best interests* are determined by ethnocentric worldviews.

The social construction of child maltreatment

Some practices, while harmful to children, are legally sanctioned, e.g. medical treatment with deleterious side effects, such as chemotherapy for juvenile leukaemia. Certain cultural or religious observances cause discomfort or pain, fasting for Ramadan or Lent, but are allowed because these are regarded as a moral good. They are also regarded as in the longer-term interests of the child as he or she becomes a recognised member of a faith community. A variety of other acts, for instance male circumcision, can be rites of passage marking important changes in the roles and expectations of children as they progress towards their majority. Physical chastisement of children by their parents is legally permitted in much of the UK, resulting in the deliberate infliction of physical pain upon children in order to correct behaviour, inculcate obedience, instil discipline or sometimes justified as morally good for the child. In most of the UK a parent can lawfully justify hitting a child on the grounds of 'reasonable punishment' under section 58 of the Children Act 2004, although 'reasonable punishment' is not a legally defined term. By contrast in most other European countries corporal punishment of children is banned, as it is in Scotland. It appears contradictory that in most of the UK hitting an adult is treated as assault and therefore unlawful, but hitting a child is permissible, even though a child is likely to be more physically vulnerable than an adult.

In the UK, the US and Australia, childhood is constructed to impose obligations on parents to look after their children, but there are no obligations on children to contribute to the wellbeing of their family. In many other societies, however, the relationship between parents and children is characterised by a set of mutual obligations and entitlements, which include the expectation that children undertake domestic chores and participate in income-generating activity (Twum-Danso Imoh & Ame, 2012). If a family perceive the contribution of children to the household as a moral good and part of their training for adulthood, is it accurate to simply interpret this as child labour and orchestrate a child protection intervention, or does it require a more considered professional response? In a cross-cultural context the scope for either misinterpreting intentions or imposing normative childcare practices are great.

There is a general consensus around what constitutes gross acts of maltreatment against children in the UK, US and Australia (Australian Institute of Family Studies, 2015; Children's Bureau, 2016b; NSPCC, 2017). While such definitions are indicative of abuse, they still leave much to be decided on the basis of professional judgement (Munro, 2008, pp. 49–50). They may only offer limited guidance to professionals confronted with concerning parental behaviours related to culture or faith. Applying these definitions, gross acts of maltreatment are easily distinguished, such as a mother's partner breaking a child's ribs with a punch when disciplining him. But, since physical chastisement of children by their parents is permitted in England, the point at which this becomes physical abuse is much less clear. In relation to sexual abuse, given the pervasiveness of sexually explicit material in advertising, on television, in films and easily viewable through the internet, at what juncture should exposure to this be considered maltreatment? Is it emotional abuse if a parent is unaffectionate, spends little time with their child and delegates most of their upbringing to paid carers or other family members? If these are the circumstances of a high-earning White British professional couple who send their young children to boarding school or employ a full-time au pair, should it be adjudged differently from similar behaviour in a first-generation Nigerian family where a relative acts as a kinship carer and working parents have intermittent contact with their children? Is it supervisory neglect if an economically disadvantaged parent of African Caribbean heritage leaves their eight-year-old child home alone while they work in premises nearby, are contactable by mobile phone, and reside in a close-knit local community?

Tethering a young child to an adult while out walking, typically using a leash attached to a young child's backpack or reins attached to a safety harness worn by a toddler, is generally regarded as acceptable parental behaviour. Conversely, tying a young child to a piece of furniture in the home would be regarded as cruelty in the UK. But, even when a parent's behaviour appears to constitute abuse, such as tying a toddler's leg to a fixed point (a common practice in some rural communities of the Levant), her motive and intention may be to protect the child from harm in a situation where she cannot keep the child in view the whole time. Accordingly, the intention accepted by social workers behind the act of tying the child, whether to keep him safe or punish him, will determine their professional response. If it is deemed to be the former, the family is likely to be assessed as in need of additional services to support childcare; if the latter, the child will be deemed at risk of abuse from a parent adopting extreme forms of discipline and this will trigger a child protection intervention.

Judgements about child neglect raise issues as to what constitutes a standard of acceptable parenting, and whether this ought to be identical across varied income groups and ethnic communities. There are norms in many societies which require children to be responsible for their self-care at an early age and to manage when left alone (Laird, 2015). British law does not set a minimum age at which children can be left unattended, so the determination as to whether leaving a child unsupervised is neglectful is reliant on the appraisal of the social worker. In relation to the conditions of the home environment, to what extent should a social worker take into consideration the socio-economic circumstances of the family in deciding whether the level of stimulation, hygiene, nutrition and leisure activity is adequate for a young child? Should the threshold be exactly the same for a low-income family as for a high-income one in determining whether there should be no social work involvement, or whether it is treated as a child in need of services, or as a child protection situation requiring investigation and mandatory intervention?

Reflective exercise

Using reflection to develop your *cultural awareness*, explore the following questions.

What are your personal beliefs, attitudes and values in relation to childrearing?

Are these all consistent with your agency's perspective, and if not why not?

How do you manage personal and professional conflicts in this area and how does it impact on your practice with parents, their partners, guardians or other carers?

Good enough parenting

As Munro (2008, pp. 52–53) suggests, the basis on which professional judgements rest as to what constitutes adequate or good parenting remains obscure. While notionally acceptable and unacceptable modes of childrearing can be understood as located at either end of a continuum of parental behaviours, where the threshold falls along its length dividing one from the other is a moot point and largely determined by the dominant ideas in a society as to what constitutes good or bad parenting. In the UK, as in the US and Australia, it is the perspective of the middle class among the White majority population which is most influential in determining childrearing norms. This means there is the potential for discrimination against those from working-class or low-income backgrounds and minority ethnic communities (Munro, 2008, pp. 53–54). Research conducted in the US has revealed that social workers, as a result of involvement with multiple abusive parents and their partners, can actually develop a lower standard of acceptable childrearing practices than that of the general population (Rose & Meezan, 1996). Notably, the same study also found that mothers from minority ethnic backgrounds held a higher standard of childcare than Americans from the White majority.

Before any discussion of *parenting capacity* it is important to conceptualise parenting. It has been argued that one of the most important tasks that adults undertake is the area of bringing up children (Abela & Walker, 2013). This is because parenting behaviour has been proven to be a central indicator of healthy child wellbeing. Indeed, Heckman (2013, p. 12) concluded that 'The proper measure of child adversity is the quality of parenting – not the traditional measures of family income or parent al education'. Parenting is complex and vital to the growth and development of all children. It comprises of: delivering basic physical care; providing affection and security; stimulating their children's innate potential; providing guidance and control; giving children appropriate responsibility as they grow; fostering children's independence and self-awareness; supporting their sense of identity; facilitating social acceptance and aiding a child to develop their personal history (Lloyd, 1999). Parents need certain qualities in order to be able to parent efficiently and effectively; primarily warmth, affection and consistency. As children's needs change and develop over time, ideally so too do parents' skills and abilities. No two children are the same, consequently for parents who have more than one child the experience of parenting previous children is useful, but not necessarily sufficient, to parent subsequent children. Children are themselves differentiated by age, ability, gender, birth order and so on and will require different skill sets to raise.

The term *'parenting'* is the verb derived from the word *'parent'*, and for the purposes of this critical analysis these terms need to be differentiated as parenting may be carried out by family members or others who are not the child's parents. Parenting has been seen by some as 'something that parents do', and according to Pugh et al. (1994) concerns a number of tasks. What parents *'do'* is influenced by many things, including genetics, their own childhood experiences, poverty, mental and physical health. An ecological perspective on parenting encourages thinking about the complicated and often interdependent relationships between the factors affecting parenting. Parenting is therefore the process whereby a particular kind of nurturing is provided to children and what others may refer to as *'upbringing'*.

There are ongoing debates about what is likely to be described as *good enough parenting*. *Parenting capacity*, according to Conley (2003) refers to *good enough parenting* in the longer term. Such a definition poses problems for social workers who are tasked with assessing whether parents are able to provide *good enough parenting* to their children. The term *'good enough'* is quite vague and subjective. This subjectivity makes it difficult to identify what might constitute *good enough parenting*. Research suggests that there can be no universal understanding of *good enough parenting* and that what one ethnic community or indeed one family considers as *good enough parenting* may not be regarded as such within a different ethnic group or family. Secondly, it is likely that the social work assessment takes place within the context of heightened anxiety, religious and cultural beliefs and potential for defensive behaviours and attitudes on the part of the parents.

Parenting usually takes place within a birth family. However, significant changes in childcare policy and practice in the UK has meant that a variety of adults can, and may, become involved in parenting. Children in foster care; adoptive families; stepfamilies; reconstituted families; or who have extended family members, may have their needs met by adults other than their biological parents. It is therefore easier to view parenting from the perspective of the child's needs rather than adhering to a rigid list of what adults should be providing. Kellett & Apps (2009) suggest that a part of being a *good enough parent* is the extent to which people prepare their children for the world outside their homes. This is an important consideration in understanding parenting behaviours as linked to the broader goals of the family. They found that there is in fact a high consensus among professionals working with families that the components of *good enough parenting* comprise:

> ➤ meeting children's health and developmental needs

> ➤ putting children's needs first

> ➤ providing routine and consistent care

> ➤ parental acknowledgement of any problems and engagement with support services

Assessing children and families from ethnic minorities

In order to establish *good enough parenting* and determine whether or not children are at risk of significant harm, assessments of parenting capacity will have to be undertaken by social workers. During assessment of parenting it is important to establish whether poor parenting is a regular occurrence or whether there are extenuating factors resulting in momentary lapses in the quality of parenting (Kellett & Apps, 2009). Exploring with family members and understanding how religious and cultural beliefs and practices impact on parenting is imperative. *Culturally sensitive* assessment is therefore central to effective practice. Milner et al. (2015, p. 2) divide assessment into five processes, which are reproduced below.

Processes of assessment

1. *Preparing* for the task

2. *Collecting data*, including perceptions of the service user, the family and other agencies of the problem and any attempted solutions.

3. *Applying professional knowledge* (practise wisdom as well as theory) to seek analysis, understanding or interpretation of the data.

4. *Making judgements* about the relationships, needs, risks, standard of care or safety, seriousness of the situation, and people's capacities and potential for coping or for change (is the progress good enough?)

5. *Deciding* and/or recommending what is to be done; plus how, by whom and when, and how progress will be reviewed.

In an endeavour to drive up standards in relation to these processes of assessment, while achieving a common systematic approach, in the United Kingdom, the Department of Health (2000) devised the *Framework for the Assessment of Children in Need and their Families*. Key features of this assessment framework have since been taken up by the World Health Organization and as a guide it has been influential in Europe, North America and Australia (Rose, 2010, pp. 50–51). At the time of its introduction it was widely welcomed by the social work profession as moving away from assessment formats which focused solely on the family and failed to take into account broader influences. The framework incorporates the conceptual work of Bronfenbrenner (1979) on ecological systems and expands assessment outwards from a focus on family dynamics to encompass the family's relationships with wider networks and the socio-economic environment. It also pioneered the notion of an assessment of a child's needs and an investigation of maltreatment constituting aspects of the same assessment process, which not only focused on dangers and family deficits, but also on needs and family strengths (Horwath, 2010; Milner et al., 2015, p. 17).

The implementation of the assessment framework in England through the strictures of the Integrated Children's System, an electronic interface with prescriptive formats and timescales, has been extensively and consistently criticised (Munro, 2008; Broadhurst et al., 2010; Featherstone et al., 2014). However, the conception of assessment as being child-centred while incorporating three distinct dimensions: the child's developmental needs; parenting capacity; and family and environmental factors, alongside the further sub-division of these into detailed elements of investigation and consideration (reproduced in Figure 10.1), has remained widely accepted. For these reasons, what has become known as the *assessment triangle* will act as an organising principle for exploring the assessment of risk with families from ethnic minorities and underpins the worked case study in the last section of this chapter.

In child protection practice, risk assessment is an inherent aspect of gathering, collating and analysing information ascertained from family, friends, neighbours and other professionals. The concept of risk is succinctly

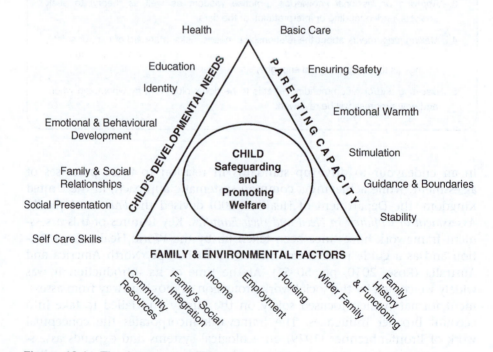

Figure 10.1 The Assessment Triangle

Department of Health (2000, p. 89)

defined by Carson & Bain (2008, p. 242) as 'an occasion when one or more consequences (events, outcomes and so on) could occur. Critically (a) those consequences may be harmful and/or beneficial and (b) either the number and/or the extent of those consequences, and/or their likelihood, is uncertain and/or unknown.' Munro (2008, p. 76) transposes this concept into a set of questions to be explored and answered by child protection social workers; these are reproduced below.

1. What is or has been happening?

2. What might happen?

3. How likely are these outcomes?

4. How undesirable are they?

5. The overall judgement of risk – a combination of the likelihood and the seriousness.

Working with families necessarily involves making child protection decisions within a limited timescale; based on partial information; when the reliability of evidence is variable; in ambiguous situations; with limited control; and in circumstances of uncertainty regarding future behaviour or events. It is this reality which introduces risk in relation to both the chances of a consequence occurring and the degree of detriment or benefit associated with it. The notion of risk historically meant the likelihood of either a desirable or undesirable outcome, but as Munro (2008) observes, contemporaneously, it is associated predominantly with an adverse outcome, particularly so in relation to child protection. Yet 'child protection workers have a duty to promote children's welfare as well as protect them, to maximise their well-being as well as to minimise any danger' (Munro, 2008, p. 59). This is consonant with a strengths-based approach to child protection and, indeed, supporting strengths can be an essential component of risk reduction (Turnell & Edwards, 1999). Paradoxically the same child protection intervention can carry risks of good and bad outcomes, making this an extremely challenging area of practice. Carson & Bain (2012) identify five levels at which inter-related risks exist and need to be addressed.

Level 1: *Risky or dangerous people, circumstances, events or articles* concerns people deemed to pose a risk and/or be at risk and includes factors affecting them and their access or exposure to dangerous objects.

Level 2: *Dangerous contexts and social settings* focuses on risk in relation to the environment people live in and the material and social context of their interactions with others.

Level 3: *Dangerous decisions* relates to the quality of decisions made by professionals undertaking the assessment, analysis and management of risk. It considers the degree to which poor decision-making can contribute to risk.

Level 4: *Dangerous management* concerns the nature of the support, supervision and guidance provided by managers to frontline professionals. It examines the extent to which poor management contributes to risk.

Level 5: *Dangerous systems* relates to organisational structures, internal agency systems regarding policies, procedures and IT alongside protocols for multi-agency communication. Flaws or gaps in these can increase the degree of risk.

Reflective exercise

Reflect on your experience of conducting risk assessments with families from racial and ethnic minority backgrounds and focus on levels 3–5 above.

What aspects of decisions, management and systems contribute to dangerousness?

Are any of these aspects of dangerousness different from those present when working with families from the ethnic majority, and if so why?

How might aspects of dangerousness more common to work with families from racial or ethnic minorities be reduced and in what ways could you contribute to this?

Actuarial risk assessment

Munro (2008, p. 71) suggests that *actuarial assessment tools*, which convert information about a family into numeric values to produce an estimate of risk, can be used to broadly categorise high-, medium- and low-risk families. She argues such tools can only assist professional judgement regarding the probability of harm at a particular point in time comprising one component in a holistic process of risk management. In the area of child protection *actuarial assessments* struggle to encompass the complexity of individual histories, family dynamics, environmental impacts and inter-related multiple problems. *Actuarial risk assessment* therefore remains underdeveloped for child protection and the majority of social workers continue to rely predominantly on *clinical risk assessment* based on structured interview schedules to collect relevant information, such as the *Framework for the Assessment of Children in Need and their Families* (Calder & Archer, 2016). Nevertheless social workers in coming to professional judgements about levels of dangerousness draw on evidence-based risk factors. The Children's Bureau (2004), an agency of the federal government of the US, in a major collation and analysis of the research literature identified the common risk and protective factors for families in relation to child maltreatment. These are reproduced in Table 10.1 and reflect the three domains of the assessment triangle.

Table 10.1   Risk and Protective Factors for Child Maltreatment

Dimensions	Risk factors	Protective factors
Child	• Premature birth, birth anomalies, low birth weight, exposure to toxins in utero • Temperament: difficult or slow to warm up • Physical/cognitive/emotional disability, chronic or serious illness • Childhood trauma • Anti-social peer group • Age • Child aggression, behaviour problems, attention deficits	• Good health, history of adequate development • Above-average intelligence • Hobbies and interests • Good peer relationships • Easy temperament • Positive disposition • Active coping style • Positive self-esteem • Good social skills • Internal locus of control • Balance between help-seeking and autonomy
Parental & Family	• External locus of control • Poor impulse control Depression/anxiety • Low tolerance for frustration • Feelings of insecurity • Lack of trust • Insecure attachment with own parents • Childhood history of abuse • High parental conflict, domestic violence • Family structure – single parent with lack of support, high number of children in household • Social isolation, lack of support • Parental psychopathology • Substance abuse • Separation/divorce, especially high-conflict divorce • Age • High general stress level • Poor parent–child interaction, negative attitudes and attributions about child's behaviour • Inaccurate knowledge and expectations about child development	• Secure attachment; positive and warm parent–child relationship • Supportive family environment • Household rules/structure; parental monitoring of child • Extended family support and involvement, including caregiving help • Stable relationship with parents • Parents have a model of competence and good coping skills • Family expectations of pro-social behaviour • High parental education

Table 10.1 *Continued*

Dimensions	Risk factors	Protective factors
Social & Environmental	• Low socio-economic status • Stressful life events • Lack of access to medical care, health insurance, adequate childcare and social services • Parental unemployment; homelessness • Social isolation/lack of social support • Exposure to racism/discrimination • Poor schools • Exposure to environmental toxins • Dangerous/violent neighbourhood • Community violence	• Mid to high socio-economic status • Access to health care and social services • Consistent parental employment • Adequate housing • Family religious faith participation • Good schools • Supportive adults outside of family who serve as role models/mentors to child

Notably many of these factors, particularly in relation to the social and environmental domain, are more likely to affect families from Black and minority ethnic backgrounds than those from the majority. People from minority ethnic backgrounds are disproportionately represented among low-income groups, living in neighbourhoods characterised by high crime and poor facilities and exposed to discrimination. If they are recent migrants or asylum seekers they may also be disproportionately affected by poor access to universal services such as health care and education, alongside higher rates of homelessness, unemployment or low wage jobs and social isolation. Children and parents or guardians from minority communities may be subject to additional stressors related to racist or sectarian behaviour from peers, feelings of insecurity and dislocation of family relationships. Consequently, practitioners can over-assess risk among families from Black and minority ethnic backgrounds due to their over-representation in relation to these risk factors. This is more likely to occur in circumstances where a practitioner has insufficient understanding of, or has not conducted adequate exploration of, the protective factors deriving from aspects of culture, faith, kinship, neighbourhood and local ethnic community.

Reflective exercise

Reflect on your practice with a family from a racial or ethnic minority and read through the list of risk factors and predictive factors above.

▶

◀

To what extent do you rely on identifying these factors in conducting a risk assessment?

How might your reliance on this list skew your perceptions of risk in a family from a racial or ethnic minority?

How might positive or negative stereotypes about a family from a minority background interact with this list to amplify or mute your perceptions of protective or risk factors?

What changes could you make to your beliefs and practices to reduce bias and the resultant over- or under-assessment of risk?

Clinical risk assessment

As Munro (2008) observes, the clinical approach is predicated on building relationships with families over time. It can be based on gathered evidence and an in-depth knowledge of particular family members, their situation and wider environment. This will include familiarity with the risk factors affecting specific children and the development of a tailored risk management strategy for the family. It involves the methodical collection and analysis of information underpinned by reflective practice (Munro, 2008). Aspects of *clinical judgement* can also rely on impressions and subjective conclusions about people and situations. *Practice wisdom* based on social workers' professional experiences often informs their intuitive understandings of family situations and the behaviour of individuals. This will necessarily be based on a limited number of abusive and non-abusive families (Munro, 2008). Professional perspectives may also be shaped by the personal experiences, values and beliefs of individual practitioners, which leaves considerable scope for stereotypes to skew professional judgement. Anxiety caused by the uncertainty created during encounters with *'strangers'* (those from other racial or ethnic groups) can prompt practitioners to retreat from engagement, resulting in superficial information gathering. For this reason social workers cannot rely on their professional experiences alone to identify risk factors for child maltreatment or make assumptions as to how commonly they occur. Calder & Archer (2016, p. 147) identify the problems associated with clinical risk assessment; these are reproduced in the text box below.

Problems of clinical risk assessments

Subjective bias of the assessor: for example, discriminatory practice, the over-identification of vivid and unacceptable risks).

Staff taking short cuts: when under pressure.

▶

◀

Over-identification with the subject of the assessment: for example, probation officers may prioritise the rights of offenders over those of the victims; social workers may prioritise the desires of parents over the needs of children.

Over reliance on the self-report of the subject of the risk assessment: for example: the accounts of offending behaviour provided by offenders, parental accounts of family interactions.

As the Serious Case Review case studies analysed in this book amply demonstrate, all of these shortcomings of clinical risk assessment are evident. This is the result of a combination of the professional challenges of cross-cultural work and the inherent complexity of risk assessment. Deciding what level of risk is posed in terms of severity, probability and immediacy in circumstances of uncertainty, and whether this meets the criterion for intervention, involves interpreting the behaviour of family members and those in close contact with the child. Understanding the motivation of individuals and the meanings they assign to their actions is essential in comprehending their likely future actions. As Munro (2008, p. 78) points out, such interpretations can blur facts and values, which is why it is vital to explore and gain knowledge of a family's culture and spiritual worldview. This requires adequate professional judgements to be made regarding acceptable parenting as opposed to normative parenting predicated on Anglocentric cultural expectations. It requires differentiating between dangerousness in parental behaviours and merely differences in childrearing practices; while comprehending how these are shaped and impacted by the wider context in which childcare is taking place. Munro (2008, p. 79) argues that 'the range of cross-cultural variability in child-rearing beliefs and behaviours makes it clear that there is no universal standard of optimal childcare or definition of abuse and neglect'.

Decision-making and heuristics

The primacy of *clinical risk assessment* in child protection, in conjunction with conditions of uncertainty; high workloads exerting time pressures; and short deadlines for urgent decision-making, mean that social workers often make determinations on risky situations and dynamics which do not clearly demonstrate evidence-based practice; transparent logical step-by-step analysis of the facts; or explicit analytic reasoning (Munro, 2008; Kemshall et al., 2013). While this may be considered poor practice, it needs to be understood in context. All human beings presented with overwhelming amounts of information rely on innate, usually unconscious, psychological mechanisms. These help them make decisions in relation to their environment without being paralysed by the quantity of data presented or undertaking virtually impossible feats of data collection and analysis in order to make choices about multiple courses of action. Innate cognitive developmental processes involve the creation of psychological shortcuts which help humans to choose responses, make decisions and take action in their daily lives.

For instance, people are generally more disposed to believe someone they like, as opposed to someone they do not, regardless of the strength of the evidence. Because individuals have limited time, they tend to rely on word of mouth from someone they like, rather than undertaking their own research into the facts. This has huge implications for practice. Imagine that a social worker intervening with a re-constituted mixed heritage family holds the negative stereotype that men of African Caribbean heritage are quick tempered and easily become aggressive. Consequently, when a father of African Caribbean heritage tells the practitioner that his White teen-aged stepson is physically assaulting him, the father's claim is dismissed by the social worker rather than explored, while the assertion of the stepson is taken at face value. This is partly because a negative stereotype inevitably induces a degree of dislike for someone. But it also demonstrates how a time-pressured practitioner can make rushed judgements which reflect a cognitive shortcut rather than *practice wisdom*.

These shortcut cognitive mechanisms, referred to collectively as *heuristics*, are particularly significant when professionals are heavily reliant on *practice wisdom*. Heuristics can culminate in 'subjective perceptions of risk' rather than objective assessments of probability and severity based on a rigorous evaluation of the available evidence, logical reasoning and cogent analysis (Kemshall et al., 2013, p. 54). When *heuristics* are used in child protection decision-making they can result in information being lost through avoidance (evidence not collected due to prior assumptions), forgetting (counter-evidence overlooked), rejecting (counter-evidence not believed) or reinterpreting (faulty interpretations of evidence). Research indicates that *heuristic intuitive* reasoning, comprising typically unconscious cognitive processes, tends to be relied upon by practitioners in situations of high uncertainty – often in relation to neglect or an indeterminate physical injury. Analytical rule-based processes are more likely to be drawn upon when there is a clearer picture of non-accidental substantial injury (Enosh & Bayer-Topilsky, 2015). As *heuristics* are innate they are unavoidable aspects of decision-making. Nevertheless, they can be recognised and brought into awareness through reflective practice, while being forestalled through the application of evidence-based practice. This minimises their distorting potential and facilitates more analytical consideration underpinned by evidence. Table 10.2 identifies key *heuristics* influencing professional judgement in relation to risk, drawn from Kemshall et al. (2013), Carson & Bain (2008) and Taylor (2013) and adapted to child protection social work. It gives examples as to how these *heuristics* can skew perceptions of risk in work with families from racial and ethnic minorities.

Table 10.2   Heuristics Affecting Child Protection Decision-Making

Heuristic	Cognitive mechanism	Child protection example
Availability bias	Risk assessed on the basis of easily obtainable information rather than the quality or comprehensiveness of information.	One member of the family speaks English while others speak little or no English. As a result the perspective of the family member who speaks English prevails over all other views from the family, as eliciting these require much more time and effort from the practitioner.
Recall bias	Recent or dramatic events are treated as more significant in the assessment of risk than mundane or earlier happenings.	Cultural or faith-related events or behaviours, which are more surprising, novel or startling to the practitioner eclipse familiar and routine aspects of family life, including demonstrable strengths.
Presumed associations	Imputing causes to correlations	A typical example of this is attributing violence against children to cultural influences or religious beliefs as opposed to disadvantaged circumstances or family isolation.
Credibility bias	According greater significance and weight to information from individuals who are liked or respected and downgrading that received from those who are disliked.	For instance, the practitioner feels more comfortable with a White British parent and therefore accepts his or her version of events as against that of their foreign-born partner and other parent, who is experienced as a 'stranger' engendering uncertainty and anxiety in the practitioner.
Hindsight bias	Over-estimate of what could have been known at the time before making a decision, due to knowing the ultimate outcome of the decision at a future point.	Risk assessment necessarily involves uncertainty regarding future events. But investigations into child deaths or serious injuries have the advantage of hindsight as to what actually happened, leading to assumptions that erroneous decisions were made and engendering precautionary child protection decisions. For example disproportionate child protection responses to Muslim children who express strong religious beliefs due to previous high-media profile cases of Islamic radicalisation.
Representative bias	Over-reliance on personal experience and thus a small number of unrepresentative cases leading to perceiving situations as similar when in fact they are different, and hence responding to new situations within established frames of reference	Superdiversity means that practitioners may only ever work with a very small number of families from a particular minority ethnic or faith group. Consequently, this kind of bias can be amplified in work with families from minority racial, ethnic or faith backgrounds.
Confirmation bias	Skewed selection of information to support an already chosen course of action while ignoring or minimising information that controverts it.	Racial and cultural stereotypes held by individuals are known to be highly resistant to change. Therefore confirmation biases can be accentuated in work with Black and minority ethnic families when sweeping but often subliminal assumptions are made about them, which subsequently feed into decision-making.

Anchoring and adjustment bias	Once an estimate of risk is made, any subsequent adjustment up or down due to new information tends to be influenced by the original estimate, which anchors and therefore reduces the magnitude of later adjustments.	Pathologising cultural or religious practices or worldviews which differ from those typically held among the ethnic majority can result in practitioners perceiving a raised level of risk. This is then little changed by subsequent information regarding the family, even when this identifies strengths.
Optimism bias	Investment of time and effort in supporting change resulting in trifling or modest progress being attributed greater significance than is objectively warranted.	Practitioners working with people from different cultural and faith backgrounds may feel assured by some positive changes in parental or children's behaviour. But fail to recognise the degree to which a cultural or faith-related belief or practice is entrenched and underpinning a risky behaviour.
Repetition bias	Giving primacy to information repeated by an individual or different individuals, as opposed to assessing its evidential robustness.	Racial, cultural or faith-related stereotypes in society act as repetitions of particular assumptions about people from different heritage backgrounds. These can become subconscious confirmations of a particular view of a family, for example that fathers of Pakistani ethnicity are oppressive figures within their families.
Compression bias	Over-estimation of catastrophic events even though statistically they are rare, resulting in a misperception of higher risk.	This bias can be amplified in work with ethnic or faith minorities, for example when a teenaged girl of Indian heritage discusses arranged marriage in school or parents originally from Nigeria emphasise the importance of their children's obedience and respect.
Prejudice	Bias in the assessment of risk created by positive or negative stereotyping of individuals and families.	Positive stereotypes such as assumptions that families of South Asian heritage live in supportive multi-generational families or that mothers from African Caribbean ethnic backgrounds are powerful matriarchs, can result in under-estimation of risk. Conversely, negative stereotypes such as assuming that Black men are more likely to be violent or Roma parents are indifferent to educating their children can result in over-estimates of risk and disproportionate child protection responses.
Over-confidence	Feeling over-confident in one's ability to accurately assess risk or assuming that the information on which it is based is of high quality and reliable.	Practitioners whose anxiety is below the minimum threshold anticipated in cross-cultural encounters, which should create a degree of uncertainty, are likely to react in routine ways. The consequent lack of reflexiveness among overly confident practitioners will result in them missing relevant clues about matters of race, culture and faith, thus failing to explore them and feed this information into decision-making.

Table 10.2 *Continued*

| Illusion of control | Innate tendency to under-estimate the degree of uncertainty in a situation and assume one has more control over events than is the case. | Practitioners from the White majority who have adopted *contact* or *reintegration* statuses can be oblivious to important aspects of a family's heritage pertinent to risk assessment, or tend to perceive differences from Anglocentric norms around family organisation and childrearing as deficits. Both assumptions are likely to mislead a practitioner into thinking they have more knowledge and therefore more control over the situation than is the case. Both these identity statuses tend to avoid recognising the uncertainty inherent in meeting people from other social groups to oneself. |
| Fundamental attribution error | Tendency to attribute one's own behaviour to the environment, but attribute the behaviour of others to their character or disposition. | This can result in under-estimating environmental factors in the behaviours of family members and over-attributing them to personal factors linked to cultural and religious motivations when working with people from minority ethnic backgrounds. Consequently practitioners may overlook or minimise the structural factors which influence the behaviours of family members. |

Reflective exercise

Reflect on your recent practice with a family from a racial or ethnic minority and read through the list of common *heuristics* above.

Which of these *heuristics* did you rely on while gathering information and assessing the degree of risk?

Why did you rely on these *heuristics*?

What aspects of your practice could you change to reduce your reliance on *heuristics*?

Cultural competence in risk assessment

This section focuses on a worked case study relating to risk assessment. This is not intended to be comprehensive, but is designed to illustrate how cultural competence can be integrated into the three dimensions of the *Framework for the Assessment of Children in Need and their Families* to deepen and enhance information gathered when family members from minority racial and/or ethnic communities are involved. Discussion within the *Assessment Framework* is followed by a risk assessment to demonstrate how a culturally competent approach can assist in making appropriate professional judgements regarding the likelihood of significant harm occurring to a child or young person from a minority heritage background. This type of assessment is also premised on the use of whole-family approaches.

Morris et al. (2008) found repeated evidence of family-based services or models which in reality were either geared towards the adult parent or the child. They emphasise the importance of working with whole-family interventions as opposed to working with individual family members. Family group conferences, which are a whole-family approach, have been found to work effectively with families generally and to provide positive outcomes for Black and minority ethnic families. Family group conferences are a process led by family members, including extended family, to make decisions and implement plans they have agreed upon to protect children at risk. Best practice in these forums permits families to self-define and decide who should attend. Therefore they can accommodate a wide variety of family forms. Every family is unique and the strategies which might work in one family might not work in another.

A study by O'Shaughnessy et al. (2010) highlighted the appropriateness of family group conferences for families from ethnic minority backgrounds particularly because these families found that that this model understood, acknowledged and respected their cultural beliefs and practices, enabling them to formulate plans which took their cultural practices seriously. Evidence suggests that Black and minority ethnic families have felt sufficiently included in this type of decision making process to own the care plan developed through the family group conference. Writing about the use of family group conferences, Valenti (2017) found that overall their availability for families where English was an additional language was scarce owing to a lack of interpreters. Even where they were employed, it was found that in at least one case, seven different interpreters had been used for one family. This meant that the social worker had to introduce each interpreter at each visit or meeting, undermining the flow and progress of the intervention with this family. A participant in the Valenti (2017, p. 130) study added in a cautionary contribution, that family group conferences 'could be seen as an opportunity for the dominant members to reproduce their oppression towards other members...[and] might reinforce the culture stereotype for men to make decisions and women and young people would not have the chance to challenge it'. Arguably, for minority families, this may be the opportunity for social workers to understand family dynamics in relation to power, gender roles and decision-making. It may also be a chance to explore with family members who they perceive as belonging or not belonging to the family, and why.

Case study on risk assessment for practitioners

Children's Social Care receives a referral from the safeguarding lead of a local school who expresses concern that two sisters of Albanian ethnicity aged 13 and 14 are describing very explicit sexual activity to other pupils and saying that they are soon to be married. You are the social worker tasked to explore this child protection concern and carry out a risk assessment.

Building initial rapport

When visiting the family for the first time you will want to quickly establish the English language competence of different family members. Do not assume this necessarily reflects the length of time that they have resided in the UK, as additional language proficiencies are often mediated by age and gender. Children, by virtue of entering the free education system, and due to their developmental stage (most particularly young children), often pick up English language skills more quickly than their parents or guardians. Older people, particularly if they were never in employment in the UK, may be less likely to speak English than other family members. In cultures where there are strong gender roles, and Albanian society is one of these, adult males are more likely to pick up English language skills through work outside the home, while the role of women oriented around domestic life may reduce their opportunities to develop English language abilities. Nevertheless, bear in mind that many of those who migrate already have, or quickly develop, proficiency in English. Customary roles for men and women may be less pronounced among wealthier, more highly educated or urbanised families. Conversely, adaptive strategies in the host country may have modified these ascribed gender roles, making them much more flexible.

If some family members speak little or no English, you will need to find out what languages people speak in Albania, whether there are different dialects which are mutually intelligible or unintelligible, and whether these are spoken by sections of the population in other countries, as this might assist you in identifying an appropriate interpreter. Finding out whether it is common for Albanians to speak other languages would also help you. There are resource costs to employing interpreters and it can be tempting to rely on English-speaking family members. This can also play into Anglocentric assumptions regarding nuclear family forms, which often leads to dismissing extended kin. Undertaking the initial stage of the assessment will require you to use research, the internet, colleagues, personal networks and community resources to build up a broad *cultural knowledge* of Albanian society. This information should be used to suggest any additional matters for discussion and not to create stereotypes which, because they generate presumptions, shut down areas of further enquiry with family members.

Other countries may not have a well-developed child protection system or social work profession and it can be challenging for families from such countries to comprehend your role. This can still be true for some families that have been settled for many years. Therefore you may need to explain this at length and double-check the understanding of family members. You will want to consider whether it is necessary to build rapport through more extended small talk. In this case it is essential to establish the English language proficiency of each family member through an opportunity for direct communication with them. This is likely to involve exploring their experiences of education in Albania, if they have lived in other countries before coming to the UK, and how long different family members have lived in this country. Finding out what activities or work they have engaged in during these periods might also help in indicating likely language ability in English or additional languages.

You will be aware of the factors that can affect an individual's English language competence and its variation over time. As a culturally competent practitioner you will be mindful that non-verbal communication can mean quite different things in different societies and cultures. Therefore you will want to double-check through the interpreter any hunches you have based on observations of family members' gestures, facial expressions and so forth. In some areas of Albania a head nod means *'no'* while turning the head from side to side means *'yes'*. It can be important to avoid relying solely on even apparently common non-verbal signals without confirming meanings through verbal communication. This is not to detract from the importance of recognising contradictions between verbal and non-verbal signals, but these can be much more difficult to read accurately when relying on an interpreter and working with family members from a cultural background unfamiliar to the practitioner. Even when communicating with family members with an apparently good level of English proficiency it will remain important to double-check verbal and non-verbal meanings.

Throughout later exchanges with the family it will be vital to have a sense of what topics of conversation are likely to be more difficult or embarrassing than others. Matters such as sex, dependency, income, religion and politics are taboo subjects across many different societies. In Albanian society, particularly for those families originally from a rural background, sexual relations tend to be more uncomfortable for people to discuss. Equally, for families arriving from large towns in Albania, or who have spent some years in the UK and may have acculturated, such customary taboos may be much less influential.

Child's developmental needs

If the children are recent migrants rather than having been born in the UK or having come to the country in infancy then how might the children's health have been impacted by their *pre-flight* and *flight* experiences? Albania is one of the poorest countries in Europe, with quite high levels of relative and absolute poverty, and therefore some sections of the population can be undernourished. What were the experiences of these children as they journeyed across the continent to the UK, and how did these affect their mental and physical health? What health care provision existed in the children's country of origin and how did this affect what treatments they received in the past? Albania's health care system was gravely disrupted by the fall of communism in the 1990s and the global financial crisis in 2008 and, while it is nominally free, expectations of payments for access to various services have led many Albanians to rely on home treatments. What experiences have the children had during *reception, settlement* or *resettlement* and what impact have these had on their health? What formal or informal education have the children received and what pedagogical approaches were adopted? What are the attitudes of the children towards formal schooling in the UK? In Albania, particularly in rural areas, a significant minority of children either do not attend school or drop out early. What is the children's level of numeracy and literacy in their first language and in English?

How do the children view their own identity and how has this been affected by experiences in their country of origin and the host country? In Albania if the children are from the rural north of the country they might have a strong clan identity in addition to identifying as Albanian. If they are from a Roma background, the children may have experienced considerable discrimination in Albania and have more in common with other Roma peoples. As migrants in the UK have they been subject to hostility, prejudice or harassment due to their ethnicity and if so what affect does this have on them? Do they have a religious identity and if so what part does this play in their lives? In Albania, the main faiths are Islam, Eastern Orthodox and Roman Catholic. The influence of communism over many years, with its emphasis on secularism, means that many people do not have a strong faith identity or none at all, while many others do. Not only is it necessary to establish if the children have a religious faith or not, but also what this means to them and how it frames their worldview and observances. Conversely, if the children have been in the UK for a number of years, or indeed if they have experienced discrimination due to their accent or appearance, they may be adopting *assimilative strategies* and be trying to merge into the ethnic majority. Therefore their heritage identity may be relatively weak, or they may feel conflicted as they strive to manage the cultural expectations of family while being accepted by or schoolchildren from the ethnic majority or other minority communities.

It will be important to understand not only what the children's level of cognitive, emotional and behavioural development is, but also what appears to be expected of them in relation to their interactions with other members of the family and self-care. In Albania many children are required to work in order to assist the household, particularly in rural communities. Boys are generally encouraged to be independent and to spend time outside of the home, while girls' dependency and orientation toward remaining in, and around, the home is typically promoted. Older children are often expected to take care of younger children and early self-care may be fostered. Early marriage is still practised in some regions of Albania and among sections of the Roma minority, although the legal minimum age of marriage in that country is 18 years. Ascribed gender roles can mean that, from an early age, girls are encouraged to take on the care of younger siblings and undertake domestic tasks, while their education is deemed less essential than that of boys. These cultural expectations may be more influential in the northern rural region of Albania and weaker for urban families or wealthier ones living in the cities. This echoes Archard's (2015) concept of *divisions* which relate to how childhood may be divided up into distinctive periods, associated with different expectations which vary cross-culturally. It also engages the social GGRRAAACCEEESSS model, which directs practitioners to consider how culture is mediated by geographic, economic and social stratification.

Parenting capacity

Where forced migration or human trafficking has occurred, you will need to explore how these experiences might have affected the mental and physical health of parents or guardians and their relationships with children. How does the immigration status of different family members affect their ability to provide care for children and keep them safe? As Albanians, the parents or guardians might have been granted refugee status many years previously or be professionals with work visas and have few problems. On the other hand they may be undocumented migrants or asylum seekers facing substantial challenges due to holding far fewer rights and entitlements than British citizens. When exploring the attachment of parents or guardians to children, it will be vital to explore family organisation; gender roles; the role of kin; and cultural or religious influences on understandings of child development, childcare and discipline. Where beliefs, values and/or practices differ from Anglocentric norms, it will be important to resist finding fault with these on the basis that they are different, rather than on the grounds of posing a risk of significant harm. Among many families in Albania, particularly those from agricultural backgrounds, extended kin remain quite central in the upbringing of children. While childcare is the preserve of mothers and female relatives, fathers typically take a much less involved role. In relation to stability in children's lives, in cultures where childcare is typically shared among a wider number of kin than is the case in Anglocentric societies, family form may be more fluid with different relatives temporarily joining and leaving the household.

You will need to understand the place of the family's heritage culture and faith in their worldview and daily lives, particularly in relation to the upbringing of children. It needs to be remembered that acculturation may have occurred during the family's residence in the UK, and modified the influences of culture and faith, so this will require exploring. Structural factors may significantly shape how parents or guardians relate to their children, which may have much less to do with culture or faith. Considera-tion needs to be given to how formative experiences, in this case in another country, might affect the current attitudes or behaviours of family members. In Albania paying for access to health services, or widespread poverty over many decades, meant that large sections of the population could not afford some health treatments or buy toys or printed material for children. This may influence parental behaviour in UK. It is crucial to enquire about what you are observing; for example, delay in seeking medical treatment or lack of stimulation for children, rather than assuming what these things mean from an ethnocentric viewpoint. It is essential to consider how Anglocentric norms inform professional judgements; in this case, how materialism in British soci-ety leads to assumptions that children are neglected because they lack toys.

Family and environmental factors

You will need to explore with family members who they perceive to be significant kin and explore their role and influence. This may be similar to Anglocentric family forms or differ in significant ways. Beyond this it will be necessary to understand the family's relationships with other households both in the UK and transnationally. Do these comprise extended kin, house-holds from the same region of the country of origin or the same clan (in the case of Albania), or sub-group of an ethnic community (e.g. Roma)? What cultural obligations are there in connection with providing or receiving assistance, and are these still influential? Among those of Albanian ethnic-ity, hospitality and kin loyalty can be significant influences and manifest in sharing accommodation with kin or friends and sending remittances back to relatives in Albania. You will want to explore how the immigration statuses of different family members and therefore their rights and entitlements impact on their living conditions and mediate aspects of culture and faith.

How do family members relate to their own heritage identity and wider ethnic community? Is this a source of support, comfort, or difficulty, or a mixture? What are the implications if the family is from a sub-group, in this case Roma, or from a particular clan background? How do experiences (if any) of prejudice and discrimination within their neighbourhood affect family members? What resources are there for the family within the local ethnic community, through virtual communities or wider national or international networks? Are there multicultural or multi-faith resources? How do different family members relate to their neighbourhood, the ethnic majority, other minorities or their local ethnic community? Unemployment rates have historically been very high in Albania, leading to many unemployed men congregating together and passing the time. In the UK, where immigration status, the language barrier or discrimination may prohibit or hinder obtaining employment, men may meet together at cafés or other community venues. By contrast, many women can be more isolated in their homes and have less opportunity for social interactions, while children, through schooling and the acquisition of English language skills, may be successfully integrating into the wider community. Appreciating how age, gender, sexuality or disability mediate dynamics of inclusion in local communities will be essential.

Exploring the influence of *collectivist norms* within this local ethnic community will assist you to consider the implications of events within the household for family/community relationships. In relation to ethnic Albanians, for instance, preserving *'honour'* and being seen to engage in *'right conduct'* can be an important consideration for some. It may be that if family members arrived in the UK as asylum seekers, they have been dispersed away from other members of their ethnic community and therefore they are relatively isolated. It is possible that conflicts in their country of origin or acculturation in the UK may lead family members to feel little affiliation with other ethnic Albanians.

Risk assessment

The first question is to establish what is happening. This means finding out whether the sisters are being sexually abused and if so by whom. Bearing in mind that discussing sex may carry a strong taboo, this may both constitute a challenge in terms of addressing the issue with family members and also be an indicator that something untoward is happening to lead these girls to discuss sexual matters. Such a taboo could be used by some family members to discourage disclosure or to hide what is actually taking place. Equally, British society is a highly sexualised one and these girls may simply have acculturated and been watching explicit material online and discussing it to gain acceptance by peers. Or it could be that they are not permitted to mention sexual matters at home and are only able to do so at school. It will also be important to explore whether there are indeed plans for an underage marriage of these girls or if notions of early marriage are being used to justify or perpetrate sexual abuse. How might these be influenced by the religious beliefs that different family members may hold? If sexual abuse is not occurring, but underage marriage is planned in accordance with religious or cultural traditions, it needs to be remembered that cultures are not monolithic and many such customary practices are contested within ethnic minorities.

Understanding how the family's structure, socio-economic situation and relationship to the local community affect dynamics, decision-making and actions will be crucial to avoiding culturising the behaviour of family members. It will mean examining and comprehending the influence of structural factors and their inter-relationship with aspects of culture and faith. Indeed, it may mean discovering that the family's heritage plays little part in their lives. This will help to reveal the perspectives and motivations of different family members. Aspects of a family's socio-economic circumstances can amplify, modify or diminish the influence of beliefs or practices deriving from culture and faith.

Aspects of faith and culture which influence day-to-day life or key events for family members can constitute strengths, create vulnerabilities or contribute directly to the risk of significant harm to a child. Sometimes norms associated with a family's heritage background have the potential to be both protective and risky, depending on how they manifest for a particular family or change over time. Understanding these is vital to effective risk assessment. For many ethnic Albanian families there are strong cultural expectations of kin loyalty and offering hospitality. This can mean that the family receives support from a wide range of relatives living in the UK, their country of origin, or elsewhere. Clan bonds may still be significant, providing another source of assistance and access to a network of co-ethnics. Conversely, these cultural expectations may impose obligations on family members to accommodate and support extended family members, clan members or other Albanians when their own resources are already inadequate to maintain the welfare of their children. If such norms also lead to multiple people passing through the household this could increase the risk to vulnerable children of sexual abuse. At the same time multiple adults in the household could provide childcare relief, enabling parents to undertake training, attend English language classes, undertake employment or simply mitigate the stress and fatigue of bringing up children. These possibilities all require investigation and evaluation.

Families often fear social work involvement in relation to child protection and for people from minority backgrounds this may be heightened due to their own experiences or those of other community members with public authorities and services. Reluctance and resistance are common initial reactions among families, whether from the ethnic majority or from ethnic minorities. Some family members from racial or ethnic minorities may resort to accusations of racism or notions of cultural privacy to impede child protection enquiries. These may be genuine or manufactured concerns on the part of family members. Either way, social workers need to reflect on how these kinds of responses from minority families affect them. It is essential to ask in the first instance: is the family justified? Is a family member's belief or way of doing things merely different, but being treated as inferior or deficient by professionals? Is the commonly mono-cultural nature of the services offered or arranged by Children's Social Care creating discriminatory practices?

These questions need to be accompanied by a consideration of how the beliefs or practices of family members, which they attribute to culture or faith, affect children's welfare and safety. Putting the child's experience at the centre of the assessment helps to protect social workers from permitting cultural respect to slip into cultural relativity in situations where children are at risk of harm. Cultural influences which pressure girls into underage marriages, apart from being illegal in the UK, also have detrimental consequences in relation to lack of freedom of choice, disrupted education and damage to health due to early pregnancy. As *bride price* – money or gifts that the groom's family sends to the bride's family – is a common feature of such early marriages, this can also mean that poverty is an additional factor. Early marriage is perhaps a cultural practice that may have had positive functions in the past in Albania where historically child mortality was high and conditions of extreme poverty reduced the ability of families to provide for all their children. While this does not make the practice of child marriage acceptable in present-day Britain, some of these factors may provide a starting point for a culturally sensitive discussion with family members. Sometimes culture may be cited by family members as a cover or justification for sexual abuse, neglect and other forms of child maltreatment. The ultimate question is always does this practice pose a significant risk of harm to the child? If it does, how likely is this detrimental outcome, if the motives for the practice are driven by aspects of culture, faith or socio-economic conditions or indeed a combination of these? This deliberation on risk assessment can be summarised through a list of key questions for culturally sensitive child protection enquiries, which are set out in the text box below.

Key questions in culturally sensitive risk assessment

1. What are the needs of family members in relation to culture and faith?

2. What are the risks posed to children by beliefs, values, attitudes or behaviours shaped by culture or faith? Where there are perceived risks are this attributable to:

    a) Harmful beliefs, attitudes or practices in relation to the child in any context?

    b) Positive beliefs, attitudes or practices in the past or in the country of origin, but which are harmful in the changed context of present-day Britain?

    ▶

◀

    c) Negatively evaluated beliefs, values or practices because they differ from those of the ethnic majority but which are in fact neutral or beneficial for children's welfare.

    d) Beliefs, attitudes or practices mediated by gender, age, language, legal status, time in host country, education, class, income, health, disability, racism and discrimination.

    e) Socio-economic or personal factors or other considerations either unconnected with or only weakly linked to the family's ethnicity, culture or faith.

3. What are the family's strengths and protective factors deriving from their cultural or religious beliefs and practices?

4. What cultural or spiritual resources can family members draw upon or access to support family wellbeing, improve the welfare of children and reduce the risk of significant harm?

5. Is a different threshold (higher or lower) for access to welfare provision or the initiation of child protection intervention being applied to a minority family as compared to that used in work with ethnic majority families and if so why? What is the justification for this difference?

Conclusion

The UN Convention on the Rights of the Child protects the right of families to express and observe their faith and cultural heritage while protecting children from harmful practices. What constitutes 'harmful' can involve disagreement between social workers and individual families from minority backgrounds or sometimes their wider ethnic community. This can be exacerbated by ethnocentric conceptions of *good enough parenting* among professionals as opposed to an impartial consideration of whether customary practices are harmful, beneficial or neutral for a child's welfare. Clinical risk assessment which relies on social workers building positive relationships with family members and exercising objective professional judgement can also be highly vulnerable to bias. An awareness of the role *heuristics* play in decision-making about risk can help practitioners to counter the effect of ethnocentrism and stereotyping. Culturally sensitive approaches to the gathering and analysis of information from families and their communities can be integrated into the *Framework for the Assessment of Children in Need and their Families*.

Appendix One: Serious Case Reviews used as Exemplar Case Studies

Bexley Safeguarding Children Board (2013) *Serious Case Review Baby F D.O.B. 01.01.2012: D.O.D. 14/06/2012*

Birmingham Safeguarding Children Board (2010) *Working Together to Safeguard Children in respect of the Death of a Child: Case Number 14*

Bradford Safeguarding Children Board (*2013) Serious Case Review: The Overview Report on Hamzah Khan*

Brighton and Hove Local Safeguarding Children Board (2017) *Serious Case Review: Siblings W and X*

Cambridgeshire Safeguarding Children Board (2015) *Serious Case Review using the Significant Incident Learning Process of the Circumstances Concerning Child J*

City of Salford Local Safeguarding Children Board (2007) *Executive Summary Report of the Serious Case Review Panel into the Death of a Child: C Aged 17 Months*

Cheshire East Safeguarding Children's Board (2011) *Serious Case Review CE001: Child B, Child C, Child D, Executive Summary.*

Coventry Safeguarding Children Board (2013) *Serious Case Review Re Daniel Pelka Born 15th July 2007 Died 3rd March 2012*

Cumbria Local Safeguarding Children Board (2014) *Serious Case Review Child J, Final Report*

Enfield Safeguarding Children Board & Haringey Local Safeguarding Children Board (2015) *Child 'CH': Serious Case Review Overview Report*

Gloucestershire Safeguarding Children Board (2011) *Serious Case Review: Redacted Overview Report Re SCR 0310*

Gloucestershire Safeguarding Children Board (2016) *Serious Case Review Lucy, Final Report*

Islington Safeguarding Children Board (2012) *Serious Case Review: Services provided to Child B and Child C January 2008-February 2011*

Kingston Local Safeguarding Children Board (2013) *The Serious Case Review Relating to Tom & Vic*

Kingston Local Safeguarding Children Board (2015) *Serious Case Review Family A*

Lambeth Safeguarding Children Board (2014) *Serious Case Review Child H*

Leeds Safeguarding Children Board (2010) *Executive Summary of the Serious Cases Review Panel: Re Child Q*

Leicester Safeguarding Children Board (2011) *Serious Case Review in Respect of the Deaths of Children known as Child 1 and Child 2: Case "A"*

London Borough of Lewisham Local Safeguarding Children Board (2009) *Executive Summary: Serious Case Review 'Child J and Child L'*

London Borough of Waltham Forest Safeguarding Children Board (2011) *Serious Case Review: Child W – Executive Summary*

Manchester Safeguarding Children Board (2010) *Executive Summary of the Serious Care Review in Respect of Child S*

Manchester Safeguarding Children Board (2016) *Serious Case Review Child B1 Overview Report*

NSPCC (2016) Serious Case Review No. 2016-C5807 *Children U, B and V*

Rochdale Borough Safeguarding Children Board (2013) *Serious Case Review in Respect of Young People 1,2,3,4,5 & 6*

Southampton Local Safeguarding Children Board (2014) *Serious Case Review Family A*

Surrey Safeguarding Children Board (2014) *Overview Report on the Serious Case Review Relating to: Young Person: Hiers*

Tower Hamlets Safeguarding Children Board (2014) *'Jamilla' Serious Case Review*

Tri-borough Local Safeguarding Children Board (2015) *Serious Case Review Sofia*

Walsall Safeguarding Children Board (2014) *Serious Case Review Child W3*

Appendix Two: Clustered Themes from Summaries of Serious Case Reviews

Table A2.1 Clustered Themes from Summaries of Serious Case Reviews

Conceptions of family form
Inter-generational relationships
Transnational families
Family reunification
Polygamous families
Visiting relationships
Confusion between a household and a family
Collectivist understandings of family
Mutual obligations of family members
Confusion between forced and arranged marriages
Kin group conflict
Fluidity of household and family membership
Culture and faith affirming family life
Understandings of privacy
Understandings of childhood
Child development theory biases
Expectations of children's self-care
Beliefs regarding children's responsibilities
Racial and ethnic identity development
Experiences of racism or sectarianism
Diversity in children's care
Childcare arrangements
Child rearing practices
Children left home alone
Kinship care of children
Parental involvement in children's care
Professional confusion around private fostering
Professional and parental expectations of children's self-care
Control and discipline of children
Child abuse linked to faith or belief

Children's education
Level of college/school attendance
Integration with or isolation from other pupils
Socialisation and acculturation
English language acquisition
School exclusion
Missing from school
Teacher/child relationships
Cultural norms around education
Faith schools
After-school religious teaching
Home schooling
Institutional racism

Gender roles and relationships
Patriarchal norms and influence
Parental stress caused by poverty
Traditional gender roles and expectations
Cultural norms regarding fatherhood and motherhood
Gender role change and adaptation
Domestic abuse
Power relationships
Religious observance regarding gender relations

Localised ethnic and faith communities
Tensions within ethnic communities due to conflicts in country of origin
Tensions between different local ethnic groups
Role of elders within communities
Influences of opinion and faith leaders
Stereotypes and prejudice
Racism and sectarianism
Structural discrimination
Collectivist norms
Faith based social networks
Community resources
Poor professional knowledge of ethnic community
Low professional expectations of community members
Community tolerance of maltreatment of women and children
Relationship between family and community

Visibility and invisibility of culture and observances
Community hostility towards professionals
Preservation of good community relations
Ambivalence towards disclosure of maltreatment
Children at risk who remain within local ethnic community
Community mediators
Individual ethnic identification and community
Gang membership
Socio-economically disadvantaged communities

Recent economic migrants
Housing mobility
Language barrier in professional communications
Lack of interpreters
Private housing providers
Unsuitable or substandard accommodation
Low paid casual work
Poverty related impacts on family
Poor communication with country consulates
Disjointed multi-agency involvement
Confused understanding of role and remit of other agencies
No recourse to public funds
Confusion regarding eligibility criteria for benefits and services
Misleading statements about family relationships
Transnational family reunification
Domestic violence against mothers
Complaints of racism
Fathers not assessed
Confusion if from outside EU but arrived via an EU country
Lack of knowledge of systems and services
Resource constraints within ethnic communities

Forced migrants, asylum seekers and refugees
Limited entitlement to benefits and services
Homelessness and extreme housing mobility
Unsuitable or substandard accommodation
Activities illegal due to immigration status
Poor communication with Border Agency
Patriarchal norms in country of origin

Domestic violence against mothers

Alcohol and drug related coping strategies

Poor mental health due to prior trauma

Poor mental health due to immigration status

Confusion over immigration status if lived in several countries

Disparate multi-agency involvement

Confused understanding of role and remit of other agencies

Lack of knowledge of systems and services

Multiple adjustments to living in new host country

Severe poverty and destitution

Misleading statements about family relationships

Fathers not assessed

Resource constraints within ethnic communities

Mental and Physical Health

Health inequalities

Systems of health care

Health care provision

Health related beliefs and practices

Beliefs and perceptions about disability

Beliefs regarding the 'good life'

Cultural norms relating to family care

Influences of family members on healthcare

Family decision-making in healthcare

Institutional racism

Social status of parents

Lack of inter-disciplinary consensus

Expectations of self-care regarding health

Cross-cultural communication

Multilingual individuals and families

Communication in an additional language

English language proficiency

Stereotyping additional language English speakers

Stereotypes related to dialects and accents

Families misleading over children's language competencies

Direct communication with children

Communication using professional interpreters

Communication without an interpreter

Use of family members as interpreters

Language proficiency and who is heard

Literacy in heritage languages and English

Use of switching dialects or languages

Reliance on non-verbal communication

Professional risk assessment

Risk assessment biases

Timescales in risk assessment

Flight responses to anxiety

Cultural relativism

Confusion over child protection thresholds

Influence of stereotypes or prejudice

Cognitive decision-making processes

Fixed notions of family form

Professional culture and norms

Organisational culture and norms

Fear of being perceived as racist

Complaints of racism or cultural insensitivity

Social worker positionality

References

Abela, A. & Walker, J. (2013) *Contemporary Issues in Family Studies: Global Perspectives on Partnerships, Parenting and Support in a Changing World,* Hoboken, NJ: John Wiley.

Ager, A. (1999) *Refugees: Perspectives on the Experiences of Forced Migration,* London: Pinter.

Ahmad, F., Riaz, S., Barata, P. & Stewart, D. (2004) 'Patriarchal beliefs and perceptions of abuse among South Asian immigrant women', *Violence against Women,* 10, 262–82.

Ahmed, A.A. (2000) 'Health and disease: An Islamic framework' in A. Sheikh & A.R. Gatrad (eds) *Caring for Muslim Patients,* Abingdon: Radcliffe Medical Press, 29–41.

Ahmed, S. (2012) *On Being Included: Racism and Diversity in Institutional Life,* Durham, NC: Duke University Press.

Ainsworth, M.D.S. (1978) *Patterns of Attachment: A Psychological Study of the Strange Situation* Mahwah, NJ: Lawrence Erlbaum Associates.

Akilapa, R. & Simkiss, D. (2012) 'Cultural influences and safeguarding children', *Paediatrics and Child Health,* 22(11), 490–5.

Alcohol Concern (2014) *Alcohol and Football,* London: Alcohol Concern.

Ali, Z., Fazil, Q., Bywaters, P., Wallace, L. & Singh, G. (2001) 'Disability, ethnicity and childhood: A critical review of research', *Disability and Society,* 16(7), 949–68.

Allen, C. (2015) '"People hate you because of the way you dress": Understanding the invisible experiences of veiled British Muslim women victims of Islamophobia', *International Review of Victimology,* 21(3), 287–301.

Anderson, B., Ruhs, M., Rogaly, B. & Spencer, S. (2006) *Fair Enough? Central and East European Migrants in Low-Wage Employment in the UK,* York: Joseph Rowntree Foundation.

Andrews, M.M. & Boyle, J.S. (1999) *Transcultural Concepts in Nursing Care,* Philadelphia, PA: Lippincott.

An-Na'im, A.A. (2009) 'Towards a cross-cultural approach to defining international standards of human rights: The meaning of cruel, inhuman, or degrading treatment or punishment' in M. Goodale (ed.) *Human Rights: An Anthropological Reader,* Chichester: Blackwell,. 68-85.

Archard, D. (2015) *Children: Rights and Childhood,* London & New York: Routledge.

Arnett, J.J. (1999) 'Adolescent storm and stress, reconsidered', *American Psychologist,* 54(5), 317–26.

Australian Institute of Family Studies (2015) *What is Child Abuse and Neglect?* https://aifs.gov.au/cfca/publications/what-child-abuse-and-neglect, date accessed 26 April 2018.

Bains, K. (2001) 'Psychotherapy with young people from ethnic minority backgrounds in different community based settings' in G. Baruch (ed.) *Community Based Psychotherapy with Young People: Evidence and Innovation in Practice,* London: Routledge, 63–72.

Barn, R., Sinclair, R. & Ferdinand, D. (1997) *Acting on Principle: An Examination of Race and Ethnicity in Social Services Provision for Children and Families,* London: British Agencies for Adoption and Fostering.

Barth, F. (1969) 'Introduction' in F. Barth (ed.) *Ethnic Groups and Boundaries: The Social Organisation of Cultural Difference,* Oslo: Universitiesforlaget, 9–38.

BASW (2014) *The Code of Ethics for Social Work,* Birmingham: The British Association of Social Workers.

Baumrind, D. (1971) *Current Patterns of Parental Authority,* Washington, DC: American Psychological Association.

Bayrakli, E. & Hafez, F. (2016) (eds) *European Islamophobia Report 2015* www.islamophobiaeurope.com/reports/2015/en/EIR_2015.pdf date accessed 18 June 2018.

Beider, H. (2011) *Community Cohesion: The Views of White Working Class Communities,* York: Joseph Rowntree Foundation.

Bent-Goodley, T.B., Chase, L., Circo, E.A. & Rodgers, S.T.A. (2010) 'Our survival, our strengths: Understanding the experiences of African American women in abusive relationships' in L.L. Lockhart & F.S. Danis (eds) *Domestic Violence: Intersectionality and Culturally Competent Practice,* New York: Columbia University Press, 67–99.

Beresford, P., Croft, S. & Adshead, L. (2008) '"We don't see her as a social worker": A service user case study of the importance of the social worker's relationship and humanity', *British Journal of Social Work,* 38, 1388–407.

Bernard, C., Fairtlough, A., Fletcher, J. & Ahmet, A. (2011) Diversity and Progression among Social Work Students in England, research.gold.ac.uk/6326 date accessed 26 May 2018.Bernard, C., Fairtlough, A.Fletcher, J. & Ahmet, A. (2013) 'A qualitative study of marginalised social work students' views of social work education and learning', *British Journal of Social Work,* 44(7), 1934–49.

Bernard, C. & Harris, P. (2016) *Safeguarding Black Children: Good Practice in Child Protection* London: Jessica Kinglsley.

Berry, J.W. (1990) 'Psychology of acculturation' in R.A. Dienstbier (ed.) *Nebraska Symposium on Motivation 1989,* Lincoln: University of Nebraska Press, 201–34.

Bhui, K., Lawrence, A., Klineberg, E., Woodley-Jones, D., Taylor, S., Stansfeld, S., Viner, R. & Booy, R. (2005) 'Acculturation and health status among African-Caribbean, Bangladeshi and white British adolescents', *Social Psychiatry and Psychiatric Epidemiology,* 40, 259–66.

Bilson, A., Cant, R.L., Harries, M. & Thorpe, D.H. (2015) 'A longitudinal study of children reported to the child protection department in Western Australia', *British Journal of Social Work,* 45, 771–91.

Birchall, E. & Hallett, C. (1995) *Working Together in Child Protection,* London: HMSO.

Blanchet-Garneau, A. & Pepin, J. (2014) 'Cultural competence: A constructivist definition', *Journal of Transcultural Nursing,* 26(1), 9–15.

Blinder, S. (2014) *Migration to the UK: Asylum,* Oxford: Migration Observatory University of Oxford.

Blinder, S. (2017) *Immigration by Category: Workers, Students, Family Members and Asylum Applicants,* Oxford: Migration Observatory: University of Oxford.

Bloch, A., Neal, S. & Solomos, J. (2013) *Race, Multiculture and Social Policy,* Basingstoke: Palgrave Macmillan.

Blos, P. (1962) *On Adolescence,* New York: Free Press.

Boamah, M. (2014) 'Stop force-feeding babies – doctors admonish' *Ghanaweb* 06.05.14 www.ghanaweb.com/GhanaHomePage/health/Stop-force-feeding-babies-Doctors-admonish-308396 date accessed 22 December 2017.

Bourdieu, P. & Wacquant, L. (1998) 'Sur les ruses de la raison impérialiste' *Actes de la Recherche en Sciences Sociales,* 121–122, 109–18 (cited in Garner, 2007 6).

Bowlby, J. (1951) *Maternal Care and Mental Health,* Geneva: World Health Organization.

Bowlby, J. (1953) *Child Care and the Growth of Love,* New Orleans, LA: Pelican.

Boyd, R. (2014) 'African American disproportionality and disparity in child welfare: Towards a comprehensive conceptual framework', *Children and Youth Services Review*, 37, 15–27.

Brah, A. (1993) '"Race" and "culture" in the gendering of labour markets: South Asian young Muslim women and the labour market', *Journal of Ethnic and Migration Studies*, 19(3), 441–58.

Brandon, J. & Hafez, S. (2008) *Crimes of the Community: Honour-Based Violence in the UK*, Trowbridge: The Cromwell Press.

Brandon, M., Bailey, S., Belderson, P., Gardner, R., Sidebotham, P., Dodsworth, J., Warren, C. & Black, J. (2009) *Understanding Serious Case Reviews and their Impact: A Biennial Analysis of Serious Case Reviews 2005–07*, London: Department for Children, Schools and Families.

Brandon, M., Sidebotham, P., Bailey, S. & Belderson, P. (2011) *A Study of Recommendations Arising from Serious Case Reviews 2009–2010*, London: Department for Education.

Broadhurst, K., Wastell, D., White, S., Hall, C., Peckover, S., Thompson, K., Pithouse, A. & Davey, D. (2010) 'Performing "initial assessment": Identifying the latent conditions for error at the front-door of local authority children's services', *British Journal of Social Work*, 40(2), 352–70.

Bronfenbrenner, U. (1979) *The Ecology of Human Development: Experiments by Nature and Design*, Cambridge, MA: Harvard University Press.

Brown, J., Newland, A., Anderson, P. & Chevannes, B. (1997) 'Caribbean fatherhood: Under-researched, misunderstood' in J.L. Roopnarine & J. Brown (eds) *Caribbean Families: Diversity among Ethnic Groups*, Greenwich, CT: Ablex Publishing, 85–114.

Burman, E., Smailes, S.L. & Chantler, K. (2004) '"Culture" as a barrier to service provision and delivery: Domestic violence services for minoritized women', *Critical Social Policy*, 24(3), 332–57.

Burnham, J. (2012) 'Developments in social GRRRAAACCEEESSS: Visible – invisible and voiced – unvoiced' in I.-B. Krause (ed.) *Culture and Reflexivity in Systemic Psychotherapy: Mutual Perspectives*, London: Karnac, 139–60.

Butt, J. & Mirza, K. (1996) *Social Care and Black Communities*, London: HMSO.

Bywaters, P., Ali, Z., Fazil, Q., Wallace, L.M. & Singh, G. (2003) 'Attitudes towards disability amongst Pakistani and Bangladeshi parents of disabled children in the UK: Considerations for service providers and the disability movement', *Health and Social Care in the Community*, 11(6), 502–509.

Bywaters, P., Bunting, L., Davidson, G., Hanratty, J., Mason, W., McCartan, C. & Steils, N. (2016) *The Relationship Between Poverty, Child Abuse and Neglect: An Evidence Review*, York: Joseph Rowntree Foundation.

Calder, M.C. & Archer, J. (2016) *Risk in Child Protection: Assessment Challenges and Frameworks for Practice*, London: Jessica Kingsley.

Campbell, C., Cornish, F. & Mclean, C. (2004) '*Social capital*, participation and the perpetuation of health inequalities: Obstacles to African-Caribbean participation in "partnerships" to improve mental health', *Ethnicity and Health*, 9(4), 313–35.

Campinha-Bacote, J. (2002) 'The process of cultural competence in the delivery of healthcare services: A model of care', *Journal of Transcultural Nursing*, 13(3), 181–84.

Cantle, T. (2008) *Community Cohesion: A New Framework for Race and Diversity*, Basingstoke: PalgraveMacmillan.

Carbaugh, D. & Berry, M. (2001) 'Communicating history, finnish and American discourses: An ethnographic contribution to intercultural communication inquiry', *Communication Theory*, 11, 352–66.

Carson, D. & Bain, A. (2008) *Professional Risk and Working with People: Decision Making in Health, Social Care and the Criminal Justice System*, London: Jessica Kingsley.

Carson, D. & Bain, A. (2012) *Professional Risk and Working with People: Decision-Making in Health, Social Care and Criminal Justice,* London: Jessica Kingsley.

Cawson, P., Wattam, C., Brooker, S. & Kelly, G. (2000) *Child Maltreatment in the United Kingdom: A Study of the Prevalence of Child Abuse and Neglect,* London: National Society for the Prevention of Cruelty to Children.

The Centre for Social Justice (2009) *Breakthrough Britain Dying to Belong: An In-Depth Review of Street Gangs in Britain,* London: The Centre for Social Justice.

Chand, A. (2000) 'The over-representation of black children in the child protection system: Possible causes, consequences and solutions', *Child and Family Social Work,* 5, 67–77.

Chao, R.K. (1994) 'Beyond parental control and authoritarian parenting style: Understanding Chinese parenting through the cultural notion of training', *Child Development,* 65, 1111–19.

Charlsey, K.A.H. & Liversage, A. (2012) 'Transforming polygamy: Migration, transnationalism and multiple marriages among Muslim minorities', *Global Networks,* 13(1), 60–78.

Charsley, K., Bolognani, M., Spencer, S., Ersanilli, E. & Jayaweera, H. (2016) *Marriage Migration and Integration Report,* Bristol: University of Bristol.

Child Poverty Action Group (2017) *The Impact of Poverty* http://cpag.org.uk/content/impact-poverty, date accessed 7 August 2017.

Children's Bureau (2004) *Risk and Protective Factors for Child Abuse and Neglect* www.childwelfare.gov/pubpdfs/riskprotectivefactors.pdf, date accessed 9 March 2018.

Children's Bureau (2016) *Racial Disproportionality and Disparity in Child Welfare* www.childwelfare.gov/pubPDFs/racial_disproportionality.pdf,date accessed 12 March 2018.

The Children's Society (2013) *A Good Childhood for Every Child? Child Poverty in the UK* www.childrenssociety.org.uk/sites/default/files/tcs/2013_child_poverty_briefing_1.pdf, date accessed 7 August 2017.

Chimba, M., Davey, D., de Villiers, T. & Khan, A. (2012) *Protecting Black and Minority Ethnic Children: An Investigation of Child Protection Interventions,* Cardiff: BAWSO.

Chinese Culture Connection (1987) 'Chinese values and the search for culture-free dimensions of culture', *Journal of Cross-Cultural Psychology,* 18, 143–64.

Choudry, S. (1996) *Pakistani Women's Experience of Domestic Violence in Great Britain Research Findings No. 43,* London: Home Office Research and Statistics Directorate.

Chowbey, P., Salway, S. & Clarke, L. (2013) 'Supporting fathers in multi-ethnic societies: Insights from British Asian fathers', *Journal of Social Policy,* 42(2), 391–408.

Cinnirella, M. & Loewenthal, K.M. (1999) 'Religious and ethnic group influences on beliefs about mental illness: A qualitative interview study', *British Journal of Medical Psychology,* 72, 505–24.

Coffin, J. (2007) 'Rising to the challenge in aboriginal health by creating cultural security', *Aboriginal and Islander Health Worker Journal,* 31(3), 22–24.

Congress, E. (1994) 'The use of culturagrams to assess and empower diverse families', *Families in Society,* 75(9), 1–9.

Conley, C. (2003) 'A review of parenting capacity assessment reports', *Ontario Association of Children's Aid Societies (OACAS) Journal,* 47(3), 16–22.

The Conversation (2017) *European Map of Implicit Racial Bias* https://theconversation.com/this-map-shows-what-white-europeans-associate-with-race-and-it-makes-for-uncomfortable-reading-76661, date accessed 7 May 2018.

Cook, K. (2016) 'Female genital mutilation in the UK population: A serious crime', *The Journal of Criminal Law,* 80(2), 88–96.

Coupland, N., Coupland, J., Giles, H. & Henwood, K. (1988) 'Accommodating the elderly: Invoking and extending a theory', *Language in Society,* 17, 1–41.

Crabtree, S.A., Husain, F. & Spalek, B. (2008) *Islam and Social Work: Debating Values, Transforming Practice*, Bristol: Policy Press.

Crittenden, C.A. & Wright, E.M. (2012) 'Predicting patriarchy: Using individual and contextual factors to examine patriarchal endorsement in communities', *Journal of Interpersonal Violence*, 28(6), 1267–88.

Crompton, R. (2008) *Class and Stratification*, Cambridge: Polity Press.

Cummins, I. (2018) *Poverty, Inequality and Social Work*, Bristol: Policy Press.

Dakil, S.R., Cox, M., Lin, H. & Flores, G. (2011) 'Racial and ethnic disparities in physical abuse reporting and child protective services interventions in the United States', *Journal of the National Medical Association*, 103(10), 1–6.

Dale, A., Fieldhouse, E., Shaheen, N. & Kalra, V. (2002) 'The labour market prospects of Pakistani and Bangladeshi women', *Work, Employment and Society*, 16(1), 5–25.

Daniel, B., Wassell, S. & Gilligan, R. (2010) *Child Development for Child Care and Protection Workers*, London: Jessica Kingsley.

Danis, F.S. & Bhandari, S. (2010) 'Understanding domestic violence: A primer' in L.L. Lockhart & F.S. Danis (eds) *Domestic Violence: Intersectionality and Culturally Competent Practice*, New York: Columbia University Press 29–66.

De Keseredy, W. & Schwartz, M. (2013) *Male Peer Support and Violence Against Women: The History and Verification of a Theory*, Boston: North-Eastern University Press.

Dengate, S. & Ruben, A. (2002) 'Controlled trial of cumulative behavioural effects of a common bread preservative', *Journal of Paediatrics and Child Health*, 38, 373–6.

Department for Communities and Local Government (2017) *Statutory Homelessness and Prevention and Relief, October to December 2016: England* www.gov.uk/government/uploads/system/uploads/attachment_data/file/602387/Statutory_Homelessness_and_Prevention_and_Relief_Statistical_Release_October_to_December_2016.pdf, date accessed 3 May 2017.

Department for Education (2014a) *Children Looked After in England (Including Adoption and Care Leavers) Year Ending 31 March 2014*, London: Department for Education.

Department for Education (2014b) *Promoting Fundamental British Values as Part of SMSC in Schools: Departmental Advice for Maintained Schools* www.gov.uk/government/uploads/system/uploads/attachment_data/file/380595/SMSC_Guidance_Maintained_Schools.pdf, date accessed 9 January 2017.

Department for Education (2017) *A Guide to Exclusion Statistics*, London: HMSO.

Department of Health (2000) *Framework for the Assessment of Children in Need and Their Families*, London: Department of Health.

Derrington, C. & Kendall, S. (2004) *Gypsy Traveller Students in Secondary Schools: Culture Identity, Achievement*, Stoke on Trent: Trentham Books.

Dominelli, L. (1997) *Anti-Racist Social Work: A Challenge for White Practitioners and Educators* Basingstoke: Macmillan.

Donnelly, J. (2002) *Universal Human Rights in Theory and Practice*, Ithaca & London: Cornell University Press.

Dubowitz, H., Newton, R.R., Litrownick, A.J., Lewis, T., Briggs, E.C., Thompson, R., English, D., Lee, L.-C. & Feerick, M. (2005) 'Examination of a conceptual model of child neglect', *Child Maltreatment* 10 173 http://cmx.sagepub/content/10/2/173 date accessed 20 February 2018.

Duffy, M.E. (2001) 'A critique of cultural education in nursing', *Journal of Advanced Nursing*, 36(4), 487–95.

Dwyer, P. & Brown, D. (2005) 'Meeting basic needs? Forced migrants and welfare', *Social Policy and Society*, 4(4), 369–80.

The Economist (2017) 'Why China's traditional medicine boom is dangerous', *The Economist* 01. 09.17 www.economist.com/china/2017/09/01/why-chinas-traditional-medicine-boom-is-dangerous, date accessed 18 May 2018.

Edmonds-Cady, C. & Wingfield, T.T. (2017) 'Social workers: Agents of change or agents of oppression?' *Social Work Education*, 36(4), 430–42.

Edwards, R., Temple, B. & Alexander, C. (2005) '"Users" experiences of interpreters, the critical role of trust', *Interpreting*, 7(1), 77–95.

Enosh, G. & Bayer-Topilsky, T. (2015) 'Reasoning and bias: Heuristics in safety assessment and placement decisions for children at risk', *British Journal of Social Work*, 45, 1771–87.

Entwistle, J. (2000) *The Fashioned Body: Fashion, Dress and Modern Social Theory*, Cambridge: Polity Press.

Equality and Human Rights Commission (2016) *Healing a Divided Britain: The Need for a Comprehensive Race Equality Strategy*, London: Equality and Human Rights Commission.

Erikson, E.H. (1963) *Childhood and Society*, New York: Norton.

Erikson, E.H. (1968) *Identity, Youth and Crisis*, New York: Norton.

ERTF & Phenjalipe (2013) *Making Early Marriage in Roma Communities a Global Concern* https://cs.coe.int/team20/cahrom/7th%20cahrom%20plenary%20meeting/item%2004%20-%20ertf%20and%20phenjalipe%20joint%20paper%20making%20early%20marriage%20in%20roma%20communities%20a%20global%20concern.pdf, date accessed 7 June 2018.

Faith Matters (2018) *Gendered Anti-Muslim Hatred and Islamophobia: Interim Report 2018* https://tellmamauk.org/gendered-anti-muslim-hatred-and-islamophobia-street-based-aggression-in-cases-reported-to-tell-mama-is-alarming/ accessed 08.12.18.

Faulker, A. (2014) *Ethnic Inequalities in Mental Health: Promoting Lasting Positive Change: A Consultation with Black and Minority Ethnic Mental Health Users* London: National Survivor User Network

Featherstone, B. (2013) Working with fathers: Risk or resource? in J.R. McCarthy, C. Hooper & V. Gillies (eds) *Family Troubles?: Exploring Changes and Challenges in the Family Lives of Children and Young, People*, Bristol: Policy Press, 315–25.

Featherstone, B., White, S. & Morris, K. (2014) *Re-Imagining Child Protection: Towards Humane Social Work with Families*, Bristol: Policy Press.

Finch, J. & Mason, J. (2000) *Passing On: Kinship and Inheritance in England*, London: Routledge.

Finney, N., Kapadia, D. & Peters, S. (2015) *How are Poverty, Ethnicity and Social Networks Related?* York: Joseph Rowntree Foundation.

Fisher, P. & Nandi, A. (2015) *Poverty Across Ethnic Groups Through Recession and Austerity* www.jrf.org.uk/report/poverty-across-ethnic-groups-through-recession-and-austerity, date accessed 10 January 2018.

Fitzpatrick, S., Bramley, G., Sosenko, F., Blenkinsopp, J., Johnsen, S., Littlewood, M., Netto, G. & Watts, B. (2016) *Destitution in the UK*, York: Joseph Rowntree Foundation.

Fluke, J., Harden, B.J., Jenkins, M. & Ruehrdanz, A. (2011) *A Research Synthesis on Child Welfare Disproportionality and Disparities*, www.cssp.org/publications/child-welfare/alliance/Disparities-and-Disproportionality-in-Child-Welfare_An-Analysis-of-the-Research-December-2011.pdf date accessed 12 March 2018.

Fluke, J.D., Goldman, P.S., Shriberg, J., Hillis, S.D., Yun, K., Allison, S. & Light, E. (2012) 'Systems, strategies and interventions for sustainable long-term care and protection of children with a history of living outside of family care', *Child Abuse and Neglect*, 36, 722–31.

Fook, J. (2012) *Social Work: A Critical Approach to Practice*, London: Sage.

Fortune, M.M., Abugideiri, S.E. & Dratch, M. (2010) 'A commentary on religion and domestic violence' in L.L. Lockhart & F.S. Danis (eds) *Domestic Violence: Intersectionality and Culturally Competent Practice*, New York: Columbia University Press, 318–42.

Foster, B. & Norton, P. (2012) 'Educational equality for Gypsy, Roma and travel-
    ler children and young people in the UK', *The Equal Rights Review*, 8, 85–113
    www.equalrightstrust.org/ertdocumentbank/ERR8_Brian_Foster_and_Peter_Norton.
    pdf date accessed 14 May 2018.
Foundation, J.R. (2013) *Home Affairs Committee Inquiry into Asylum: Evidence from the
    Joseph Rowntree Foundation and the Housing and Migration Network*, York: Joseph
    Rowntree Foundation.
Fox, J.E., Moroşanu, L. & Szilassy, E. (2015) 'Denying discrimination: Status, 'race' and
    the whitening of Britain's new Europeans', *Journal of Ethnic and Migration Studies*,
    41(5), 729–48.
Frankenburg, R. (1993) *White Women, Race Matters: The Social Construction of Whiteness*,
    Minneapolis, MN: University of Minnesota Press.
Freud, A. (1969) 'Adolescence as a developmental disturbance' in G. Caplan & S.
    Lebovici (eds) *Adolescence: Psychological Perspectives*, New York: Basic Books, 5–10.
Frost, L. (2001) *Young Women and the Body: A Feminist Sociology*, Basingstoke: Palgrave.
Furbey, R., Dinham, A., Farnell, R., Finneron, D., Wilkinson, G., Howarth, C., Hussain,
    D. & Palmer, S. (2006) *Findings Informing Change: Faith as Social Capital*, York: Joseph
    Rowntree Foundation.
Furness, S. (2005) 'Shifting sands: Developing cultural competence', *Practice*, 17(4),
    247–56.
Furness, S. & Gilligan, P. (2010) *Religion, Belief and Social Work: Making a Difference*,
    Bristol: Policy Press.
Gair, S., Miles, D., Savage, D. & Zuchowski, I. (2014) 'Racism unmasked: The experi-
    ences of Aboriginal and Torres Strait islander students in social work field place-
    ments', *Australian Social Work*, 68(1), 32–48.
Galanti, G. (2008) *Caring for Patients from Different Cultures*, Philadelphia, PA: University
    of Pennsylvania Press.
Gangoli, G., McCarry, M. & Razak, A. (2009) 'Child marriage or forced marriage? South
    Asian communities in North East England', *Children and Society*, 23, 418–29.
Gatrad, A.R. & Sheikh, A. (2000) 'Birth customs: Meaning and significance' in A. Sheikh
    & A.R. Gatrad (eds) *Caring for Muslim Patients*, Abingdon: Radcliffe Medical Press.
Garner, S. (2007) *Whiteness: An Introduction* London: Routledge.
Gervais, M. & Jovchelovitch, S. (1998) *The Health Beliefs of the Chinese Community in
    England: A Qualitative Research Study*, London: Health Education Authority.
Ghelani, T. (2001) *Performing 'Blackness': The Appropriation of Commodified African-
    American Culture by South Asian Youth in Britain Unpublished M.Phil.*, Birmingham:
    University of Birmingham http://etheses.bham.ac.uk/3605/1/Ghelani02MPhil.pdf
    date accessed 13 October 2017.
Gibbons, J., Convoy, S. & Bell, C. (1995) *Operating the Child Protection System*, London:
    HMSO.
Gilchrist, L., Ireland, L., Forsyth, A., Laxton, T. & Godwin, J. (2014) *Roles of Alcohol in
    Intimate Partner Abuse*, London: Alcohol Research UK.
Gill, A. (2004) 'Voicing the silent fear: South Asian women's experiences of domestic
    violence', *The Howard Journal*, 43(5), 465–83.
Gilligan, P. & Akhtar, S. (2006) 'Cultural barriers to the disclosure of child sexual abuse
    in Asian communities: Listening to what women say', *British Journal of Social Work*,
    36, 1361–77.
Gilroy, P. (1987) *There Ain't No Black in the Union Jack: The Cultural Politics of Race and
    Nation*, London: Hutchinson.
Gleeson, K. & Frith, H. (2004) 'Pretty in pink: Young women presenting mature sexual
    identities in A. Harris (ed.) *All About the Girl: Culture Power and Identity*, London:
    Routledge, 103–14.

Goldstein, B.P. (1999) 'Black, with a white parent, a positive and achievable identity', *British Journal of Social Work*, 29(2), 285–301.

Goldstein, B.P. (2002) '"Catch 22" – Black workers' role in equal opportunities for black service users', *British Journal of Social Work*, 29(2), 285–301.

Government, H.M. (2018) *Working Together to Safeguard Children: A Guide to Inter-Agency Working to Safeguard and Promote the Welfare of Children.* https://assets.publishing.service.gov.uk/government/uploads/system/uploads/attachment_data/file/729914/Working_Together_to_Safeguard_Children-2018.pdf, date accessed 7 August 2018.

Graham, M. (1999) 'The African-centred worldview: Developing a paradigm for social work', *British Journal of Social Work*, 29(2), 252–67.

Graham, M. (2002) *Social Work and African-Centred Worldviews*, Birmingham: Venture.

Graham, M. & Robinson, G. (2004) '"The silent Catastrophe" institutional racism in the British educational system and the underachievement of Black boys', *Journal of Black Studies*, 34(5), 653–71.

Graham, J. R., Bradshaw, C., & Trew,J. L. (2009) 'Adapting social work in working with Muslim clients *Social Work Education*, 28(5) 544-561.

Grant, C. (2009) *Altruism and Christian Ethics*, Cambridge: Cambridge University Press.

Greenberg, J. Pyszcynski, T. Solomon, S. Rosenblatt, A., Veeder, M., Kirkland, S. & Lyon, D. (1990) 'Evidence for terror management theory: II. The effects of mortality salience on reactions to those who threaten or bolster the cultural worldview' *Journal of Personality and Social Psychology* 58 308-318.

Greenfields, M., Schaub, J. & Wager, N. (2010) *BME Children Subject to a Child Protection Plan or Who are Looked After (2006-2010): An Evaluation on Behalf of Buckinghamshire County Council*, High Wycombe: Buckingham New University.

Griffin, C. (2004) 'Good girls, bad girls: Anglocentrism and diversity in the constitution of contemporary girlhood' in A. Harris (ed.) *All About the Girl: Culture Power and Identity*, London: Routledge, 29–44.

The Guardian Online (2011) 'Nurse jailed for killing her baby by force-feeding' www.theguardian.com/uk/2011/nov/11/nurse-jailed-baby-force-feeding, date accessed 7 August 2018.

Gudykunst, W.B. (2005) 'An anxiety/uncertainty management (AMU) theory of effective communication: Making the mesh of the net finer' in W.B. Gudykunst (ed.) *Theorizing About Intercultural Communication*, Thousand Oaks, CA: Sage, 281–322.

Hall, E.T. (1989) *Beyond Culture*, New York: Anchor Books.

Hall, G.S. (1904) *Adolescence: Its Psychology and its Relations to Physiology, Anthropology, Sociology, Sex, Crime and Religion*, Massachusetts: D. Appleton and Company.

Halme, N., Åstedt-Kurki, P. & Tarkka, M. (2009) 'Fathers' involvement in their pre-school-age children: How fathers spend time with their children in different family structures', *Child Youth Care Forum*, 38, 103–19.

Harman, V. (2010) 'Social work practice and Lone White Mothers of mixed-parentage children', *British Journal of Social Work*, 40, 391–406.

Harris, P. & Rees, R. (2000) 'The prevalence of complementary and alternative medicine use among the general population: A systematic review of the literature', *Complementary Therapies in Medicine*, 8, 88–96.

Harrison, G. & Turner, R. (2011) 'Being a "culturally competent" social worker: Making sense of a murky concept in practice', *British Journal of Social Work*, 41(2), 333–50.

Hasan, R. (2010) *Multiculturalism: Some Inconvenient Truths*, London: Politico's.

Hasegawa, T. & Gudykunst, W.B. (1998) 'Silence in Japan and the United States', *Journal of Cross-Cultural Psychology*, 29, 668–84.

Hawkins, O. (2015) *Migration Statistics: Briefing Paper Number SN06077*, London: House of Commons Library.

Hayden, C. (2004) 'Parental substance misuse and child care social work: Research in a city social work department in England', *Child Abuse Review*,13(1), 18–30.

Health Resources and Services Administration (2007) *Study on Measuring Cultural Competence in Health Care Delivery Settings* www.hrsa.gov/culturalcompetence/measures/ sectioniii.htm, date accessed 7 May 2007.

Heckman, J.J. (2013) *Giving Kids a Fair Chance: A Strategy that Works,* Cambridge, MA: The MIT Press.

Helms, J.E. (1990) *Black and White Racial Identity: Theory, Research and Practice,* New York: Greenwood Press.

Hendrick, H. (1997) *Children, Childhood and English Society 1880–1900,* Cambridge: Cambridge University Press.

Henley, A. & Schott, J. (1999) *Culture, Religion and Patient Care in a Multi-Ethnic Society: A Handbook for Professionals,* London: Age Concern.

Hickman, M., Crowley, H. & Mai, N. (2008) *Immigration and Social Cohesion in the UK: The Rhythms and Realities of Everyday Life,* York: Joseph Rowntree Foundation.

Higazi, A. (2005) *Ghana Country Study: A Part of the Report on Informal Remittance Systems in Africa, Caribbean and Pacific (ACP) (Ref: RO2CS008),* Oxford: Centre on Migration, Policy and Society, University of Oxford.

Hofstede, G. (2011) 'Dimensionalizing cultures: The Hofstede model in context', *Online Readings in Psychology and Culture,* 2(1) http://scholarworks.gvsu.edu/cgi/ viewcontent.cgi?article=1014&context=orpc date accessed 7 August 2017.

Holland, K. & Hogg, C. (2001) *Cultural Awareness in Nursing and Healthcare,* London: Arnold.

Holloway, M. & Moss, B. (2010) *Spirituality and Social Work,* Basingstoke: PalgraveMacmillan.

Home Office (2017) *Individuals Referred to and Supported Through the Prevent Programme, April 2015 to March 2016* www.gov.uk/government/uploads/system/uploads/ attachment_data/file/662824/individuals-referred-supported-prevent-programme-apr2015-mar2016.pdf accessed 10.01.18.

Horwath, J. (2007) *Child Neglect: Identification and Assessment* Basingstoke, Hampshire: Palgrave Macmillan.

Horwath, J. (2010) 'Assessing children in need: Background and context' in J. Horwath (ed.) *The Child's World: The Comprehensive Guide to Assessing Children in Need,* London: Jessica Kingsley, 18–33.

Horwath, J., Lees, J., Sidebotham, P., Higgins, J. & Imtiaz, A. (2008) *Religion, Beliefs and Parenting Practices,* York: Joseph Rowntree Foundation.

Hua, Z. (2014) *Exploring Intercultural Communication Language in Action,* London: Routledge.

Hurcombe, R., Bayley, M. & Goodman, A. (2010) *Ethnicity and Alcohol: A Review of the UK Literature,* York: Joseph Rowntree Foundation.

Hussein, S., Stevens, M. & Manthorpe, J. (2011) 'What drives the recruitment of migrant workers to work in social care in England', *Social Policy & Society,* 10(3), 285–98.

Hussein, S. & Manthorpe, J. (2014) 'Structural marginalisation among the long-term care workforce in England: Evidence from mixed-effect models of national pay data', *Ageing and Society,* 34 (1), 21–41.

Institute of Alcohol Studies (IAS) (2013) *UK Alcohol Related Crime Statistics* accessed online at www.ias.org.uk/Alcohol-knowledge-centre/Crime-and-socialimpacts/Factsheets/UK-alcohol-related-crime-statistics.aspx!, date accessed 14 October 2014.

Ismail, H., Wright, J., Rhodes, P., Small, N. & Jacoby, A. (2005) 'South Asians and epilepsy: Exploring health experiences, needs and beliefs of communities in the north of England', *Seizure,* 14, 497–503.

Jacobson, J. (1997) 'Religion and ethnicity: Dual and alternative sources of identity among young British Pakistanis', *Ethnic and Racial Studies,* 20(2), 238–56.

James, A.L., Jenks, C. & Prout, A. (2007) *Theorizing Childhood,* Cambridge: Polity Press.

James, N. (2009) *Politics of Alcohol: A History of the Drink Question,* Manchester: Manchester University Press.

Jay, A. (2014) *Independent Inquiry into Child Sexual Exploitation in Rotherham 1997–2013* www.rotherham.gov.uk/downloads/file/1407/independent_inquiry_cse_in_rotherham, date accessed 6 August 2017.

Jayaweera, H. & Choudhury, T. (2008) *Immigration, Faith and Cohesion: Evidence from Local Areas with Significant Muslim Populations,* York: Joseph Rowntree Foundation.

Jenkins, R. (1997) *Rethinking Ethnicity: Arguments and Explanations,* London: Sage.

Jenks, C. (1996) *Childhood,* London and New York: Routledge.

Jobanputra, R. & Furnham, A. (2005) 'British Gujarati Indian immigrants' and British Caucasians' beliefs about health and illness' *International Journal of Social Psychiatry* 51(4) 350-64.

Johnstone, M. & Kanitsaki, O. (2007) 'An exploration of the notion and nature of the construct of cultural safety and its applicability to the Australian healthcare context', *Journal of Transcultural Nursing,* 18(3), 247–56.

Kai, J. & Hedges, C. (1999) 'Minority ethnic community participation in needs assessment and service development in primary care: Perceptions of Pakistani and Bangladeshi people about psychological distress', *Health Expectations,* 2, 7–20.

Katbamna, S., Ahmad, W., Bhakta, P., Baker, R. & Parker, G. (2004) 'Do they look after their own? Informal support for South Asian carers', *Health and Social Care in the Community,* 12(5), 398–406.

Keating, F. & Robertson, D. (2004) 'Fear, black people and mental illness: A vicious circle?' *Health and Social Care in the Community,* 12(5), 439–47.

Kellett, J. & Apps, J. (2009) *Assessments of Parenting and Parenting Support Need: A Study of Four Professional Groups,* York: Joseph Rowntree Foundation.

Kemshall, H., Wilkinson, B. & Baker, K. (2013) *Working with Risk,* Cambridge: Polity.

Kim, M. (2002) *Innovative Strategies to Address Domestic Violence in Asian and Pacific Islander Communities: Examining Themes, Models and Interventions,* San Francisco: Asian and Pacific Islander Institute on Domestic Violence.

Koenig, H., McCullough, M. & Larson, D. (2001) *Handbook of Religion and Health,* Oxford: Oxford University Press.

Laird, S.E. (2008) *Anti-Oppressive Social Work: A Guide for Developing Cultural Competence,* London: Sage.

Laird, S.E. (2013) *Child Protection: Managing Conflict, Hostility and Aggression,* Bristol: Policy.

Laird, S.E. (2014) 'The law, professional ethics and anti-oppressive social work' in C. Cocker & T. Hafford-Letchfield (eds) *Re-Thinking Anti-Discriminatory and Anti-Oppressive Theories for Social Work Practice,* Basingstoke: PalgraveMacmillan, 45–59.

Laird, S.E. (2015) 'If parents are punished for asking their children to feed goat's': Supervisory neglect in sub-Saharan Africa', *Journal of Social Work,* 16(3), 303–21.

Laird, S.E., Morris, K., Archard, P. & Clawson, R. (2017) 'Working with the whole family: What case files tell us about social work practices', *Child and Family Social Work,* 22(3), 1322–29.

Lambert, R. & Githens-Mazer, J. (2010) *Islamophobia and Anti-Muslim Hate Crime* http://library.college.police.uk/docs/Islamophobia-Lambert-2010.pdf, date accessed 16 January 2018.

Laming, W.H. (2003) *The Victoria Climbié Inquiry: Report of an Inquiry by Lord Laming,* Cmnd. 5730, London: HMSO.

Lattanzi, J.B. & Purnell, L.D. (2006) (eds) *Developing Cultural Competence in Physical Therapy Practice,* Philadelphia: F.A. Davis Company.

Le Bas, D. (2014) 'Yes, Gypsies lag in education, but the reasons are complex and cultural', *The Guardian Online* 22.01.14 www.theguardian.com/commentisfree/2014/jan/22/gypsies-lagging-education-gypsies-travellers, date accessed 14 May 2018.

Le Vine, R.S. & Miller, P.M. (1990) 'Special topic – cross-cultural validity of attachment theory – commentary' *Human Development*, 33, 73–80.

Le Vine, S. & Le Vine, R. (1983) 'Child abuse and neglect in sub-Saharan Africa' in J.E. Korbin (ed.) *Child Abuse and Neglect: Cross-Cultural Perspectives*, Berkley: University of California, 35–55.

Leigh, J.W. (1998) *Communicating for Cultural Competence*, Boston: Allyn & Bacon.

Leigh, P.R. (2003) 'Interest convergence and desegregation in the Ohio Valley', *Journal of Negro Education*, 72(3), 269–96.

Leininger, M. & McFarland, M.R. (2002) *Transcultural Nursing: Concepts, Theories, Research and Practice*, New York: McGraw-Hill.

Lesane-Brown, C.L. (2006) 'A review of race socialisation within Black families', *Development Review*, 26(4), 400–26.

Lewis, G. (2000) *Race, Gender and Social Welfare: Encounters in a Postcolonial Society*, Cambridge: Polity Press.

Lindley, A. (2005) *Somalia Country Study: A Part of the Report on Informal Remittance Systems in Africa, Caribbean and Pacific (ACP) (Ref: RO2CS008)*, Oxford: Centre on Migration, Policy and Society, University of Oxford.

Lloyd, E. (1999) *Parenting Matters: What Works in Parenting Education* Ilford: Barnardo's

Lonne, B., Harries, M. & Lantz, S. (2012) 'Workforce development: A pathway to reforming child protection systems in Australia', *British Journal of Social Work* http://bjsw.oxfordjournals.org/content/early/2012/05/22/bjsw.bcs064, date accessed 7 July 2016.

Lustig, M.W. & Koester, J. (2013) *Intercultural Competence: Interpersonal Communication Across Cultures*, Upper Saddle River, NJ: Pearson.

Maiter, S. (2009) 'Using an anti-racist framework for assessment and intervention in clinical practice with families from diverse ethno-racial backgrounds', *Clinical Social Work Journal*, 37(4), 267–76.

Maiter, S., Alaggia, R. & Trocmé, N. (2004) 'Perceptions of child maltreatment by parents from the Indian subcontinent: Challenging myths about culturally based abusive parenting practices', *Child Maltreatment*, 9(3), 309–24.

Malek, M. (2004) 'Understanding ethnicity and children's mental health' in M. Malek & C. Joughin (eds) *Mental Health Services for Minority Ethnic Children and Adolescents*, London: Jessica Kingsley, 23–48.

Mama, A. (1996) *The Hidden Struggle: Statutory and Voluntary Sector Responses to Violence Against Black Women in the Home*, London: Whiting and Birch.

Manning, V., Best, D.W., Faulkner, N. & Titherington, E. (2009) 'New estimates of the number of children living with substance misusing parents: Results from UK national household surveys', *Journal of Public Health*, 9, 377 www.ncbi.nlm.nih.gov/pmc/articles/PMC2762991/ date accessed 23 January 2017.

Marcia, J.E. (1966) 'Development and validation of ego-identity status', *Journal of Personality and Social Psychology*, 3(5), 551–8.

Markova, E. & Black, R. (2007) *East European Immigration and CommunityCohesion*, York: Joseph Rowntree Foundation.

Marshall, E.S., Olen, S.F., Mandleco, B.L. & Dyches, T.T. (2003) 'This is a spiritual experience', *Perspective of Latter-Day Saint Families Living with a Child with Disabilities' Qualitative Health Research*, 13(1), 57–76.

Martin, J.N. & Nakayama, T.K. (2010) *Intercultural Communication in Contexts*, New York: McGraw Hill.

Mason, D. (2000) *Race and Ethnicity in Modern Britain,* Oxford: Oxford University Press.

Mathews, I. (2009) *Social Work and Spirituality,* Exeter: Learning Matters.

Matsumoto, D. & Juang, L. (2004) *Culture and Psychology,* Belmont, CA: Wadsworth/ Thomson.

Mazzucato, V. & Schans, D. (2011) 'Transnational families and the well-being of children: Conceptual and methodological challenges', *Journal of Marriage and Family,* 73, 704–12.

Mbarushimana, J. & Robbins, R. (2015) '"We have to work harder": Testing assumptions about the challenges for Black and Minority Ethnic social workers in a multicultural society', *Practice,* 27(2), 135–52.

McLean, C., Campbell, C. & Cornish, F. (2003) 'African-Caribbean interactions with mental health services in the UK: Experiences and expectations of exclusion as (re) productive of health inequalities', *Social Science and Medicine,* 56, 657–69.

McPhatter, A.R. (1997) 'Cultural competence in child welfare: What is it? How do we achieve it? What happens without it?', *Child Welfare,* 76(1), 255–78.

Meissner, F. & Vertovec, S. (2015) 'Comparing super-diversity', *Ethnic and Racial Studies,* 38(4), 541–55.

The Migration Observatory (2013) *Migration in the News: Portrayals of Immigrations, Migrants, Asylum Seekers and Refugees in National British Papers, 2010–2012,* Oxford: Migration Observatory, University of Oxford.

Miller, D. (1994) *Modernity: An Ethnographic Approach,* Oxford: Berg.

Miller, K.M., Cahn, K. & Orellana, E.R. (2012) 'Dynamics that contribute to racial disproportionality and disparity: Perspectives from child welfare professionals, community partners, and families', *Children and Youth Services Review,* 34(11), 2201–207.

Milner, J., Myers, S. & O'Byrne, P. (2015) *Assessment in Social Work,* London: PalgraveMacmillan.

Mirza, H.S. (1992) *Young, Female and Black,* London: Routledge.

Mlcek, S. (2014) 'Are we doing enough to develop cross-cultural competencies for social work?' *British Journal of Social Work,* 44, 1984–2003.

Modood, T., Berthoud, R., Lakey, J., Nazroo, J., Smith, P., Virdee, S. & Beishon, S. eds. (1997) *Ethnic Minorities in Britain: Diversity and Disadvantage, The Forth National Survey of Ethnic Minorities,* London: Policy Studies Institute.

Monaghan, K. (2012) 'Early childhood development policy: The colonization of the world's childrearing practices' in A. Twum-Danso Imoh & R. Ame (eds.) *Childhoods at the Intersection of the Local and the Global,* Basingstoke: PalgraveMacmillan, 56–74.

Moore, S. & Rosenthal, D. (1993) *Sexuality in Adolescence,* London: Routledge.

Morris, K., Hughes, N., Clarke, H., Tew, J., Mason, P., Galvani, S., Lewis, A., Loveless, L., Becker, S., & Burford, G. (2008) *Think Family: A Literature Review of Whole Family Approaches* London: Social Exclusion Task Force: Cabinet Office.

Morris, K. (2012) 'Think family? The complexities for family engagement in care and protection', *British Journal of Social Work,* 42(5), 906–20.

Morris, K., White, S., Doherty, P. & Warwick, L. (2017) 'Out of time: Theorizing family in social work practice', *Child and Family Social Work,* 22, 51–60.

Morton, C.M., Ocasio, K. & Simmel, C. (2011) 'A critique of methods used to describe the overrepresentation of African Americans in the child welfare system', *Children and Youth Services Review,* 33(9), 1538–42.

Moseley-Howard, S. & Burgan Evans, C. (2000) 'Relationship and contemporary experiences of the African-American family: An ethnographic case study', *Journal of Black Studies,* 30(3), 428–45.

Munro, E. (2008) *Effective Child Protection,* London: Sage.

Munro, E. (2011) *The Munro Review of Child Protection, Interim Report: The Child's Journey* www.gov.uk/government/uploads/system/uploads/attachment_data/file/206993/ DFE-00010-2011.pdf, date accessed 24 January 2016.

Murray, L. & Barnes, M. (2010) 'Have families been rethought? Ethic of care, family and 'whole family' approaches' *Social Policy and Society*, 9(4), 533–44.

Myers, M. & Bhopal, K. (2018) 'Muslims, home education and risk in British Society', *British Journal of Sociology of Education*, 39(2), 212–26.

Nandy, S. & Selwyn, J. (2013) 'Kinship care and poverty: Using Census data to examine the extent and nature of kinship care in the UK', *British Journal of Social Work*, 43(8), 1649–66.

NASW (2015) *Standards and Indicators for Cultural Competence in Social Work Practice*, Washington, DC: National Association of Social Workers.

Nazroo, J. (1997) *The Health of Britain's Ethnic Minorities: Findings from a National Community Survey*, London: Policy Studies Institute.

NEC (1990) *Caring for Everyone: Ensuring Standards of Care for Black and Ethnic Minority Patients*, Cambridge: National Extension College.

Neuliep, J.W. (2018) *Intercultural Communication: A Contextual Approach*, Thousand Oaks, CA: Sage.

NHS (2017) *Statistics on Alcohol England, 2017* file:///C:/Users/lqzsel/Downloads/alc-eng-2017-rep.pdf date accessed 19 December 2017.

NHS Greater Glasgow and Clyde (2010) *Mosaics of Meaning: Partnerships with Black and Minority Ethnic Communities to Promote Mental Health: Handbook*, Glasgow: NHS Greater Glasgow and Clyde.

Nixon, J. & McDermott, D. (2010) 'Teaching race in social work education', *Enhancing Learning in the Social Sciences*, 2(3), 1–14.

Noller, P. & Fitzpatrick, M.A. (1993) *Communication in Family Relationships*, Englewood Cliffs, NJ: Prentice Hall.

Northern Territory Government (2007) *Report of the Northern Territory Board of Inquiry into the Protection of Aboriginal Children from Sexual Abuse*, Darwin: Northern Territory Government.

Nsameng, A.B. (1992) *Human Development in Cultural Context: A Third World Perspective*, Newbury Park, CA: Sage.

NSPCC (2017) *Definitions and Signs of Child Abuse* www.nspcc.org.uk/globalassets/documents/information-service/definitions-signs-child-abuse.pdf, date accessed 7 August 2018.

Nzira, V. (2011) *Social Care with African Families in the UK*, London: Routledge.

O'Neale, V. (2000) *Excellence Not Excuses: Inspection of Services for Ethnic Minority Children and Families*, London: Department of Health.

O'Reilly, A. (2001) *Mothers and Sons: Feminism, Masculinity, and the Struggle to Raise Our Sons*, London: Routledge.

O'Shaughnessy, R., Collins, C. & Fatimilehin, I. (2010) 'Building bridges in Liverpool: Exploring the use of family group conferences for Black and minority ethnic children and their families', *British Journal of Social Work*, 40, 2034–49.

Oakley, L.R. & Kinmond, K.S. (2014) 'Developing safeguarding policy and practice for spiritual abuse', *Journal of Adult Protection*, 16(2), 87–95.

Observatory, M. (2012) *Migrants in the UK: An Overview*, University of Oxford: Migration Observatory.

Observatory, T.M. (2014) *Bulgarians and Romanians in the British National Press: 1 December 2012 – 1 December 2013*, Oxford: Migration Observatory, University of Oxford.

Office for National Statistics (2011) *2011 Census Data* www.ons.gov.uk/census/2011census/2011censusdata, date accessed 10 May 2018.

Office for National Statistics (2018) *Why do People Come to the UK? (4) For Family Reasons* www.gov.uk/government/publications/immigration-statistics-october-to-december-2017/why-do-people-come-to-the-uk-4-for-family-reasons, date accessed 10 April 2018.

Office, H. (2018) *Guidance Domestic Violence and Abuse* www.gov.uk/guidance/domestic-violence-and-abuse, date accessed 7 August 2018.

Office of National Statistics (2017) *Families and Households in the UK: 2017* www.ons.gov.uk/releases/familiesandhouseholdsintheuk2017, date accessed 2 June 2018.

Ofsted (2011) *Ages of Concern: Learning Lessons from Serious Case Reviews: A Thematic Report of Ofsted's Evaluation of Serious Case Reviews from 1 April 2007 to 31 March 2011*, www.ofsted.gov.uk date accessed 17 June 2017.

Oliver, C. & Jayaweera, H. (2013) *The Impacts of Restrictions and Entitlements on the Integration of Family Migrants*, Oxford: Centre on Migration, Policy & Society, University of Oxford.

Owen, C. & Statham, J. (2009) *Disproportionality in Child Welfare: The Prevalence of Black and Minority Ethnic Children within the 'Looked After' and 'Children in Need' Populations and on Child Protection Registers in England*, London: Department for Children, Schools and Families.

Owusu-Bempah, K. (1994) 'Race, self-identity and social work', *British Journal of Social Work*, 24, 123–36.

Papadopoulos, I. (2006) 'The Papadopoulos, Tilki and Taylor model of developing cultural competence' in I. Papadopoulos (ed.) *Transcultural Health and Social Care: Development of Culturally Competent Practitioners*, London: Churchill Livingstone, 7–24.

Papadopoulos, L. (2010) *Sexualisation of Young People Review* http://webarchive.nationalarchives.gov.uk/20100418065544/http://homeoffice.gov.uk/documents/Sexualisation-of-young-people2835.pdf?view=Binary date accessed 27 March 2017.

Parker, J. & Bradley, G. (2007) *Social Work Practice: Assessment, Planning, Intervention and Review*, Exeter: Learning Matters.

Parrott, L. (2009) 'Constructive marginality: Conflicts and dilemmas in cultural competence and anti-oppressive practice', *Social Work Education*, 28(6), 617–30.

Parrott, L. (2013) *Social Work and Poverty*, Bristol: Policy Press.

Patel, K. & Strachan, R. (1997) 'Anti-racist practice or heuristics?' *Practice*, 9(3), 15–26.

Patterson, S. (2013) 'Religion, spirituality and health care: Confusions, tensions, opportunities' *Health Care Analysis*, 21, 193–207.

Payne, M. (2014) *Modern Social Work Theory*, Basingstoke: PalgraveMacmillan.

Peach, C. (1998) 'South Asian and Caribbean ethnic minority housing choice in Britain', *Urban Studies*, 35(10), 1657–80.

Peach, C. (2005) 'Social integration and social mobility: Spatial segregation and intermarriage of the Caribbean population in Britain' in C. Peach (ed.) *Ethnicity, Social Mobility and Public Policy*, Cambridge: Cambridge University Press, 178–203.

Pearce, M.J., Medoff, D., Lawrence, R.E. & Dixon, L. (2016) 'Religious coping among adults caring for family members with serious mental illness', *Community Mental Health Journal*, 52, 194–202.

Pease, B. (2016) 'Critical social work with men: challenging men's complicity in the reproduction of patriarchy and male privilege', *Social Alternatives*, 35(4), 49–53.

Pedersen, D.M. & Frances, S. (1990) 'Regional differences in privacy preferences', *Psychological Reports*, 66, 731–36.

Pemberton, S., Sutton, E., Fahmy, E. & Bell, K. (2014) *Life on Low Income in Austere Times Poverty and Social Exclusion in the UK* www.poverty.ac.uk/sites/default/files/attachments/Life%20on%20a%20low%20income%20in%20austere%20times_final_report.pdf, date accessed 5 August 2017.

Penny, S. & Kingwill, P. (2018) 'Seeds of the future/Somali programme: A shared autoethnography on using creative arts therapies to work with Somali voices in female genital mutilation refusal in the UK,' *International Journal for the Practice and Theory of Creative Writing*, 15(1), 55–64.

Perry, J. (2012) *UK Migrants and the Private Rented Sector,* York: Joseph Rowntree Foundation.

Petch, H., Perry, J. & Lukes, S. (2015) *How to Improve Support and Services for Destitute Migrants,* York: Joseph Rowntree Foundation.

Petro, M.R., Rich, E.G., Erasmus, C. & Roman, N.V. (2018) 'The effect of religion on parenting in order to guide parents in the way they parent: A systematic review', *Journal of Spirituality in Mental Health,* 20(2), 114–39.

Phillips, M. (2007) 'Issues of ethnicity' in K. Wilson & A.L. James (eds) *The Child Protection Handbook: The Practitioner's Guide to Safeguarding Children,* Sidcup: Baillière Tindall, 142–60.

Phinney, J.S. (1993) 'A three-stage model of ethnic identity development in adolescence' in M.E. Bernal & G.P. Knight (eds) *Ethnic Identity: Formation and Transmission among Hispanics and Other Minorities,* Albany, NY: State University of New York Press, 61–79.

Phoenix, A. & Husain, F. (2007) *Parenting and Ethnicity,* York: Joseph Rowntree Foundation.

Pierson, J. (2011) *Understanding Social Work: History and Context,* Maidenhead: Open University Press.

Pietkiewicz, I. & Smith, J.A. (2012) 'Praktyczny przewodnik interpretacyjnej analizy fenomenologiczney w badaniach jakościowych w psychologii Czasopismo Psychologiczne 18(2) 361–369. (English language version) www.academia. edu/7609849/A_practical_guide_to_using_Interpretative_Phenomenological_ Analysis_in_qualitative_research_psychology accessed 04.01.18

Pohjola, A. (2016) 'Language as a cultural mediator in social work: supporting Sámi culture with services in Sámi' *International Social Work,* 59(5) 640– 652.

Popple, K. (2015) *Analysing Community Work: Theory and Practice,* Maidenhead: Open University Press.

Powell, A. (2010) *Sex, Power and Consent,* Cambridge: Cambridge University Press.

Power, A. (2007) *City Survivors: Bringing up Children in Disadvantaged Neighbourhoods,* Bristol: Policy Press.

Price, J. & Spencer, S. (2015) *Safeguarding Children from Destitution: Local Authority Responses to Families with 'No Recourse to Public* Funds' www.compas.ox.ac.uk/ fileadmin/files/Publications/Reports/PR-2015-No_Recourse_Public_Funds_Las.pdf, date accessed 4 May 2017.

Prior, L., Chun, P.L. & Huat, S.B. (2000) 'Beliefs and accounts of illness. Views from two Cantonese-speaking communities in England', *Sociology of Health and Illness,* 22(6), 815–39.

Public Health England (2017) *Public Health Outcomes Framework: Health Equity Report: Focus on Ethnicity* https://assets.publishing.service.gov.uk/government/uploads/ system/uploads/attachment_data/file/629563/PHOF_Health_Equity_Report.pdf, date accessed 11 April 2018.

Pugh, G. (1994) *Confident Parents, Confident Children: Policy and Practice in Parent Education and Support,* London: National Children's Bureau.

Pulsifer, M.B., Gordon, J.M., Brandt, J., Vining, E.P.G. & Freeman, J.M. (2001) 'Effects of ketogenic diet on development and behavior: Preliminary report of a prospective study' *Developmental Medicine and Child Neurology,* 43, 301–306.

Putnam, R. (2000) *Bowling Alone: The Collapse and Revival of American Community,* New York: Simon & Schuster.

Radford, L., Corral, S., Bradley, C., Fisher, H., Bassett, C., Howat, N. & Collishaw, S. (2011) *Child Abuse and Neglect in the UK Today* www.nspcc.org.uk/globalassets/ documents/research-reports/child-abuse-neglect-uk-today-research-report.pdf, date accessed 8 January 2018.

Ramsden, I. (2002) *Cultural Safety and Nursing Education in Aotearoa and Te Waipounamu,* Wellington: University of Wellington.

Revans, L. (2003) 'Foreign social workers "Abandoned" without Information', *Community Care*, 22, May 2003.

Reynolds, T. (1997) '(Mis)representing the black (super)woman' in H.S. Mirza (ed.) *Black British Feminism: A Reader*, London: Routledge ,97–112.

Reynolds, T. (2001) 'Black mothering, paid work and identity' *Ethnic and Racial Studies*, 24(6), 1046–64.

Robinson, D. & Reeve, K. (2006) *Neighbourhood Experiences of New Immigration: Reflections from the Evidence Base*, York: Joseph Rowntree Foundation.

Robinson, D., Reeve, K. & Casey, R. (2007) *The Housing Pathways of New Immigrants*, York: Joseph Rowntree Foundation.

Robinson, L. (2007) *Cross-Cultural Child Development for Social Workers*, Basingstoke: PalgraveMacmillan.

Roland, A. (1988) *In Search of Self in India and Japan: Towards a Cross-Cultural Psychology*, Princeton, NJ: Princeton University Press.

Rose, S. & Meezan, W. (1996) 'Variations in perceptions of child neglect' *Child Welfare*, 75, 139–60.

Rose, W. (2010) 'The assessment framework' in J. Horwath (ed.) *The Child's World: The Comprehensive Guide to Assessing Children in Need*, London: Jessica Kingsley, 34–70.

Royal Geographic Society (2010) *Consumption Controversies: Alcohol Policies in the UK*, London: Royal Geographic Society.

Ruby, M. (2012) 'The role of a grandmother in maintaining Bangla with her granddaughter in East London', *Journal of Multilingual and Multicultural Development*, 33(1), 67–83.

Runnymede Trust (1997) *Islamophobia: A Challenge for Us All*, London: The Runnymede Trust.

Salway, S. & Chowbey, P. (2009) *Understanding the Experiences of Asian Fathers in Britain*, York: Joseph Rowntree Foundation.

Salway, S., Powell, K., Carter, L., Turner, D., Mir, G. & Ellison, G.T.H. (2014) *Race Equality and Health Inequalities: Towards More Integrated Policy and Practice*, London: Race Equality Foundation.

Sawrikar, P. & Katz, I.B. (2014) 'Recommendations for improving cultural competency when working with ethnic minority families in child protection systems in Australia', *Child and Adolescent Social Work Journal*, 31(5), 393–417.

Scanzoni, J. & Polonko, K. (1980) 'A conceptual approach to explicitly marital negotiation', *Journal of Marriage and Family*, 42(1), 31–44.

Schnoll, R., Burshtey, D. & Cea-Aravena, J. (2003) 'Nutrition in the treatment of attention-deficit hyperactivity disorder: A neglected but important aspect', *Applied Psychophysiology and Biofeedback*, 28(1), 63–75.

Scholar, H. (2013) 'Dressing the part? The significance of dress in social work', *Social Work Education*, 32(3), 365–79.

Secker, J. & Harding, C. (2002) 'Users' perceptions of an African and Caribbean mental health resource centre', *Health and Social Care in the Community*, 10(4), 270–76.

Sewell, T. (1997) *Black Masculinities and Schooling: How Black Boys Survive Modern Schooling* Stoke on Trent: Trentham Books.

Shaikh, Z. & Reading, J. (1999) *Between Two Cultures: Effective Counselling for Asian People with Mental Health and Addiction Problems*, Hounslow: Ethnic Alcohol Counselling in Hounslow.

Sidebotham, P., Brandon, M., Bailey, S., Belderson, P., Dosworth, J., Garstang, J., Harrison, E., Retzer, A. & Sorensen, P. (2016) *Pathways to Harm, Pathways to Protection: A Triennial Analysis of Serious Case Reviews 2011–2014* www.gov.uk/government/uploads/system/uploads/attachment_data/file/533826/Triennial_Analysis_of_SCRs_2011-2014_-__Pathways_to_harm_and_protection.pdf, date accessed 23 January 2017.

Singer, A. (2008) *Charity in Islamic Societies,* Cambridge: Cambridge University Press.

Singh, S. (2013) 'Anti-racist social work education' in A. Bartoli (ed.) *Anti-Racism in Social Work Practice,* St Albans: Critical Publishing, 25–47.

Skeggs, B. (1997) *Formations of Class and Gender: Becoming Respectable,* London: Routledge.

Skrivankova, K. (2014) *Forced Labour in the United Kingdom,* York: Joseph Rowntree Foundation.

Smaje, C. & Le Grand, J. (1997) 'Ethnicity, equity and use of health services in the British NHS', *Social Science and Medicine,* 45(3), 485–96.

Smedley, A. (1993) *Race in North America: Origin and Evolution of a Worldview,* Boulder: Westview Press.

Smith, M.G. (1986) 'Pluralism, race and ethnicity in selected African countries'. In J. Rex & D. Mason (eds.) *Theories of Race and Ethnic Relations* Cambridge: Cambridge University Press.

Smith, J. (1998) 'Youth homelessness in the UK: A European perspective', *Habitat International,* 23(1), 63–77.

Smith J.A., Flowers, P. & Larkin, M. (2009) *Interpretive Phenomenological Analysis: Theory Method and Research* London: Sage.

Smith, N.R., Kelly, Y.J. & Nazroo, J.Y. (2011) 'The effects of acculturation on obesity rates in ethnic minorities in England: Evidence from the health survey for England', *European Journal of Public Health,* 22(4), 508–13.

Smolak, A., Gearing, R.E., Alonzo, S. & McHugh, K. (2013) 'Social support and religion: Mental health service use and treatment of schizophrenia', *Community Mental Health Journal,* 49, 444–50.

South East Wales Women's Aid Consortium (2010) *Domestic Abuse and Equality: Gypsy and Traveller Women* www.equalityhumanrights.com/en/file/6231/download?token=XyDGlOUh, date accessed 7 June 2018.

Sproston, K., Pitson, L., Whitfield, G. & Walker, E. (1999) *Health and Lifestyles of the Chinese Population in England,* London: Health Education Authority.

Stanley, J. & Goddard, C. (2002) *In the Firing Line: Violence and Power in Child Protection Work,* Chichester: Wiley.Stanley, T., Guru, S. & Coppock, V. (2017) 'A risky time for Muslim families: Professionalised counter-radicalisation networks', *Journal of Social Work Practice,* 31(4), 477–90.

Stevenson, L. (2015) 'High court judge praises social worker's 'outstanding contribution' to radicalisation case', *Community Care* www.communitycare.co.uk/2015/08/28/high-court-judge-praises-social-workers-outstanding-contribution-radicalisation-case/, date accessed 10 January 2018.

Stokes, J. & Schmidt, G. (2011) 'Race, poverty and child protection decision making', *British Journal of Social Work,* 41(4), 1105–21.

Stokes, L., Rolfe, H. Hudson-Sharp, N. & Stevens, S. (2015) *A Compendium of Evidence on Ethnic Minority Resilience to the Effects of Deprivation on Attainment* https://assets.publishing.service.gov.uk/government/uploads/system/uploads/attachment_data/file/439861/RR439A-Ethnic_minorities_and_attainment_the_effects_of_poverty.pdf accessed 19.06.18

Strug, D. & Wilmore-Schaeffer, R. (2003) 'Fathers in social work literature: Policy and practice implications', *Families in Society,* 84(4), 503–11.

Sudbery, J. (2009) *Human Growth and Development: An Introduction for Social Workers,* Abingdon: Routledge.

Sue, D.W., Rasheed, M.N. & Rasheed, J.M. (2016) *Multicultural Social Work Practice: A Competency Based Approach to Diversity and Social Justice,* Hoboken, NJ: John Wiley & Sons.

Sue, D.W. & Sue, D. (2008) *Counselling the Culturally Diverse: Theory and Practice,* Hoboken, NJ: John Wiley & Sons, Inc.

Sveinsson, K.P. (ed.) (2010) *Ethnic Profiling: The Use of 'Race' in UK Law Enforcement,* London: Runnymede.

Sveinsson, K.P. (ed.) (2012) *Criminal Justice v. Racial Justice: Minority Ethnic over Represen-tation in the Criminal Justice System,* London: Runnymede.

Taylor, B.J. (2013) *Professional Decision Making and Risk in Social Work,* London: Learning Matters.

Taylor, E. (1998) 'A primer on critical race theory', *Journal of Blacks in Higher Education,* 19, 122–24.

Tedam, P. (2013) 'Developing cultural competence' in A. Bartoli (ed.) *Anti-Racism in Social Work Practice,* St. Albans: Critical Publishing, 48–65.

Tedam, P. (2014) 'When failing doesn't matter: A narrative inquiry into the practice learning experiences of black African social work students in England', *International Journal of Higher Education,* 3(1), 136–45.

Tedam, P. (2015) 'Enhancing the practice learning experiences of BME students: Strategies for practice education', *Journal of Practice Teaching and Learning,* 13(2–3), 130–45.

Tedam, P. (2016) 'Safeguarding children linked to witchcraft' in C. Bernard & P. Harris (eds) *Safeguarding Black Children,* London: Jessica Kingsley, 181–99.

Tedam, P. & Adjoa, A. (2017) *The W Word: Witchcraft Labelling and Child Safeguarding in Social Work Practice,* St Albans: Critical Publishing.

Tell MAMA (2017) *A Constructed Threat: Identity, Prejudice and the Impact of Anti-Muslim Hatred: Annual Report 2016* https://tellmamauk.org/wp-content/uploads/2017/11/A-Constructed-Threat-Identity-Intolerance-and-the-Impact-of-Anti-Muslim-Hatred-Web.pdf, date accessed 18 June 2018.

Thiara, R. & Gill, A. (2010) 'Understanding violence against South Asian women: What it means for practice' in R. Thiara & A. Gill (eds) *Violence Against Women in South Asian Communities: Issues for Policy and Practice,* London: Jessica Kingsley, 29–54.

Thomas, T.N. (1995) 'Acculturative stress in the adjustment of immigrant families: Dilemmas of dependence, integration and isolation', *Journal of Social Distress and the Homeless,* 4(2), 131–42.

Thompson, A. (2001) 'Refugees and mental health', *Diverse Minds Magazine,* 9, 6–7.

Thompson, N. (2016) *Anti-Discriminatory Practice: Equality, Diversity and Social Justice,* Basingstoke: PalgraveMacmillan.

Tibury, C. (2008) 'The over-representation of indigenous children in the Australian child welfare system', *International Journal of Social Welfare,* 18(1), 57–64.

Tibury, C. & Thoburn, J. (2009) 'Using racial disproportionality and disparity indica-tors to measure child welfare outcomes', *Children and Youth Services Review,* 31(10), 1101–6.

Ting-Toomey, S. (2005) 'Identity negotiation theory: Crossing cultural boundaries' in W.B. Gudykunst (ed.) *Theorizing About Intercultural Communication,* Thousand Oaks, CA: Sage, 211–33.

Tizard, B. & Phoenix, A. (2003) *Black, White or Mixed Race: Race and Racism in the Lives of Young People of Mixed Parentage,* London: Routledge.

Townsend, M. (2016) 'Modern slavery and human trafficking on the rise in the UK', *The Observer* 10.07.16 www.theguardian.com/law/2016/jul/10/modern-slavery-on-rise-in-uk, date accessed 18 April 2017.

Turnell, A. & Edwards, S. (1999) *Signs of Safety: A Solution and Safety Oriented Approach to Child Protection,* New York: Norton.

Twum-Danso Imoh, A. (2012) 'From central to marginal? Changing perceptions of kin-ship fosterage in Ghana', *Journal of Family History,* 37(4), 351–63.

Twum-Danso Imoh, A. & Ame, R. (2012) 'Introduction' in A. Twum-Danso Imoh & R. Ame (eds). *Childhoods at the Intersection of the Local and the Global,* Houndmills: PalgraveMacmillan, 1–14.

Twum-Dansoh Imoh, A. (2012) 'Rites vs rights: Female genital cutting at the crossroads of local values and global norms', *International Social Work,* 56(1), 37–50.

UK Council for International Student Affairs (2015) *International Student Statistics: UK Higher Education* www.ukcisa.org.uk/Info-for-universities-colleges–schools/ Policy-research–statistics/Research–statistics/International-students-in-UK-HE/#International-(non-UK)-students-in-UK-HE-in-2013-14, date accessed 11 August 2015.

Ungar, M. (2008) 'Resilience across cultures', *British Journal of Social Work,* 38(2), 218–35.

Valenti, K. (2017) 'Family group conferences with BME families in Scotland', *Practice,* 29(2), 121–36.

Vargas-Silva, C. (2014) *Migration Flows of A8 and Other EU Migrants to and from the UK,* Oxford: The Migration Observatory, University of Oxford.

Vargas-Silva, C. & Markaki, Y. (2016a) *Long-Term International Migration Flows to and from the UK,* Oxford: The Migration Observatory, University of Oxford www.migrationobservatory.ox.ac.uk/wp-content/uploads/2016/04/Briefing-LTIM_FLows_UK-1.pdf date accessed 18 April 2017.

Vargas-Silva, C. & Markaki, Y. (2016b) *EU Migration to and from the UK,* Oxford: The Migration Observatory, University of Oxford www.migrationobservatory.ox.ac.uk/wp-content/uploads/2016/04/Briefing-EU_Migration_UK.pdf date accessed 18 April 2017.

Vincent, C., Ball, S., Rollock, N. & Gillborne, D. (2013) 'Three generations of racism: Black middle class children and schooling', *British Journal of Sociology of Education,* 34(5–6), 929–46.

Wah, Y.Y., Avari, B. & Buckley, S. (1996) *British Soil Chinese Roots,* Countrywise: Liverpool.

Ward, C. (1996) 'Acculturation' in D. Landis & R.S. Bhagat (eds) *Handbook of Intercultural Training,* Thousand Oaks, CA: Sage 125–47.

Wardak, A. (2000) *Social Control and Deviance: A South Asian Community in Scotland,* Aldershot: Ashgate.

Warrier, S. (1994) 'Gujarati Prajapatis in London: Family roles and sociability networks' in R. Ballard (ed.) *Desh Pardesh: The South Asian Presence in Britain,* London: Hurst & Company, 191–21.

Watts, B., Johnsen, S. & Sosenko, F. (2015) *Youth Homelessness in the UK: A Review of the OVO Foundation,* Edinburgh: Heriot-Watt University.

Weller, R.P., Huang, C.J., Wu, K. & Fan, L. (2017) *Religion and Charity: The Social Life of Goodness in Chinese Societies,* Cambridge: Cambridge University Press.

Westin, A.F. (1967) *Privacy and Freedom,* New York: Atheneum.

White, D.R. (1988) 'Rethinking polygyny: Co-wives, codes, and cultural systems', *Current Anthropology,* 29(4), 529–72.

White, P. (1998) 'The settlement pattern of developed world migrants in London', *Urban Studies,* 35(10), 1725–44.

Whiteley, P., Rodgers, J., Savery, D. & Shattock, P. (1999) 'A gluten-free diet as intervention for autism and associated disorders: Preliminary findings', *Autism,* 3(1), 45–65.

Wilkin, A., Derrington, C., White, R., Martin, K., Foster, B., Kinder, K. & Rutt, S. (2010) *Improving the Outcomes for Gypsy, Roma and Traveller Pupils: Final Report* http://dera.ioe.ac.uk/11566/1/DFE-RR043.pdf, date accessed 19 June 2018.

Williams, C. & Johnson, M.R.D. (2010) *Race and Ethnicity in a Welfare Society,* Maidenhead: McGraw-Hill, Open University Press.

Williams, R. (1997) *Cultural Safety What Does It Mean for Our Work Practice* https://pdfs.semanticscholar.org/357f/fdc5e19dabe642266f10bad9961b7c7a54e1.pdf, date accessed 22 October 2018.

Wilson, L. (1982) *The Skills of Ethnic Competence* unpublished resource paper. Seattle: University of Washington, School of Social Work.

WIN/Gallop International (2015) *Global Tables for Religion Data, Survey 2014* http://gallup-international.bg/en/Publications/2015/223-Losing-Our-Religion-Two-Thirds-of-People-Still-Claim-to-Be-Religious accessed 28.12.18.

WIN/Gallop International (2016) *Global Tables for Religion Data, Survey 2016* www.wingia.com/en/services/end_of_year_survey_2016/10/, date accessed 9 October 2017.

Wood, R. (2010) 'UK: The reality behind the 'Knife Crime' debate', *Race and Class*, 52(2), 97–103.

Workman, L. & Smith, H. (2008) *The Effect of Accent on Perceived Intelligence and Attractiveness* Paper Presented at the Annual Conference of the British Psychological Society Dublin April.

World Health Organization (2008) *Eliminating Female Genital Mutilation: An Interagency Statement*, Geneva: World Health Organization.

Wyss, B. (2001) 'Gender and cash child support in Jamaica', *Review of Radical Political Economics*, 33, 415–39.

Yamey, G. & Greenwood, R. (2004) 'Religious views of the 'medical' rehabilitation model: A pilot qualitative study', *Disability and Rehabilitation*, 26(8), 455–62.

Yin, R.K. (1994) *Case Study Research: Design and Methods*, London: Sage.

Yok-Fong, P. (2015) 'The roles of life course resources on social work minority students' educational aspirations', *International Journal of Lifelong Education*, 34(2), 121–38.

Zapf, M.K. (1991) 'Cross-cultural transitions and wellness: Dealing with culture shock', *International Journal for the Advancement of Counselling*, 14, 105–19.

Index